READINGS CASES MATERIALS IN CANON LAW

A Textbook For Ministerial Students

By

Jordan F. Hite, T.O.R.

Gennaro J. Sesto, S.D.B.

Daniel J. Ward, O.S.B.

THE LITURGICAL PRESS

COLLEGEVILLE, MINNESOTA

Library of Congress Cataloging in Publication Data

Hite, Jordan F 1938-
Readings, cases, materials in canon law.

Bibliography: p. 358
1. Canon law. I. Sesto, Gennaro, J., 1921- joint author. II. Ward, Daniel J., 1944- joint author. III. Title.
LAW 262.9 79-24977
ISBN 0-8146-1081-1

Nihil obstat: Joseph C. Kremer, S.T.L., *Censor deputatus. Imprimatur:* +George H. Speltz, D.D., Bishop of St. Cloud, January 21, 1980.

Printed in the United States of America.

Contents

B. THE UNIVERSAL CHURCH

C. THE LOCAL CHURCH

D. INSTITUTES OF CONSECRATED LIFE

E. THE LAITY

PART III: CANONICAL NORMS AND SELECT PROCEDURES

A. GENERAL PRINCIPLES OF CHURCH LAW

B. SELECT PROCEDURES

Acknowledgments

The authors acknowledge, with gratitude, permission to reprint the following materials.

Part I

"Law in the New Testament" by John L. McKenzie from *The Jurist* 26 (1966), 167-80.

"Towards a Theological Conception of Canon Law" by Ladislas Orsy from *The Jurist* 24 (1964), 383-92.

"The Spirit of Canon Law, Teachings of Pope Paul VI" by Francis G. Morrisey from *Origins* 8 (1978), 34-40.

"Canon Law in the Age of the Fathers" by Justin Taylor. This article appeared originally in the *Australasian Catholic Record,* April 1977 (Vol. LIV, No. 2, pp. 151-68) and is here reproduced with permission.

"Canon Law" by Peter Huizing. Reprinted with permission from *Encyclopaedia Britannica,* 15th edition, ©1974 by *Encyclopaedia Britannica,* Inc.

"Principles Which Govern the Revision of the Code of Canon Law," translation by Roger Schoenbechler. The Latin text appeared in *Communicationes* 2 (1969), 77-85.

"The Revision of the Code of Canon Law" by Francis G. Morrisey from *Studia Canonica* 12 (1978), 177-98.

Part II

"What Belonging to the Church Has Come to Mean" by Yves Congar from *Communio* Summer (1977) 146-60.

"Pope" by Michael Schmaus from *Sacramentum Mundi: An Encyclopedia of Theology* edited by Karl Rahner. Copyright ©1970, Herder KG. Used by permission of the publisher, The Seabury Press.

"Council" by Hans Kung from *Sacramentum Mundi: An Encyclopedia of Theology* edited by Karl Rahner. Copyright ©Herder, KG. Used by permission of the publisher, The Seabury Press.

"Synod of Bishops" by D. R. Foley from *New Catholic Encyclopedia* 16 (1974), 439-41.

"The Roman Curia" from *The Official Catholic Directory* (1978), 4-5.

The Bishop as Head of the Local Church and Its Discipline" by Eugenio Corecco from *Concilium* 38 (1968), 88-104.

"Senate of Priests" by T. J. Green from *New Catholic Encyclopedia* 16 (1974), 411-13.

"Structural Arrangements of the Parish," by William J. LaDue from *The Jurist* 30 (1970), 314-27.

"Episcopal Conferences" by Frederick R. McManus from *New Catholic Encyclopedia* 16 (1974), 157-59.

"The Spirit of the Proposed New Law for Institutes of Consecrated Life" by Francis G. Morrisey from *Studia Canonica* 9 (1975), 77-94.

"The Right of the Church People to Participate in Ecclesial Decision-Making" by William J. LaDue from *Studia Canonica* 7 (1973), 179-90.

Part III

"The Church Society and the Organization of Its Powers" by William H. Onclin from *The Jurist* 27 (1967), 1-17.

"The Canons on Ecclesiastical Laws Revisited: *Glossae* on Canons 8-24" by Ladislas Orsy from *The Jurist* 37 (1977), 112-59.

"Return to the Lay State: The Meaning, Practice and Reform of Laicization" by Terence E. Tierney from *Studia Canonica* 8 (1974), 277-94.

"On Due Process" (revised edition March 1972), 4-18. Publications Office, United States Catholic Conference.

"The Conveyance of Ecclesiastical Goods" by Francis G. Morrisey from *Proceedings of the Canon Law Society of America* (1976), 123-37.

Part IV

"The Canonical Ordering of the Sacraments" by Tomas Garcia Barbarena from *Concilium* 38 (1968), 6-15.

"Liturgical Law and Difficult Cases" by Frederick R. McManus. Reprinted from *Worship* 48 (1974) with permission.

Preface

This book emerged as a result of a seminar for teachers of canon law at the 1978 convention of the Canon Law Society of America in St. Louis. In a round-table discussion of the materials and methods used by each teacher of church law, two points became clear: 1) materials for introductory courses were in such scattered sources that both teachers and students had difficulty coordinating their use, and 2) some teachers use the case method in as far as possible. These points became the basis of this book.

A survey of the subject matter of present courses shows that the majority of seminaries offer two basic courses in church law, an introductory course and a course on marriage. This book is intended for an introductory course. The assembled readings and cases are probably more than can be covered in one quarter or semester. Instructors and students can then choose the material they believe to be most important. The readings represent an introduction to or a discussion of a particular area by a qualified author. Several readings were selected because of their scriptural base and theological content, which are the foundations of church law. The renewal of church law is founded on the principle that good law flows from the self-understanding of the Church expressed in the Scriptures and sound theology. Church law is viewed as a vital means of the pastoral ministry of the Church. These readings express that most important thrust.

The use of cases has had an honored place in the teaching of moral theology and canon law. It has enjoyed a resurgence in secular studies and most recently in theological and canonical studies. The cases in this text follow the form of factual presentation, exercise, and references. Some of the fact patterns are based on real situations, others are fiction. They are designed to involve students in a concrete situation in order to apply the principles of law. The exercises range from direct questions which focus on a particular area to directions to do research or produce argumentation supporting a certain point. The references are composed of readings, documentation, or canons that should aid in completing the exercise. The canons referred to are from the 1917 Code. Although the proposed schemas are available and should be used by instructors, the unsureness of the canons' numbering in a future draft or promulgated law is the reason for their omission. The purpose of the cases is to introduce students to the source and style of church law. The cases can only be approached by going to the Code, other promulgated laws, digests, commentaries, and other sources. Although the readings and cases were assembled primarily for the future minister, much of this material will be valuable to those ministers already serving God's people. In their ministry they have met or currently do meet many of these cases. Some answers are not yet entirely clear, yet the contribution of those now in ministry will be of great value to brother and sister ministers and students.

Part I is an introduction to the roots and sources of church law in Scripture and theology. The renewal of church law is intended to be based on the principle that church law grows out of and is dependent on Scripture and theology. Without such a foundation, church law flounders and becomes an insulated science without reference to the constant and ongoing inspiration of the Holy Spirit.

Part II deals with the immense topic of the People of God. The subject is introduced by a theological essay exploring what it means to belong to the Church, a subject which touches everyone exclusive of role or function. Next, a series of church structures is examined. That the order begins with the papacy and concludes with the laity is not a clue to an underlying ecclesiology since the order could be reversed and in fact can be studied in reverse. An instructor may choose to begin with the ministries of the universal Church and conclude with those of the local church or vice versa.

Part III looks at the general principles of law and a series of selected procedures. Again, at least the section on the principles of law, which apply to all laws, could be taught early in a course. The procedures were chosen because of the frequency with which the minister is likely to be involved in such cases.

Part IV provides a brief introduction to liturgical and sacramental law. At present there is a division of approach to this material. In some schools the canonical material is taught in the sacramental and liturgical courses while in others it remains in a law course. These materials should serve to introduce and explain the general principles of liturgical and sacramental law.

Finally, the glossary lists commonly used canonical terminology that should be helpful to anyone studying church law.

The original publication of the articles in the respective journals and reference works differs, as would be expected, from one to the other in certain points of style such as capitalization, footnoting, handling of quotations, British vs. American spellings, etc. The authors of this volume, wishing to keep the integrity of the articles' original publication intact, have only corrected an infrequent error in typesetting which was noted in the original.

The authors extend a special note of gratitude to the American Theological Society whose funding and support has made their efforts possible and to the several authors and publications who have granted permission to use their works.

Foreword

In the early sixties there was a minor revolution in American canonical circles. It was parallel to the Second Vatican Council and later much influenced by the Council. It embraced a fresh look at the canon law of the Western Church, a fresh appraisal of the role of law in the Christian community, and a reorientation of canonical studies.

This book, a happy combination of studies and cases, shows the progress made since that time. The reflective studies suggest the breadth of a new orientation that goes beyond a positivistic view of the letter of the law to the purposes of church order and discipline. The concrete, pastoral cases test the applicability of theory to practice in the life of the Church.

In 1959 Pope John XXIII announced both the Second Vatican Council and the project of revising the 1917 Code of Canon Law, which had been operative in the Western or Latin Church since 1918. Although that Code did not by any means exhaust the ecclesiastical law at the time of its publication, it was the clearest symbol of church order and discipline, and Pope John's announcement, although less dramatic than the convocation of a general council, seemed to set in motion strong forces of canonical change. The formal work of revision would have to await the completion of the Council in 1965; the philosophizing and theologizing about the canon law, more important by far, would move rather quickly. And, perhaps unexpectedly, the forces in motion among professional canonists and scholars, were just as evident on the pastoral scene. For better or worse, the fixed form of the Church's canon law was simply not taken so seriously as before.

The 1917 Code had built within it the dimensions of future change: the abrogation of laws and their replacement; the possibility of new canons and decrees and norms; the force of customary usage. But the spirit and tone of the Code of Canon Law were stability and permanence if not perpetuity. Such a concept of legal codification or even of the law itself is illusory. In the forty-five years before the Second Vatican Council large volumes were needed to print new legislative enactments for the Western Church. It was not so much the flaws in the 1917 Code that needed correction—by and large it was a technically sound redaction of canons—but the changes in the Church and in human society and thought. These changes were multiplied several times over in the conciliar years of 1962 to 1965 and have continued in the succeeding decade and a half, even as the new revision of the Code of Canon Law has been going on.

This book comes at an opportune time: after that decade and a half during which church law has proliferated, sometimes replacing the canons of the 1917 Code and other preconciliar legislation, sometimes covering new situations of the Christian community. It appears on the eve of the promised codification. Its brief studies will serve to introduce today's canon law and the new Code itself—and indeed to help critique the new Code. Its cases ask the very questions that in some measure must be faced by the new Code when it appears.

Whether the forthcoming revision of the Code is successful or not, there will be need for this volume of studies and cases. Traditional interpretative and exegetical commentaries on the canons, decrees, constitutions, and statutes that make up the canon law will always have their place, but we now know that they are insufficient by themselves. The experience of a generation of canonical instruction in seminaries, for example, has revealed a much greater need than mere comprehension of the written ecclesiastical law, word by word, line by line. It is not enough to know the letter of the law, although this too is essential: those who study the law or live by it must situate it theoretically in a sound ecclesiology and practically in the ongoing experience of the Christian people which is our tradition.

A commonplace of canonical interpretation is that the law should be understood in its text and context. Today we would broaden that context to include not only the body of church law but the whole context of ecclesial life. Both the studies and the cases in this book serve to deepen and clarify that necessary context.

Another axiom of canon law is that the reason for the law is not part of the law. But this is a less wholesome aphorism and smacks of a positivism or even absolutism that would be rejected by Catholic legal philosophers in any other system of law. Admittedly, the language of the law and the intent with which it is promulgated must stand by themselves and be honestly understood. The reason for the law, including the canon law, is what makes it an ordinance of reason; if there is no reason, there is no law. Again, both the studies and the cases in this book serve to explore the reason for the law.

A foreword is a kind of recommendation, and this volume deserves the warmest recommendation—to those engaged in studies for the ministry (and not for the ordained ministry alone) and to those already engaged in the pastoral ministry.

Frederick R. McManus

The Catholic University of America
December 28, 1979

Readings, Cases, Materials in Canon Law

PART I: *Foundations of Church Law*

A. THEOLOGY AND LAW

Law in the New Testament

John L. McKenzie

The Jewish law is one of the most important theological topics in the New Testament, and one of the topics most frequently mentioned. An approach to the New Testament attitude towards law must begin with the law of Judaism. We can say at the beginning of this discussion that the approach must also end there. In a recent paper I attempted to add some weight to the opinion of most New Testament interpreters that the New Testament has no attitude towards the natural law; natural law is simply ignored.[1] In the present context it seems unnecessary to discuss the attitude of the New Testament towards civil law. It is sufficient to notice that the New Testament recommends that the civil law be observed unless it contravenes the Christian conscience. What we take up here is the place of law within the religious community; and we must begin with the law of Judaism, because no other ancient religion is known to us which had a religious law.

Let us sum up the meaning of the law in Judaism as it is reflected in the literature of Judaism and in the New Testament, without adverting to the solidity of the historical basis of this meaning in all details.[2] The law in Judaism was regarded as the revealed will of God determining a peculiarly Jewish way of life both for the individual and the community. The law was revealed to Israel by Moses and interpreted by his spiritual heirs, the scribes, who sat in the chair of Moses. Fidelity to the law assured the Jews of continued good revelations(sic) with the God who had revealed his law, who historically had punished Israel severely for its rebellion and had shown his forgiving mercy by preserving Israel after its catastrophe, thus insuring that there would continue to be a community in which his law was known and observed. By New Testament times, the messianic element in Israelite faith had become somewhat dimmed; the reality achieved by God's saving will was Judaism, the people of the book and the law. While we find ample traces of messianic theories and messianic groups in Judaism, the dominant

1. J. L. McKenzie, "Natural Law in the New Testament," *Biblical Research 9 (1964) 1-13.*

2. See Walter Gutbrod in Gerhard Kittel, Theologisches Worterbuch zum Neuen Testament (Stuttgart: Kohlhammer, 1942), pp. 1046-1077.

element was the type of Judaism associated with the scribes.[3] The messianic theories remained theories concerning a remote or eschatological future. When the messianic theories were put into practice by the Zealots, they issued in a disaster which nearly eliminated Judaism and assured that only the Judaism of the law would survive.

We are speaking of Jewish esteem of the law, not of Jewish observance of the law; it is impossible to estimate the degree to which pharisaic observance or anything approaching it was found within the Jewish community. The rabbinical writings themselves refer to the *am haarez,* the contemptuous designation given to the Jew who either did not know the law or was not observant.[4] Nor can we make a clear distinction between the observance of the law in Palestine and in the diaspora, although it seems clear that the law sat more lightly on the Jews of the diaspora. But the position we have outlined above was the official Jewish position, and the only official Jewish position. To the Jew the law was the most sacred of all realities. It is necessary to bear this in mind when we read of the words of Jesus about the law and his attitude towards at least some of its observances, and when we study Paul's controversies about the law. Jesus and Paul departed more violently from the conventions than we can easily realize.

Interpretations of the attitude of Jesus towards the law vary somewhat. This is due in the first place to the fact that his words as reported in the Gospels reflect the process through which the apostolic Church reached a stable position about the law. This does not imply historical skepticism about the words of Jesus, and still less that apostolic tradition distorted his words; it means only that the apostolic Church made no clear distinction between the words of Jesus and its own teaching. The uncertainties in interpretation are also due to the fact that interpreters come to the problem with their own convictions and presuppositions. Theology too often exhibits an effort of theologians to employ the words of the Bible in order to support conclusions already reached on other grounds. The words of Jesus have been used to support both legalistic and antinomian theses. It is not because the words are ambiguous that this has been possible, but because those who used his words made no effort to reach an understanding of his mind. I am convinced that his words are clear and that their meaning is unambiguous; but it is no more than fair to point out that the interpretation which I propose has been argued.

The time available does not permit a full examination of all the passages which can be introduced into the discussion. No one will dispute that Jesus did not accept the pharisaic understanding and observance of the law.[5] Nor

3. See Rudolf Schnackenburg, *God's Rule and Kingdom* (Eng. tr., New York: Herder and Herder, 1963), pp. 41-75.

4. Joseph Bonsirven, S.J., *Le judaisme palestinien au temps de Jesus-Christ* (Paris: Beauchesne, 1934), I, 60-61; II, 233.

5. Matthew 23:1-46; Luke 11:39-42, 47-51; 20:45-47.

can it be disputed that he treated the law as its master and not as its subject. In certain areas such as that of legal cleanliness and the Sabbath observance he did not observe the law and taught others not to observe it.[6] Here a distinction may be made between the law as the text of the Pentateuch and the law as the text with the interpretation of the scribes, that interpretation which was called "the tradition of the elders." The Jews treated these as a single complex, and it is not at all clear that Jesus accepted the law as the text while rejecting the traditions of the elders. What he proclaimed was not a new interpretation of the law.

In the Sermon on the Mount we find that passage called the Antitheses, "You have heard . . . I say to you."[7] This passage is introduced by a declaration that Jesus has come not to destroy the law but to fulfill it, and that he that does and teaches the commandments is great in the Reign of God. This verse should not be taken apart from its immediate context nor from its general context in the Gospels. What Jesus meant by fulfilling the law was more than observance of the law. The antitheses deal with some of the basic moral precepts of the decalogue. In each instance Jesus shows that the law, apart from its interpretation by the scribes, prescribes a lower degree of moral perfection than he himself demands. The law touches only the external act. The moral teaching of Jesus touches the interior dispositions, the heart; it is here that true "cleanliness" is to be found. A clean heart goes beyond the prescription of the law; and a clean heart is judged by the acts which the persons perform. By their fruits you shall know them. The law is here declared insufficient for entrance into the Reign; and the blessing given to him who does and teaches refers to the moral teaching of Jesus, not to the law.

In a passage which is often quoted with reference to vocations and the "evangelical counsels" an inquirer asks Jesus what he must do to obtain eternal life.[8] He is told to observe the commandments, which are enumerated more or less in agreement with the decalogue. The inquirer asks what is still lacking. Why should he feel that something is lacking? The answer of Jesus does not suggest it. We must postulate something in the personal impact of Jesus or in his words which leads the inquirer to see that the law does not assure communion with God. In answer to the second question, Jesus invites him to become a disciple and thus to enter into the Reign of God. The man refuses the invitation; and it should be noticed that he was not invited to become more of a disciple than any one else. Again the law is declared insufficient for entrance into the Reign of God and for discipleship.

I take these two passages as samples because they contain the most affirmative statements concerning the law which are found in the Gospels. In

6. Matthew 12:1-14; Mark 2:23-28, 3:1-6; Luke 6:1-11; Matthew 15:1-20; Mark 7:1-23.

7. Matthew 5:17-48.

8. Matthew 19:16-30; Mark 10:17-31; Luke 18:18-30.

both we can see that the attitude of Jesus is not simply affirmative. The law is insufficient; what does Jesus propose which is more? At the risk of oversimplifying, we can reduce his demands to two items under which all others can be included. The first of these is faith in him, a faith which is not imposed by the Old Testament or by the law or by the principles of Judaism. In Jesus God reveals himself anew; he is more than Moses, he is the fullness of Israel into which the Israelite must be incorporated. The believer must accept Jesus as the supreme revelation of God, and must give him a total surrender beyond the demands of the law. The will of God revealed in the law yields place to the saving will of God revealed in Jesus. A new era, the Reign of God, is begun, in which the law will not be the dominant revelation and the dominant moral force.

The second item is the reduction of the entire law to the double commandment of love. This commandment comprises all of one's duties to God and to one's fellow man; one who loves as Jesus teaches and empowers to love has achieved moral perfection. The Gospels contain no detailed catalogue of particular duties through which this commandment is to be executed. This is the renewed and the clean heart, and from the heart each individual will discover his own way of fulfilling the commandment of love. The Gospel defines no minimal obligation of love, and gives no occasion for a scale of calculation of love. An obligation which does not involve love is not a Christian moral obligation. Love is the great and ultimately the only moral imperative in the Gospel.

It is safe to say that Jesus takes from the law the Jewish assurance that it was a complete and secure means of salvation. The salvation of the Gospel is achieved by faith and love. It is safe to say that Jesus removes the law as a mediation between God and man. He himself becomes the sole mediator; he replaces the law, and in this sense he fulfills it. The law can lead to faith, and that is all it can do. It is less obvious, but I believe it is a clear conclusion from his words, that Jesus denies that the Christian way of life can be codified in law. There is no safe ceiling above which the Christian may be sure he need not rise. There is no explicit annulment of the law in the words of Jesus; but when one asks what place the law can have in the Reign, it is hard to find an answer. All that the law was intended to do is done more fully by the proclamation of Jesus and by his saving act; and all the obligations of the law are met by faith and love. In such areas as those mentioned, legal cleanliness and the Sabbath observance, where no personal relations are involved, one observes that Jesus is indifferent to them.

When we turn from the Gospel to Paul—whose writings are earlier than the Gospels—we observe that the question of law is more sharply and urgently posed. It is a mark of the fidelity of apostolic tradition that while the controversy concerning the law is reflected in the Gospels, the words of Paul are not put in the mouth of Jesus. Paul felt that he was a faithful interpreter of the teaching of Jesus, and the early Church agreed with him. A brief review of this controversy is necessary.[9]

The primitive Palestinian community felt no obligation to deviate from Jewish observances. They were Jewish messianists, and they proclaimed the Messiah to their fellow Jews. It seems that the question of the law did not arise until Gentiles believed in Jesus. It seems also—the uncertainty here is due to the incomplete records of the events—that there were two ways in which Gentiles were admitted to the Christian community, and that both were followed independently for some time. One was to make a Jew of the Gentile convert; the other was simply to receive him by baptism. It is clear that the second way was Paul's way, and we do not know how many others followed it. The first way is associated in the New Testament with the church of Jerusalem; again we do not know how many others followed it. Nor is it clear who first saw that the two ways were irreconcilable, nor when it was seen. Paul became the spokesman of the second way; the first way is found in the New Testament only in writings of men who disagreed with it.

Paul attacked the problem primarily from the nature of the saving act of Jesus. If the law was necessary for salvation, then Jesus was not a total savior. The question seems to have had its roots in cultic practice; the Judaizers demanded circumcision as well as baptism. It is doubtful that any one before Paul saw that this destroyed the symbolism of baptism. But since it was circumcision which imposed the yoke of the law, the Gentile could not become subject to the law. Hence Paul's reiterated declarations that the Gentiles are free from the law. Nothing could be required besides faith and baptism; to add something was, in Paul's phrase, to nullify the grace of God.[10] Thus even more explicitly than the Gospels and on a basis which is not declared in the Gospels Paul denies any saving power to the law.

What of the Jewish Christian? Here Paul was neither the first nor the last Christian leader to show less than perfect consistency between his principles and his practices. It seems that he himself observed the law when he was in Jewish company and abandoned it in Gentile company.[11] His excuse was that he should not scandalize; he should not cause the Jews to think him irreverent, nor should he suggest to Gentiles that they would be better Christians if they observed the law. But we find no polemic against the circumcision of children of Jewish Christians; and if Paul were perfectly consistent he should not have allowed this. One may conclude from this that in the area of law even so clear-headed a man as Paul is easily confused. His practice of adapting his observance to his company evades the question of the value of the law rather than resolves it; in principle he should not have allowed Jews to observe the law, because he knew quite well that they attached a saving efficacy to the observance.

9. See Johannes Munck, *Paul and the Salvation of Mankind* (Eng. tr., Richmond: John Knox Press), pp. 87-134.

10. Galatians 2:21.

11. 1 Corinthians 9:19-22.

It is this belief in the efficacy of the law which Paul controverts by his thesis that man is rendered righteous by faith and not by works.[12] Works is too literal a rendering of Paul's language in modern times; by works he means the observance of the law, and he denies any saving value to this observance. It is necessary to explain that Paul does not mean moral anarchy by this position, and we shall explain it; but it is clear that observance of the law contributes nothing to the Christian life. More than this, the Christian who observes the law as a salutary act effectively denies the efficacy of the redeeming death. It is the works of the law precisely as observance of the law which are rejected. The Christian who refrains from murder, adultery, theft, and such activities does not abstain from a motive of observance, but from another motive; if he abstains because of the law, his observance is not salutary.

Moral anarchy is removed by Paul's fidelity to the Gospel in reducing the law to the single commandment of love. One who loves his neighbor has fulfilled the law.[13] An act which is not an act of love is not a Christian moral act. It is true that Paul does not limit himself to this classic statement. The epistles often exhibit exhortations to particular virtues and warnings against particular vices; these exhortations become longer and more detailed in the deuteropauline epistles, and they are the first examples in the long history of Christian homiletic.[14] But in New Testament morality these are specifications of the work of love. Paul does indeed discuss particular moral problems at length; the first epistle to the Corinthians exhibits a number of examples of this,[15] and the motivation of love is not always studied thoroughly by Christian moralists—it need not be always explicit; and we can safely conclude that this motivation was no less explicit in his gospel. The Christian is guided and moved in all his acts by the indwelling spirit, and the spirit is the gift and the principle of love.

Paul's controversy took him so far that he had to answer the question about the place of the law in the scheme of salvation. After all, the law was the revealed will of God; and how could it now be dismissed as irrelevant to the saving work of Christ? The writings of Paul show that he did not reach a position on this without some struggle; and here it should be remembered that Paul was a Jew and a Pharisee.[16] It is difficult for us to imagine the reversal which was involved in this position unless we have gone through a similar reversal ourselves. The law, he declared, was the pedagogue, the slave who takes the boy to school; once the boy has arrived at the school, the work of the slave is finished.[17] The law is a disclosure of man's moral impotence, which it does not heal; in a way it actually seems to make man's condition worse by imposing upon him obligations which it does not enable

12. Romans 3:30, 27; 9:32; Galatians 2:16 ; 3:2.

13. Romans 13:8; Galatians 5:14.

14. Ephesians 5:3-6:14; Colossians 3:5-4:6; Thessalonians 4:3-12; Titus 3:1-11.

15. Corinthians 5:1-8:12.

16. Romans 9-11.

17. Galatians 3:23-4:7.

him to fulfill.[18] But Paul discerns in this a salutary purpose. Unless man knows that he needs to be saved and cannot save himself, he will not believe that only Jesus Christ can save him.

To us Paul's position on the law may seem to go beyond the needs of controversy. He may himself have wondered at times whether he had talked himself into a position which was difficult to defend on some fronts. Yet the bases of the position which we have reviewed here are fundamental in Pauline theology and in Christian theology. We are too remote from the Judaism of the time to understand fully how Paul could see the law as an attack on the dogma of salvation through Christ. The Christian is saved by a rebirth, a regeneration, a new creation. This is absolutely new; it is the saving work of God which man can only receive. By the saving act man receives a new life, new powers, and a new dimension of living. It appears that Paul did not realize at once not only that the Gentile need not become a Jew, but also that the Jew must cease to be a Jew. The unity of Christians in Christ and in a new life makes any other factor unimportant. If any other factor is given undue importance, it may endanger the integrity of the life in Christ. Such a factor in Paul's time was the law; we may think of others.

It is clear that the law of Moses has no place in the Christian scheme; but is the gospel a new law? Let us notice that "new law" is not a biblical phrase; it has not been traced in Christian literature earlier than the epistle of Barnabas. John's allusion to the new commandment (Jn. 13:34) explicitly refers to the commandment of fraternal love. Paul's allusion to the law of the spirit (Rom. 8:2) is an oxymoron; the spirit liberates from the law of sin and death, and thus it is a higher power. The law of Christ (Gal. 6:2) is explicitly the law of fraternal love, as is the royal law of James 2:8; and to this law James applies the rabbinical principle that he who fails in one commandment transgresses the entire law. We are in the same world of thought in these phrases. The New Testament does not suggest that the gospel is seen as a new law; it is a gospel, which is something different. It fulfills the law in the sense that it does what the law did; it is the revelation of God's saving will, it is a medium of salvation, it is a way of life. But all these features are incorporated into the person of the Incarnate Word.

We come now to the final and the most difficult question: granted that the gospel effectively annuls the law of Moses and is not itself a new law, does the New Testament reject the principle of law in the Christian life? I specify "in the Christian life"; for the New Testament has nothing to say about the principle and the practice of civil law as such. Before we can answer this question it will be necessary to define the principle of law, which is not the same thing as a definition of law; I mean the principle on which the legislative power rests, the principle which affirms that law is necessary and good and that there is a natural legislative power in society which arises from its very constitution. The question is not daring. If the New Testament

18. Romans 7.

rejects the only religious law which it knew and erects no other law in its place, we ask only whether this is a rejection in principle or in a particular practice. The fact that the church of the New Testament shows no law does not prohibit the postapostolic church from making laws; neither does the absence of law in the New Testament give the postapostolic church any authority to make law. It would appear that the existence of this power will have to be settled on other than biblical grounds, and in this hypothesis I should gracefully retire at this point; but an interpreter should have something to say on the principle implicit in the New Testament, or whether there is a principle implicit in the New Testament. It is hardly necessary to call your attention to the fact that at this point the interpreter speaks less from his erudition and the erudition of his colleagues than from his personal interpretation of the evidence. With these cautions and with some diffidence I proceed to the task.

The philosophical base of law is the common good of the society and the existence of an authority which is empowered to secure the common good. Law expresses the will of this authority, and it implies a judgment made by authority concerning means apt to secure the common good. Law is not directed to the individual personal good except in so far as the individual personal good depends on the common good. Thus authority demands the surrender of the life of some of its citizens in order to preserve the common good against extreme threats. In such cases the individual personal good is not secured by law, but is rather sacrificed. In other less extreme instances the law inhibits the exercise of personal freedom and the use of personal goods; the common good cannot permit the uninhibited pursuit of the individual personal good. The law is not directed to the improvement of the person in his personal goods or in his use of real goods. It is not intended to make the citizen a better man, but to prevent him from doing things which will prevent others from sharing in the common good. Law has no interest in the motives of those who observe it, but simply in the observance; and only the observance comes under its competence. This is said generally and I believe the accuracy of this description is not affected by the fact that malice aforethought is one of the legal factors in a trial for murder. The law is not interested in why a man does not kill his neighbor; it is satisfied if he does not for any reason.

There are some reasons for doubting that the principle of law has a meaningful function in the Christian life. One who would wish to define the "common good" of the Church might find himself involved in impossible difficulties. The New Testament knows no other end of the Church than the incorporation of persons into Christ. The Church can have no accomplishment and no fulfilment which is not expressed in terms of individual persons. Renunciation is, of course, essentially involved in the Christian fulfilment; but Christian renunciation has this vitally important quality, that it is not Christian and salutary unless it is an entirely free choice of the person who renounces. The office of authority in the Church is to lead Christians to that renunciation which their faith demands of them, not to impose it. It cannot make personal decisions for its members. The supreme motive of the Christian moral act, we have seen, is love; and the introduction of any type of pressure, even if it be no more than social pressure, attacks the integrity of Christian love. Compulsion is alien to the genius of Christianity; and if there is a type of law which is not compulsive, no one has yet discovered it. Jesus did not remove the law of Judaism in order that it might be replaced by another law which would do the same thing.

These reflections, I must repeat, are personal; to my knowledge they do not represent a consensus of biblical scholarship, and they might not mean much if they did. They may deserve some attention, and that is all that can be asked for them. It is an obvious fact that the Church has had law for most of its history. It has not always been easy to see how law in the Church has differed in form, structure, and purpose from civil law. It would be naive to say that Church authority has never employed the compulsion of law. To say that law has no place in the Christian life specifically as such need not imply that law has no place in the Church at all. The organization of the Church has become vast and complex as its membership has grown, and as its activities have expanded beyond the proclamation of the word and the administration of the sacraments. It would be idle to discuss whether this growth has always reflected the true mission of the Church, or always helped the mission of the Church. We deal with existing realities. I do not mean to say that the discussion of the activities of the Church should never be carried on by any one. All we can do here is face the fact that law has proved the easiest way in which the authorities of the Church have been able to manage the business of the Church.

As long as law is confined to the business of the Church, and as long as the Church has business to manage, there appears no convincing reason at the moment why legal processes should not be employed. But observe that I speak of the business of the Church. Law, it seems, should not touch the Christian life of the Church; here it is an intrusion of a secular factor. The Church is empowered to exercise leadership in the Christian life, but this is not a leadership of the law. It is leadership of another type, and not every member of the Church is capable of this type of leadership. As long as the mission of the Church is clearly perceived, it is hard to see how any one could think of appealing to another type of leadership. Only when something other than the true mission of the Church is the objective are we likely to turn to means which are quite suitable to these objectives; and I mean the use of power. Power is profane and adapted to profane purposes; but why should the Church have profane purposes? Order can be achieved by other means than law; and in this age of self-examination of the Church, we can ask whether the failures of the Church may not be connected with our failures to achieve a truly ecclesiastical order.

Towards a Theological Conception of Canon Law

Ladislas Orsy

Christian thought of today endeavors to find a more unified vision of the world than we had yesterday, and to co-ordinate all sciences into a harmonious one in which theology would reign again as queen among her handmaids. Yet there is a difference: now this queenship would be constitutional. While in former times theology tended to take the place of natural sciences, now their autonomy is being respected. The particular inspiration of all branches of learning is upheld, and theology contents itself with declaring their ultimate meaning and significance, which is to proclaim the glory of God in a way that is their own. Thus we have now a theology of earthly things, *des réalités terrestres,* a theology of the state, a theology of work and leisure, and so on.

For one who is a professional lawyer it is impossible not to notice the crying absence of a *theology of canon law* in this new orchestration. Such a theology is really needed and should have been written long ago. There is, however, no point in speculating whether the omission is the fault of theologians who lost interest in the practical life of the Church (are they not accused sometimes of surveying divine and human things from their own ivory tower?), or whether it is the omission of the canonists (who are blamed by good Christians for upholding the law and forgetting the spirit). There is no point in apportioning the blame. The times are bad, and we should start to work out this new theology of canon law. By *we* I mean theologians and canonists together, since for the sake of balance both are needed. The purpose of this article is to begin the work, hoping that others will soon come and do it better than the present writer. Thus within a reasonable time we shall have a theological vision of the sacred canons. From this new vision, in which theology and canon law will be united, the Church will profit and will build up a richer life of spotless faith and unfailing practical charity.

After the introduction definitions should follow, *ne parvus error in initio magnus sit in fine,* as St. Thomas would say.

To begin with the obvious, *by theology* I do not mean faith in the strict sense, but the human science that is built on the words and deeds of God as they have been revealed to us. If the data of revelation are the pillars of divine wisdom for a mortal man, theology is the connecting link between those pillars: it shows the order and unity in God's plan.

Canon law is principally concerned with the practical life of the Church and of every single Christian. It contains norms of action for the whole community and for each member. Basically it springs from the will of Christ, but its minute and detailed rules come from human agents who carry the dignity of being the divinely instituted shepherds of the Church, that is, the pope and the bishops.

From these very general definitions it follows that theology and canon law can never be entirely separated. To some extent they overlap and have a mutual impact on each other. It is by reflecting on the words and deeds of God that I conclude what the whole Church should do, how the smaller Christian communities should live, and what the right practical balance should be between the universal and local needs in the Church.

Vice versa: the practical life of the Church has an immense impact on theology. (If theologians would always remember this, perhaps they would be less abstract.) The rules for the formation of the clergy, those about men and women religious, those for the administration of the sacraments, for punishing and forgiving offenses and crimes, reflect a practical attitude that always had and will have repercussions on theological thinking. Thus, the way our clergy is educated decides to a large extent what sort of theology the priest will cultivate—or avoid. Some good practical rules about the celebration of the Mass and distribution of holy Communion may help to increase the devotion towards the sacrifice of Christ and his holy Body in the whole Church, and this devotion may give a new inspiration to theological thinking. Finally, the more merciful the Church is with her failing sons and daughters, the more the mercy of God will be manifest to all.

As I said above, theology and canon law overlap and interpenetrate. This, however, is a general statement and the time has come to go into more detail and ask the question with more precision: what is the exact relationship between the two sciences? On the one hand, in formulating the answer I shall try to show that at times a text of canon law is no more than an expression of a rule of faith; and that canon law depends on theology as its norm and its inspiration. On the other hand, I hope to demonstrate that canon law should contribute to the deepening of theological thought, and that the practical life of the Church should be kept in high regard. Finally, I shall try to say some words about the triple relationship between theology, philosophy, and canon law. This last paragraph will be necessary, because philosophy of law is widely taught and discussed in legal circles.

I.

Frequently in the body of canon law we find rules that are simply the restatements of a revealed truth. These immutable rules are the principles on which canon law is based. Without them our laws would simply collapse. This is self-evident. When the Code affirms the supreme power of the pope or of the ecumenical council, when it states that the bishop has (under the pope) legislative, judicial, and executive power, a theological truth is stated in legal terms. Thus far there is not much difference between theology and canon law. Their ways part only when canon law is drawing practical conclusions from the first truths of the faith. While, for instance, the preoccupation of the theologian will be to determine after historical and speculative research the exact relationship between primacy and episcopacy, the interest of the lawyer will lie more in finding the right practical balance between the two. But obviously he will depend on the research of the theologian. Actions ought to be inspired by ideas, and practical rules should be the fruit of right theories. Hence, in the understanding of first principles the canonist has to lean on the theologian, and in the drafting of practical rules he will have to take his inspiration from his colleague in theology. If not, we shall fall into a state of things in which action precedes thinking, a procedure which cannot meet with approval.

But the tableau is not complete. Sometimes the practice of the Church in understanding the principles of the faith can be more inspired than the reflections of the theologians. Let us consider an example: today we all accept the fact that episcopal consecration is a sacrament. Yet, for a long time, for many centuries, theologians could not agree on this point, and they remained divided till the very eve of the Second Vatican Council. Nevertheless, the practice of the Church was uniform: no person was ever considered to be a bishop unless he was consecrated by another bishop. The practice was uniform and constant, but not so the theological speculation. Some theoreticians went as far as to say that if the episcopate was not a sacrament, there was no reason why a presbyter could not be consecrated bishop by a deacon, delegated, of course, by the pope. The Church never listened to such theoreticians or to anyone else who would make the episcopal consecration a sort of canonical installation without the intervention of the Holy Spirit. The practice reflected the mind of the Church better than many of the theories. Hence the rules of canon law may express the deepest conviction of the Church better than theology. This shows that the practical and "canonical" life of the Church should never be separated from the theological reflection. Canon law can be and more than once *is* spontaneous expression of a deep understanding of a tradition that theological reflection has not brought to the surface. In this context legal rules may be simply the vital expressions of the riches of the Church. It will be to a large extent the theologian's duty to separate this type of rule from the rest and to show their theological relevance. Theology and canon law are more interwoven in the essentials than we might have expected.

II.

Not every legal rule is an expression of a divine truth. The bulk of laws is man-made. To ensure that they are *well* made, theology must play an important part in their formulation. It can do this in many ways.

a) The legal system of the Church ought to be an *open* system, i.e., so composed that it may be enriched by new rules and legal institutions according to the needs of the time and the inspiration of the Spirit.

The reason is that the Church is somehow the living Christ on earth, engaged in distributing the treasures of divine revelation to every person. Her soul is the Spirit of Christ who continually inspires her. Now, in order to put into practice the new inspirations of the Spirit which may come at any time and which may lead the Church in any direction that he may choose, the legal rules must be formulated in such a way that the door remains open for the wind and the fire of the Spirit. Although the Church possesses the fullness of revelation, we have not reached the stage (and never will reach it) where our understanding and our expressions will equal the internal riches of the Gospel. In order to adapt our practical life to a deeper understanding of the faith it is necessary that the body of laws should have an open character, so that they should be able to receive and to assimilate the new without destroying what is good in the old.

An example will throw light on this issue: much is being said today about a more intense participation of all Christians in the life of the Church. Books and articles are advocating a fair share for the laity in building up the Church. Now, it would be crippling if our Code ever defined with precision what lay men and women can and cannot do in the Church. We live in a period of transition, and we do not know exactly where the spirit and the reflection of responsible theologians will lead us, and how the practice of the Church will develop. Hence, it is better not to make many laws about lay people, so that the system can remain open, and be able to receive the infusion of new wine when it has matured after the present fermentation. This openness is surely a theological necessity in the legal system of the Church.

Another example may confirm the necessity of this openness in our canonical system. There is a deeper understanding of the relation between primacy and episcopacy in the Church, but we have not reached the final point of our reflection, and probably it will take a long time before a definite balance is achieved. Whatever the outcome of the present research and speculation may be, there will be practical consequences of considerable importance. But if we tried to give an ultimate definition of the rules for episcopal conferences too soon when the doctrinal background is not clear we would be sinning against this postulate of openness, which is so essential for us.

It follows also that a legal system that is entirely sealed in the form of a Code, and does not leave any reasonable freedom for customs and usages, is somehow opposed to the best theological conception of the Church. This is why the wish has been expressed that the main part of a future Code of Canon law should only contain the most basic laws and principles. They should be promulgated with the authority of the Holy See and they should not be easily changed. Then perhaps a secondary part could contain less important and more detailed rules. Here the possibility of change should be made easier. This would mean really to leave behind the old Roman division that we have in the Code, and to approach more closely the modern division of legal codes and science: constitutional law should come first, and the rules of less importance should follow.

b) Legal rules should promote in every possible way the expansion of the Kingdom of God. In other words a dynamic apostolic spirit should be evident in the various books of the Code. In the chapter on the rights and duties of the parish priest, his duty to visit the parishioners should be clearly stated; similarly his duty to make the Gospel known to those who are not of our flock. In the chapter on men and women religious, the great principle should be laid down that in apostolic orders and congregations the observance of external formalities should not be an impediment to the practice of the works of charity. The same apostolic spirit will postulate that all rules of natural law should be observed and *seen* to be observed in our legal proceeedings: there should be no unnecessary delays, no one condemned before he has had the opportunity to defend himself, and so forth.

c) It is sound theology that will help to appreciate both universality and diversity in the Church. Things of universal value should be principally under the care of the universal bishop, that is, the pope. Things of particular value should be left as far as possible to the local bishop. Thus there will be a balance between universal and particular values, as the nature of the Church, which is an organic unity, postulates. This provides us with a very cogent theological reason for having one general code with the universal laws of the Church, and several particular codes for the particular needs of a nation or a community.

When the natural values of a people or a nation are good and holy, they can be and should be incorporated into the legal system of the Church. An obvious example would be the incorporation of local marriage ceremonies into the formalities of the sacrament, whenever and wherever this is practicable.

III.

The structure of the Church is both supernatural and natural. These two elements, divine and human, blend into one reality, and they cannot be separated without doing harm to the whole. The separation of the soul from the body writes death for man; the separation of the divine element from the human in the Church would also mean death. Of course, the Church cannot die, the Spirit of Christ keeps her alive. The evil forces will never be able to overcome the strength of God. Nevertheless the right balance between the supernatural and the natural elements can be disturbed. And here I am touching a point of some importance.

In the traditional canonical literature we find stated frequently that the Church is perfect society. From this principle many other statements are deduced. One of them is—in many writers—that the Church has a right to inflict capital punishment on her members. The reason is that every perfect society has a right to inflict capital punishment. This sort of reasoning betrays a complete lack of theological method. The Church is surely a perfect society, but it is also a *sui generis* institution in the supernatural order, far above any human society. From the nature of a merely human society of a lower order (as the state is) one has no right to conclude that the nature of the Church is the same. There is some analogy between the two, certainly, but there is no genuine identity. The Church is Christ living on earth, who came to save and to sanctify, and not to judge. Hence, without proof from revealed sources no one has any right to state that the Church is entitled to deprive human persons of their mortal life.

The application of proper theological method, even when we are dealing with the human side of the Church, is essential. Without it one is bound to go astray and to transfer human ideas to divine reality.

Here we touch the problem of the application of philosophical ideas to the Church. How far is this permissible, and how far can we hope truly to reach the whole reality, divine and human, by using them?

The answer is that philosophical principles and ideas can be helpful in understanding the nature of the Church, provided they are kept in the place of a handmaid and do not take that of the mistress of the house.

God's plan has taken flesh in a human society that is ruled by the ordinary laws of human nature. These laws have been assumed into the fullness of the divine reality that is present in the Church. Therefore the nature of the Church should *first* be determined from revelation, and *secondly* the gaps should be filled by human reasoning, using all the sound principles that philosophy has discovered. For instance, the principle of subsidiarity will help to organize the legal structure of the Church in such a way that the proper competence and personality of each will be respected.

At the same time philosophy should be kept in the place of a handmaid, subordinate to theology. This practical subordination should be reflected also by the program of canonical faculties. At present philosophy of law is taught in every canon law school, and not without some fruit. One would like to see, however, a course on the theology of canon law taking the first place. This would correspond to the real nature of ecclesiastical laws far better than mere philosophical considerations, and would bear better fruit in the mind of the students. All arguments from the nature of perfect society could be reduced to the minimum necessary, since the difference between the two societies is so great that the analogy in particular cases can be misleading. An example can be found in the term *power*, which in a civil society means political power, whereas in the Church it means the right and duty to feed and to serve the flock. On analysis, one concept after the other turns out to be different, and any shift in emphasis away from theology and towards natural philosophy may be misleading for the students.

In conclusion let us say that there is no other true conception of the canon law than the theological conception. We have been influenced too much by philosophy (in itself very good, provided it is kept in its place), and to some extent we have lost sight of the living reality of the life of Christ in the Church.

This article is of course no more than a short sketch that draws the attention of the reader to the very urgent need of working out a theology of canon law. Our legal principles should be rethought in the light of the new developments in theology, which should instill new life into every legal concept.

If there is to be a reform of canon law, theologians should not be absent from the working committees. I mean, of course, theologians blessed with a great practical sense.

No doubt such theological revision of canon law is bound to take a long time: and one wishes that the reform should not come within a short period. Even when it comes, it would be wise to introduce it in much the same way as the liturgical reform has been introduced: by stages and by experiments. How good our laws will be if they reflect the deepest understanding of our faith that we can reach. Thus the laws of the Church will be the framework in which the Spirit of God can freely operate and re-create the face of the earth.

The Spirit of Canon Law and the Teachings of Pope Paul VI

Francis G. Morrisey

Over the past 15 years since he became Pope, Paul VI has spoken on some 40 occasions[1] about the role of canon law in the life of the church, its importance in the renewal currently underway, and its essential place in the life of every believer. While, hopefully, he will deliver many more addresses on the subject during the course of his reign, I believe that we are now in a position to determine some of the principal thrusts of his teaching regarding the spirit of ecclesial legislation and the role it is expected to play in leading all Christians to a greater understanding of the plan of God for the salvation of the world.

The foundation of his teaching is to be found in the statement that "the church, as a society, is not exactly the same as a civil society. It is unique and singular because, by virtue of its specific goal and the means it uses to reach this goal, it is a supernatural and spiritual society."[2]

This being the case, the church, as a society, has within it an authority whose "original reason for being . . . is that of service. But this should not cause us to misconstrue the source of authority itself."[3] It has been established "for the guidance and salvation of the people of God."[4]

The authority which we find in the church is not in opposition to what is known as "The church of charity." As Pope Paul stated on Jan. 25, 1966, "the church which is founded juridically, with the pontiff at its head, is the very church of Christ, the church of charity and the universal family of Christians."[5]

In this context, we can easily make our own the words which the Holy Father used in 1970: "Do not be afraid of the church; instead, you should love her."[6] Within this framework, then, of the church as a society founded on love we shall try to determine the spirit of the ecclesial law. To do so, we shall first consider the sacramental or sign value of justice in the church, then proceed to examine canon law as an expression of justice, and conclude by trying to determine what characteristics are to be assigned to the new law.

I. "SACRAMENTAL" OR SIGN VALUE OF JUSTICE IN THE CHURCH

While it might be surprising to speak of justice in the terms of a "sacrament," we find that on at least three occasions Pope Paul uses this word to express the reality of juridical life in the church.[7] The "church's juridical activity is, as it were, a sacramental sign of salvation just as the church herself is—except that this sign is not restricted to juridical activity . . . of the church (which) can have no other aim but to manifest and serve the life of the Spirit."[8] In other words, the ecclesial juridical structure is unique because it shares in the sacramental nature of the church.[9]

We immediately see then that when we are considering canon law as a means of providing for the administration of justice, we are placing ourselves in an entirely different perspective: we are no longer simply at an external level, but we raise ourselves to partake, as it were, in God's providential plan. This being so, let us see how this sign or sacramental value is to be applied to the notions of justice, equity and law.

A. Justice in the Church

Any social life of humans has as its foundation the practice of justice, which is not based on a subjective approach, on situation ethics or on a philosophy of doing what is opportune.[10] Rather, justice is that which brings peace to others. "There is no true peace except in justice. And true justice is not to be found in a legislation that is imposed by one or another group because of its strong position in society. It is found, on the contrary, in the concern for assuring even better protection for natural rights."[11] The first blessing which justice brings forward is indeed peace: "peace with God and peace among the faithful."[12] Justice, therefore, and the juridical life of the church, have no other purpose, it seems, than of being "a pastoral means of constantly fostering and preserving peace."[13] The insistence upon the word "pastoral" leads immediately to another question: who provides for the administration of justice?

In one of his earlier addresses, Pope Paul speaks of the man of law as a *sacerdos iustitiae,* a person who defends and seeks out justice, who gives it its own image; a priesthood which provides for the common good of society and for the good of each person. The jurist is a "priest of justice" because his ministry is to be faithful and above reproach.[14] As a priest of justice, he has as a special role to develop a sense of justice in others which will "be proof against the weaknesses caused by attention to special interests."[15] This sense of justice will be developed by protecting, affirming and defending those values which possess an undeniable authority and which have been declared sacred.[16]

A sense of justice is not identified with a spirit of rigidity. It calls very often for flexibility and true pastoral concern which do not mean "any departure from the standards of truth and justice which must be scrupulously observed."[17] What is, in fact, flexibility? It is something, opposed to "legalism," which is founded on the "concern for assuring even better protection of natural rights."[18]

The judge will, if inspired by this true sense of justice, "take into account all the promptings of charity and seek to avoid the rigor of the law and the rigidity of its formal expression. He will avoid the letter of the law that kills and try to imbue his interventions with the charity that is the gift of God's liberating and vivifying Spirit."[19] This spirit which is to characterize each man of law, will also, necessarily, have to characterize the law of the church itself. "Do not stifle the Spirit," the Pope stated on Feb. 4, 1977, repeating the words of St. Paul; to avoid doing so, we must therefore make certain that all our juridical activity is truly guided by the Holy Spirit, letting the wind blow where it will.[20]

Justice will be protected in the new Code of Canon Law for a number of reasons: one of these is that "the communion of the church embraces both the faithful and their pastors."[21] Justice is not something which is to be used only on the level of those in authority; the communion of all in Christ is such that all have a right to justice and an obligation to provide for it.

Consequently, we are able to come to a new view of the way in which justice is to be considered. It is here, I believe, that Pope Paul makes one of his most important contributions to legal theory in the church when he states emphatically that "justice will be protected in the new code . . . (since) the juridical will no longer appear to dominate every area of the church's life. It will appear rather as but one facet of that life: an important one, indeed, but also one which serves the life of the communion as such and leaves to the individual believer the freedom and responsibility he needs in building up the body of Christ."[22] This will entail, of course, a respect for the values of the "cultures which now exist in the various parts of the world (and) are to be more fully acknowledged and accepted, provided the unity of the faith is safeguarded."[23]

Justice, therefore, will not be something standing on its own. It will be but one star or jewel in a multifaceted crown. It will be mounted, as it were, on a background of equity, another virtue which plays such a significant role in the renewal of law.

B. Canonical Equity

Canonical equity, the fruit of benignity and charity,[24] is "justice tempered with the sweetness of mercy."[25] It is the qualitative character of the precepts of law and the norm of their application.[26] Especially, "it is an attitude of mind and spirit that tempers the rigor of the law. It is a human corrective element and a force for proper balance."[27]

Our present code, undoubtedly, provided for equity, mercy and humanity (cf. Canon 1929); it also called for a higher form of justice with a spiritual goal in mind. Yet, for Pope Paul, this does not seem to be enough. He asks whether "we shall have to rethink the notion of canonical equity in the light of the council, in order to imbue it with even greater Christian value and more strongly pastoral import."[28]

This is a call to all of us—a call that we shall examine in more detail in the second part of this study. Suffice it for the moment to state that "in canon law it is equity which governs the application of norms to concrete cases, with the salvation of souls as the goal which is always kept in view. Equity takes the form of mildness, mercy and pastoral charity and seeks not a rigid application of law but the true welfare of the faithful."[29]

There is a third aspect to be considered under the heading of the sacramental or sign value of justice in the church: it is law at the service of truth.

C. Law at the Service of Truth

Our pastoral service is twofold: it is a service of charity and a service of truth.[30]

This is very clearly stated in one of the Holy Father's most important addresses on the subject of law, his allocution of Jan. 28, 1971. In this address, Pope Paul clearly states that "the law is not for the law's sake, nor judgment for the sake of judgment, but both law and judgment are at the service of truth, justice, patience and charity—virtues which constitute the essence of the Gospel and which today more than ever should stamp the character of the ecclesiastical judge."[31]

This is going to lead to what he calls a "pastoral style," a spirit of understanding. "Thus there opens before our eyes," he says, "as a good omen, the vision of the administration of ecclesiastical justice permeated with this pastoral style. It is characterized, indeed, by the essential and indispensable requirements of order, and at the same time by that progressive discovery of dignity of the human person to which the church, our mother and teacher, today leads us."[32]

Against this background, we can now move one step further; let us try to determine how canon law, according to Pope Paul, is to be an expression of justice, equity and truth.

II. Canon Law as an Expression of Justice

There are many possible ways of considering what canon law is, or should be. But all of these ways presuppose, it seems, a justification of the need for a juridical order. Therefore, having established this, we can try to see what would be the role assigned to canon law in assisting the individual and the community. With this background, it will then be possible, I hope, to provide some type of descriptive definition of canon law as it is to exist in the church today.

A. The Need for a Juridical Order

We often find today "an appeal to liberty against law, against any law whatever. And there is an appeal to the Gospel to support this. It is true that the Gospel reminds us of the preeminent liberty of the spirit."[33] We have only to think of the preaching of Jesus "against pharisaical legalism in behalf of the love and liberty of the children of God" to be aware of this.[34] But, "the teaching of the Gospel and of the apostles does not end there. The same Jesus who preached love and proclaimed the interior life and freedom, laid down practical and moral regulations binding his disciples to faithful observance, and he willed . . . an authority provided with fixed powers, in the service of man."[35]

The positive law which we have in the church has as its purpose to safeguard human goods, arrange and foster the common good, and guarantee the inviolable, "responsible autonomy of the individual against all eventual interference and abuse. It is this autonomy that makes it possible for every human being to develop his own personality in a fruitful manner. Freedom and authority are not opposing terms, but rather values that complement each other; their mutual cooperation promotes the growth of the community and, at the same time, the capacities for initiative and enrichment of the individual members."[36]

This judicial order presupposes a hierarchical structure in the church, an authority established to provide for the necessary order. Canon law, then, as an expression of this juridical order, "devotes the first place to the spirit which is its supreme law, but it also responds to a need inherent in the church as an organized community. It gravitates toward spiritual values; it scrupulously protects and safeguards the administration of the sacraments, which are the focal points of its rules."[37]

While the Holy Father recognizes that there exist "certain antiquated or overly arbitrary or excessively severe forms of exercising judicial power," he also reminds us that the use of such power, in the proper form and within reason, is at the source of the rights of the individual as well as of community order.[38] This order has as its goal to protect the individual and the community.

B. Law at the Service of the Individual

The proper goal of all sacred institutions is the salvation of others.[39]

In this regard, law which has its foundation in Jesus Christ, has the value of a sign of the internal action of the Spirit. It thus has a number of roles assigned to it in relation to the individual: 1) it must express the life of the Spirit at work within each believer; 2) it must produce the fruits of the Spirit which Paul tells us are love, joy, peace, long suffering, gentleness, goodness, faith, meekness and temperance (Gal. 5:22-23) and against which there is no law.

It must also 3) reveal the image of Christ which is within us, enabling us to be signs to others of the love of Christ which urges us on.[40]

That is why the individual will consider canon law as a hierarchical law, a missionary law, a bond of communion, an instrument of grace and a law of the church.[41] Indeed, we have traced out for us an entire program which presupposes deep inner convictions. This instrument of grace, however, will not be only for ourselves; it will produce its effects in the community as a whole.

C. Law at the Service of the Community

The juridical function in the church derives from the power of jurisdiction which finds its strength and reason for being in Christ.[42]

This function has been assigned a number of roles in the life of the community. First, it is to be a bond of unity in a line that is distinct and subordinate to the sacraments, which are of divine institution. Second, it must be pastoral, giving the church a more human characteristic, making it more sensitive to the charity that law should promote and guarantee in the ecclesial community. Third, it is to be service, ministry and love.

Given these characteristics, we could state that the primary function of canon law in regard to the community is to help structure Christian institutions by seeing to order and promoting concord. Law has, then, the practical role of guiding the faithful to maturity in Christ.

As a result of this order and concord, canon law is to provide, by its norms, for the social protection of rights. It has a special role to play, not only as an instrument of personal renewal, but also for the development of society: it is not a fixed status of things, but rather a dynamic plan for action.

Consequently, Pope Paul assigns four basic roles to canon law in its service to the community: 1) It defines institutions; 2) provides for the necessities of life by means of laws and decrees; 3) completes the essential features of juridical relations between the faithful, pastors and laity by means of its rules, which are in turn counsels, exhortations, directives of perfection, pastoral indications. 4) Finally, it defends the human person and forms the Christian so that he may participate in a community way in Catholic life.[43]

If it is to be faithful to its mission of being the exterior sign of the internal life of the Spirit in the church, canon law must then: 1) be consistent with the doctrine and teachings of the church; 2) be aware of its end, the sanctification of the faithful, and provide means of reaching this goal through order and peace; 3) be attuned to the dignity of each Christian in the church-communion, in whom the Spirit of God dwells; 4) determine the manner in which the relations between the faithful are to be carried out.[44]

D. What Is Canon Law?

Having seen the role ascribed to canon law both in regard to the individual and to the community, we can now try and provide a description of this sacred science. The Holy Father has spoken on a number of occasions on this particular subject.[45]

First of all, the Pope states that canon law is "a norm that tends for the most part to interpret two laws—a higher divine law and an internal, moral one of conscience."[46] It provides balance between rights and corresponding duties, between liberty and responsibility, between the dignity of the individual and the sovereign requirements of the common good.[47]

It is "the law of a society that is indeed visible but also supernatural."[48] It is a sacred science entirely distinct from the civil law, proceeding from the very will of Christ.[49] The juridical structure of civil society cannot be applied to the church without risk.[50] Once we move away from a law patterned on civil law, we move to a law based on doctrine. This, I believe, is the very point of Pope Paul's projected renewal. He has very strong words to say on this subject. "With the Second Vatican Council there has ended, once and for all, the time when certain canonists refused to consider the theological aspect of the disciplines studied, or the laws that they applied."[51]

Or again, "If churchmen cannot escape the charges of juridicism and formalism, even when they must make laws and govern, rest assured that these accusations are also leveled at canonical studies that cling to the old positions of juridical positivism or of juridical historicism. Be able to see in the church, beyond the veil of her secularity, the society of the spirit."[52]

The charter of the new canon law is to be found in the following injunction: "To limit ecclesial law to a rigid order of injunctions would be to violate the Spirit who guides us toward perfect charity in the unity of the church. Your first concern will not be, therefore, to establish a juridical order modeled on civil law, but to deepen the work of the Spirit which must be expressed also in the church's law."[53]

These words provide us with the new understanding that is required if we are to be in line with the proposed renewal of law. Our law is to be based on the Spirit, be an instrument of grace, determine the rights and obligations of believers, and be a dynamic plan for action.

It is easy to see that such has not always been the case. Indeed, Pope Paul explicitly states so: "It cannot be denied that the church, in the course of her history, has taken from other cultures (Roman law is a well-known example, but it is not the only one) certain norms for the exercise of her judicial power. It is unfortunately true that the church, in the exercise of her power, whether judicial (procedural) or coercive (penal), has in the course of the centuries borrowed from civil legislations certain serious imperfections, even methods which were unjust in the true and proper sense, at least objectively speaking.''[54]

Let us see now what characteristics he is assigning to the renewed canon law, and let us use these as background against which to evaluate our own canonical ministry.

III. A Renewed Canon Law

Having seen the importance of law as a means of expressing justice and providing for equity and truth, and having considered the role assigned to law today, let us now turn our thoughts toward the future to see how Pope Paul envisages the renewal of law. He will express this in a number of ways, especially by considering the role of the judge as he applies ecclesial legislation, and by describing the spiritual characteristics of law.

A. Renewal of Law in the Church in General

As a society of the Spirit, ''no longer having any temporal power of her own, and with no ambition to recover the burden and advantages of that power, the church's only desire is to be effectively assured of the free exercise of her spiritual and moral mission, by means of equitable, fair and stable delineations of respective spheres of competence.''[55]

Consequently, ''a church in which an external and formalistic canon law would depart from the spirit of the Gospel, or prevail over theological speculation, or stifle the formation of a conscience enlightened by self-determination . . . would not correspond to the renovating orientations of the council.''[56] The spirit of juridicism, then, is not the spirit which animates the man of law; rather it is the spirit of the Catholic Church which calls for clear displays of integrity, firmness and goodness.

B. The Exercise of Judicial Power in Particular

To a great extent, the law of the church is to be applied by the judge who must also have those characteristics which correspond to the traits of the new law itself.

The qualities of the canonist were outlined in the address of Jan. 28, 1978: he is to be a person who exercises moral qualities, leads an upright life, has excellent doctrine and gives enlightened judgments.[57] But even more than this, we need impartiality that presupposes a profound and unshakable honesty. We need disinterestedness, to avoid undue pressure; we need care and concern to take the cause of justice to heart.[58] Finally, the judge is to be characterized by integrity, firmness and goodness.[59]

The integrity of the judge will manifest itself by avoiding ''an excessive rigorism which refuses to grant reasonable confidence to the plaintiff and risks harming a person who is within his rights, all of which leads to direct consequences for his eternal salvation if it is a question of providing a remedy for sad moral situations.''[60] This is an important point: to recognize the trustworthiness of others and to apply this in our judgments. An illustration of this can be found in the address given by Cardinal Felici some months ago in which he described the manner of building up proof in a case through arguments of credibility when no other means were available.[61]

Because of these traits, the church's juridical activity becomes, as mentioned earlier, "a sacramental sign of salvation"[62] since it has "no other aim but to manifest and serve the life of the Spirit, that is, the divine life of the faithful and charity in particular . . . The revision of the Code of Canon Law . . . will be nothing but an application of this teaching."[63] Or, in other words, "when he is proclaiming the law and guaranteeing order, the judge lets himself be penetrated by a sense of humanity, which is both humble and wise, and which makes of him a master, a guide, a father and a friend."[64]

Since the ecclesiastical judge is essentially that "certain inspired justice," he must understand and fulfill his mission in a priestly spirit. "Over and above the requisite knowledge . . . he must also acquire a great and habitual self-mastery. He must strive to grow in virtue, lest he should eventually obscure with the filter of a defective and distorted personality the heavenly rays of justice, which the Lord grants to him for a correct exercise of his ministry."[65]

This exercise will also call for diligence. On at least three occasions, Pope Paul has mentioned that the administration of law is to be carried out with diligence and speed. "You want to exercise justice with canonical equity, and you want it to be speedier, more gentle, more even-tempered. As far as being speedier is concerned, it is certainly true that prudence is not necessarily to be identified with a sluggish pace, which sometimes leads to real injustice and great danger to souls."[66]

Or again, in January 1978: "Another element is speed, with regard to which it seems to us opportune to say a few words, since it is certainly desirable and must be constantly sought, but always as a method subordinate and geared to the primary aim of justice. Speed will thus be a further expression of the above-mentioned diligence. It will mean solicitude in the study and definition of the cases, in order to avoid the two opposite obstacles of haste and of slowness which deprive the parties in question of timely answers to their problems."[67]

A third mention of this important aspect is to be found in his address of Jan. 11, 1965: "Any suspicion of injustice will again be avoided in the pursuit of a trial by suppressing any delay which would not be required by the particular character of special circumstances of a given case, and by proceeding with great care, *sedulo et cito* . . . You know that any culpable delay in the carrying out of the execution of justice, caused by negligence or by other occupations, is, in itself an injustice of which every member of a tribunal will strive to avoid even the risk."[68]

If, at this point, we still feel that we can respond to these high ideals, we can ask ourselves how now can we envisage the new law.

C. The Manner of Renewing Canon Law

As Pope Paul clearly and emphatically stated on Feb. 4, 1977, the revision of the code "cannot mean simply improving the earlier code by introducing a more appropriate order of material, adding what seems worthwhile and omitting what is no longer relevant. Rather the code must become an aid to contemporary church life in the post-Vatican age."[69]

A new element has now entered into the study and formulation of canon law: the canonist is obliged "to search deeper in sacred scripture and theology for the reasons for his own teaching. This fact has upset his way of doing things, for he was accustomed to basing his teaching for the most part on a centuries-old, unquestioned tradition and to supporting it with a comparison to and contribution from Roman law first of all . . . and then with the laws of the nations to which the church had directed her evangelizing mission."[70] The new element consists in deriving canon law "from the very essence of the church of God, for whom the new and original law, that of the Gospel, is love."[71] This closer relationship between theology and canon law will infuse new characteristics into the latter to make it "a fostering and protecting law."[72]

"Today it is impossible to carry out studies on canon law without a thorough theological training. The close relationship between canon law and theology is raised, therefore, with urgency."[73] Today there is necessary a theology of law which takes up everything that divine revelation says about the mystery of the church. In the various aspects in which are expressed the person and the organization in the church, the action of the Spirit, secret and yet manifest exteriorly, is present: and this action must constitute the object of your reflection."[74]

Given this, in addition to the roles assigned above, Pope Paul attaches a further role to canon law: "It is meant to preserve, protect and encourage all those common undertakings designed to make us more faithful and more persevering in the practice of Christian living."[75] It does this by devoting "the first place to the spirit which is the supreme law."[76]

Since they are to be based on doctrine, the norms "are not ends in themselves. They are means by which the blessings God entrusts to the church may actually reach the faithful in a regular, orderly way."[77] The new code, then, must "have a more evident spiritual character. This is because the function derives from the sacramental nature of the church and is exercised within the communion of the church."[78] Consequently, "the laws of the code should breathe the spirit of charity and restraint, kindness and moderation, which must distinguish the new code from every purely human legislation. The purpose of the entire array of laws is to help the faithful in their spiritual life, which must be inspired by personal conscience and a sense of responsibility rather than by precepts."[79]

One further point is that the new law "must state that the principle of protection by the law applies equally to superior and subject, so that even the suspicion of arbitrariness may be eliminated from ecclesiastical government."[80]

The role of the new code can, then, be summed up in the following points: 1) to impose proper order on the various powers; 2) to administer the help which brings us grace; 3) to define and protect the rights and duties of the faithful toward one another and toward the community as a whole; 4) to prepare a fruitful soil for pastoral action, "namely a just social order in which the ultimate end not only can be attained but is, in fact, attained."[81]

At the end of this lengthy study we are able to draw a few conclusions.

Pope Paul states that law is not an end unto itself; it is based on the Gospel; it provides for proper pastoral action. The law will remain a dead letter if it is not applied by persons of integrity, honesty and zeal.

Just as he told us not to be afraid of the church, Pope Paul also calls upon us not to stifle the spirit by "keeping the heart open to every genuine action of the Holy Spirit." And as he says, repeating the words of scripture, "Let him who has ears heed the Spirit's words to the churches."[82]

NOTES

1. The following addresses were used as a basis for preparing this presentation: Sept. 21, 1963; Dec. 12, 1963; Nov. 4, 1964; Jan. 11, 1965; Nov. 20, 1965; Jan. 23, 1966; April 23, 1966; Aug. 17, 1966; Oct. 12, 1966; Oct. 19, 1966; Dec. 23, 1966; Jan. 11, 1967; Jan. 23, 1967; May 27, 1967; Feb. 12, 1968; May 25, 1968; Jan. 15, 1969; Jan. 27, 1969; June 23, 1969; Oct. 4, 1969; Nov. 12, 1969; Jan. 19, 1970; Jan. 29, 1970; June 17, 1970; June 23, 1970; July 8, 1970; Jan. 28, 1971; Dec. 13, 1971; Jan. 28, 1972; Dec. 9, 1972; Dec. 13, 1972; Feb. 8, 1973; Sept. 17, 1973; Dec. 14, 1973; Jan. 31, 1974; March 18, 1974; Jan. 30, 1975; Feb. 9, 1976; Feb. 4, 1977; Feb. 19, 1977; Jan. 28, 1978.
2. Paul VI, Jan. 27, 1969, in *The Pope Speaks*, 14 (1969-1970), p. 40.
3. Id., ibid.
4. Id., ibid.
5. Id., Jan. 25, 1966, in *La Documentation catholique*, 63 (1966), col. 306.
6. Id., Jan. 19, 1970, in *The Pope Speaks*, 15 (1970-1971), p. 74.
7. Feb. 4, 1977 (two occasions), Feb. 8, 1973.
8. Paul VI, Feb. 8, 1973, in *The Pope Speaks*, 18 (1973-1974), p. 77.
9. Id., Feb. 4, 1977, in *The Pope Speaks*, 22 (1977), p. 175.
10. Id., cf. Jan. 23, 1965, in *La Documentation catholique*, 64 (1967), col. 291.
11. Id., Oct. 4, 1969, in *The Pope Speaks*, 14 (1969-1970), p. 374.
12. Id., Feb. 4, 1977, loc. cit., p. 174.
13. Ibid., p. 179.
14. Cf. Id., Jan. 11, 1967, in *La Documentation catholique*, 62 (1965), col. 198.
15. Id., Jan. 30, 1975, in *The Pope Speaks*, 20 (1975-1976), p. 84.
16. Cf. ibid.
17. Ibid., p. 87.

18. Id., Oct. 4, 1969, loc. cit., p. 374.
19. Id., Feb. 8, 1973, loc. cit., p. 81.
20. Cf. Id., Feb. 4, 1977, loc. cit., p. 176.
21. Ibid., p. 177.
22. Ibid., p. 177.
23. Ibid.
24. Cf. Id., Feb. 8, 1973, loc. cit., p. 75.
25. Ibid., p. 78.
26. Cf. ibid., p. 79.
27. Ibid.
28. Ibid.
29. Id., Feb. 19, 1977, in *The Pope Speaks*, 22 (1977), p. 171.
30. Cf. Id., Jan. 27, 1969, in *The Pope Speaks*, 14 (1969-1970), p. 41.
31. Id., Jan. 28, 1971, in *The Pope Speaks*, 16, (1971-1972), p. 77.
32. Ibid., p. 78.
33. Id., Jan. 29, 1970, in *The Pope Speaks*, 15 (1970-1971), p. 54.
34. Ibid.
35. Ibid., p. 55.
36. Ibid.
37. Ibid., p. 56.
38. Cf. ibid., pp. 57-58.
39. Cf. Id., Jan. 29, 1970, loc. cit., p. 51.
40. Cf. Id., Sept. 17, 1973, in *Origins*, 3 (1973-1974), p. 272.
41. Cf. Id., Feb. 8, 1973, loc. cit., p. 78.
42. Cf. Id., Jan. 27, 1969, loc. cit., p. 39.
43. Cf. Id., Sept. 17, 1973, loc. cit., p. 272.
44. Cf. Francis G. Morrisey, "The Role of Canon Law Today," in *Chicago Studies*, 15 (1976), pp. 240-241, where a collation is made of a number of addresses of Pope Paul VI.
45. For instance, Jan. 19, 1970; Dec. 13, 1972; Feb. 8, 1973, etc.
46. Paul VI, Jan. 19, 1970, loc. cit., p. 73.
47. Cf. ibid.
48. Cf. Id., Dec. 13, 1972, in *The Pope Speaks*, 17 (1972-1973), p. 376.
49. Cf. ibid., p. 377.
50. Cf. Ibid.
51. Id., Sept. 17, 1973, loc. cit., p. 263.
52. Id., Jan. 19, 1970, loc. cit., p. 74.
53. Id., Sept. 17, 1973, loc. cit., p. 272.
54. Id., Jan. 28, 1971, loc. cit., p. 76.
55. Id., Jan. 19, 1970, loc. cit., p. 74.
56. Id., Jan. 27, 1969, loc. cit., p. 41, Cf. p. 42 for sources for the following sentence.
57. Id., Jan. 28, 1978, in *L'Osservatore Romano*, English edition, Feb. 9, 1978, p. 7.
58. Id., Jan. 29, 1970, loc. cit., p. 53.
59. Cf. Id., Jan. 27, 1969, loc. cit., p. 42.
60. Id., Jan. 11, 1965, loc. cit., col. 199.
61. Cf. *Communicationes*, 9 (1977), No. 1.
62. Paul VI, Feb. 8, 1973, loc. cit., p. 77.
63. Ibid.
64. Id., Jan. 25, 1966, loc. cit., col. 306.
65. Id., Jan. 28, 1971, loc. cit., p. 77.
66. Id., Feb. 8, 1973, loc. cit., p. 82.
67. Id., Jan. 28, 1978, loc. cit., p. 3.
68. Id., Jan. 11, 1967, loc. cit., col. 199.
69. Id., Feb. 4, 1977, loc. cit., pp. 173-174.

70. Id., Jan. 19, 1970, loc. cit., p. 72.
71. Ibid., p. 73.
72. Ibid.
73. Id., Sept. 17, 1973, loc. cit., p. 263.
74. Ibid., p. 272.
75. Id., May 25, 1968, in *The Pope Speaks*, 13 (1968-1969), p. 221.
76. Id., Jan. 29, 1970, loc. cit., p. 56.
77. Id., Feb. 4, 1977, loc. cit., p. 174.
78. Ibid., p. 176.
79. Ibid., p. 178.
80. Ibid.
81. Cf. Id., Feb. 19, 1977, loc. cit., p. 170.
82. Ibid., p. 176.

Case 1

Theology and Law

In the attempt to draft a constitution (*Lex Fundamentalis*) for the Church, a disagreement has occurred centered on the placement of certain proposed canons. One group of those drafting a constitution wants to begin with canons describing the universal call of all people to holiness, the Church as a means to holiness, and the rights and duties of all the faithful. Next would follow a description of the offices and ministries of the Church that are to be of service to the People of God. Their theological rationale is that the model of the Church presented in the New Testament is based on the call of the Christian to be holy with its ministers as servants of the people.

Another group wishes to begin with a description of the structure and offices of the Church, outlining in broad terms their authority and jurisdiction, followed by a list of the rights and duties of the faithful. They prefer to omit any reference to the call of holiness as purely theological. Their theological rationale is that the New Testament describes the Church in terms of apostolic authority and order and that these principles should be expressed in the basic law of the Church.

Exercise

1. Given the many theologies of the Church and the proposition that law is dependent on theology, what do those commissioned to draft church law do when presented with draft laws based on different theological principles?

2. Should the Church attempt to combine plural theological viewpoints in one church law? Is it possible to do so?

3. Should the Church omit making laws in areas where there is considerable theological disagreement? What would be the effect of endorsing one theological approach in preference to another?

References

Dulles, A., *Models of the Church* (Garden City, New York: Doubleday, 1974).

Green, T., "Reflections on the People of God Schema," *Canon Law Society of America. Proceedings of the Fortieth Annual Convention,* St. Louis, Missouri, October 6-12, 1978, 13-33.

LaDue, W., "A Written Constitution for the Church," *The Jurist* 32 (1972), 1-13.

B. HISTORY OF CHURCH LAW

Canon Law in the Age of the Fathers

Justin Taylor

This paper will deal with the origins and early development of Church law.

The first important point about early canon law is that it existed. The Church has always had a law. It may appear whimsical to underline this fact as I am doing. The implications of the fact are not always, perhaps, sufficiently appreciated. They amount to this: the Church, in her own understanding of herself, is the sort of body that has a law, and a true law at that, comparable to the legal system of any nation. We know that the Greek word which we translate as "church"—ecclesia—was chosen as the equivalent of the Hebrew word qahal.[1] Both words are from roots meaning "to call". The Hebrew word depicts God's people Israel as, at least in notion, a sacred assembly summoned before Jahweh. The Greek word explicates or reinforces the political associations of the original. For an ecclesia in ancient Greece was a sovereign assembly of the citizens of a city-state, summoned—"called out" by the herald. The spread of Hellenism had made it a familiar institution in the near East. The qahal, the ecclesia, of Old Israel had a law, viz. the law of the Covenant which determined the relations between God and His people and among the people themselves. By virtue of the Covenant Israel was constituted a nation. The law arising from the Covenant, a law which underwent a progressive development throughout the history of Israel, governed the entire life of the nation. It comprised articles moral, civil, criminal, ritual, set down cheek by jowl and evidently making up a system which—whatever distinction might later be made, for instance between its moral and its ceremonial precepts—was originally all of a piece.

The Christians deliberately assumed the inheritance of Israel. They

**Father Justin Taylor S.M. is a member of the teaching staff of Mount St. Mary's House of Studies, Greenmeadows, Hawkes Bay, N.Z.*

1. See Mason, A.J., "Conceptions of the Church in Early Times", in Swete, H.B. (ed.), *Essays on the Early History of the Church and the Ministry,* London, 1918, pp. 5-6; also generally the article "The Church" (Schmidt, K.L.) in *Bible Key Words from Gerhard Kittel's Theologisches Woerterbuch zum Neuen Testament* (Eng. tr. and ed. Coates, J.R.), New York, 1951, pp. 1-34.

regarded themselves as the renewed, or as the new, People of God.[2] They expressed their self-understanding by applying to their body the name ecclesia. The word ecclesia, it should be noted in passing, was applied in the first place to the whole body of Christians regarded as assembled in Christ before God. Of that universal assembly, the local congregation was, not the part, but the microcosm or compendium, the representation in miniature, and so also could be called ecclesia.[3] It is perhaps not out of place to give some little emphasis to this understanding. For too often the local church has been seen simply as a part of the whole, or, on the other hand, the universal Church is regarded as simply a federation of local churches. Both these views are mistaken.

It accords with the Church's understanding of herself as God's People in some way like Israel, that she would have a law in some way like Israel's. This assumption has, however, been called into question. Rudolf Sohm, who did in the field of Church law what Adolf Harnack did in the field of dogma, maintained that law is in fact incompatible with the Gospel and was introduced as the result of the "secularization"—in this case the "Romanization"—of Christianity.[4] It must be admitted that such a view is not without evidence which at least appears to recommend it. Jesus, we know, had hard things to say about "the doctors of the law".[5] He expressly rejected a number of legal rulings which were current, and indeed spoke critically of the "human traditions", those man-made elaborations of the revealed law which too often imposed an excessive burden or alternatively obscured or frustrated the command of God.[6] Even the Torah itself could be reduced to two "simple" commandments, to love God and to love the neighbour.[7] In every age there have not been lacking those who have supposed that Our Lord would apply the same strictures to many of His own followers, even that He would declare that He did not intend them to be governed by law. The case appears to be even clearer with St. Paul. He protests constantly that through the death of Christ the law has lost its force.[8] Many have inferred from his writings, especially from the Epistles to the Corinthians, that in Paul's view Christians were to be governed not by law but uniquely by the Holy Spirit, that the Church's structure should be not "juridical" but purely "charismatic".

The weight of this evidence is, however, more apparent than real. Jesus is portrayed in the Gospels as carefully observant of the Law, even of its ritual

2. Mason, "Conceptions of the Church", pp. 7-9; "The Church" *(Kittell),* p. 49.

3. Mason, "Conceptions of the Church", pp. 19-24; "The Church" *(Kittell),* p. 7.

4. Sohm, R., *Kirchenrecht,* vol. I, Leipzig, 1892.

5. Luke xi. 45-52.

6. Mark vii. 1-13.

7. Matthew xxii. 34-40.

8. Romans vii; Galatians iii, 23-29.

prescriptions.[9] He said He had come not to abolish but to complete the Law, not, indeed, in the way of "carrying into effect each single injunction of the old Law but of bestowing on that Law a new and definitive form by raising it to a higher plane through the spirit of the Gospel".[10] Our Saviour's attitude to the Law is to be understood as that of a reformer and a renewer. Finally, in a passage which undoubtedly represents the authentic speech of Jesus, He declared His intention of building His ecclesia, His qahal.[11] The Christians' understanding of themselves as a people—not unlike a nation or a state—with all that that implied of government and law, was true to the intention of their Master. As for St. Paul, he himself was careful to exclude the antinomianism that some appear to have inferred from his teaching.[12] He was certainly no anarchist. The Acts of the Apostles depicts him establishing episcopoi (or alternatively presbyteroi) in churches which he founded.[13] With regard to the "charismatic" church of Corinth, R.E. Brown points out that, far from assuming such a structure to have been the rule in Paul's churches, one should recognize that, according to the evidence, it seems rather to have been exceptional. Brown suggests that it may indeed have been an experiment, and a none too successful one at that.[14] At any rate, by the turn of the first century, the church at Corinth has its presbyteroi.[15] Indeed, it is becoming clear that to oppose "juridical" and "charismatic" in any absolute sense is to beg the question.[16]

The Church by and large did not use the ordinary Greek word for law—nomos—but another which she made peculiarly her own: kanon. The fundamental meaning of this word is a straight rod or bar, especially one which is used to keep something else straight.[17] In its literal sense it is used of things like a weaver's rod, a mason's or carpenter's line, even a curtain-rod. Metaphorically, kanon meant a rule or standard, and was used in art to signify a model or standard (we talk about "canons of taste"), and in grammar a general rule; it could also be equivalent to a philosophical principle. Further afield, the word was used in astronomy and chronology of a table,

9. On Jesus' attitude to the Law, see the article "Law" (Kleinknecht, H. and Gutbrod, W.) in *Bible Key Words from Gerhard Kittell's Theologisches Woerterbuch zum Neuen Testament* (Eng. tr. and ed. Barton, D.M. and Ackroyd, P.R.), London, 1962, pp. 79-92.

10. Matthew v. 17 and note in *The Jerusalem Bible* (Eng. tr. and ed.), London, 1966.

11. Matthew xvi. 18; see Cullmann, O., *Peter, Disciple, Apostle, Martyr,* 2nd. Eng. ed., London, 1962, pp. 192 ff.; also "The Church" *(Kittell),* pp. 35-56. The Aramaic word used by Our Lord was probably either qehala or kenishta (which can also mean a "house".)

12. Romans vi. 15-19; I Corinthians vi. 12. On Paul and the Law, see now Drane, J.W., *Paul, Libertine or Legalist?* London, 1976.

13. Acts xiv. 23.

14. Brown, R.E. *Priest and Bishop,* London, 1971, pp. 69-72.

15. Epistle of Clement to the Corinthians, ed. Lightfoot, J.B. and Harmer, J.R. *The Apostolic Fathers,* London, 1891, pp. 5 ff.

16. "The Church" *(Kittell),* p. 69.

17. Liddell, H.G. and Scott, R., *Greek-English Lexicon* (rev. ed. Jones, H.S.), Oxford, 1968, s.v. Kanon.

e.g. of dates, and in public administration for an assessment of taxation; it could also mean a limit or boundary. The Church made, and still makes, extensive use of the word Canon in a wide number of different but related senses. Thus we speak of the Canon of the Mass and of the Canon of Sacred Scripture; a "canon" is a priest "on the list" of the clergy of a cathedral or collegiate church—formerly the word could have been used of any priest "on the books" of any church; the saints who have been raised to the honours of the Church are "canonized"; a "canon" is also a rule of faith.[18] The word kanon had already been used of law, so that the Church had a precedent for employing it in this sense.[19] It means in this context a rule or a standard of how to act, and one may usefully refer back to its basic literal meaning of something, a rod or a line, which keeps something else straight. Thus St. Paul uses the word kanon to mean a regulative principle of christian life.[20] There is interest in the fact that the Church should have used her own word for law, and not the word in ordinary use, nomos—which word, incidentally, was used in Scripture for the Law of Moses. However, not too much should be read into this: a canon is a precept to which one is obliged, not simply an ideal to which one is encouraged.

The sources of Church Law, in the sense of "fontes cognitionis", are many, as they are set out in treatises such as that of Cardinal Cicognani.[21] They can, however, be reduced to a few heads. The classic enumeration of these heads is: Scripture; Tradition and Custom; and Particular and Positive Enactment.[22]

I wish to speak first of Scripture as a source of Church law. To the first Christians, of course, "Scripture" meant what we know as the Old Testament: the formation of the New Testament was precisely the production of writings by the Christian community which were recognized by the Church as having to be placed alongside the "Scripture" of old Israel.[23] The first Christians were, as we know, faced with the question how far, if at all, they were bound by the "Old Law".[24] Jewish Christians only gradually emancipated themselves from it. Gentile Christians in mixed communities were at first held by the "Council of Jerusalem" to observe part of it. St. Paul declared—and the other Apostles agreed—that in principle Christians were not obliged as such by it (although, as we have noticed, such a doctrine had apparent consequences that were at least inconvenient). The eventual solution of the difficulty was to distinguish in the Mosaic law a body of "moral

18. For these and similar uses see Bright, W., *Notes on the Canons of the First Four General Councils,* Oxford, 1882, pp. 2-3.

19. The orator Lycurgus, cited by Liddell and Scott.

20. Galatians, vi. 16, where it refers to the irrelevance of circumcision.

21. Cicognani, A.G., *Canon Law* (Eng. tr.), Philadelphia, 1934. pp. 60 ff.

22. Thus Reichel, O.J., *The Canon Law of Church Institutions,* vol. I, London, 1922, p. 73.

23. See Kelly, J.N.D., *Early Christian Doctrines,* 4th ed., London, 1968, p. 56.

24. See "Law" *(Kittell),* pp. 92-101.

precepts" which were still binding, though subordinately to the law of the Gospel, and a body of "ceremonial precepts" which had ceased to be of obligation.[25] It is a fact, however, that the ceremonial law came to be revived, at least in part, in the Church. Such a second life was given when this or that precept was regarded as applying, in some sense, to Christians. So in the Didache the Jewish law of first fruits was continued for Christians and even extended beyond agricultural produce to income of any kind. In the same document the command to pay first fruits to the priests was continued in favour of the Church's ministers.[26] Indeed the Christian clergy, in particular, thus came to be governed by precepts drawn from the Levitical law.[27] The foundation of this development was the identification of the Christian clergy with the Israelite priesthood, in this way that they were seen as the fulfilment of what had been foreshadowed, antitype to type. The identification of Christian clergy with Israelite priesthood is apparent in the Epistle of Clement to the Corinthians.[28] Such a view seemed to flow naturally from the overall view of the Church as the renewed or the new Israel: everything in the old should have its counterpart in the new. In this way the ceremonial law as a whole came to be seen as symbolic of the life and worship of the Christian Church and so as offering models for laws regulating them.[29]

Before leaving the subject of the Old Testament, I wish to draw your attention to an element in the New Testament which is derived from the Jewish legal tradition, viz. Halakhah.[30] This is a form of midrash, i.e. of the interpretation of Scripture in a way which develops and applies it with the current situation in mind. Halakhah was midrash of a legal text, an interpretation of that text in view of a new state of affairs, in an attempt to extend the old prescription to cover the new facts, to stretch it even, or to reinterpret it so as to make it apply to a situation which the original legislator had not envisaged. Halakhah thus provided a means of changing the law by way of a sort of legal fiction—one of the classic resources of societies which hesitate to meet their needs by way of outright legislation.[31] In the past, the progressive development of the Covenant Law of Israel had enabled it to re-

25. Such a distinction is already clear in Irenaeus, *Adv. Haereses,* IV, (especially xiii-xviii); compare Harnack, A., *Lehrbuch der Dogmengeschichte,* 3rd ed., Freiburg i, B., 1894, vol. I, pp. 578 ff.

26. Didache, 13, ed. Lightfoot and Harmer, *Apostolic Fathers,* p. 223: the Christians are to give their firstfruits "to the prophets, for they are your chief-priests".

27. E.g. the law that a priest's wife must be a virgin, drawn from Leviticus xxi. 13 f., found in *Apostolic Constitutions,* II, ii, and in later synodical and papal legislation, e.g. c.3 of Council in Trullo and Siricius, Ep. i. cap. ix.

28. Ep. Clem., 40, ed. Lightfoot and Harmer, *Apostolic Fathers,* p. 27.

29. Thus St. Thomas Aquinas, *Summa Theologiae,* I IIae. ciii. 3.

30. See Bonsirven, J., *Palestinian Judaism in the Time of Jesus Christ* (Eng. tr.), New York, 1964, pp. 83-89 ("The Written and the Oral Law").

31. Compare Maine, H.S., *Ancient Law* (ed. Pollock F.), London, 1906, pp. 29 ff.

main the law of the nation despite the many changes, economic, social, and political, which the people went through, so that Deuteronomy could be drawn in unbroken continuity from the Ten Commandments. In the time of Our Lord, Halakhah was a living tradition of exegesis which re-interpreted the Torah, which had long reached a fixed form, and applied it to yet more new situations. For it was beyond doubt that the Torah had answers for every question, even for one which arose from new and previously unimaginable circumstances. The art of Halakhah was the art of making the Torah answer those questions. It was a necessary art, even if some of its products drew down on them the criticisms of Our Lord. Halakhah is, as I said, an element in the New Testament. It is part of the mental furniture of St. Paul and helped to produce some of those peculiar lines of thought which strike us as far from luminously self-evident.[32] The method can be seen clearly in I Cor. 9/9, where Paul proves from Deut. 25/4—"You must not put a muzzle on the ox when it is treading the corn"—that the Christian missionary has a right to be supported by his people. When the provisions of the Old Law were applied to the Church in the manner described above, it was, in fact, by way of a Christian Halakhah.

The New Testament contains a number of prescriptions belonging to a specifically Christian law. Many of these are attributed to the Lord. Among them are reported sayings of Jesus, such as that which restores the original indissolubility of marriage, or that which orders that one who refuses to accept the correction of the Community is to be excluded from it.[33] Clearly this New Law is not a matter of general exhortation to virtue, and the Church which Jesus intended to found has, as we should say, got "teeth", coercive power: "whatever is bound on earth shall be considered bound in heaven, whatever is loosed on earth shall be considered loosed in heaven".[34] Other ordinances of Christ are reported on the authority of another.[35] The New Testament also contains rulings or directions which are attributed to an Apostle rather than to the Master, such as the famous "Pauline Privilege".[36] Thus too the Pastoral Epistles set out the qualities necessary in an episcopos, presbyteros, or diaconos. So St. Paul in I Tim. 3/2 says that an episcopos should be temperate, discreet, courteous, etc., and that he "must not have been married more than once".[37] It is evident that the current law of the Church has continued to draw on such rules of the New Testament.

I turn now to Custom and Tradition as a source of Church law. I wish to

32. Compare "Law" *(Kittell),* p. 118.

33. Matthew xix. 3-9; Matthew xviii. 15-17.

34. Matthew xviii. 18.

35. I Corinthians vii. 10-11.

36. I Corinthians vii. 12-16.

37. For a discussion of this last prescription, see Lyonnet, St., "Unius Uxoris Vir", *Verbum Domini,* 45 (1967), pp. 3 ff.

stress however, that custom is not merely a source of law. It is law. To make this point I feel I can do no better than to quote at some little length from Professor Clive Parry who thus writes of custom and the English Common Law: "(General custom) *is* the common law itself—a set of largely unformulated principles fundamental to legal relations and considered inherent". He goes on: "(T)he transformation of custom which is not law into custom which is can be judged of only after the event. We find that what we have in fact done binds us. But we also find that only that which we have done in the conviction that it is already binding so binds us . . . (W)hat we seek is 'a general practice accepted as law'. A practice not so accepted will not suffice. What is relevant is only what was done because it was considered what must be done. Or, as Blackstone put it, a custom must be supported by the *opinio necessitatis*".[38] The original law of the Church is, I would maintain, to be found in just such customs, i.e. in the practice of the Church considered as binding on her members.

The rules of discipline in the early Church are referred to by contemporary writers as "canons", to which were regularly attached the adjectives "ecclesiastical", "ancient", or "apostolic".[39] It should be noted that, as this usage reveals, the word canon referred in the first place not to a particular enactment of a competent lawgiver in the Church, but to a rule of conduct which had been received generally in the Church and was considered to have been handed down from earlier times, even from the Apostles themselves. That is to say, a "canon" was a rule which was to be found in Custom and in Tradition. In a particular instance, an ecclesiastical authority might have formulated such a rule. But there was no question of innovating legislation. Quite the reverse. The authority concerned had no thought of doing anything other than to state "the good old law", the traditional, indeed apostolic canon. It might need to be stated or reformulated at a particular time in view of particular circumstances, but it was not thought to take its origin then and there. It was a rule of the universal Church and had always been so. It had been observed everywhere since the time of the apostles, and if it had been "made" it was made by them. After that, it was simply "found". Such a rule, then, was regarded as deriving its authority not from its immediate promulgation, but from what was believed to be its traditional nature and its apostolic origin. This, as we shall shortly see, was made abundantly clear in the form in which these rules were expressed in the first ages. Later, it is true, the legislative activity of Councils or Popes became clearer and in practice was acknowledged. But even so, the old idea of a canon as a traditional rule was never entirely lost sight of.

With the note of antiquity or apostolicity attached to the canons was closely connected the note of universality. In fact, a particular rule might

38. Parry, C., *The Sources and Evidences of International Law,* Manchester, 1965, p. 61.

39. Percival, H.R., *The Seven Ecumenical Councils of the Undivided Church,* Oxford, 1900, p. 592, citing earlier authorities.

have developed in peculiar local circumstances or have been formulated to meet local requirements. It was nevertheless thought of as the universal rule of the Church. There was no question of deliberate local adaptation or creation. Again, quite the reverse. A local community had no intention to do other than what the universal Church received as proper and in accordance with the rule received everywhere. Consequently, when such rules find a formal expression, they are invariably couched in terms which imply that they are of general, indeed of universal application. Belief in the apostolic origin of the canons reinforced the notion of their universality. For it was to be presumed that the Apostles would have been of one mind. So rules which descended from them would be uniform. In fact, we find that canonical rulings emanating from Church authorities which were regarded as repositories of apostolic tradition did receive widespread acceptance. Thus the Epistle of Clement of Rome to the Corinthians was accepted as authoritative in churches far away from Corinth, and in many places was read publicly in the liturgy.[40] In various later documents Clement figures as the medium through which the Apostles issue their decrees.[41] It was possible, however, for there to be a clash between apostolicity and universality. Thus in the 2nd century, Pope Victor wished to bring the churches of Asia Minor into line with the rest of the Church in the matter of the date of Easter; they, however, resisted in the name of the tradition which they claimed to have received from the Apostle John.[42]

In the nature of things, customary law gets written down. A number of documents have come down to us from the first three or four centuries which contain rules of procedure or conduct in the Church. They are not attributed to Councils or Popes, but rather appear to be private compilations. They are essentially witnesses to the traditional law of the Church to that which was "done because it was considered what must be done". They state what is the rule of the Church—the canon—with regard to various matters. All the documents have this in common, that the discipline which they describe purports to come from the Apostles, whether from the Apostolic College generally or from individual Apostles.

The oldest of these documents is the *Didache* or "Teaching of the Lord to the Gentiles through the Twelve Apostles".[43] Upon its discovery in 1883, it was immediately seen to be the most important text of the subapostolic period.[44] Indeed the great Duchesne was of the opinion that it was of apostolic authorship; internal evidence would, however, dissuade from this view, and the usual judgment is that it was composed early in the 2nd cen-

40. Lightfoot, J.B.,*S. Clement of Rome,* London, 1869, pp. 9-13.

41. See the *Apostolic Constitutions* below (p.159); compare also the series of pseudo-Clementine writings which sprang up in the 2nd and 3rd centuries.

42. Eusebius, *Historia Ecclesiastica,* V. xxiii-xxiv.

43. Ed. Lightfoot and Harmer, *Apostolic Fathers,* pp. 217-225.

44. Compare Quasten, J., *Patrology,* Utrecht-Antwerp, 1962, vol. I, pp. 29 ff.

tury in Syria. As it is, the usages which the Didache describes are of great antiquity: indeed its author or compiler claims for them no less than the authority of the Apostles, even of Christ Himself. This brief work is in fact the oldest source of ecclesiastical law which we possess. In the words of J. Quasten, "we have here the oldest Church-Order and the venerable prototype of all the later collections of Constitutions or Apostolic Canons with which ecclesiastical law in the East and the West began".[45] It is worth taking note of the ecclesiology of the Didache. Quasten again: "The concept 'Church' has in the Didache the connotation of universality. In the foreground of Christian consciousness is the idea of the all-embracing world church. The word ekklesia means not only the congregation of believers assembled for prayer, but also the new people or the new race of Christians that shall one day be firmly established in God's kingdom. The attributes *one* and *holy* are particularly stressed. The symbol of this unity of all unities is the Eucharistic bread which from a multitude of grains becomes one bread".[46] Among a number of Church Orders descended from the Didache is the *Didascalia Apostolorum* or "Catholic Teaching of the Twelve Apostles and Holy Disciples of Our Saviour".[47] This was composed early in the 3rd century for a community of Christian converts from paganism in northern Syria.[48] Its author appears to have been of Jewish descent. He aimed principally at moral instruction and canonical regulation for the maintenance of the constitution and order of the Church. The Didascalia was modelled on the Didache and in its turn became the main source of Bks. 1-6 of the Apostolic Constitutions, which we shall shortly see.

Another fundamental witness to early canon law is the *Apostolic Tradition* of Hippolytus.[49] The tradition in question mainly consists in laws for church organization and the conduct of worship.[50] This slim book was composed about the year 217, explicitly in order to state the traditional rules of the Church against innovations. The usages therein described represent the normal practice at Rome (and elsewhere) when Hippolytus was a young man, in the latter half of the 2nd century. The author sincerely believed them to be apostolic and so unalterable. They are in fact rules of real antiquity and of widespread observance, as a number of them are attested by others, such as Tertullian. Harnack remarks: "Here is the richest source that we in any form possess for our knowledge of the polity of the Roman church in the oldest time, and this Roman polity may, in many regards, be

45. Ibid., p. 30.

46. Ibid., p. 35.

47. Ed. Funk, F.X., *Didascalia et Constitutiones Apostolorum,* Paderborn, 1905; Eng. tr. Connolly, R.H., *Didascalia Apostolorum,* Oxford, 1929.

48. Quasten, *Patrology,* vol. II, pp. 147 ff.

49. Eng. ed. Easton, B.S., *The Apostolic Tradition of Hippolytus,* Cambridge, 1934.

50. See Easton's Introduction, pp. 24 ff; compare Quasten, *Patrology,* vol. II, pp. 180 ff.

accepted as the polity held everywhere".[51] Hippolytus wrote his Apostolic Tradition "for the Churches", i.e. for Christendom at large. Here is a case of a prophet not being without honour except in his own country. The work was neglected at Rome and in the West generally. In the East, however, and especially in Egypt and Syria, it was highly regarded. In fact "Hippolytus, more than any other Church Father, gave the laws and the liturgy of the Eastern Church their permanent form".[52] From the Apostolic Tradition are descended *The Testament of Our Lord,* composed in the latter part of the 4th century in Syria or Asia Minor, and *The Canons of Hippolytus,* composed in the 5th century in Egypt.[53]

The Apostolic Tradition of Hippolytus was also used largely in the composition of Bk 8 of the *Apostolic Constitutions.*[54] We have already seen the influence of the Didascalia Apostolorum and ultimately of the Didache on Bks 1-6 of this work, which therefore brings the two streams together.[55] The Apostolic Constitutions are in fact the most ambitious of all the Church Orders. The work undertakes to provide a practically complete treatise on Church laws and liturgies by collecting and revising earlier authorities. It has the appearance of a systematic code, as the various statements of traditional discipline are gathered under the broad headings of eight books as follows:

Concerning the Laity; Concerning Bishops, Priests and Deacons; Concerning Widows; Concerning Orphans; Concerning the Martyrs; Concerning Schisms; Concerning Christian Life, and the Eucharist, and the Initiation into Christ; Concerning Gifts, and Ordinations, and the Ecclesiastical Canons. It will be seen that the work is fairly comprehensive. In style, however, it is prolix and homiletic—the reverse of what one expects to find in a book of laws. The author of the Apostolic Constitutions is unknown, but he appears to have worked about 375 in Syria or at Constantinople. Consistently with the literary genre, the Constitutions are attributed to "the Apostles and Elders" as sources, sometimes to individual apostles, and to "Clement, Bishop and Citizen of Rome" as compiler and transmitter.

To the Constitutions are appended 85 so called *Apostolic Canons,* which were compiled, apparently by the same author, partly from the Constitutions and partly, its seems, from unspecified synods.[56] The Canons have a succinctness lacking in the prosy Constitutions. It is interesting to note that they do not have the same order as the Constitutions, nor do they cover the whole ground of the subjects of the Constitutions. In fact, most of the

51. Cited by Easton, p. 26.

52. Easton. p. 27.

53. Ibid., pp. 14-15.

54. Ed. Funk, *Didascalia et Constitutiones Apostolorum;* Eng. tr. in *Ante-Nicene Christian Library,* vol. XVII, Edinburgh.

55. Easton, *Hippolytus,* p. 12 f.

56. Ibid., p. 13.

Canons are concerned with the clergy, and within the whole collection the order is rather haphazard. In the course of time, the Canons became detached from the parent document and have a separate history. The Constitutions as a whole were not accepted as apostolic, and various local Councils branded them as apocryphal—for one thing, Arian tendencies can be discerned in them. Nevertheless, later writers do quote individual passages from them as authoritative. The Canons, on the other hand, were generally received as authoritative. The Eastern Church treated them as the fundamental part of ecclesiastical law. As such they were solemnly recognized by c. 2 of the Council in Trullo of 692.[57] They became known in the West in a Latin translation of the first 50 Canons made by Dionysius Exiguus early in the 6th century, which were included in his canonical collection.[58] Shortly afterwards, Pope Hormisdas, in re-issuing the Decree "De Libris Recipiendis et Non Recipiendis" of Pope Gelasius, rejected the Canons as apocryphal.[59] Notwithstanding, the authority of Dionysius continued to recommend them in the West. Gratian used them in the Decretum,[60] and after that they were usually accepted as authoritative.

Among the Apostolic Canons are, we have remarked, some which seem to have originated from various synods. That brings us to the Synod as a legislative body and to its enactments as a source of canon law. The practice of bishops of a region to meet in order to discuss matters of common concern is of such obvious utility that it can be assumed to have occurred from earliest times. It was certainly well established by the end of the 2nd century when, in the time of Pope Victor, Councils were convened in a number of places to discuss the date of Easter.[61] No. 37 of the Apostolic Canons orders that there should be a meeting of the bishops twice a year, in the fourth week after Easter and in the middle of October, "and let them examine amongst themselves the decrees concerning religion and settle the ecclesiastical controversies which may have occurred". By the early 4th century, such a practice had become the rule in the Eastern Church, and it was enjoined by the Council of Nicaea.[62] The region which each synod represented was there defined as the civil province; the assembly was to meet in its chief city or metropolis and was presided over by the bishop of that city, the metropolitan. The practice of holding synods established itself more slowly in the West, where in most parts bishops were literally few and far between. Africa, however, which had a fairly dense Christian population already in the 3rd century, knew regular meetings of its numerous

57. See below, p. 164

58. See below, ibid.

59. Migne, J.P., *Patrologia Latina,* vol. xix. pp. 166 ff.

60. Thus No. 17 of the Apostolic Canons was taken up by Gratian (c. 1, Dist. XXXIII) and so, as the footnote to CIC reveals, became a romote source of the modern c. 984.

61. Compare above, p.158, Eusebius, *H.E.* V. xxiii. 2.

62. Canon 5.

bishops at Carthage and other main centres.[63] In Italy too there were frequent synods; but they were of a different type, the patriarchal synod—not so much meetings of equals as convocations of the subordinates of the Pope.[64] Canons have also come down of Councils held at Elvira in Spain in 305 and at Arles in Southern Gaul in 314. The procedure of the ancient synods was closely modelled upon that of the Roman Senate and of the provincial assemblies and town councils which imitated the Senate.[65] Members spoke in turns by seniority, each bishop stating his *sententia;* examples are the so-called "canons" of the Council of Sardica, which are really a kind of Hansard report of the discussion. After each such intervention the assembly voted, and when a *sententia* obtained a majority of votes it was thereby adopted. After the Council had risen, its resolutions were drawn up in a clear and concise form which could be published, and which again resembled that of the *senatusconsulta.*

Synods, as the Apostolic Canon already cited implies, were often called on to judge in case of disputes or of charges brought against someone. Certain of their resolutions were therefore judicial sentences or alternatively the rules or principles upon which they had reached a particular judgment.[66] Others had a more general purpose. Synods decided in accordance with "the canons", those rules which were to be "found" in Sacred Scripture or in ecclesiastical tradition.[67] The bishops might also think it necessary or opportune to restate the canon on a particular matter or to provide for its application in various new cases; or they might have been asked to declare what the canon was on this or that, or which canon governed a particular case. Thus Nicaea stated explicitly: "Concerning those who have been excommunicated by the bishops in the different provinces, let the sentence of the canon prevail, which pronounces that those persons who have been cast out by one bishop are not to be received again into communion by any other".[68] Here the "canon", which Nicaea merely endorsed, was a presumably traditional rule which is also found in No. 32 of the Apostolic Canons. Although no synod would have regarded itself as doing anything except restating the ancient rule, in fact of course its proceeding was in many instances really equivalent to legislation. In a system where law is thought of as something that is found not made, as Maitland observed,

63. From early in the 3rd century; thus Duchesne, L., *The Early History of the Christian Church* (Eng. tr.), Vol. I, London, 1909, p. 288.

64. See below, p. 164.

65. See Hess, H., *The Canons of the Council of Sardica,* Oxford, 1958, pp. 24 ff.

66. Thus, presumably, a number of the decisions of the Council of Nicaea, such as canon 16, which awards the penalty of excommunication for clerics who refuse to go back to the churches to which they originally belonged.

67. Thus, of Nicaea, canon 2, which bases its prohibition of ordaining recent converts on I Timothy iii. 6; and canon 13, which maintains "the ancient and canonical law (nomos)" concerning the administration of Holy Viaticum to the dying.

68. Canon 5.

"the function of declaring law was scarcely to be distinguished from that of making law".[69] Because the law declared by the synods was regarded as the good old law of the Church, its authority was derived less from those who reformulated it than from those who were believed to have first given it, the Fathers and indeed the Apostles.[70] Again, although a synod may well have acted in view of local circumstances or have promulgated a discipline which had been developed locally, it thought of the canon which it was stating as not only ancient and apostolic, but also as of universal application. It was no more and no less than the rule supposed to be known and observed throughout the Church. Thus each synod purported to speak in the name of the whole Church and in this sense, as Sohm put it, "each synod claimed oecumenical status".[71] In the same way, the statements of each synod were to be regarded as equally and universally binding. Conciliar resolutions were frequently given wide publicity in the Church and might be received far from their place of origin. So the decrees of a local council in Asia Minor could become the law of the universal Church.[72] In practice, however, some councils were branded as heretical and their rulings were not received, while others were regarded as especially authoritative. Chief among these latter was the Council of Nicaea of 325, which was the first to get the epithet "oecumenical".

The name "canon" was extended from the rule which the synods were supposed to be stating to their statement of the rule.[73] From the 4th century collections of these synodical enactments were made. The origins of what has been called "the ancient Code of the Universal Church" are to be found in Asia Minor.[74] The nucleus of this great collection is formed by the canons of the Council of Ancyra (314) and Neocaesarea (315). To them were added the canons of Nicaea (325), which thenceforth took first place in the corpus, and of the Council of Gangra (343). Later this collection was augmented by the canons of the Councils of Antioch (341), of Laodicea (date unknown), of Constantinople (381), and of Ephesus (431). Thus was gathered the ancient corpus of canon law, which was confirmed by the Council of Chalcedon (451) in its first canon: "We have judged it right that the canons of the Holy Fathers made in every synod even until now, should remain in

69. Maitland, F.W., *Roman Canon Law in the Church of England,* London, 1898, p. 103.

70. It is of interest that at Nicaea, although canon 9 seems to allude to a ruling already given at the Council of Neocaesarea (c. 9), there is no reference to the previous synodical enactment, but only to "the Canon".

71. *Kirchenrecht,* vol. I, p. 317.

72. See below, p. 163.

73. It appears that the Council of Constantinople (381) was the first to refer to one of its own rulings as a "canon" (c. 2).

74. On the ancient collections generally, see Cicognani, *Canon Law,* pp. 192 ff.

force''. The canons of Chalcedon also became part of the code.[75] This collection, of Eastern origin, was also received in the West. The Church of Rome had a Latin version of the canons of Nicaea, to which were added those of the Council of Sardica (343)—without being distinguished from the canons of Nicaea, so that in the early 5th century Popes were quoting canons of Sardica as canons of Nicaea.[76] It is matter for dispute whether at that time Rome and the West acknowledged other Eastern councils.[77] The African Church had its own Latin version of the Nicene Canons.[78] From the councils which were held regularly at Carthage there issued a body of canons which were accumulated and which reached a classical form at the 17th Council of Carthage in 419.[79] This is the so called ''Code of the Canons of the African Church'', which made no small contribution to the development of law in the Church universal. In the course of the 5th century, translations of the Greek corpus were made into Latin—the so called ''Hispana'' or ''Isidoriana'' and ''Itala'' or ''Prisca'' collections.[80] The great Latin collector, who could justly be called the Founding Father of systematic canon law in the West, was Dionysius Exiguus. Before the year 500, he produced a revision of the Eastern code as received in the West (including Sardica), to which he added 50 of the Apostolic Canons and also the African Code.[81] The ancient canon law of the Eastern Church received its final form in the Council in Trullo (692).[82] The Trullan collection includes the old Eastern Code, to which it adds the African Code, canons of a Council of Constantinople of 394, and its own new canons.

Despite the frequency with which synods were held and the multitude of their decrees, synodical enactment was not, however, regarded as the sole source of Church law. It was not forgotten that a *canon* was supposed to be a traditional rule which had been observed everywhere from the time of the Apostles. Accordingly, the Trullan Council gave first place to ''the eighty-five canons, received and ratified by the holy and blessed Fathers before us,

75. For editions of the canons in this ''Code'': from the Councils of the 4th century, Jonkers, E.J., *Acta et Symbola Conciliorum Quae Saeculo Quarto Habita Sunt,* Leiden, 1954; from the Councils of the 5th century, Schwartz, E., *Acta Conciliorum Oecumenicorum.* Strasbourg, Berlin and Leipzig, 1914-1940; for Eng. tr. Percival, H.R., *The Seven Ecumenical Councils.*

76. Hess, *Sardica,* p. 49.

77. Innocent I declared: ''Whichever were drawn up at Nicaea, those canons alone ought the Catholic Church to follow, and these we recognize'' (Ep. vii. 3, *P.L.* xx. 505).

78. Hess, loc. cit.

79. Ed. Labbe, P. and Cossart, G., *Sacrasancta Concilia,* Paris, 1671, vol. II, pp. 1041 ff., Eng. tr. Percival, *The Seven Ecumenical Councils,* pp. 437 ff. The collection included also canons of a Council of Milevis and of another of Hippo.

80. The classic edition of the Latin collections is that of Turner, C.H., *Ecclesiae Occidentalis Monumenta Iuris Antiquissimi,* Oxford, 1899-1930.

81. See Cicognani, *Canon Law,* p. 215.

82. Ed. Labbe and Cossart, *Concilia,* vol. VI, pp. 1135 ff; Eng. tr. Percival, *The Seven Ecumenical Councils,* pp. 355 ff.

and also handed down to us in the name of the holy and glorious Apostles".[83] Moreover, such a rule could also be stated by one of the Fathers of the Church, in which case it would have as much authority as if it had been issued by a Council. So, the same canon 2 of the Council in Trullo "sets its seal" also upon "the canons" of the Twelve Fathers of the Eastern Church and even upon a canon attributed to St. Cyprian.

A final note. When any of these great synodical collections is called a "Code", one should not therefore expect to find a systematic law book. "Corpus" or "Collection" would be a less misleading term. The synods issued their statements on matters that came before them, and there is no necessary order among the canons of any one synod or in the collection as a whole. Similarly, no collection makes any claim to be a comprehensive statement of the entire law of the Church then deemed to be in force. The written law was never more than a partial enunciation of the unwritten law, which retained its authority and was regarded as the ultimate source of the particular enactment.

Finally, we come to the Apostolic See of Rome as a source of Church law in the age of the Fathers. The Roman Church and See was regarded in the early Church as the repository *par excellence* of apostolic tradition, since upon it, as Tertullian said, the Apostles Peter and Paul had "poured forth all their doctrine with their blood".[84] It was in virtue of this belief that Clement had told the Church of Corinth how to settle its affairs and that Victor had commanded the Churches of Asia to conform to the practice of the rest of the Church in the celebration of Easter.[85] The Roman See was eminently the place from which to seek authoritative statements of the canon, the traditional rule of the Church handed down from the Apostles. Clement, we have already seen, was frequently represented as the ideal channel through which the rulings of the Apostles reached the later Church.[86] The legislative activity of the papacy was closely connected with the Pope's competence as supreme tribunal for the whole Church. Rome was traditionally regarded as a final recourse from the judgments of bishops and synods in all parts of the Church and as a supplementary tribunal when lower courts were lacking—so much, at least, can be taken as certain here. Any court of superior jurisdiction, as well as deciding particular cases in accordance with the law, will also be called upon to make authoritative statements of what the law is, i.e. to give "authentic interpretations" of the law. This function is closely akin to legislation. For to declare with binding force what the law is, when other sources are silent or doubtful or in conflict, is really to make new law. So the Bishop of Rome acted as witness to the rules handed down by the Apostles, but he nonetheless acted as a lawgiver.

83. Canon 2.

84. *De Praescriptione Haereticorum,* 36.

85. See above, p. 161.

86. See above, p. 157.

The customary function of the papacy as supreme tribunal in the Church was being formulated in the 4th century, for instance by the Council of Sardica (343) and by the Constitution of the Emperor Gratian which was prompted by the Council of Rome of 381.[87] It is no mere coincidence that the position of the papacy as authentic interpreter of the canons, which also belonged to the practice of the Church, should have received a formal shape about the same time. That shape was in fact closely modelled upon the similar position of the Roman Emperor with regard to civil law.[88] It had long been a function of the Emperor to state the law in reply to the queries of officials or private persons. An inferior judge, for example, might write to the Emperor asking for direction on a point of law before him. Such a request was known as a *relatio,* a "reference" or "report". The Emperor's written reply, in the form of a letter *(epistula),* was called *rescriptum.* Usually he would simply cite an existing rule of law. Occasionally, however, a new rule might be laid down or a new principle introduced to meet the case. According to the dictum of Gaius, the imperial rescript, like other forms of *constitutio principis,* had the force of law, i.e. of statute.[89]

The Popes were asked from time to time what was "the canon" regarding such or such a matter, i.e. they were asked for "authentic interpretations" of Church law. Their replies can be documented from the time of Damasus (366-384).[90] If there was a relevant rule of a recognized synod, the Pope would apply it to the point in question and make any necessary clarification. Thus Innocent I (401-417) was able to answer several of the questions put by the Bishop of Rouen simply by citing canons of a Roman Synod of 386.[91] Where, however, there was no enacted canon, it fell to the Pope to "find" and state the rule or principle which governed the particular matter and apply it. Thus the same Pope explained to the Bishop of Toulouse that he would tell him "what docile reason persuaded, or the authority of reading showed, or the series of what had been observed through the ages demonstrated, should be followed".[92] The "authority of reading" meant above all the Bible, which was used as a book of law, and also the Fathers, especially his own predecessors. A rule could also be inferred from the practice of the Church, that is to say from Custom. That practice might, however, be abrogated by decision of the competent authority for a sound

87. On the "appeal canons" of the Council of Sardica, see Hess, *Sardica,* pp. 109-127; for Gratian's Rescript *Ordinariorum Sententias* and the Synod's Petition, see *P.L.* xiii, 575 ff.

88. See Jolowicz, H.F., *Historical Introduction to the Study of Roman Law,* 2nd ed., Cambridge, 1967, pp. 378 ff.

89. *Institutiones* I. v: "Constitutio principis est, quod imperator decreto vel edicto vel epistula constituit. Nec umquam dubitatum est, quin id legis vicem obtineat".

90. Frequent references will be made in what follows to letters of Pope Siricius, in *P.L.,* vol.xiii, pp. 1131 ff., and to letters of Pope Innocent I, in *P.L.,* vol. xx, pp. 463 ff.

91. Ep. ii; compare Siricius, Ep. v.

92. Ep. vi.

reason.[93] No ecclesiastical Gaius wrote that these replies of the Popes "have the force of a canon", but that was bound to be the effect of their authoritative statements of the Church's law. Such at least was the intention of the Popes themselves. Siricius in 385 explicitly put "the decisions of the Apostolic See" on the same level as "the venerable definitions of the canons".[94] The Popes in the letters containing their replies consciously imitated the style and language of the imperial constitution.[95] Thus the query sent up by a Bishop of Tarragona or of Thessalonica was called a *relatio.* The Popes did not, however, describe their replies as *rescripta,* although the verb *rescribere* was used. They preferred instead to call them *responsa;* but Siricius employed the term *decretalia constituta* to describe his replies and others like them, and it is as "decretals" that such papal replies on points of law are known.[96]

Relationes came in to Rome from Italy, Gaul, Spain and Illyricum.[97] In the case of Italy, the local bishops were traditionally in close contact with the Bishop of Rome, who was really their Patriarch.[98]

In the other Western provinces named, intermediate structures such as metropolitan see and synod were only slowly being elaborated, and the local bishops had more need to look to Rome for guidance. The bishops of Africa and the East were not in the habit of referring questions of law to Rome, for the same reason in both cases, namely that they had institutions of government superior to the local bishop and could therefore be for the most part self-governing. There is, however, an example of a decretal sent by Pope Innocent I in the early 5th century to Alexander Bishop of Antioch, who appears to have asked about several matters of concern to his own Church:[99] it is to be observed that Alexander, as a Patriarch, had no immediate superior under the Pope (unless the Patriarch of Constantinople, whose powers, at that time were still in the process of development). In their *responsa* some Popes, such as Innocent, were careful to seem to be doing no more than to state the existing law.[100] With others, the emphasis was upon

93. Thus in reply to the question whether incontinent clerics could be admitted to Penance and Communion, Innocent replied that a "consuetudo prior" had allowed them Penance but not Communion, but he declared that it had been decided ("placuit"), apparently by himself, that they might be admitted to Communion before they died, "lest we seem to follow the asperity and hardness of the heretic Novatian, who denied pardon".

94. Ep. i. 20.

95. See Getzeny, H., *Stil und Form der Aeltesten Papstbriefe bis auf Leo d. Gr.,* Guenzburg a. D., 1922, pp. 27 ff.

96. Siricius, Ep. i. 1 and 20.

97. Thus among Innocent's decretals are letters to the Bishops of Gubbio (Ep. xxv). Toulouse (Ep. vi), the Synod of Toledo (Ep. iii), and to the Bishop of Thessalonica (Ep. xvii).

98. See my article "The Early Papacy at Work: Gelasius I (492-496)", *Journal of Religious History,* 8 (1975), pp. 317 ff.

99. Ep. xxiv.

100. The characteristic of Innocent's decretals; see Getzeny, *Stil und Form,* p. 51 f.

their own ordinance as governors of the Church.[101] One of the earliest extant decretals, of Pope Siricius to Himerius of Tarragona, goes well beyond any simple statement of the law in force and decides with the authority of St. Peter what is to be done about the matters proposed.[102] Pope Zosimus, Innocent's successor, made striking use of such an unmistakably legislative formula as "placuit apostolicae sedi, ut. . .".[103] The questions dealt with in these early decretals were various: liturgical practice, the rules governing clerical appointments, the procedure to be followed in the Church courts, clerical and monastic life, the penitential discipline (often with reference to marriage).[104] Sometimes the letter included or was even mostly taken up with judgments delivered by the Pope on individual cases which had been referred to him.[105]

Although the decretals were replies to particular questions put by individuals, they were held to have universal force. This was in part because of the universal authority of the Bishop of Rome who issued them. But it was also because they were regarded as statements of the "canons", the rules deemed to have been handed down and observed throughout the Church since the time of the Apostles. So the decretals were of much more than purely private interest, as they were documents containing the law of the Church, and were of interest to the whole Church. Copies of them were circulated, and collections were made. The great collection of the early papal decretals was that made in the 6th century by Dionysius Exiguus.[106] He was persuaded to make a collection of papal letters to replace the defective collections which were then in use, and he produced a collection of thirty-eight decretals of Popes from Siricius (384-399) to Anastasius II (496-498) inclusive. Some years later he combined this collection of decretals with the collection of canons which he had already made. Thus was formed the "Collectio Dionysiana" which for several centuries was used generally at Rome and in Italy and was widely diffused throughout the West and even the East and exercised a great influence upon subsequent Western collections. By combining papal and synodical enactments in a single code, Dionysius was demonstrating his conviction that popes and councils were comparable sources of Church Law. In the last analysis, as the presence in the "Dionysiana" of the Apostolic Canons suggests, both were seen as authoritative witnesses to the "canons"—"those rules of old discovered not devised".

With the compilations of Dionysius Exiguus and of the Council in Trullo,

101. The characteristic of Zosimus' decretals; see Getzeny, p. 54.

102. Ep. i, which abounds in such expressions as "volumus", "iubemus", "inhibemus".

103. Ep. i. 1, *P.L.* xx. 642.

104. Among Innocent's decretals, Ep. xxv, Ep. xxxvii, Ep. ii. 5-6, Ep. ii. 13-16, Ep. vi.

105. Innocent to the Synod of Toledo, Ep. iii. 5, 6, 8.

106. Cicognani, Canon Law, p. 215 f.

the age of the Fathers in canon law comes to an end. In the West, further development is along the lines already laid down, and is represented by conciliar enactments and papal legislation. There are new collections made, largely based on the Dionysian. It would be outside the scope of this paper to discuss the False Decretals of the 9th century. The systematic study and codification of the ancient canon law was stimulated by the 11th century controversies surrounding the Investiture Contest between the Regnum and the Sacerdotium, and produced its classic work in Gratian's Decree. In the East too councils continued to be held. A notable part of the growing body of Eastern Church law consisted of imperial legislation. The Codes of Civil Law produced under Theodosius II in the 5th century and Justinian in the 6th contained a great many imperial laws—nomoi—pertaining to religion and the Church. Soon they were being excerpted and placed alongside the collections of synodical canons to make what was known as the *Nomocanon.*

Eventually in the early 7th century there appeared the classic form of the Nomocanon, a digest of church law in which was presented under each of its fourteen titles all the relevant legislation, both conciliar and imperial. The great systematic compiler of the Eastern Church, who occupies a similar position to that of Gratian in the West, was Photius, Patriarch of Constantinople in the 9th century. His collection in two parts—a chronologically ordered compilation of synodical canons and a revision of the Nomocanon—formed and still forms the classic source of ancient Church Law for the Greek Church.[107]

107. On the formation of the Nomocanon and the work of Photius, see Cicognani, *Canon Law,* pp. 200 ff.

Canon Law

Peter Huizing

Father Huizing's article begins at its midpoint so that it starts at the approximate point in history where Father Taylor's article ends.

. . . From *c.* 300 until *c.* 550, canon law in Western churches had a certain unity through the acceptance of the Eastern and North African councils and the binding factor of the papal decretal law (answers of popes to questions of bishops in matters of discipline), which did not exist in the East. The African canons, like the Eastern canons at Chalcedon, were read out at the councils of Carthage and, if confirmed, included in the Acts, which contained the newly enacted canons. Thus, at the third Council of Carthage (397), the Compendium of the Council of Hippo (393) was included. The collection of the 17th Council of Carthage (419) was soon accepted in all of the East and West. In Spain the canons of Nicaea I (325) and Chalcedon (451) and also African and south Gallican canons and Roman decretals were taken over, as well as their own canons, but the later *Hispana* (Spanish collection) crowded out all earlier collections. The Council of Elvira (295-314) in Spain was the first that set up a more complete legislation, followed by Gaul in the first Council of Arles in 314. Texts from the East, Spain, and Rome, including the *Quesnelliana* (an early 6th-century canonical collection named for its publisher, the 17th-century Jansenist scholar Pasquier Quesnel), circulated there. Gennadius, a priest from Marseilles (in France), *c.* 480 wrote the *Statuta ecclesiae antiqua* ("Ancient Statutes of the Church"), principally inspired by the *Constitutiones apostolicae.* A tendency toward the unification of canon law revealed itself most clearly in Italy against the disintegrating situation that existed between the eastern and western churches—*i.e.,* the so-called Acacian Schism (484-518), occasioned by the patriarch Acacius of Constantinople and the emperor Zeno's neglect of the legislation of the Council of Chalcedon—and the breakup of the Western Empire soon after the fall of Rome (476), at the time of the 30-year "Gelasian renaissance," beginning during the reign of Pope Gelasius I. There also existed in Rome translations of Eastern councils: *Vetus Romana, Versio Hispana* ("Ancient Roman, Spanish Version"), *Isidoriana, versio Prisca* ("The Isidorian, Priscan Version"), and *Itala*

("Italian"). By far the most important is that of the *Liber canonum* ("Book of Canons") of the 6th-century Roman theologian Dionysius Exiguus, *c.* 500. The first two versions contain 50 *Canones apostolorum,* Greek canons, and the African canons of the 17th Council of Carthage. Dionysius Exiguus also composed a *Liber decretorum* ("Book of Decretals") from Pope Siricius to Pope Anastasius II. Together, the books form the *Corpus* ("Body") or *Codex canonum* ("Code of Canons"). The *Quesnelliana* and other Italian collections are of less importance.

Until the end of the 7th century a greater decentralization and less mutual contact occurred in the separate Geman kingdoms. Elements of German law found their way into Roman canon law. The *Collectio Avellana* ("Avellen Collection"), written in Rome, *c. 555,* which was a western nomocanon, the *Collectio Novariensis* ("Novarien Collection"), and the *Epitome Hispanica* ("Spanish Abridgment") entered Italy from Spain. In Africa, the first, albeit primitive, systematic collections appeared: the *Breviatio canonum* ("Abridgment of Canons") of (Fulgentius) Ferrandus, deacon of the Church of Carthage (*c.* 546), and the *Concordia canonum Cresconii* ("Harmony of the Canons of Cresconius," a 6th- or 7th-century author), a systematic compilation of the *Dionysiana,* subsequently found in different manuscripts in Gaul. Here the collections were local ones: every cathedral and monastery had its own *liber canonum.* The church of Arles, the metropolis of southern Gaul, had the *Liber auctoritatum ("Book of Authorities"; i.e.,* legal texts), a nomocanon of its privileges. The first systematic Gallic *Collectio Andegavetis* ("Andegavenan Collection"), from the end of the 7th century, was an attempt to unite the ancient law with the native.

In Spain, after the conversion of King Recared in 587, the church of the Visigothic kingdom became a well-knit national church with a classical provincial structure under metropolitan jurisdiction, closely linked to the crown. The national councils of Toledo preserved the unity of law and respect for the ancient law. The *Capitula* ("Chapters") of Martinus, bishop of Braga (*c.* 563), was included completely in the *Hispana* and was also copied outside Spain. The *Collectio Novariensis* was related to the *Epitome Hispanica* ("Spanish Abridgment"), the code of the hierarchy that was temporarily halted at the fourth Council of Toledo (633). The *Hispana* was recognized by popes Alexander III and Innocent III as the authentic *corpus canonum* of the Spanish church. Shortly before the *Hispana,* systematic indices (called *tabula*) were written and were subsequently expanded into *excerpta* ("excerpts") and finally into complete texts, the *Hispana systematica* ("Systematic Spanish [Code]"). After the 10th century, the *Hispana* was also called the *Isidoriana,* attributed to Isidore of Seville, a Spanish encyclopaedist and theologian, who was the author of the *Etymologiae* ("Etymologies"), a universally distributed early medieval book of doctrine.

The most disparate picture is offered by the church in the British Isles.

The church there was concentrated around heavily populated monasteries, and discipline outside them was maintained by means of a new penitential practice. In place of ancient canons about public penance, the clergy and monks used *libri poenitentiales* (''penitential books''), which contained detailed catalogs of misdeeds with appropriate penances, and were a counterpart of the *Wehre* (lists of punishments) of the *Leges barbarorum* (''Laws of the Barbarians''). They were private writings without official authority and with very disparate content. From the monasteries founded in Europe by the Irish monk Columbanus and other missionaries of Anglo-Saxon background, the *libri poenitentiales* spread all over the continent, where once again new versions emerged. The *Collectio Hibernensis* (''Hibernian [or Irish] Collection''), *c.* 700, used texts from Scripture, mainly from the Old Testament, for the first time in canonical collections, and texts from the Greek and Latin early Church Fathers in addition to canons. The *Liber ex lege Moysi* (''Book from the Law of Moses''), an Irish work, drew exclusively from the Pentateuch.

The reorganization of the Frankish church began with the Carolingian reform in the middle of the 8th century. The canon law was set down especially in the *Capitularia ecclesiastica* (''Ecclesiastical Articles'') of the prince, as well as in the *Capitularia missionum* (''Mission Articles''); *i.e.,* instructions given by the prince to the bishops and abbots who visited in his name. The *Capitularia* (''Short Articles'') of Charlemagne, the founder of the Holy Roman Empire, and his son, the emperor Louis the Pious, were collected in 827 by the abbot Ansegisus. Following this model the bishops composed terse *capitula,* the oldest known diocesan statutes, for their clergy. The penance books were condemned and replaced by new ones that were more closely related to tradition. The reception of the *Dionysiana* and the *Hispana* is of importance for the transmission of the text and for the Carolingian cultural renaissance. In 774 Charlemagne received from Pope Adrian I a completed *Dionysiana,* the *Dionysiana-Hadriana,* which was accepted at a national synod in Aachen in 802, but it never was adopted as an official national code. About 800 the *Hadriana* and the *Hispana* were developed into a systematic whole, the *Dacheriana* (canonical collection named for its 17th-century publisher, a French scholar, Jean-Luc d'Achéry)—the principal source of the collections before 850—which was of influence until the Gregorian reform in the 11th century.

After Louis the Pious, the central power of the prince was increasingly divided among counts and barons. German law—which linked the right to govern with land ownership, without distinction between public and private law—expressed itself in the medieval forms of the system of private churches. This northern law looked upon dioceses, churches, and monasteries—with their rights and privileges—as lucrative possessions that deserved to be confiscated, by fraudulent means if necessary.

Such situations became the occasion *c.* 850 for the massive falsifications (*i.e.,* forgeries) of the Pseudo-Isidorian collections: the *Hispana Augustodunensis* ("Spanish Collection of Autun"), the *Capitula Angilramni* ("Chapters of Angilramnus," bishop of Metz), the *Capitularia Benedicti Levitae* ("Frankish Imperial Laws of Benedict the Levite," a fictitious name), and the *Pseudo-Isidorian Decretals.* The central goal of the anonymous Frankish group of authors of these collections was to strengthen the position of the bishops and to rectify the poor condition of ecclesiastical-state affairs. This was accomplished by means of falsified and forged texts that were attributed to the esteemed authority of the old law (*i.e.,* the popes) and the Carolingian princes. They did not have much influence on the real development of canon law, although later collections drew from them abundantly. Only the Magdeburg Centuriators, authors of the *Centuries,* a 16th-century Lutheran church history, denied the genuineness of all the decretals of pseudo-Isidore; the lack of authenticity of the other three works was discovered later.

Before 1000 several collections appeared: about 882 of them in northern Italy in the *Collectio Anselmo dedicata* ("Collection Dedicated to Anselm"), a papally oriented, systematic work; in Germany in the *Libri duo de synodalibus causis et disciplinis ecclesiasticis* ("Two Books Concerning Synodical Causes and Church Discipline") of Regino, abbot of Prüm (906), a manual for the bishops for the judicial interrogation of jurymen during a visitation; and in France in the collection of Abbon, abbot of Fleury (*c.* 996), which defended the legal position of his monastery against the king and bishop. Intended as a doctrinal book for the young cleric, the Decree of Burchard—bishop of Worms (bishop 1000-25)—became the canon-law manual in the cathedral schools and in the curias (administrative bureaucracies) of bishops and abbots in Germany, France, and Italy. Burchard was a promoter of moderate imperial reform. He did not reject the system of private churches; he only rejected the misuses proceeding from it, such as simony (buying or selling church offices) and the violation of celibacy.

The slogans of the Gregorian reformation, initiated by Pope Gregory VII, who reigned 1073-85, were *libertas Ecclesiae* ("liberty of the church") and *puritas Ecclesiae* ("purity of the church"): freedom from the system of private churches on all levels; freedom from papal dependence on the Roman nobility and emperor; freedom from dependence of the village priest on his *senior* (the beginning of the fight against investiture); and purity from simony and from the total collapse of celibacy (which was exhibited in the practice of hereditary parishes and bishoprics). Fundamental principles of Gregorian canon law included: only canon law that is given or approved by the pope is valid; papal legates (representatives) stand above the local hierarchies and preside over synods; for possession of every ecclesiastical office, choice and appointment by church authorities is demanded, along with the exclusion of lay investiture; every form of simony makes the appointment invalid; the faithful must boycott the services of married priests. New material was sought, especially for the confirmation of papal primacy, in archives and libraries. The principal new sources were: the *Breviarium* of Cardinal Atto (*c.* 1075), the *Dictatus Papae* ("Dictates of the Pope") of Gregory VII (*c.* 1075), the *Collectio 74 titulorum,* or "Collection of 74 Titles" (1074-76), the collection of Bishop Anselm of Lucca (*c.* 1083) and that of Cardinal Deusdedit (*c.* 1085), the *Liber de vita Christiana* ("Book Concerning the Christian Life") of Bonizo, bishop of Sutri (*c.* 1090).

The investiture battle over the conflicting asserted rights of lay or ecclesiastical officials to invest a church official with the symbols of his spiritual office ended in France, England, and Germany (Concordat of Worms, 1122) in compromises. Gregorian law, which now seems too strict, had to be reconciled with the established traditions. Ivo, bishop of Chartres from 1091 to 1116, contributed to the settlement of the investiture problem by his political activities; his extended correspondence; and his three law collections, *Tripartita* ("Tripartite Collection"), *Decretum* ("Decrees"; *i.e.,* collection of decrees or canons), and *Panormia* (collections of "All the Laws"), the last two practically a fusion of Burchard's Decree with Gregorian law. The famous Prologue, written by Ivo for either the *Decretum* or the *Panormia,* indicated for the first time a method by which the bishop must handle the conflicting strict and liberal texts, with *justitia* ("justice") or *misericordia* ("mercy"). Bernold of Constance, in his little tractates, written between 1070 and 1091, listed several criteria for the reconciliation of conflicting texts: authenticity of the text; identity of the author; difference between law, counsel, and dispensation, between universal and local law, of time and place; different meanings of a word. A Liège (Belgium) canon lawyer, Alger, in his *Liber de misericordia et justitia,* or "Book Concerning Mercy and Justice" (*c.* 1105), applied Ivo's criteria to the problem of the effect of sacraments administered by heretics and persons guilty of simony. The great medieval theologian Abelard developed the method of reconciling texts that are for or against a theological position in his *Sic et non,* or "Yes and No," (1115-17). The same methods were applied by the first writers of glosses (commentaries or interpretations) at the law school in Bologna on the *Pandecta* of Justinian, which was rediscovered *c.* 1070.

The Corpus Juris Canonici (c. 1140-c. 1500). *The "Decree of Gratian."* About 1140 the monk John Gratian completed his *Concordia discordantium canonum* ("Harmony of Contradictory Laws"), later called the *Decretum Gratiani* ("Decree of Gratian"); it became not only the definitive canonical collection of the entire preceding tradition, but also a systematic application of the scholastic method (utilizing reason) to all legal material. The *Concordia* dealt with the sources of the law, ordinations, elections, simony, law of procedure, ecclesiastical property, monks, heretics, schismatics, marriage, penance, and sacraments, and sacramentals. Primitive as it was, it provided a foundation for systematic compilation of the legal material by canonists, and for the expansion of decretal law. It provided a basis for the education in canon law which began in the schools of Bologna, Paris, Orleans, Canterbury, Oxford, Padua, and elsewhere. It was accepted everywhere in the ecclesiastical administration of justice and government.

The Corpus Juris Canonici. From the time that the Gregorian reformation introduced a more centralized ecclesiastical administration, the number of appeals to Rome and the number of papal decisions mounted. New papal laws and decisions, called decretals, first added to Gratian's *Concordia,* were soon gathered into separate collections, of which the best known are the *Quinque compilationes antiquae* ("Five Ancient Compilations"). The first, the *Breviarium extravagantium* ("Compendium of Decretals Circulating Outside"; *i.e.,* not yet collected) of Bernard of Pavia, introduced a system inspired by the codification of Justinian, a division of the material into five books, briefly summarized in the phrase *judex* ("judge"), *judicium* ("trial"), *clerus* ("clergy"), *connubium* ("marriage"), *crimen* ("crime"). Each book was subdivided into titles and these in turn into *capitula,* or canons. This system was taken over by all subsequent collections of decretals. These compilations were the foremost source of the *Liber Extra* ("Book Outside"; *i.e.,* of decretals not in Gratian's Decree) or *Liber decretalium Gregorii IX* ("Book of Decretals of Gregory IX"), composed by Raymond of Penafort, a Spanish canonist, and promulgated on September 5, 1234, as the exclusive codex for all of canon law after Gratian. On March 3, 1298, Pope Boniface VIII promulgated *Liber Sextus* ("Book Six"), composed of official collections of Innocent IV, Gregory X, and Nicholas III, and private collections and decretals of his own, as the exclusive codex for the canon law since the *Liber Extra.* The *Constitutiones Clementinae* ("Constitutions of Clement") of Pope Clement V, most of which were enacted at the Council of Vienne (1311-12), were promulgated on October 25, 1317, by Pope John XXII, but they were not an exclusive collection. The *Decretum Gratiani,* the *Liber Extra, Liber Sextus,* and *Constitutiones Clementinae,* with the addition of two private collections, the *Extravagantes* of John XXII and the *Extravagantes communes* ("Decretals Commonly Circulating"), were printed and published together for the first time in Paris in 1500. This entire collection soon received the name *Corpus Juris Canonici* ("Body of Canon Law").

The science of canon law was developed by the writers of glosses, the commentators on the Decree of Gratian (decretists), and the commentators on the collections of decretals (decretalists). Their notations, or glosses, were based on the system used by Gratian: next to the texts of canons parallel texts were noted, then conflicting ones, followed by a *solutio* ("solution"), again with text references. In connection with this the glosses of other canonists were also introduced. In this way the *apparatus glossarum,* continuous commentaries on the entire book, arose. The *glossa ordinaria* (''ordinary explanation'') on the different parts of the *Corpus Juris Canonici* was the apparatus that was used universally in the schools. After the classical period of the glossators (12th-14th centuries), terminated by the work of a lay Italian canonist, John Andreae (*c.* 1348), followed that of the postglossators. In the absence of new legislation in the time of the Babylonian Captivity (1309-77)—named after the 6th-century-BC biblical captivity or exile of the Jews to Babylon for 70 years (traditionally)—when the papacy was situated at Avignon, France, and the Great Schism (1378-1417), when there were at least two popes reigning simultaneously, the commentaries on decretals continued, but with a larger production of special tracts; *e.g.,* regarding the laws of benefices and marriage and of *consilia* (advice about concrete legal questions).

From the Council of Trent (1545-63) to the Codex Juris Canonici (1917). *The end of decretal law.* Toward the end of the Middle Ages decretal law ceased to govern. The medieval Christian society (called the *Christianitas*) became politically and ecclesiastically divided, according to the principle of *cuius regio, illius et religio* (*i.e.,* the religion of the prince is the religion of the land). In Protestant areas the former Roman Catholic church buildings and benefices were taken over by other churches; and even in the lands that remained Catholic the churches found themselves in an isolated position as secularization forced the churches to reorganize. With the end of the medieval social system known as feudalism, canon law dealing with benefices, chapters, and monasteries, which were closely bound to the feudal structure, changed. The territorial, material, and economic character of canon law and the decentralization allied with it disappeared. The decision of the reform councils from Pisa (1409) until the fifth Lateran Council (1512-17), affected, in particular, benefices, papal reservations, taxes, and other such ecclesiastical matters. In the same period various concordats (agreements) permitted the princes to intervene in the issue of ecclesiastical benefices and property. Canon law took on a more defensive character with prohibitions regarding books, mixed marriages, participation of Catholics in Protestant worship and vice versa, education of the clergy in seminaries, and other such areas of concern.

At the Catholic reform Council of Trent (1545-63) a new foundation for the further development of canon law was expressed in the *Capita de reformatione* (''Articles Concerning Reform''), which were discussed and accepted in 10 of the 25 sessions. Papal primacy was not only dogmatically affirmed against conciliarism (the view that councils are more authoritative than the pope) but was also juridically strengthened in the conduct and implementation of the council. The central position of the bishops was recovered, over against the decentralization that had been brought about by the privileges and exemptions of chapters, monasteries, fraternities, and other corporate bodies that sprang from Germanic law, as well as caused by the rights granted to patrons. In practically all matters of reform the bishops received authority *ad instar legati S. Sedis* ("like delegates of the Holy See"). Strict demands were made for admission to ordination and offices; measures were taken against luxurious living, nepotism, and the neglect of the residence obligation; training of the clergy in seminaries was prescribed; prescriptions were given about pastoral care, schools for the young, diocesan and provincial synods, confession, and marriage; the right to benefices was purified of misuse; the formalistic law of procedure was simplified.

The council gave the duty of execution of the reform to the pope. On January 26, 1564, Pius IV confirmed the decisions, reserved to himself their interpretation and execution, and on August 2, 1564, established the Congregation of the Council for that purpose. The congregations of cardinals, which proceeded from the former permanent commissions of the *consistorium,* (the assembly of the pope with the College of Cardinals), were organized by Pope Sixtus V in 1587. Since then the administrative apparatus of the Curia has consisted of congregations of cardinals together with courts and offices. This apparatus made it possible for the Latin Church to acquire a uniform canon law system that was developed in detail.

Law for the missions. The medieval church knew nothing of "missions." Expansion of the church brought with it expansion of the ordinary hierarchical episcopal structure. This was true also for the new colonies under the right of patronage of the Spanish and Portuguese kings. In the other mission areas and in the areas taken over by the Protestants, where the realization of the episcopal structure and the decretal law adopted by Trent was not possible, the organization of mission activity was taken from missionaries and religious orders and given to the Holy See. The congregation *De Propaganda Fide* ("For the Propagation of the Faith") was established for this purpose in 1622. Missionaries received their mandate from Rome; the administration was given over to apostolic vicars (bishops of territories having no ordinary hierarchy) and prefects (having episcopal powers, but not necessarily bishops) who were directly dependent on the *Propaganda,* from which they received precisely described faculties. A new uniform mission law was created, without noteworthy native influence; this sometimes led to conflict, such as the Chinese rites controversy in the 17th and 18th centuries over the compatibility of rites honouring Confucius and ancestors with Christian rites.

Late Developments in Roman Catholic Canon Law

The first Vatican Council (1869-70) strengthened the central position of the papacy in the constitutional law of the church by means of its dogmatic definition of papal primacy. Disciplinary canons were not enacted at the council; but the desire expressed by many bishops that canon law be codified did have influence on the emergence and content of the code of canon law.

The Codex Juris Canonici (1917). Since the closing off of the *Corpus Juris Canonici* there had been no official or noteworthy private collection of the canon law, except for the constitutions of Benedict XIV (pope 1740-58). The material was spread out in the collections of the *Corpus Juris Canonici* and in the generally very incomplete private publications of the *acta* of popes, of general and local councils, and the various Roman congregations and legal organs, which made canon law into something unmanageable and uncertain. The need for codification was recognized even more because of the fact that since the end of the 18th century, secular law had undergone a period of great codification. Several private attempts to do this had met with little success.

Preparations for reorganization of the Code of Canon Law. On March 19, 1904, Pius X announced his intention to complete the codification, and he named a commission of 16 cardinals, of which he himself was chairman. Bishops and university faculties were asked to cooperate and to make their desires known. The schemas of the five books that were prepared in Rome—universal norms, personal law, law of things, penal law, and procedural law—were proposed in the years 1912-14 to all those who would ordinarily be summoned to an ecumenical council, and with their observations were then reworked in the cardinals' commission. The entire undertaking and all the drafts were under the papal seal of secrecy and, as a matter of fact, were not published. Meanwhile, Pius X introduced various reforms that were to a great degree the results of the commissions's work. In July 1916 the preparations for the *Codex Juris Canonici* (Code of Canon Law) were completed. The code was promulgated on Pentecost Sunday, May 27, 1917, and became effective on Pentecost Sunday, May 19, 1918.

The Code of Canon Law. In contrast to all earlier official collections this code was a complete and exclusive codification of all universal church law then binding in the Latin Church. Out of fear of political difficulties, a systematic handling of public church law, especially what concerned the relations between church and state, was omitted. Its main purpose is to offer a codification of the law, and only incidentally adaptation, and so it introduces relatively little that is new legislation. The 2,414 canons are divided into five books that no longer followed the system of the collections of decretals but did follow that of the Perugian canonist Paul Lancelotti's *Institutiones juris canonici* ("Institutions of Canon Law"), Perugia, 1563, which in turn went back to the division of the 2nd-century Roman lawyer Gaius' *Institutiones: personae* ["persons"], *res* ["things"], *actiones* ["actions"], and is based on the fundamental idea of Roman law; *i.e.,* subjective right. Book I, general norms, deals with the area covered by the codex, the relation between old and new law, laws, customs, the way of reckoning time, rescripts, privileges, and dispensations. Book II, about persons, deals with persons in general, corporate bodies, clerics, religious, and laity. Book III, about things, deals with sacraments and sacramentals, consecrated places and times, worship, church teachings, authority, benefices, church property, and foundations. Book IV, on processes, deals with general and special trials, beatification and canonization, and special procedures. Book V, on crimes and punishments, deals with crimes, punishments in general, special punishments, and punishments for extraordinary crimes. In some editions the sources that were used by the editors are indicated at the individual canons. Since the publication of the codex these sources belong to the history of the law. Older general and particular law, in conflict with the codex, has been given up; and, insofar as it is not in conflict with it, serves only as a means for interpreting the code. The old law of custom in conflict with the code and expressly reprobated by it is rendered null; when not reprobated and 100 years old or immemorial it can be allowed by ordinaries for pressing reasons. Acquired rights and concordats in force remain in force. With this change, an independent science of the history of canon law has become necessary, in addition to the dogmatic canonical science of canon law on the basis of the code.

Canon law after the Codex Juris Canonici. In order to ensure the unity of the codification and the law, a commission of cardinals was established on September 15, 1917, for the authentic interpretation of the new code. At the same time it was decided that the cardinals' congregations should no longer make new general decrees, but only instructions for the carrying out of the prescriptions of the code. Should a general decree appear necessary, it was determined, the commission would formulate new canons and insert them into the code. Neither of these decisions was carried out. Only two canons were altered and congregations have promulgated numerous general decrees. New papal legislation has complemented and altered the law of the code. The law on judicial procedure was extended by instructions of the Congregation for the Sacraments to the diocesan courts in cases concerning annulment of ordinations and its attached obligations and of marriages; the Congregation for Religious gave detailed prescriptions for five-year reports of pontifical religious institutes and the papal cloister for religious women; an excommunication *latae sententiae* ("of a sentence already pronounced"; *i.e.,* incurred immediately upon the commission of the offense) was imposed by the Congregation of the Council on violations of the prohibitions against business engagement for clerics and religious, and the Sacred Penitentiary reserved the excommunications of married priests most strictly to the Holy See. The *responsa* of the commission for the interpretation of the code and the documents of the Roman Curia concerning canon law are published in the order of the canons in various private collections. The Sacred Roman Rota (court) developed an extensive jurisprudence regarding marriage law: every year an official publication of the verdicts of the tenth year previous appears. The numerous commentaries on the code are principally concerned with the exegesis (critical interpretation) of the text of the canons; this is prescribed in seminaries and faculties of canon law as the basic text for instruction.

The Eastern churches in union with Rome. The principle for the Catholic Eastern churches (churches in union with the Roman Catholic Church) is that they retain their own traditions in liturgy and church order, insofar as these are not considered to be in conflict with the norms taken by Rome to be divine law. In 1929 Pius XI set up a commission of cardinals for the codification of canon law valid for all uniate churches in the East. In the following year a commission was established for the preparation of the codification and one for the collection of the sources of Eastern law, in which experts of all rites were involved. These collections were published in three series, begun respectively in 1930, 1935, and 1942.

In 1935 the preparatory commission became the Pontifical Commission for the Redaction of the *Codex Juris Canonici Orientalis* ("Body of Oriental Canon Law"). The cooperation of all Eastern ordinaries (bishops, patriarchs, and others having jurisdictions) was requested, and the drafts of the various documents were sent to them. Since then four parts have been published: in 1949, on marriage law; in 1952, on the law for monks and other religious, on ecclesiastical properties, and a title *De Verborum Significatione* ("Concerning the Meaning of Words"), a series of definitions of legal terms used in the canons; and in 1957, on constitutional law, especially of the clergy. The still incomplete codification follows the Latin code with the assimilation of the authentic interpretation and with textual corrections, and also with the insertion of the general law proper to the Eastern churches, including the Orthodox churches, regarding the patriarchs and their synods, marriage law, the law of religious, and other matters. The promulgation was made in Latin, with official translations in Greek, Slavic, Arabic, and Egyptian. The Catholic Eastern churches came under the Congregation for the Eastern Churches that was established on January 6, 1862, by Pius IX as part of the *Propaganda Fide,* and was made independent by Benedict XV on May 1, 1917, and expanded considerably by Pius XI on March 25, 1938. Roman legislation as well as the jurisdiction of a congregation of the Roman Curia was criticized as being incompatible with the traditional autonomy of the Eastern churches in legislation and administration.

Vatican II and Postconciliar Canon Law

Vatican II. Fundamental to the development of canon law in the Roman Catholic Church is the second Vatican Council's (October 11, 1962-December 8, 1965) vision of the church as the people of God. In this connection the former concept of the church as *societas perfecta* (the "perfect society"), founded by Christ through the mission of the Apostles and their successors, to which one belongs through subjection to the hierarchy, is replaced by a vision of the church as a community in which all possess the sacramental mission to live and proclaim the Gospel, and all have a function in the service of the whole. The legislative and administrative functions remain related to the hierarchy, but this is much more expressly seen as a service for the religious life of the community. The idea of collegiality, resting on the recognition of the vocation received by each one from the Lord, works itself out in the relationship existing among the bishops and with the pope, of the bishops with the clergy, and of the clergy with the laity. Related to this is a tendency to co-responsibility and the democratization of the church structure. Independence has been returned to the Eastern uniate churches, and in regard to their patriarchal synods, greater autonomy is set forth for the bishops in their own dioceses and for the episcopal conferences in their territory, and also an autonomy for the laity to exercise individually and collectively the Christian Mission proper to them; viz., to bring the spirit of Christ also into the secular life of mankind. The right of clergy and laity to a share in the leadership of bishops and pope is recognized. The vision of the people of God as *sacramentum mundi,* a sign of redemption for all mankind, gave a new insight into the relationships with the Protestant churches, the other world religions, and the nonreligious atheistic and humanistic movements. In this view, freedom of religion and philosophy became the most fundamental right of man.

Postconciliar legislation. From a schematically chronological survey of the principal conciliar and postconciliar legislation a new era apparently began for canon law—*e.g.,* in 1960, establishment of the Secretariate for Promoting Christian Unity; in 1963, various faculties, previously reserved to Rome, were given to the bishops; in 1964, reorganization of the papal commission for communications media; also in 1964: establishment of the Secretariate for Non-Christians, lifting of the prohibition against cremation, and various faculties, previously reserved to Rome, given to the superiors general of religious institutes. Other legislative changes indicating a new era included several regulations that could not have been proposed with any possibility of their being accepted prior to Vatican II: *e.g.,* in 1965, pre-eminence in the College of Cardinals is given to Eastern patriarchs, after deacon and subdeacon and after the cardinals of the dioceses of the province of Rome; also in 1965, establishment of the Secretariate for Non-Believers, and the Holy Office (formerly the Inquisition) became the Congregation for the Doctrine of the Faith, with emphasis on the positive fostering of theological research; in 1966, greatly reduced prescriptions for fasting and abstinence were adopted, the Index of prohibited books became a moral guide instead of obligatory law, and in implementation of the conciliar decree on the episcopal office, the principle according to which ordinaries (*e.g.,* bishops) dispense from universal laws only when this is allowed by law or special faculties was replaced by the principle that ordinaries can always dispense unless it is explicitly reserved to Rome—and such reserved dispensations in question are indicated. In addition to these changes, still further canonical regulations were proposed and accepted as follows: in 1966, new regulations for mixed marriages were adopted, and norms were established for the implementation of the conciliar decrees on the office of bishops and priests, religious life, missionary activity, personal and material aid to needy churches, salaries and social insurance for priests and others in the service of the church, introduction of priests' councils and pastoral councils of priests, religious (*i.e.,* monks and nuns), and laity as advisory groups for bishops, international episcopal conferences and their mutual relationships, and other concerns. From 1967 to 1970 more changes were made in canonical regulations—*e.g.,* in 1967, total revision of the norms for indulgences, establishment in the Roman Curia of the council of laymen and the study commission, *Justitia et Pax* ("Justice and Peace"), new dispensation rights for Eastern bishops, directory for ecumenical cooperation with Christian churches, regulations of the office of diaconate, also for married men, reorganization of the Roman Curia; in 1970 a mandate to the secretary of state to discuss with the world episcopacy the question of celibacy and ordination of married men in areas that need priests, and new rules for mixed marriages.

Characteristics of the new law are: a searching for structures to allow all members of the church to have a voice in ecclesiastical decision making; decentralization and autonomy of local churches; regulations from Rome are kept to the general, with ample room for local adaptation; the giving up of the Index and the prohibition of cremation, the minimal fasting regulations and so forth, all point to the emancipation of personal religious life from laws and sanctions. In addition, new regulations are to be enacted only after extensive and open inquiry and tested by experience, with possibilities for experimentation. In place of regulations of religious behaviour, canon law may be becoming an ordering of the cooperation of all members of the Roman Catholic Church for the realization of its mission in the world. . . .

Case 2

Selection of Bishops: Church History and Tradition

The National Conference of Catholic Bishops has appointed a special committee to discuss ways of implementing the *Norms for the Selection of Candidates for the Episcopacy in the Latin Church.* Two issues before the committee have provided controversy. You have been asked to offer an opinion on the two issues. The majority of the committee supports the position that clergy and laity in the diocese through a representative body (such as the Diocesan Pastoral Council) be given the power to approve or disapprove of a candidate for ordinary of a diocese. The minority argues that this would in effect give such a body veto power in regard to the papal appointment of bishops.

The majority of the committee also believes that bishops should have a limited term of office. They feel if an error is made in an appointment and the bishop proves to be a poor shepherd, it makes it easier to remove him at the end of a term. Those against the proposal say that the pope, upon receiving proper information can remove a bishop at any time, making a term of office unnecessary. You are asked to study these issues and report back to the committee with recommendations.

Exercise

1. Research the scriptural sources on the office of bishop to determine if Scripture sheds any light on the above positions.

2. Research the history and tradition of church practice and law regarding selection of bishops and term of office. Are there any precedents or analogous practices in church history that would be helpful in arriving at a position?

3. In responding to the committee directives what is your opinion on the role of Scripture, theology, and history in trying to make helpful church regulations?

References

Procedure for Selection of Bishops in the United States (A suggested implementation of present papal norms), CLSA, 1973.

Report of the Selection of Bishops Committee (Part I), CLSA, 1970.

Auer, et al., "Limited Term of Office for Resident Bishop," *Bishops and People,* Swidler and Swidler, eds. (Philadelphia: Westminster Press, 1970), 22-37.

Benson, "Election by Community and Chapter: Reflections on Co-Responsibility in the Historical Church," *The Jurist* 31 (1971), 54-80.

Lynch, "Presbyteral Colleges and the Election of Bishops," *The Jurist* 31 (1971), 14-53.

Neumann, J., "Election and Limitation of Term of Office in Canon Law," *Bishops and People,* Swidler and Swidler, eds. (Philadelphia: Westminster Press, 1970), 54-70.

Case 3

Celibacy: Church History and Tradition

"A bishop must be above reproach, the husband of one wife" (1 Tim. 3:2). Ministers in the early Church were usually married. This was the ordinary practice until local churches legislated obligatory celibacy (Elvira 305). From the fourth to the twelfth centuries in the Latin Church, priestly celibacy grew in practice until it became universal law at Lateran I in 1123. However, the Eastern Catholic Churches always maintained the discipline of optional celibacy.

The Ukrainian Church was guaranteed they could maintain the tradition of a married clergy in the Synod of Brest-Litovsk in 1596. However, decrees of the Sacred Congregation for the Propagation of the Faith in 1890 and the Sacred Oriental Congregation in 1929 made celibacy obligatory in North America. Notwithstanding the policy, married priests have been ordained in Europe and serve the Toronto Ukrainian diocese in Canada.

In 1975 a Ukrainian bishop ordained three married seminarians in Toronto. The Latin Rite bishops protested but received a reply from the Ukrainian bishop stating:

> This matter does not concern you. It is an internal question of our own. It is our decision to make whether or not to ordain married seminarians to the priesthood. We are completely within our rights to do this once such a decision has been made. A married clergy is part of our Church tradition and rite.

Catholics of Eastern Rites argue that the refusal to allow a married clergy was the reason many Eastern Catholics joined the Orthodox Churches.

The Vatican II *Decree on Oriental Churches* (no. 6) provided that

> All Eastern rite members should know and be concerned that they can and should always preserve their lawful liturgical rites and their established way of life, and that these should not be altered except by way of an appropriate and organic development. Easterns themselves should honor all these things with the greatest fidelity. Besides, they should acquire an even greater knowledge and a more exact use of them. If they have improperly fallen away from them because of circumstances of time or personage, let them take pains to return to their ancestral ways.

Exercise

1. What are the implications for law making in the Church because it is united in adherence to Scripture and doctrine, but pluralistic in its history and tradition?

2. Are there social and cultural conditions present in the Church today that call for a review of the traditions of the Rites of the Catholic Church concerning celibacy?

3. Can it be argued that to allow a married clergy for Eastern Rite Catholics in North America would undermine the Latin tradition of celibacy?

4. Why did the Latin Church adopt the discipline of celibacy? Why must Eastern Rite bishops be celibate?

References

Lawrence, C. H., "The Origins and Development of Clerical Celibacy," *The Clergy Review* 60 (1975), 138-46.

Pope Paul VI, Encyclical Letter, "Sacerdotalis Caelibatus," *The Pope Speaks* 12 (1967), 291-319.

Pospishil, V., "Compulsory Celibacy for Eastern Catholics in the Americas," *Diakonia* 11 (1976), 133-56.

Shorter, A., "Marriage, Celibacy, and Ministry in Africa," *The Clergy Review* 60 (1975), 444-52.

C. THE REVISION OF CHURCH LAW

Principles Which Govern the Revision of the Code of Canon Law*

The Latin text of this document is found in "Acts of the Commission for the Revision of the Code," Communicationes *2 (1969), 77-85. It has been translated by Roger Schoenbechler, O.S.B.*

The principles proposed in this present document for the revision of the Code of Canon Law are the fruit of careful study and attentive consideration given to the Decrees of Vatican II. They are the fruit also of careful consideration of the general principles of law, that vast treasure house of laws and jurisprudence accumulated by the Church in the course of centuries. Furthermore, special attention has been focused on the spirit of canon law itself and on the special concern which the Church has for ecumenism.

All of this research has assisted us in expressing the principles of law better and more clearly. We have found assistance in recent studies of Holy Scripture, and we have discovered new helps through our research in the field of juridical science and in our study of the history of canon law, which has developed significantly since the promulgation of the Code of Canon Law. All of these fruits of research have been a great help to us. Added to the above, as already indicated, is the spirit of renewal of Vatican II, which already permeates the laws and regulations of the Church with new vigor and is already showing the way for accommodating the laws of the Church to the needs of our times.

Moreover, the observations of the Consultors have been very useful, made as they were according to the mind and direction of the Eminent Cardinal members of the Commission and of the Episcopal Conferences, which in their turn were asked to offer their opinions. The Consultors, in fact, in

*Included here in their entirety are: the Document in which the revision of the Code of Canon Law was discussed in the first session of the General Synod of Bishops, September 30 to October 4, 1967; also the *Relatio* and Responses of Cardinal Pericle Felici, the *Relator*, together with the expressed opinion of the Fathers of the Synod.

working on the canons to be revised for their first preparatory *schemata*, very often felt the need for certain principles to guide them so that their work of revision could proceed faster and with greater confidence and sureness. We may, therefore, conclude that the principles now presented as a result of the work of the Commission be considered a good set of principles, agreed upon by the Commission.

INTRODUCTION

We are here considering the revision of the Code of Canon Law after the close of Vatican II in which the Church brought to a close the immense task of laying down directions for the renewal of the Church itself. The revision of the Code of Canon Law is, as it were, complementary to this work of renewal. Since times and conditions have changed, the canon law, established in the Code of Popes Pius X and Benedict XV fifty years ago, must without doubt be accommodated to the new circumstances of our times and adapted to the present needs of our age. His Holiness Pope Paul VI[1] pointed out two things to be observed in the work of revising the Code of Canon Law: ". . . Canon Law must be accommodated to the new manner of thinking, in accord with Vatican II, which stresses very much the pastoral ministry. Canon Law must, therefore, consider the new needs of the people of God." The Holy Father appropriately observes that the work of revision of Canon Law must be brought about "with prudence."

From this we gather that the Holy Father intended to express certain principles to serve as guidelines in the work of revising canon law. For the Code of Canon Law, as Pope Paul VI observed, retained very often the discipline prevailing in the Church at the time the Code was composed (canon 6). Now, however, it is evident that certain changes must be made in the Code. For the Code of Canon Law has the function of serving as a guide, while Vatican II presents the general plan of the new Code of Canon Law.

THE JURIDIC CHARACTER OF THE CODE

1. The newly revised Code of Canon Law must of necessity depend as a whole on certain principles as on many hinges. In the first place, the revised Code must above all retain a juridic character and a spirit all its own. When we speak of "juridic character" we mean that character demanded by the social nature of the Church,[2] which is founded on the power of jurisdiction handed over to the hierarchy by Christ Himself. We should, therefore, avoid or rather keep out of the revised Code of Canon Law any concepts,

1. Allocution of Paul VI to the Cardinals and Consultors of this Pontifical Commission, October 20, 1965, in *A.A.S.* 57 (1965), 988.

2. Cf. The Dogmatic Constitution of the Church *Lumen Gentium,* nn. 1 and 8 and the previous Note of explanation, n. 2. Cf. also the Allocution of Paul VI, p. 988.

expressions, or suggestions recently spread abroad in various writings, according to which the future Code would have to have as its principal end solely the regulation of faith and morals. The Christian faithful, in the canons of the Church proposed to them, must be able to learn what manner of religious life they are to lead, if they wish to share in the spiritual goods which the Church offers them, so that they may attain eternal salvation.

The principal and essential object of Canon Law is to determine and safeguard the rights and obligations of each individual person with respect to the rights and obligations of others and of society at large, and certainly this can be done in the Church in all that pertains to the worship of God and the salvation of souls.

The Position of the External and Internal Forum in Canon Law

2. It is, however, necessary to confirm both the juridic character of our Code of Canon Law in all that pertains to the external forum and the need of the internal forum which has, for excellent reasons, prevailed in the Church for centuries. The revised Code of Canon Law will, therefore, incorporate all such norms which are necessary for making clear the provisions of the internal forum in so far as the salvation of souls demands.

It is necessary that in the Code of Canon Law there be perfect harmony and coordination between the external and internal forum, so that any conflict between the two may be dissipated or reduced to a minimum. This should be provided for especially in the canons dealing with the sacraments and in the penal section of the Code.

Certain Means for Fostering the Pastoral Ministry in the Code

3. The sacred and organically structured nature of the Church as a community manifests that the juridic character and all the institutions of the Church exist for the purpose of promoting the supernatural life. Hence the juridic ordering of the Church, with the laws and precepts, rights and duties, which flow from it, must be in accord with the supernatural end or purpose of the Church. For law, in the mystery of the Church, takes on the nature of a sacrament or sign of the supernatural life of the Christian faithful; it signifies that life and promotes it. Of course, not all the juridic norms are aimed directly toward a supernatural end or at directly promoting pastoral care. Yet it is necessary that the Church's law be in harmony with the attainment of the supernatural end by all men. Hence, the laws of the Code of Canon Law must shine forth with the spirit of charity, temperance, humaneness, and moderation, which as so many supernatural virtues distinguish the laws of the Church from every human or profane law.

In establishing law, the Code of Canon Law must foster justice as well as a wise equity, which is the fruit of kindness and charity; and in order to foster these virtues, the Code must seek to arouse the discretion and knowledge so necessary for pastors and judges. The norms of Canon Law should not impose duties and obligations, when instructions, exhortations, persuasions, and other pastoral means are evidently sufficient for fostering a spirit of unity among the faithful in order that the end of the Church may more easily be obtained. Nor should the Code easily establish laws that would render juridic acts null and void or that would impose ecclesiastical punishments upon members of the Church, unless the reason for such punishment or censure be a matter of grave importance and the punishment be necessary for the public good and Church discipline.

A reasonable amount of discretionary power and authority should be left in the hands of pastors and those having the care of souls to determine the duties of the faithful and to strike a happy balance between the duties of each individual and the conditions and circumstances surrounding his or her life, as has been done, for example, in the Apostolic Constitution *Paenitemini.*

Furthermore, the good of the universal Church evidently demands that the norms of any future Code should not be too rigid. In fact, a somewhat greater freedom given to Ordinaries, especially in certain circumstances, as in mission places, can contribute much toward imbuing the Code of Canon Law with a truly pastoral spirit and character.

The Incorporation of Special Faculties in the Code Itself

4. In view of what has just been said, it seems that the system of extending faculties to Ordinaries and other superiors, as has heretofore been the custom, should be radically revised. In the first place, we must avoid what in the present legislation not infrequently takes place, namely, making dispensations from the general laws of the Church depend entirely on recourse to the Apostolic See. The Holy See thus either does not grant the dispensation at all, or it is forced to grant liberal faculties in order to expedite and offer a solution to problems surrounding church law.

In the revised Code of Canon Law, the office of the bishop should be defined in a positive way and the extent of the bishop's power and authority should be determined according to the prescriptions of the Decree on the Pastoral Office of Bishops in the Church *Christus Dominus,* n. 8, a; and the cases which are reserved to the Holy See or to some other authority should be listed. Furthermore, the Code should indicate clearly which dispensations from the general laws of the Church are reserved to the Holy See or to some other authority, such as are today listed, for example, in the Apostolic Letter *De Episcoporum Muneribus.*

Application of the Principle of Subsidiarity in the Church

5. What has just been said pertains without doubt to the application of

the *principle of subsidiarity* in Canon Law. Yet, what has been said above is still a far cry from the broader and more complete application of the same principle to church legislation. The function of this principle of subsidiarity is to strengthen and confirm legislative unity in all the fundamental and major pronouncements of law of any society that is complete and compactly structured within itself. This principle of subsidiarity also has the function of defending the reasonableness or need especially of individual institutions to provide for their own advantage by particular laws enacted by themselves as well as by a reasonable amount of autonomous executive power and authority.

"Bishops, as the successors of the Apostles, in the dioceses committed to them, have *per se* all ordinary, proper, and immediate authority which is needed for exercising their pastoral office, without prejudice to the supreme power and authority which the Roman Pontiff, in virtue of his office, has for reserving cases to himself or to some other authority" (The Decree on the Pastoral Office of Bishops in the Church *Christus Dominus,* n. 8, a). In the revised Code of Canon Law, all reserved cases must be indicated most clearly. It is proper that the supreme power of the Pope, who is the ultimate authority in regulating the bishops in the exercise of their power, should have the authority to set certain limits to the power of the bishops for the good of the Church and of the faithful. And in setting such limits he should do so with great clearness and precision. It is evident that this cannot be done by merely providing a list of reserved cases; at least this would not be very convenient under present-day conditions. In the revised Code of Canon Law, these reserved cases should be mentioned in their proper place, as opportunity demands.

The system of Canon Law must be one unified system for the whole Church with regard to basic principles, with regard to the fundamental institutions of the Church, as also with regard to the description of the means proper to the Church for attaining its supernatural end. The system of Canon Law must finally be one with regard to legislative technique. All these proposals are offered as being most fitting for the common good of the Church.

This particular spirit of rewriting Canon Law has been observed by Vatican II especially in enacting its disciplinary decrees. By this new manner the unity of ecclesiastical law has been eminently strengthened and at the same time restrained somewhat by the very many decisions left to the competence of particular legislators.

Yet it seems rather foreign to the mind and spirit of Vatican II—apart from the particular disciplines of the Oriental Churches—that there be in the Western Church special statutes which seem to be like the laws of national churches. But nevertheless this need not be taken to mean that greater broadness of power and autonomy is not desirable for particular legislation, especially when it concerns laws enacted by national and regional councils, so that the special characteristics of the individual churches could be clearly apparent. The importance of particular legislation should be more accurately described in the new Code of Canon Law, especially in the matter of temporal administration, since the control of temporal goods must be governed for the most part by the laws of the respective nations concerned.

In regard to procedural law, grave doubts have arisen as to whether or not decentralization (as it is called) in this matter should be admitted to a greater extent than is now practiced—that is, so that decentralization would extend to autonomy of the regional and national tribunals. Indeed, everyone knows that the arrangement of tribunals, their ranks, their manner of procedure, the proofs admitted by them to establish truth, and the like, can be greatly influenced in individual nations and regions by the procedural rules of the various places. And yet, because of the primacy of the Roman Pontiff, it is the right of each individual faithful throughout the entire Catholic world to bring his case to the Apostolic See, even though it has been judged in a lower tribunal or is still in litigation. It is certainly clear that for the administration of justice, one must preserve at different steps a certain amount of unified organization; the lack of such organization and unity might give occasion or offer an excuse for uncertainty of judgment, or give rise to fraud and many other disagreeable consequences, or finally cause the matter to be brought to the attention of the Apostolic See. We must, therefore, think of broadening the procedural law in the new Code of Canon Law, giving it a more general and universal form and leaving to the respective regional authorities the faculty to enact rules or norms to be observed in their tribunals of justice. Thus they would determine what pertains to the constitution of the tribunals, to the office of the judges and of other officials of the tribunal. The regional authorities would also adapt the laws of the Code to the character and style of the laws prevailing in their respective regions. In this matter very often the court procedures of the land can serve as an example.

Safeguarding the Rights of Persons

6. A very important problem must be solved in the future Code of Canon Law, namely, how can the rights of persons be defined and safeguarded? It is clear that power is one and the same, whether it resides in the Supreme Authority or in a person of lesser authority, namely, in the Roman Pontiff or in the diocesan bishops within their respective sphere of jurisdiction. Each one is totally competent to exercise his juridic power for the service of the community to which he has been assigned. This strengthens and establishes the unity of his power, and no one will doubt that this is of great benefit for the pastoral care of one's subjects.

The use of this power in the Church, however, must not become arbitrary, because natural law prohibits such arbitrary use of power, as do also positive divine law and the law of the Church itself. The rights of each and every faithful must be acknowledged and safeguarded, both the rights which they have by natural law and the rights contained in divine positive law, as also the rights which are duly derived from these laws because of the social condition which the faithful acquire and possess in the Church.

Everyone does not have the same function in the Church, and the same statute or law does not apply to all in the same way. It has, therefore, been rightfully proposed that in the future Code of Canon Law, because of the radical equality which exists among all the faithful by reason of their human dignity and of their baptism, a *juridic statute* (bill of rights?) common to all the faithful should be legislated, before the rights and duties which pertain to the various ecclesiastical offices are listed.

Establishing a Procedure for Safeguarding Subjective Rights

7. Nor is it enough to say that the safeguarding of human rights is adequately provided for in our legislation. We must also acknowledge the truly personal subjective rights, without which a juridically organized society cannot be imagined. In Canon Law we must, therefore, proclaim that the principle of the juridical protection of rights applies with equal measure to superiors and subjects alike, so that any suspicion whatsoever of arbitrariness in church administration may completely disappear.

This can only be brought about by means of recourses wisely provided for by the law, so that if anyone thinks that his rights have been violated at a lower instance, he can effectively have them restored in a higher instance.

Although it is generally thought that recourses and judicial appeals are sufficiently provided for in the Code of Canon Law according to the demands of justice, it is nevertheless the common opinion of canonists that administrative recourses are still lacking considerably in church practice and in the administration of justice. Hence the need is everywhere strongly felt to set up in the Church administrative tribunals of various degrees and kinds, so that the defense of one's rights can be taken up in these tribunals according to proper canonical procedure before authorized officials of different ranks. Having accepted this principle, that the rights of the faithful must be safeguarded, then the various functions of ecclesiastical power can be clearly distinguished—namely, the legislative, the administrative, and the judicial. Then, too, we can also properly determine what special functions are to be exercised by each arm of the law.

It will be the task of the new Code of Canon Law to determine which actions may be brought before administrative tribunals, to determine the rules of administrative procedure, and to establish structures to deal with those actions.

It is evidently rather easy to apply administrative justice to administrative acts, but it is more difficult if recourse must be granted and the norms of a lower administrative organ must be applied, especially when these norms are in contradiction to those of a superior administrative organ.

It is to be hoped that, as a general rule, every trial be public, unless the judge in certain cases decides that the trial be held in secret because of special circumstances surrounding the persons involved or the subject matter of the trial itself. It is, however, necessary that in any procedure, whetherer judicial or administrative, the one who has lodged a recourse or has been accused must be informed of all the charges made against him.

Territorial Structure of the Church

8. The question arises as to whether we should continue to link the exercise of church jurisdiction to the territorial structure of the Church. From the documents of Vatican II it seems that we can deduce the following principle: the pastoral purpose of a diocese and the good of the entire Catholic Church require clear and definite territorial divisions, so that, regularly, the organic unity of each diocese may be properly safeguarded with regard to persons, offices, and institutions, after the manner of a living body. On the other hand, it seems that because of the exigencies of the apostolate in our day, there are weighty reasons to set up unified jurisdictional units for specific pastoral ministries. These jurisdictional units could exist in an entire nation or region or in a diocese. Examples of such an arrangement already exist in the Church today. They could or should be sanctioned in the Code of Canon Law as special dispositions of the law. Finally, it is urged that the future Code of Canon Law permit such jurisdictional units to be set up not only by special Apostolic Indult but also by the competent territorial or regional authority whenever they are required by the pastoral needs of the People of God.

Since this problem has various aspects, it seems that the following principles derived from the teaching of Vatican II could be proposed: Particular churches very certainly cannot today be defined as territorial parts or units, constituted in the Church. According to the teaching of the Decree *Christus Dominus,* n. 11, particular churches are "a portion of the People of God, which is entrusted to the spiritual care of the Bishop with the cooperation of the priests. . . ." When, however, we set about to determine and define this portion of the People of God which constitutes a particular church, the territory in which the faithful live might often serve as a criterion. Territory retains its importance, not indeed as a constitutive element, but as an element determining a specific portion of the People of God, by which this Church is defined and identified. Hence, we could accept it as a rule that a portion of the People of God is determined by the territory in which they live. However, there is nothing to prevent us from adducing other criteria—such as the liturgical rite of the people, their ethnic origin, and the like—for determining a particular community of the faithful.

Revision of the Penal Law

9. In the revision of the penal law of the Church, there is general agreement that the number of penal laws in the Code should be reduced. But no canonist seems willing to admit that all church penalties be suppressed, since the Church cannot do away with coercive power, which is proper to every perfect society.

It is generally agreed that penal laws be *ferendae sententiae,* inflicted only *in foro externo,* and remitted likewise only *in foro externo*. As for penal laws *latae sententiae,* while the abolition of all of these has been proposed by not a few canonists, we suggest that they be reduced to the smallest possible number and concern only the gravest of crimes.

A New Systematic Arrangement of the Code of Canon Law

10. To carry out in practice the principles which have been proposed in these pages evidently demands a completely new structure of the revised Code of Canon Law. It follows, therefore, that the very order and arrangement of the material in the new Code must be completely revised. From the very beginning of the publication of the current Code, its systematic order was considered by the most eminent canonists to be defective or faulty, especially in the disposition of the material in Books II and III. At the present time the disposition appears even more faulty than ever. The new arrangement of the material of the revised Code of Canon Law must, therefore, be made according to the mind and the spirit of the Decrees of Vatican II and according to the scientific requirements of canonical legislation.

It is evidently a very difficult task to establish a systematic and orderly arrangement *a priori.* This we know from the various attempts, certainly laudable attempts, made by various authors. It has, therefore, been considered wiser to determine the order and arrangement of the revised Code only after the revision of the individual parts has progressed sufficiently. This is the lesson taught by the history of the work of every new codification.

The Revision of the Code of Canon Law*

Francis G. Morrisey

In early 1978, Episcopal Conferences and other organisms received from the Pontifical Commission for the Revision of the Code of Canon Law, five draft schemata representing the work of some six of the sub-commissions established to revise the Code. This signifies the end of the first phase in the preparation of the new Code. From what has been stated in various circles, it appears that the Commission intends to proceed in the very near future in submitting its finalized version to the Holy Father. Indeed, the second phase — consultation — is scheduled to be completed by the end of 1978, and the third phase — revision and coordination — is already well underway for those schemata which have already been distributed.

Since we now have available the entire draft of the proposed new Code, we are in a position to examine it and to evaluate some of its particular characteristics. Before doing so, however, it would be worthwhile to examine the revision process itself and to take note of some of the characteristics of the new law as it is proposed to our attention.

I. The Revision Process

In an address to the Plenary Congregation of the Commission for Revision, May 24, 1977, Cardinal Pericle Felici, President of the Commission, briefly outlined the various steps that have been taken to bring about the revision of ecclesial law.[1] Using this address, and other sources, we can examine the various stages of the project, studying the historical facts, the consultation process, and the statements about the eventual promulgation of the Code.

a. The Historical Facts

It was on January 25, 1959, that Pope John XXIII called for the revision of the Code of Canon Law; on that same day he announced that he intended to convoke an ecumenical council and to call a Roman synod.

The next few years were taken up primarily with the organization of the Council, but, on March 28, 1963, shortly before he died, Pope John left, as it were, his testament to Canon Law by establishing the Pontifical Commission for the Revision of the Code of Canon Law, and by appointing some forty Cardinals to this commission. The group held its first meeting on

*Paper presented at the thirteenth Annual General Meeting of the Canadian Canon Law Society, Banff, Alberta, October 2-5, 1978.

1. *Communicationes*, 9 (1977), pp. 62-79.

November 12, 1963, during the second session of the Council. It was decided at that time not to undertake the work of the revision until the Council was concluded. Nevertheless, preliminary plans were prepared and made ready.

A consultative commission was established by Pope Paul VI on April 17, 1964, with 70 consultors appointed.[2] After the Council, Episcopal Conferences were asked to suggest other names. Eventually, sixty-six members were appointed to the Commission together with one hundred and twenty-five consultors.

One of the first major questions facing the Commission was to study Pope Paul's suggestion, made on November 20, 1965,[3] and determine whether there would be one Code for the universal Church, or whether separate Codes should be prepared for the Latin and the Oriental Churches, together with a fundamental law containing elements common to all Churches. It was decided to proceed in the latter way. The Oriental Commission was established on June 10, 1972, with Cardinal Joseph Parecattil as president; it was subsequently divided into ten sub-commissions.[4] Since the work of the Oriental Commission has not yet been distributed for general consultation, we shall limit our remarks here to the proposed Latin Code, as it now stands.

In 1966, then, the Commission began the preparation of a series of principles to guide the members in their work. These ten norms were eventually approved by the first Synod of Bishops in 1967 and will be examined later in this study.

Sub-commissions for the Latin Code were eventually established as follows: the systematic organization of the Code, the Fundamental Law of the Church, General Norms, Sacred Hierarchy, Institutes of Perfection, the Laity and Associations of the Faithful, Physical and Moral Persons in general, Matrimony, the Sacraments (except marriage), Ecclesiastical Magisterium, Patrimonial Law, Procedures, Penal Law. Eventually, a central commission was established, and the commission on General Norms united to the one established to revise the norms on physical and moral persons. Another sub-commission was later set up to examine administrative procedure in the Church.

The plan of the new Code was determined after a certain number of meetings, and differs greatly from the plan of the present Code. Abstracting from the Fundamental Law of the Church, it would comprise seven books: (1) General Norms, (2) The People of God, (3) The Church's Teaching Mis-

2. *Ibid.*, 1 (1969), p. 35.

3. *Ibid.*, 1 (1969), p. 41.

4. Cf. *Nuntia*, 1 (1973), pp. 1-19, mimeographed edition.

sion, (4) The Sanctifying Mission of the Church, (5) Patrimonial Law, (6) Penal Law, (7) The Protection of Rights. There was to be no special book on the third mission of the Church: to govern, since this matter was to be found in many parts of the Code as a whole, and would simply constitute a repetition of norms.

Cardinal Felici provided some statistics in 1977 on the work carried out to date on the revision: a total of 206 study sessions (mostly lasting five days) had been held up to that time for a total of 2087 days of meetings.[5] Since that time, and in the months to come, there have been and will be many more such sessions. The expenses involved in such an undertaking are quite high, yet, it seems, necessary since the Code must reflect the thinking of the universal Church.

b. The Consultation Phase

In 1971 the Bishops of the world were consulted for the first time regarding actual texts of the proposed new law. The draft "Lex Ecclesiae Fundamentalis" was distributed for study and the reaction which followed was highly publicized. In fact, this was the only document, to date, of the new Code which received extensive coverage in the secular press. In the following years, additional parts of the Code were distributed for consultation: 1972: Administrative Procedure, 1973: Penal Law, 1975: Marriage and the other Sacraments, 1976: Procedures, 1977: Institutes of Consecrated Life. The time alloted for submitting observations on these sections has now elapsed.

The five drafts which were received in 1978 cover Book I: General Norms, Book II: The People of God (parts), Book III: The Magisterium, Book IV: Sanctification (parts), Book V: Patrimonial Law. The consultation period was to end on October 31, 1978, but was later extended to December 31, 1978.

While the texts are marked "reservatum" (reserved), they are not subject to the norms regarding the Pontifical secret.[6] The intention of the Commission was that they not be publicized in the secular press. During the 1974 Synod of Bishops regret was expressed, however, that certain periodicals had already published the draft texts of some of the canons which had not yet been distributed to the Bishops;[7] even so, no measures seem to have been taken to prevent further disclosures. The matter is now simply academic since the entire text has been made available, and even translations prepared in many instances.

A number of difficulties have arisen concerning the consultation process. One important factor was the short length of time allotted to prepare

5. *Communicationes,* 9 (1977), p. 70.

6. Cf. *ibid.,* 1 (1969), p. 98.

7. Cf. *ibid.,* 6 (1974), pp. 159-160.

responses. This was felt especially in large countries where distances made it difficult for committees to be readily organized. Indeed, on a number of occasions, some countries received the draft schemata two or three months before others did. It was often felt that six months were not long enough to prepare observations on texts that were eight years in the making.

A second factor — which was almost unavoidable — is the fact that the texts were prepared in Latin so that only a small percentage of interested people had direct access to the text. This problem will undoubtedly be compounded in the years ahead. It could be asked, though, whether there should not have been broad consultation among the clergy and the laity on a matter of such importance. This would have implied the preparation of official translations, something that probably could not have been done in the short time available.

A third, and probably the most disconcerting difficulty was the lack of response to the consultation. Only one hundred and thirty-four responses were received to the consultation on Penal Law;[8] sixty-five responses were received on Administrative procedure;[9] one hundred and seventy-two responses were received on portions of the schema on Sacramental Law,[10] while seventy-six general observations were received on the draft.[11] These last included twenty-five responses from individual Bishops, and twenty-one responses from national Episcopal Conferences, to which should be added two responses from regional Conferences of Bishops, and four from international Conferences. When we consider the number of Episcopal Conferences in the world (approximately one hundred), we can ask the question the *Relator* asked when referring to the schema on Sacraments:

> An important question arises: what should we think about those Conferences, Dicasteries, Bishops, Universities and Patriarchates whose observations were not received? The question is not without importance, because we must consider the number of replies received to be quite small when we take into account the number of physical and moral persons who were asked for their opinion. Is this silence to be taken as an approval?[12]

The lack of response is probably due to many factors: Bishops have many priorities, and Canon Law is not necessarily the highest on the list; lack of qualified personnel to study the drafts and respond is certainly another cause; lack of interest in the new law as a whole might also be an explanation.

There might also be other reasons. One suggested cause is that about one-half of the world's Bishops have been appointed since the end of Vatican II

8. Cf. *ibid.,* 7 (1975), p. 93.
9. Cf. *ibid.,* 5 (1973), p. 236.
10. Cf. *ibid.,* 9 (1977, p. 117.
11. Cf. *ibid.,* 9 (1977). p. 323.
12. *ibid.,* 9 (1977), p. 324.

and, consequently, were not involved in the elaboration of the conciliar texts and might not have had the opportunity to deepen their knowledge of the teachings. For instance, in one Conference, there is only one Bishop left who attended all four sessions of the Council as a Bishop (Sri Lanka); similar situations most likely exist elsewhere.

Perhaps the most pernicious reason is that people feel it would be worthless to spend time studying the documents since, after all, their remarks will change little in the law. This could be a defeatist attitude that goes against a number of principles accepted by the Second Vatican Council and the norms of application, in particular: co-responsibility and subsidiarity. Nevertheless, the fact is there.

Yet, in many instances, this reasoning has been proven wrong. For example, a study of the revisions to be made in the canons on marriage[13] reveals that a number of significant changes were introduced into the text, improving it greatly. Among these changes we could mention the new descriptive definition of matrimonial consent, placing an equal emphasis on the good of the spouses; a revision of the incapacities for consent; the elaboration of norms regarding marriage preparation; a clearer description of the subject of marriage, and so forth.

On the other hand, though, it could be noted that the thrust of the work of the sub-commission on penal law was reversed by subsequent consultations and decisions. The *coetus,* or sub-commission, seems to have made one of its key points the separation between the internal and the external fora in relation to the application of penalties. Yet, after study by the Commission of Cardinals, it was decided to re-integrate the two.[14] While the sub-commission had proposed that an excommunicated person could receive the sacraments of Reconciliation and Anointing of the Sick, the central Commission decided it was preferable to retain the terms of the present legislation. (It could be asked whether the option of the sub-commission was not preferable and that the decision should be re-considered in the light of current legal theory.)

A thorough study of the accounts in *Communicationes* referring to the Fundamental Law also reveals that a number of worthwhile changes were incorporated into the finalized version. We do not have many detailed accounts in *Communicationes* of revisions incorporated into the other schemata. It could be mentioned in passing that the publication of the revisions in *Communicationes* could be considered to a certain extent as a second round of consultation since people would be free to write in their observations.

Lately, Episcopal Conferences have been grouping together, on an unof-

13. Cf. *ibid.,* 9 (1977), pp. 117-146, 345-378.

14. Cf. *ibid.,* 9 (1977), pp. 80, 213, 322.

ficial basis, to study some of the more important schemata. This enables them to present unified recommendations, while adding remarks that are of more particular concern to their own territories. It will be interesting to see whether these studies, representing about one-quarter of the world's Bishops will have a great impact on the final version. Such joint studies have the added advantage of having canonists in various parts of the world coordinating their thinking and observations.

c. The Promulgation of the Latin Code

One of the questions that is foremost in the minds of many people is: when will the new Code be promulgated? The Holy Father has consistently avoided setting a determined date, at least publicly. Otherwise, the consultation process would inevitably be thwarted. On the other hand, members of the Code Commission seem to be speaking about possible promulgation by the end of the decade. Whatever the date chosen, it seems accepted now that the new Code will not be the final word in Church law. It will constantly have to be revised and up-dated, since so many points are not settled.

A number of Episcopal Conferences feel that it is not yet the opportune time to promulgate a Code. They want a second round of consultation on the draft as a whole to see how the matter stands. Many changes have occured since the first consultation began in 1971 and it is felt necessary now to consider the earlier documents in the light of some of the later ones. There has been no indication whether a second round of consultation will take place officially, but it is becoming more and more evident that such would be advisable. (See, for instance, the intervention of Archbishop Gilles Ouellet, now President of the Canadian Conference of Catholic Bishops, October 20, 1977, at the Synod of Bishops).[15] If such a second round takes place, it would provide an excellent opportunity for Episcopal Conferences to work together on a presentation. It could even be asked whether it would not be opportune to have an extraordinary session of the Synod of Bishops to study the entire document before it is promulgated.

One of the reasons for the hesitation is that many persons seem to be of the opinion that we are not yet ready to issue legislation on such matters as senates of priests, diocesan pastoral councils, ecumenism, priestly formation, and so forth.[16]

15. *Ibid.*, 9 (1977), p. 215.

16. Cf., for instance, T. J. Green, "The Future of Penal Law in the Church", in *The Jurist,* 35 (1975, pp. 212-275; Id., "The Revision of the Code: The First Decade", in *The Jurist,* 36 (1976), pp. 353-441; Id., "The Revision of Marriage Law: An Exposition and Critique", in *Studia Canonica,* 10 (1976), pp. 363-410; Id., "The Revision of Sacramental Law: Perspectives on the Sacraments other than Marriage", in *Studia Canonica,* 11 (1977), pp. 261-327.

II. Characteristics of the Proposed New Law

a. The Thinking of Pope Paul VI

When the Code Commission met with Pope Paul VI on November 20, 1965, he gave it a mandate which could be summarized as follows: the new Code must be faithful to the Gospel message of Christ, and it must be faithful to the orientations of the Second Vatican Council.[17] The Pope also stated at a later date that the revision of the Code

> cannot mean simply improving the earlier code by introducing a more appropriate order of material, adding what seems worthwhile and omitting what is no longer relevant. Rather the code must become an aid to contemporary church life in the post-Vatican age.[18]

As is well known, the Holy Father has also insisted on numerous occasions on the fact that the new law must be based on doctrine, thus bringing about a closer relationship between theology and law.[19] The Pope reminds us that the norms of the Code are not to be taken as ends in themselves, but that they are means, instruments of grace, which must have a spiritual character, distinguishing the Code from every purely human legislation.[20]

Some of Pope Paul's strongest words regarding the new Canon Law are to be found in his allocution of January 27, 1969 when he stated that

> a Church in which an external and formalistic canon law would depart from the spirit of the Gospel, or prevail over theological speculation, or stifle the formation of a conscience enlightened by self-determination. . . would not correspond to the renovating orientations of the council.[21]

Let it be mentioned, by way of parenthesis, that it is not certain that the importance of this and other statements of the Holy Father has been ascertained by all parties.

It is evident that the Pope, when referring to the characteristics of the new law, did not enter into particular details. Therefore, the Commission found it necessary to prepare a series of criteria by which to judge the particular canons. Let us now mention some of these principles.

b. The Criteria for Revision

A number of general criteria, ten in all, were approved by the participants in the first Synod of Bishops, September 30 - October 4, 1967.[22] These prin-

17. Cf. *Communicationes,* 1 (1969), pp. 38-42.

18. Pope Paul VI, Allocution of February 4, 1977, in *The Pope Speaks,* 22 (1977), pp. 173-174.

19. Cf. Francis G. Morrisey, "The Spirit of Canon Law. Teachings of Pope Paul VI", in *Origins,* 8 (1978-1979), pp. 33, 35-40.

20. Cf. Pope Paul VI, February 4, 1977, *loc. cit.,* p. 178.

21. Id., Allocution of January 27, 1969, in *The Pope Speaks,* 14 (1969-1970), p. 41.

22. Cf. *Communicationes* 1 (1969). pp. 77-85; Richard T. Cunningham, "The Principles Guiding the Revision of the Code of Canon Law", in *The Jurist,* 30 (1970), pp. 447-455.

ciples would enable the drafters to remain within certain parameters, while at the same time having sufficient freedom to draft a law to answer the needs of the Church.

1) The first principle was that the Code was to be a juridical text. It is not, then, to be a textbook of theology, spirituality or exegesis. The principal purpose of the canons will be to outline the rights and obligations of all members of the Church and to provide means for their protection and implementation.

2) The second principle was that the new Code would consider all those elements which pertained to the external forum, and, where necessary, would also refer to certain aspects of the internal forum, but in such a way as to avoid conflicts between the two. We must never forget that it is impossible to reduce — or raise — everything in life to the level of law. One cannot legislate for love, generosity, service, devotion, and many other such values. Conflicts between the internal and the external fora can arise mostly on two levels today: the sacrament of Reconciliation, and the admission of the divorced and remarried to the sacraments. A third area, which is not directly of the internal forum, concerns the publicity to be given to testimony and proofs brought forward in the marriage courts. There might also be possible conflicts arising when the administrative tribunals are set in motion because a superior will not always feel free to reveal information that could be damaging or detrimental to a person's reputation.

3) Next, it was stated that the norms of the Church must be such as to foster pastoral care. They must therefore be imbued with a spirit of charity, temperance, humanity and moderation. Consequently, the law must not only favour justice but also prudent equity. The law should not impose obligations when it would be sufficient to give exhortations; in other words, the norms must not be too rigid so that their pastoral dimension would always be evident. This principle must apply to all believers, both those in authority and those under their jurisdiction. It would be of little avail to force superiors to act in such a way that there would be no room for a prudent application of equity. A number of observations made on the Code have been too one-sided, it seems, with the consequence that they would paralyze superiors in the exercise of their office. The importance of "equity" as a means of application of law cannot be underestimated.

4) All special faculties are to be included in the new Code, defining clearly and in a postitve manner the office of Bishops and the extent of their jurisdiction. In this way, as has been the case since the Council, Bishops would be able to dispense from the general laws of the Church, except in those cases reserved to a higher authority.

5) The principle of subsidiarity is to be applied in the new Code, allowing decisions to be taken at the most appropriate level. This also calls, in certain instances, for decisions to be taken at the national or regional level. We shall return to this point further on. Suffice it to state here that it seems that

this is the first time that the principle of susidiarity has been officially recognized in Canon Law. While the Council referred to it on three occasions (*Gaudium et Spes,* No. 86; *Gravissimum Educationis,* 3 and 6) it used the term to mean either decentralization or intervention by higher authorities, and in a civil context. Indeed, before the Council, the expression has been used mostly in relation to civil governments.[23] Yet, Pius XII, in his address of February 20, 1946,[24] had foreseen a prudent adaptation of the norm to the legislation of the Church. Today, the principle of subsidiarity is generally used to describe the fact that decisions are taken at the most appropriate level, while the expression "decentralization" is used in reference to sharing of authority.

6-7) The rights of persons are to be defined and protected, so that the use of power will not be arbitrary. This calls for the definition of a juridical status common to all the faithful. But, in addition to this sixth principle, a seventh one states that there must be means of protecting the subjective rights of all members of the Church; administrative tribunals will have to be established in each diocese to study cases of alleged violation of rights. All such trials would be public, unless decided otherwise by the judge, and a person would have the right to know the charges brought against him.

8) The eighth principle maintained the notion of territorial jurisdiction in the Church. Nevertheless, in certain instances, personal jurisdictions could be established, as is the case today with national parishes, military vicariates, and so forth. This principle also finds its foundation in the Conciliar teaching that the residential Bishop is the vicar and ambassador of Christ (*Lumen Gentium,* No. 27); it will not be surprising, therefore, to see in the new legislation a strong insistence placed on the local Bishop and on his role in the life of the Church.

9-10) Finally, the Synod approved principles whereby penal law was to be revised, removing, where possible, automatic penalties. Likewise, the Code was to have a new plan or systematic organization, based on the various missions of the Church.

These ten criteria were supplemented in some instances by additional principles developed by the sub-commissions themselves. For instance, the sub-commission on Institutes of Consecrated Life also determined a number of guidelines to be followed. These were explained in the introductory notes to the schema.[25] Likewise, the sub-commission on Divine Worship agreed on a series of guidelines.[26]

These criteria, however, are at times contradictory, at least on the sur-

23. Cf. R. Metz, "La subsidarité, principe régulateur des tensions dans l'Eglise", in *Revue de Droit canonique,* 22 (1972), pp. 155-176; G. Lesage, "Le principe de subsidiarite et l'état religieux", in *Studia Canonica,* 2 (1968), pp. 99-123.

24. Cf. Pope Pius XII, Allocution of February 20, 1946, in *A.A.S.,* 38 (1946), pp. 144-145.

25 *Cf. Communicationes,* 9 (1977), pp. 54-58.

26. Cf. *ibid.,* 5 (1973), pp. 42-43.

face. For instance, the *coetus* on Consecrated Life found it necessary and opportune to include doctrinal principles, while the *coetus* on Divine Worship excluded such statements.[27] This will call for coordination in the final stages of development.

It is evident to anyone who studies the schemata attentively that all the sub-commissions did not work in the same way. Only a few of the schemata (Consecrated Life, Administrative Procedure, Fundamental Law) could be said to be truly new. In other sectors substantial changes were made (v.g., Patrimonial Law, Penal Law), but in numerous cases the commissions were satisfied simply to take the present Code and update it where necessary.

c. Application at the Local Level

One of the most significant changes introduced in the proposed new Code is the application of the principle of subsidiarity through a careful effort at decentralization. This calls for a number of decisions to be made at national or local levels.[28] In this regard, the Roman Curia will eventually be seen more as a service of the particular Churches than as a legislative body settling all questions in a peremptory manner.

This decentralization also calls for an intelligent application of the great principles of law at the local level. Such principles regard the interpretation of laws and the use of prudent equity.

There are many advantages to such a system. Episcopal Conferences, within the framework of the general law, would be able to adapt some of the legislation to local and particular needs and customs. This principle had already been adopted for the liturgical renewal and will now be of great assistance in some cases related to the general law. It will also remove somewhat the monolithic character of Church law, which, to a certain extent, characterizes the present legislation.

However, the benefits that can be derived from such a system will also cause some problems that we must not be afraid to face. If there is little interest in responding to the consultation, what interest will there be in preparing laws adapted to particular situations? The new law will call for a second book, as it were, outlining the particular law of the territory. This will have to be prepared with great care — and will call for the contribution of qualified people. At the 1977 Synod of Bishops, objections were raised against this innovation[29] because, it was stated, small Conferences do not have the available expertise to carry out these plans. However, the Secretary of the Code Commission replied that the law cannot distinguish between large and small Conferences, all of which, in certain instances, have legislative power.

27. Cf. *ibid.*, 5 (1973), p. 43, No. 3.

28. See, for instance, the schema on Divine Worship, canons 25, 26, 28, 37, 45, 48, 52, and so forth.

29. Cf. *Communicationes,* 9 (1977), pp. 220-221.

This facet of the new Code, as well as many others, draws attention clearly to the fact that people must be prepared in various dioceses for the implementation of the legislation. It also means that the work of preparing the new law will not be terminated once the universal Code is promulgated, because there will still have to be national and local legislation prepared.

It also raises the serious question about the legislative role of the local bishop in regard to that of the Episcopal Conference.

The proposed new law for Institutes of Consecrated Life respected this principle throughout the draft, with almost half the canons calling for application in the particular legislation of the Institute.

d. Application of the Proposed New Law at This Time

While it is evident to everyone that the proposed new canons are not yet law in the formal sense of the word, it has been asked in many circles whether the drafts could not be used at the present time as a supplementary source of law.

Many of the revised canons simply codify the existing post-Conciliar legislation and any changes introduced are more of a stylistic nature. There should be no difficulty in following the draft texts on this score.

Furthermore, a distinction should be made between laws which are binding for validity and those which are more directive in nature. Again, there does not seem to be much difficulty in applying the second category, while it seems that the former should not be used.

It has been a principle of law that when the legislation did not provide for a certain situation, in addition to other means, the opinions of approved authors could be followed (cf. canon 20). It seems that the members of the Code commission would readily fit into this last category and that the drafts reflect their understanding of what the Second Vatican Council was teaching.

Indeed, it is important to remember that many of the proposed new canons simply translate the Council's teaching into juridical language. Since the teachings of Vatican II are already obligatory — oftentimes expressing the natural law itself[30] — we have no choice but to apply the norms. An illustration of this point could be found in the canons on marriage where the doctrine of *Gaudium et Spes* is presented in a more succinct form.

Again, Religious Institutes preparing the definitive version of their Constitutions would be very imprudent to ignore the trends and thrusts of the new law, and should provide for those points foreseen in the new law, even though they are not necessarily binding today.

Having given these general facts, let us now proceed to the third, and most difficult, part of this study: an overall evaluation of the work carried out to date on the revision of the Code.

30. Cf. J-M. Serrano-Ruiz. "Le droit à la communauté de vie et d'amour conjugal comme objet du consentement matrimonial; aspects juridiques et évolution de la jurisprudence de la Sacrée Rote Romaine", in *Studia Canonica,* 10 (1976), p. 293.

III. Evaluation of the Proposed New Code

When we examine the new Code, we are able to see at a glance that there are many positive features. Likewise, though, there are a number of points which would call for improvement. Let us now mention some of these.

a. Positive Features

1) One very positive feature of the new Code is its plan which sets forth in a more logical order the various canons that are to be considered. The place of the "Lex Fundamentalis" will have to be determined, however, since many canons refer directly to it and to its statutes. The new plan is a courageous and worthwhile attempt to pass from legislation based on Roman Law to legislation having a doctrinal basis.

It has been asked whether there should not have been a section on liturgical legislation, providing a framework within which to present the various liturgical laws that will be issued. So many points of the Code directly or indirectly refer to liturgy that it might seem advisable to have this section developed.

Likewise, it could be asked whether it might not have been preferable to have a section on the mission of governing, leaving the general aspects of the law on persons to a separate book. However, the Commission felt that it was not opportune to do so. The new plan, in spite of this, is certainly more in line with the Church's doctrinal roles, and removes from the category "De Rebus" such subjects as Sacraments, sacramentals, cemeteries, seminaries, holidays and feasts, and so forth. It also places more emphasis on the role of the Church as a living society.

The original plan had indeed called for a separate section on the mission of governing, but the entire organization was revised a few times.[31]

2) A second positive feature of the new Code is that it provides us with an authentic interpretation on many points of the teachings of the Second Vatican Council. It enables us now to build up the Church of tomorrow in a more orderly way. However, since the Council could even be considered to be obsolete in many respects, it can be asked whether the Code itself will not also be considered obsolete before it is promulgated, given the sources on which it is based. This is quite possible in some areas. Nevertheless, no one should expect the Code by itself to change the life of the Church or the mentality of people overnight. We must be willing to wait for many years to see what effects it will have. Indeed, it must be recognized — with regret — that in many parts of the world, the study of the Code is not and will not be a priority.

3) Perhaps the greatest advantage of the new Code is the fact that it will provide us with an organized synthesis of the Church's legislation. In the past fifteen years there has been an abundance of legislation that is not always easy to find or to apply. Of course, it won't be long till changes will

31. Cf. *Communicationes,* 1 (1969), pp. 111-112; 9 (1977), p. 229.

have to be introduced even in the new Code, and it is hoped that a uniform method of promulgation will be applied. This organized synthesis contains no surprises because, in most instances, the Commission is simply codifying existing legislation. It would be important, though, to avoid a multiplicity of additional laws, even though these are foreseen: for instance, special norms for the Roman Tribunals, for causes of beatification and canonization, for the functioning of the Roman Curia, for the election of the Pope, for the organization of Universities, and so forth, not to mention the numerous particular laws of countries, dioceses and religious Institutes.

4) The Code will also have an advantage referred to above: possibility of adaptation to local needs. This includes a recognition of worthwhile customs as part of the legal heritage of the local and particular Churches. We would mention, though, that only certain points of law may thus be applied. Excepted from such possibilities are the laws regarding the operation of the marriage courts. It is exactly here, however, that it would have been necessary to provide better for local needs. The present universal system cannot continue to be applied as it stands, and if we are to meet the true needs of the people, we must be able to provide them with competent and efficient service.

5) Significant advantages are also to be found in three of the schemata. The proposed new law for Institutes of Consecrated Life enables each Institute to prepare its own legislation — within certain limits — and this will allow many communities to give themselves a new thrust and a chance to return to their original sources. Of course, some of the smaller Institutes will find this difficult and already are asking for more specific guidelines in this respect. Such requests, if numerous, could result in the withdrawing of such applications of subsidiarity and would not be healthy, it seems, for the universal Church.

The new law on marriage has numerous innovations of practical importance to Christian families. Likewise, the proposed new penal law simplifies radically the number of automatic penalties imposed for various crimes, and provides a much more open legislation.

6) We cannot expect to find substantial changes in the General Norms of the Code — even though there are many — since most of these canons are based on time-honoured and proven legal principles which are almost essential to any society. The changes in the other books are mostly of a cosmetic nature and are, in fact, of little importance in the day to day life of the Church. They have, however, the advantage of providing us with a synthesis of law that will make it easier to apply the Church's legislation.

In spite of these advantages, there are a number of points concerning the new law which could well be improved. Let us now look at some of them.

b. Aspects Which Possibly Could Be Improved

As it stands, the draft of the new Code is not a finalized document. Therefore, it is only reasonable to expect that a number of modifications or changes could still be introduced. Let us refer, then, to a number of objections that have been raised against the text as it now stands. These are not all of equal importance, but they do express the thinking of numerous writers and commentators.

1) One thing that strikes the reader is that the doctrinal inspiration is not the same throughout the text. There seems to be a lack of unity among the various parts. This is inevitable because of the way the text was prepared; however, a coordinating committee might be able to do something to remedy this situation.

One could ask respectfully if all the sub-commissions have really listened to Pope Paul's call to have a law based on doctrine, and not a law patterned after civil legislation. If they did so, the results are not always as evident as they could be. I feel that this will be a serious weakness that will discredit the new law since the legislation will not always live up to the expectations we had a right to have.

2) Another factor that has been criticized in many places is the fact that in some sections reference is made to Vatican II but without changing the realities underlying the former law. This is evident in the schema on the People of God. Indeed, it is not sufficient to change a name to change a reality (like changing from "Esso" to "Exxon" — but it is the same gas!). The canons in the schema on the People of God still seem to present a pyramid system of Church organization, in spite of the new name. Another example is to be found in the introduction to the canons of Procedure, where it is stated that some changes reflect the spirit of Vatican II.[32] One seeks in vain for such changes. Likewise, in a number of instances, it can be asked whether the quotes from Vatican II are correct: it happens that certain modifying clauses have been omitted which change somewhat the nature of the text. One example, out of many, suffices.

In the canons on the Magisterium, canon 28, par. 3, referring to *Christus Dominus,* No. 35, 1, states that

> members of Institutes of consecrated life also, men and women, should willingly cooperate in providing catechetical formation for the people; superiors of Institutes of consecrated life, even the exempt, are bound personally or through their membership to offer catechetical formation to the Christian people.

Christus Dominus adds the important clause that: "the special character of each religious institute should be taken into consideration".

Similar examples were found in the first drafts of the *Lex Fundamentalis,* but numerous modifications were introduced into the revised text.

There is a danger here of petrifying the teachings of the Council, without allowing room for necessary tolerance. This would be a serious weakness in the new Code.

3) A third criticism that has been levelled against the Code as a whole is

32. Cf. *ibid.,* 8 (1976), p. 185.

that little consideration is given to the status of women in Church Law. A number of prescriptions, which could appear to be arbitrary, still prevent access of women to positions in the Church where there is no reference to the power of orders. Of course, the entire problem of the distinction between jurisdiction and office has not yet been aptly solved. The best example of a case where the status of women is not equal is to be found in the law on procedures where lay men are allowed access to various offices in the tribunal, including that of judge, while women are systematically excluded. A number of objections were raised against this exclusion, and it is not impossible to hope for changes in this respect.

4) In examining the Code as a whole, it is evident that some points are given more importance in relation to other points than they actually deserve. Examples in point are the canons on Mass stipends, on indulgences, on the use of the pallium, and so forth. The final revision might be able to make some adjustments.

5) Perhaps the most vehement objections were raised in some circles by those who opposed the fact that the schemata were settling disputed theological points before the doctrine was sufficiently elaborated. Among such questions we could mention: the requirement of faith for a sacramental marriage, the institution of Mass stipends, ministerial possibilities for women, the sacraments as mysteries of faith, the trans-physical dimensions of consummation of marriage, the legislative competence of the universal Church and the particular Churches, and so forth.[33]

6) Personally, the section I am most disappointed with is the schema "De Processibus" which perpetuates a situation that is considered by many to be unacceptable. It is very interesting, for instance, to compare the text of the proposed Latin Code with the *relatio* prepared for the Oriental Code. While the Latin Commission insisted on classifying marriage cases under the heading of contentious cases, the Oriental Commission decided — and rightly so, it seems — that such cases do not fit under this particular heading.[34] This latter opinion was shared by many who submitted observations on the Latin schema. A change is this perspective would remove much of the artificiality now necessarily found in marriage cases, at least in those ones which are non-contested.

What is of primary importance in this regard is to remove the adjudication of marriage cases from any civil context. Each diocese could have an office for the family, a section of which would be entrusted with the study of requests for declarations of nullity. The solemn court apparatus would neither be required nor opportune. However, I don't think the climate is ripe yet for such a change.

If the *summary* contentious procedure were applied to the study of mar-

33. Cf. T. J. Green, "The Revision of Marriage Law: An Exposition and Critique", *loc. cit.*, pp. 407-408.

34. Cf. *Nuntia* (printed edition), No. 5, 1977, p. 7.

riage cases, the schema would be — in spite of its weakness — of assistance to us.

7) The schema on the teaching office of the Church is prepared in what might possibly be considered as a ''triumphalistic'' approach. Of course, it must be admitted that considerable effort went into the updating of the norms, even though the final product still leaves much to be desired. It would be necessary, it seems, to correct the impression given by the text, so that a document that has been well re-worked would fit in with the other parts of the Code. This applies more particularly to the section on Universities and similar institutions.

Naturally, not everyone will agree with all of the above remarks and observations. Nevertheless, they summarize what a number of writers have been saying — at times in stronger terms — and should be considered carefully before the new Code is promulgated.

Conclusion

The foregoing remarks present some observations on the new Code. The principles for revision are very well established and their application has, generally, been carefully observed.

Yet, the question still remains: should we have a Code at this time? If one is promulgated now, should it not be ''ad experimentum'' for some time so that corrections of a more permanent nature could be incorporated at a later date?

Personally, I am in favour of a second round of consultation before the text is promulgated. In this way we would be able — and perhaps this time in a more coherent manner — to review the trends to be found in the document as a whole, not relying on piecemeal evaluations.

However, no matter which road the Holy Father decides to follow, it must be recognized that the sub-commissions tried to carry out their work carefully and studiously. While the new Code is not always the breath of fresh air that might be needed, it is certainly a marked improvement over the present legislation. Let us only hope that it will be an instrument of grace for the People of God in the years to come.

Case 4

Ongoing Revision of Church Law

A Task Force for the Revision of the Code of Canon Law has before it a proposal suggesting that a procedure be established to provide for ongoing legislation in the Church. The proposal states:

> During our study of the strengths and weaknesses of the 1917 Code of Canon Law, one of the glaring weaknesses was that the Code of 1917 became outdated very quickly and that there was no organ or procedure to provide the universal church with legislation in an ongoing manner. The Committee for the Interpretation of the 1917 Code was not adequate because it could only interpret existing legislation. The Supreme Pontiff has the power to make universal laws but there is no organ or procedure in place, except for his Curia, to aid him in the process. We therefore propose to the full commission that it develop a procedure and suggest a structure through which the church could legislate continuously.

The proposal met with a variety of comments.

I. IN FAVOR OF THE PROPOSAL

A. The Church allowed itself to fall behind by failing to provide up-to-date legislation.

B. If a method for continuous legislation is approved, it should provide for broad participation by all elements of church membership.

C. Such a proposal is acceptable only if the pope remains the supreme legislator.

D. Many other Christian Churches have a legislative body.

II. AGAINST THE PROPOSAL

A. The Church has never had such a procedure in the past and does not need one now.

B. There is no body in the Church that could efficiently operate as a church legislature.

C. There is no scriptural basis for such a procedure in the Church.

D. Such a proposal is little more than an imitation of civil governments which do not operate very efficiently anyway.

E. The Church is not a democracy or republic.

Exercise

1. How would you evaluate the strengths and weaknesses of the proposal and the reasons for and against it?

2. Could the Synod of Bishops fulfill this legislative role?

References

Brown, E. "Co-Responsibility in Church Governance. Some Protestant Experiences," *The Jurist* 31, (1970), 187-222.

Müller, A., ed., "Democratization of the Church," *Concilium, Religion in the Seventies* 63 (New York: Herder and Herder, 1971).

Orsy, L., "The Creative Role of Constitutional Law in the Church," *Studia Canonica* 2 (1968), 307-24, especially 315-18.

PART II: *The People of God*

A. MEMBERSHIP IN THE CHURCH

What Belonging to the Church Has Come to Mean

Yves Congar

CLASSICAL PRE-VATICAN II POSITIONS

We will not give a historical account of the question "de membris"—even though such a study would not be uninteresting, were it only to show how many approaches there were to the question. St. Cyprian's was not St. Augustine's. In the Middle Ages even, there were several different positions on how sinners can belong to the Church. But the classical theology of our question, as well as its ecclesiastical cadre, was determined by the great authors of the Counter Reformation, the successors to the Scholastic tradition. The leaders of the Reformation and the creeds of the reformed Churches had not posed the question *"Was ist das Kirche"* ("*What* is the Church?") but rather *"Wer ist das Kirche?"* ("*Who* is the Church?"). The response had been: true believers, and consequently, the true community they formed.[1] Catholic apologists have been led to deal with the Church from the angle of its visibility, of its guarantee of apostolic authenticity, from having to focus on the question: who belongs and who does not belong to the Church?[2]

The overall conjuncture of circumstances and events was as follows. First of all, there was Christendom, where, in the case of marriage, for example, civil and social validity coincided with validity in the eyes of the Church. Situations were clearly defined and evaluated according to canon law. And, on the whole, the mentality was one of exclusion, rather than warm welcome. That mentality played a decisive role in the division of the sixteenth century. Until quite recent times, for example, children of divorced persons were not admitted into seminaries and novitiates. As late as 1946, the Sisters of the Assumption, whose work is caring for the sick in their own

1. Cf. B. Gassmann, *Ecclesia reformata (Die Kirche in den reformierten Bekenntnisschriften)* (Herder, 1968).

2. Cf. P. Eyt, "L'ordre du discours et l'ordre de l'Eglise" (Hypothesis on the deep structures of the text "Controversies" by Bellarmine), in *Melanges d'Histoire offerts à Mgr. E. Griffe, Bull. de Littér. Eccl.,* 73 (1972), 229-249.

homes, were barred from exercising their ministry in the households of divorced persons.[3]

Another element in the overall picture: Catholics all participated in a culture world shaped by the Church. This culture had a sort of harmony, a homogeneity, a compatibility with the affirmation, norms, and practices of a Church, effectively directed by clerics. Thus a connaturality and a concordance existed between the values one lived by, or professed to live by, and the rules of the ecclesiastical institution.

The Church was defined juridically in social categories as *societas perfecta,* a complete, autonomous society, having all the juridical attributes of such a society, in particular that of *"potestas coactiva."* In this cadre, the situation of persons admitted of an exact description or juridical definition.[4] Each baptized individual is a person in the Church, possessing the rights and duties of Christians, except, insofar as the rights go, when a censure stands in the way or an *obex* prevents ecclesiastical communion. This is canon 87.[5] The obligations, for their part, remain in force.

Baptism confers the grace of union with Christ. In Patristic times and in the Middle Ages, the questions that were raised had to do with the status of baptized persons in the state of sin: do they remain members of the Body of Christ, within the ecclesial unity? If so, what sort of unity? Baptism also confers a mark which remains on the soul even when it has been damned, by virtue of which any marriage contracted between baptized persons, even *"in infidelitate,"* is *eo ipso* the sacrament of matrimony.[6]

Categories to which the interdictions of *obex* and *censura* apply were given precise definitions. Apostates, heretics, and schismatics were laid under excommunication. These categories were defined by canon 1325, 2.[7] The beautiful conciseness of the Latin formulas translates into formidable specifications. A heretic is defined as a baptized Christian who, while still professing the Christian faith, denies in an obdurate way—not just any error constitutes heresy; *pertinacia* is a necessary element—a truth one is

3. On this detail, see Lucienne Vannier, *Sur le roc* (Paris, 1975).

4. *De Ecclesia* and A.C. Gigon, *De membris Ecclesiae Christi* (Fribourg, 1949); L. Boisvert, *Doctrina de membris Ecclesiae iuxta documenta Magisterii recentiora* (Montreal, 1961); A. Hagen, quoted below n. 9. Applied to Protestants: E. Du Mont, *La situation du protestant baptisé* (Saint Maurice, 1959), and the criticism by J. Kaelin in *Nova et Vetera,* 35 (1960), 119-122.

5. "Baptismate homo constituitur in Ecclesia Christi persona cum omnibus christianorum iuribus et officiis, nisi ad iura quod attinet, obstet obex ecclesiasticae communionis vinculum impediens, vel lata ab Ecclesia censura."

6. This is the well-known canon 1012 on which we will have more to say.

7. "Post receptum baptismum si quis, nomen retinens christianum, pertinaciter aliquam ex veritatibus fide divina et catholica credendis denegat, aut de ea dubitat, haereticus; si a fide christiana totaliter recedit, apostata; si denique subesse renuit Summo Pontifici aut cum membris ei suiectis communicare recusat, schismaticus est." For a short history and elaboration of the notions of schism and heresy, cf. our *L'Eglise, une, sainte, catholique et apostolique, Mysterium Salutis* (Paris, 1970), pp. 65-121.

bound to believe, because it has been revealed by God *and* is declared to be divine revelation by the Church (*fide catholica*). Even if a baptized person places such a truth in doubt (*aut de ea dubitat*), he is a heretic. This definition seems terribly extensive even when applied to a case of openly professed doubt. A schismatic is someone who refuses to submit to the Sovereign Pontiff or to be in communion with those who do. The notion of schism, as we have seen, has become increasingly centered on submission to the pope, whereas originally it had been defined as raising altar against altar within the context of the local Church.[8] According to the *Codex Iuris Canonici,* an apostate is a person who has completely withdrawn from the Christian faith. One should not make leaving the Church, as in the legislation and context of Germany's *Bundesrepublik,* tantamount to apostasy.[9]

Members of the Church were deprived of certain rights by their situation (public sinners), by a censure of excommunication, or in the case of clerics by a censure of suspension.

This canonical doctrine, which clearly has theological foundations, was given dogmatic expression in the encyclical *Mystici corporis* by Pius XII on June 29, 1943: Only those are really to be included as members of the Church who have been baptized and profess the true faith and who have not unhappily withdrawn from the Body-unity, or for very grave faults, been cut off from it by legitimate authority, (n. 21).

The same encyclical lists the elements or conditions for communion or unity: "profession of the same faith, sharing in the same sacred rites, participation in the same sacrifice, practical observance of the same laws. Above all, everyone must be able to see the Supreme Head, who gives effective direction to what all are doing in a mutually helpful way toward attaining the desired end. We mean the Vicar of Christ on earth" (n. 69). Under these conditions, what will be the situation of those not recognizing the authority of the pope in relation to the Mystical Body which, on earth, is identical to the Roman Catholic Church? The encyclical answers this question in n. 101: "Unsuspectingly they are related by desire to the Mystical Body of the Redeemer."[10]

Elements of the spiritual life are not totally disregarded in the encyclical any more than they were by Bellarmine, but when applied to the question of belonging to the Church and even to the Body of Christ, they are subordinated to those norms of visible belonging susceptible of juridical definition. For Bellarmine, and for C. Pesch and Lercher, among the recent authors, Baptism simply *held* as valid suffices to constitute a member of the Church.

8. See our article, "Schisme," in *Dictionnaire de Théologie Catholique,* XIV, col. 1286-1312.

9. We would therefore disagree with A. Hagen, *Die Kirchliche Mitgliedschaft* (Rotenburg, 1938), p. 56.

10. "Etiamsi inscio quodam desiderio ac voto ad mysticum Redemptoris Corpus ordinentur" (*Acta Apostolicae Sedis,* p. 143).

How the Real Questions Are Being Posed in a New Way

A. The Council has left behind the narrow boundaries of a concept of the Church as society, *"societas inaequalis, societas perfecta,"* in favor of a vision of the Church as communion.[11] Already the socio-institutional interpretation that the encyclical gave to the notion of the Mystical Body had been frequently criticized. The Council did not take up this interpretation again; it gave a rather exegetical description of the theme of the Mystical Body, without making it serve as *definition* of the Church, as it had for the First Vatican Council, for Franzelin, and for Pius XII.[12] In the theme of the Body, the Council saw primarily the relationship between the faithful and Christ, and only afterwards did it affirm its ecclesiastical value. But even then the Council did not identify the Mystical Body purely and simply with the Roman Catholic Church, or even with the Church of Christ. "This Church. . .subsists in the Roman Catholic Church, *subsistit in Ecclesia catholica,* although many elements of sanctification and truth can be found outside her visible structures."[13] By expressing the matter in this way, the Council established the possibility of recognizing other Christians as truly belonging to the Body of Christ and of speaking of the relation of other Churches and ecclesial communities with the Catholic Church in terms of a real, although imperfect, communion.

The Council intentionally avoided speaking of *"membris."* The Council Fathers had in fact perceived that this vocabulary led to difficulties for which no solution could be found. In the sub-committee of the doctrinal Commission, in which we participated, it was realized that the way in which one spoke of the membership of Catholics in the Church implied a particular concept of the Church. If only external elements were brought into play, one was left with a completely external, juridical concept of the Church. Therefore it was essential to mention an interior, spiritual element without, however, transforming the whole notion of belonging to the Church into something invisible as with Wyclif or Huss. Hence this wording of n. 14, 2 of *Lumen Gentium:* "They are *fully* incorporated into the society of the Church who, *possessing the Spirit of Christ,* accept her entire system of organization. . . ."

B. The post-Conciliar period was different yet from the Council. There is a changed situation to face with regard to conditions for belonging to the Church. We can worry over this and in fact there are disquieting aspects to the current situation; we can deplore it as well, but it is legitimate, even wholesome and necessary, to recognize clearly what that situation is. This is what we want to try to do.

11. Cf. Antonio Acerbi, *Due ecclesiologie (Ecclesiologia giuridica ed ecclesiologia di communione nella "Lumen Gentium")* (Bologna, 1975).

12. Vatican I: The annotations to the first schema *De Ecclesia, Collectio Lacensis* VII, 578; Franzelin, *Theses de Ecclesia* (posthumous Opus) (Rome, 1887), p. 308; Pius XII, encyclical *Mystici corporis,* n. 13 *(Acta Apostolicae Sedis,* p. 199).

13. *Lumen Gentium* n. 8, 2. The lucky find *subsistit in* appears again in the decree on ecumenism, n. 4, 3 and in the declaration on religious freedom, n. 1, 2.

The excellent document, *Pro Mundi Vita,* which studies the behavior of French youth with regard to the Church, recognizes the fact that young people today no longer actually leave the Church; many are still to some extent in the Church. "Quite often, they are neither in the Church nor out of it."[14] Similarly, priests engaged in pastoral ministry to youth in Switzerland have stated: "We cannot simply enter the young people in our books as Christian. They have a right to stay in no man's land."[15]

The reason for this is that we are no longer living in the world Bellarmine knew, or even in the world of the Council. What has happened? The many great movements, arising simultaneously and working in concert, have profoundly altered the cultural horizon and cracked the foundations for the attitude of belief. The right of entry has been given to these "enlighted ones," in a Church which hitherto had set against them the closed doors of refusal and the high walls of refutation. The Council for its part did away with the kind of unconditional attitude that had prevailed in the theological, canonical, sociological, and psychological system derived from Scholasticism, the Counter Reformation, and the Roman Catholic Restoration of the nineteenth century. The result has been the loss of a certain simplicity in matters of faith. That it can be found once again after all the upheavals is possible, we think, but this will not come about right away, nor easily, nor will it be for everyone. Everything has become subject to interpretation, to the all too famous hermeneutics, which so often is tantamount to asking *our* questions of the text, to substituting our subjectivity for its sovereign objectivity. The result is pluralism, which is an earmark of our times. Naturally, this pluralism in principle has its limits, those placed on it from respect for the apostolic profession of faith.[16] But some of the questions pursued are of such a radical nature, with their philosophical frame of reference so poorly construed, that pluralism seems to overrun its legitimate domain. "We are all sentenced to private judgment."[17]

It is strange: while the sciences thrive on objectivity, we are bound, in all that touches spiritual convictions and the meaning of life, to the world of subjectivity. Here everything is centered on man—which in a sense is both Biblical and Christian—but even more, all is centered on personal subjectivity. Hence the pursuit of sincerity above all, the distrust of whatever

14. *Pro Mundi vita,* n. 33 (1970) (Western Youth and the Future of the Church), p. 12. Pierre Eyt also noted the problem posed by the difficulty of knowing whether one is in or out of the Church: "En marge de la réforme du Code de droit canonique. . . ." in *Nouvelle Revue théologique,* 97 (1975), 842-853 (845).

15. In *Orientierung* (Zurich), 38 (June 13, 1974), 126.

16. The international Commission of theologians published on this subject a rather remarkable declaration (cf. *Docum. Cathol.,* n. 1633 [1973], 526-29) based on studies which, until then, had appeared only in German. Written from a rather pastoral point of view, our study "Unité et pluralisme" appeared in *Ministerès et Communion ecclésiale* (Paris, 1971), 229-260.

17. M. Despland, in *Les mutations dans la foi chrétienne* (Montreal, 1974), p. 18.

seeks to set itself up as given, ready-made, or normative: rejection of Tradition claiming value as such, criticism of all that is institution, establishment, juridical determination. What will happen, in these conditions, to the rules and categories handed down in the matter of belonging to the Church?

What of "heresy"? Or "apostasy"? Heresy, properly defined, is not rejection of the content of the Christian faith, let us say the *quod,* but rejection of its ecclesial teaching, let us say the *quo.* In Catholicism, this is the authority of the magisterium safeguarding and interpreting the deposit of faith and Tradition. Now, today, what counts above all is that to which one personally chooses to adhere. We are pledged to what can be called "interpretive thought." Each one as it were re-creates faith, his faith. He accepts some things and discards others, or doubts them, leaving them in question. He does not leave the Church, but one day he realizes that he is out of the Church on one account and in the Church on another.[18] This is what is called partial concurrence or partial identification.[19] "Secularism has created a new kind of person. This new person perceives the relativity of all systematization. A pragmatic, he notes a pluralism in the many paths, forms of thought, ways of life, and spiritual families. He realizes that his own institutions have no monopoly on anything."[20] In the sphere of ecumenism, this is why young people especially want to receive communion together, and believe thay can do so even when the doctrines of their respective Churches only partially concur. This is also why ecumenism tends toward settling down to a situation of peaceful, fraternal co-existence, which obviously entails a certain abdication from the ideal of unity. Now will the question of heresy still be raised? The document from the theological Commission, to which we subscribe, rightly states on the question of pluralism: "In view of presentations of doctrine, where there is serious ambiguity, even incompatibility with the faith of the Church, the Church has the power to discern wherein lies the error, and the duty to reject it, even to the formal pronouncement of heresy as an extreme measure to safeguard the faith of the people of God." Will schism still be spoken of? The Holy Father, Paul VI, deplores the existence of a ferment that is practically schismatic.[21] What is the reality of the matter, what do the facts

18. Cf. for example the statement of P. Roqueplo (author of *La Foi d'un mal-croyant*) in *Esprit,* November, 1971, 530-531. This partial identification is the case of almost all of the authors (17 Catholics, 14 Protestants) of the German collection, *Warum bleibe ich in der Kirche?* ed. by Dirks and Stammler (Stuttgart, 1971) as they tell why they remain in the Church.

19. It is this situation that François Roustang analyzed, in a famous article, "Le troisième homme," in *Christus,* n. 52 (1965), 561-567. See J.-B. Metz. *Die Antwort der Theologen* (Dusseldorf, 1968), p. 19; *Herder-Korrespondenz,* 23 (1969), 427-433; also the question of the magisterium: "Notre Eglise a-t-elle besoin d'une nouvelle réforme?" *Concilium,* n. 54 (1970), 75-85.

20. Jacques Grand'Maison, "L'Eglise en dehors de l'Eglise" (*Cahiers de Communauté chrétienne,* 4) (Montreal, 1966), p. 48-49.

21. Holy Thursday, April 3, 1969. We commented on this grave warning in *Informations Catholiques Internationales,* n. 335 (May 2, 1969), pp. 4-6 and 31-32.

themselves say? A historian of contemporary Christianity observes

> communities, movements, or groups, sometimes very much in opposition, even on the content of faith, setting themselves up and fighting without dreaming of ceding ground and without an authority resolving to choose from among them. While it is by no means short of prophets, the new schism delays in coming. In Churches questioning themselves on their own identity, the threshold of rupture seems to recede indefinitely and the notion of dissent loses its meaning.[22]

When we open our eyes to the situation as it actually stands and speak of "baptized persons who have no faith," the question of their marriages arises: is the contract between all baptized persons automatically a sacrament (canon 1012)?[23] Surveys sufficiently reliable to clarify this question, inform us that 88% of the French people wish to see their children baptized, although more than half of them do not recognize Jesus Christ and two-thirds do not believe in the resurrection. . . .

Is this a new situation? What precisely did the baptized people of the nineteenth century believe in, those who never questioned anything? What did the "implicit faith" of the *minores* of the Middle Ages hide? Montaigne the skeptic writes: "Some people want to fool the world into thinking they believe what they do not believe. The others, who are in the majority, fool themselves, not knowing how to penetrate into what it truly means to believe."[24] It is true that these Christians had the benefit of a society and culture where everything was related to the faith of the "Church," that is, its magisterium, and that none of these things was called into question. This is not to be underestimated. This is the reason why we cannot go along with those who propose to suppress the recitation of the Creed at Mass, arguing that the majority of the faithful do not know the meaning of many of the articles of faith. Regrettably, this is often true. At least, they profess in word and in *intention* to believe what the "Church" believes. That might have sufficed before the onslaught of doubt, but does it now? Let us hear what a student, Marie-Helène Cazes has to say:

> When I speak with my mother, who has an extraordinarily simple faith, I perceive that even if the people of her generation had any doubts about their faith, they never expressed them. Things were perfectly clear: either you left the Church or you belonged to the Church and would never even dream of questioning the faith. Whereas now, even those who are in the Church, experience no hesitations in questioning it.[25]

22. E. Fouilloux, in *L'Histoire religieuse de la France, 19e-20e siècles (Problèmes et Méthodes)* (Paris, 1975), p. 170.

23. The participants in a colloquy held in 1974 at the Faculté de Droit canonique of the Catholic Institute in Paris unanimously requested a modification of this canon: *Foi et sacrement de mariage: Recherches et perplexités* (Lyon, 1974).

24. *Essais,* Book II, Chapter 12.

25. "Des jeunes et la foi"—"Des etudiants s'expriment," *La Vie spirituelle,* n. 160 (September-October,1975), 688.

Let us go one step further. The fasciculus of *Pro Mundi Vita* that we quoted (n. 14) also states that what interests young people is less the models than the values. Models would force themselves upon me, while values express my intention. Let us read on:

> What is graver yet is that they see more and more that the values they live by, in other words, those that seem important to them in daily life, remain important regardless of their doctrinal justifications. Peace, equality, scientific and technological progress, authenticity, respect for interpersonal relationships, democratic issues are for them values independent of doctrinal systems, and in the final analysis they hold that ideologies, much more than values, create opposition among men.

Naturally, we refuse to apply the label of ideology to Christianity, recognizing all the while that historically it has sometimes taken on that role. The important thing for our subject is to see that Christianity is currently considered as a value, insofar as it is *for man*. Here we have a rather ponderous subject, that has been well analyzed by M. de Certeau.[26] The Church is as it were dispossessed of Christianity in favor of what in Christianity appeals to men, dispossessed of the person of Jesus. Christianity, taken as a value for one's life, is removed from the structures and mediations of the Church.[27] In theological categories, we would say that this means remaining attached to the *res,* but without the *sacramentum,* a diagnosis we will illustrate using significant examples. This thinking represents the opposite of the old theology *"de membris,"* which, as we have seen, took its criteria from the side of the *sacramentum.* Have we examples?

What did people go to look for in Boquen, if not for the values of Christianity with a kind of freedom from the forms of the Church? What do so many young Catholics find in Taizé, if not what is essential to Catholic values without the apparatus of the Church?

In the present day practice of the Eucharist, the need so many young people feel to receive communion together, regardless of what their Church may require, shows that the Eucharist, for them, is taken chiefly as an occasion for exchange and communication, as a brotherly meal, with little interest in its reality as sacrifice or even in the "Real Presence," that is its *res et sacramentum.*

Many young people (and even some who are not so young) will receive communion as readily at a Protestant Last Supper as they will at a Catholic Eucharist. They scarcely question whether the minister is qualified from a dogmatic and sacramental point of view. For them, the important thing is that he be a warm and spiritual person.

What of marriage? How many shun the Church celebration altogether, or

26. M. de Certeau and J.-M. Domenach, *Le christianisme éclaté* (Paris, 1974).

27. We could cite here Jean-Louis Barrault, *Souvenirs pour demain* (Paris, 1972), p. 301; P.G. Wacker. "Christus ohne Kirche?" in *Theologie und Glaube,* 64 (1974), 1-28.

simply find no interest in it, who nonetheless instill their union with Christian marriage values, minus their dogmatic spiritual, and ecclesial context. . . .

Sound practice (*orthopraxie*) has replaced sound doctrine (*orthodoxie*) as a priority. A Christian is someone who practices justice and love rather than someone who frequents the Sacraments and follows the rules of the Church. Time and again this observation is made. Msgr. R. Coffy: "For contemporary man, the first mark of the faith is no longer receiving the Sacraments but taking part in action by the Church directed toward the liberation of the oppressed and brotherly love among individuals and among peoples."[28] The minister, Georges Casalis, calls to mind "other periods in history when the sense of belonging to a religious group was more important than concern for participating in a human adventure, inspired by a relationship with Jesus of Nazareth."[29] Rev. Pinto de Oliveira: "The feeling of belonging to a religion is too easily compatible with injustice, while faith in the living god absolutely rules this out. In the Old Testament the prophets stigmatized the abuses of a devotion which was only exterior."[30]

These traits delineate a new way of experiencing the Church, of living the Church, of being in the Church, or rather of bringing the Church itself into existence. Instead of positing first and foremost an institution anterior to ourselves, with its own structures and norms, we see a Church being created as a result of the living out of Christianity by men involved in the life of the world, in the fight for justice and for the liberation of the oppressed.[31] That poses many questions. Certain formulas, radicalizing these tendencies and confirming their negative aspects, are certainly to be severely criticized.[32]

Within this perspective, the "ecclesiality" of others is measured in ways that would have been impossible according to the dogmatico-juridical criteria of the Counter Reformation. In "secular ecumenism," unity appears bound, not to doctrinal agreement or sacramental conformity, but to the common action of Christians in the great human causes. This certainly brings much that is positive and salutary, but it also leaves some important questions unresolved.[33] We would be left with unity among Christians without real unity among the Churches, and the facts today point clearly in this direction. . . .

28. *Eglise, signe de salut au milieu des hommes* (Paris, 1972), p. 47; compare p. 28 and 65.

29. In *Politique et Foi* (Strasbourg, 1972), p. 204.

30. In *L'Anthropologie de Saint Thomas,* Ed. Luyten (Fribourg, 1974), p. 202, note 27.

31. A rather characteristic example, very positive, moreover: A. Savard "Vivre en chrétien à Grenoble," in *Informations Catholiques Internationales,* n. 475 (March 1, 1975), 2-16.

32. We have given examples: "Les groupes informels dans l'Eglise: un point de vue catholique," in *Les groupes informels dans l'Eglise* (Strasbourg, 1971); cf. pp. 297 note 26; 297.

33. We quote ourselves once more: "Les problèmes nouveaux du monde seculier rendent-ils l'oecumenisme superflu?" in *Concilium,* n. 54. (1970), 11-19; "Le développement de l'évaluation ecclésiologique des Eglises non-catholiques: un bilan," in *Revue de Droit canonique,* 25 (March-December, 1975), 168-198; "Formes prises par l'exigence oecuménique aujourd'hui," to appear in *Mélanges P. Simon* Dockx.

The Ecclesiastical Question Thus Posited

The question is both pastoral and dogmatic. For us, three attitudes seem possible.

(1) To hold on to everything, to adopt an all or nothing stance, but in that case, to be resigned to becoming a small flock. Just as in the early centuries? No, for the world is no longer what it was. We would not have a *"tertium genus,"* but a ghetto. Moreover, we cannot simply erase the fact that there once existed a very large Church, a Christendom even; that there would always be, in multitudes well worth considering, baptized persons, imperfect Christians, who would not enter into the all or nothing.

(2) To maintain a theoretical *status quo*, realistically accepting the large zone of so-called popular "religion," involving, in other words, observance without much emphasis on an enlightened, personalized, motivated faith, and allowing for special cases. When all is said and done, this is what is currently being practiced. But the growing number of special cases may force us toward the third solution.

(3) To accept and even encourage the existence of two *regimes,* making a distinction between a link with Christ, even with the Church, and the *Sacrament.* In any case, to provide areas which would represent a kind of threshold Church, a Church for catechumens, in order to support the spiritual life of those whose faith is unsure and, above all, of those who are unable to participate fully in the sacramental life. In the Gospels, we find diverse degrees and types of visible links with Christ: there were the occasional hearers of the Gospel; there were those who sought aid from Jesus (sinners, sick people); there were the disciples, and among them, a Nicodemus; there was the post-pentecostal community. It is true that we are a post-Pentecost Church, but the Church is not ready-made, it is still adding new members, and it is always made up of men, who, for their part, find themselves in very diverse circumstances. We know that the question of polygamists and their wives arises in many African countries. In Senegal, Rev. Gravrand founded "Amis des chrétiens" for them.[34] Those who are attracted to the Christian faith and wish to belong to it are given instruction; they receive a Christian name; they are taught to pray; they promise to raise their children in the Catholic faith and to have themselves baptized at the point of death.

That has to do with a situation which is not our own. We would have to find forms, varied and adaptable, that would respond to the analogous need for a threshold community within our own context.

Is not the most urgent task facing those, whoever they may be, who are respon-

34. Cf. P. Gravrand, *Visage africain de l'Eglise* (Paris, 1962), (C.R. in *Parole et Mission,* n. 18 [July, 1962], 477-481).

> sible for the destiny of the Christian community, precisely that of assuring to all the flow of life between institution and the non-institution? For the Church today is of both sides. To recognize this, and to live accordingly, is the foremost duty.[35]

Under what conditions would a proposal of this nature not be unsound? On condition that such a creation not be taken for the "Church," or for another Church, an alternative Church, that, on the contrary, it depends on an integral Church, vibrantly alive. On condition, too, that such threshold communities be very open, expressly maintaining a status of moving, of opening toward a total heritage, with the necessary means of transition. Such threshold structures would not have complete autonomy. Such threshold structures would not have complete autonomy. They would have legitimacy only by reference to the Church in its fullness. The Church is the gathering of catechumens before being the assembly of the faithful celebrating and partaking in the Sacraments, principally that of the Body and Blood of the Lord.[36] The Church itself is the fullness of communion with the fullness of the gifts God gives through Christ and in the Spirit.

Are these perspectives chimerical? But if our analysis of the current situation is correct, what other response can one offer to the burning questions it poses?

Translated by Frances M. Chew. This article first appeared in *Revue Catholique International: Communio* (May, 1976), under the title "Sur la transformation du sens de l'appartenance à l'Eglise."

35. Paul Ricoeur in *Le Monde,* July 19, 1973.
36. On this dynamic sequence in building the Church, cf. A. P. Liégé, "Théologie de l'Eglise et problèmes actuels d'une pastorale missionnaire," in *La Maison-Dieu,* n. 34 (1953), 5-19.

B. THE UNIVERSAL CHURCH

Pope

Michael Schmaus

I. Theological

A. Definition

The Pope is the vicar of Jesus Christ, the successor of the Apostle Peter, the head of the Catholic Church and also Bishop of Rome, Patriarch of the West, Primate of Italy, Archbishop and Metropolitan of the ecclesiastical province of Italy, Sovereign of the Vatican City (cf. *Annuario Pontificio*). In ancient times, the title "Pope" ("Father") was given to bishops. It was widely used in monastic circles and became the ordinary title of a priest in the Orthodox Churches, as also in the Romanic parts of the Roman Catholic Church. In Egypt, it was the prerogative of the Bishop of Alexandria. From the middle of the 6th century on, the title came to be restricted in the West to the Bishop of Rome. This usage was juridically established by Gregory VII.

B. Biblical Foundations

The papacy can only be understood in the framework of the Church as a whole and in connection with the hierarchical structure of the Church. The Church cannot be properly understood either as a papal or as an episcopal Church. But it does not exist except with the Pope as the visible representative of Christ, the invisible head of the Church. According to Catholic faith, the papacy grew out of the mission of the apostle Peter, who, according to reliable testimonies (not, however, universally accepted), ended his life in Rome. In the NT, Peter appears as the first of the apostles in rank. The gospels show him as their spokesman (Mk 58:29; Mt 18:21; Lk 12:41; Jn 6:67f.). In the lists of the apostles given in the synoptics he is always named first (Mk 3:16-19; Mt 10:1-4; Lk 6:12-16; cf. Acts 1:13; Mk 1:26; Lk 9:32; Mt 16:7). A most important point is that, in what is obviously a traditional formula, Peter is named by Paul as the first to whom the risen Christ appeared, though chronologically he was not the first (1 Cor 15:5). The

Easter apparition is a revelation of his call. Since the formula in 1 Cor 15 is a very ancient piece of tradition, it is an expression of the primordial conviction that Peter was the primary witness to the resurrection. Three texts in particular bring out specifically the special place of Peter: Mt 16:13-19; Lk 22:31 f.; Jn 21:15 ff. In the first text, the authenticity of which as part of the gospel cannot be seriously doubted, though its place in the arrangement of the text is perhaps due to the redaction, Jesus gives Simon a new and symbolic name, by calling his *Petros* (Kephas = Rock). Jesus promises the apostle that he is to be the rock foundation of the Church which he planned. Peter is to guarantee stability and security, permanence and unity. Christ is himself the foundation of the Church, but this foundation appears visibly in Peter. The other apostles are also included in this function (Eph 2:19f.). One must also remember that according to the Letter to the Ephesians, the Church is also founded on the prophets, i.e., the charismatics. None of these elements should be overlooked. Though Peter alone was given a special charge, it is clear that he can only exercise it in unity with and in conjunction with the rest of the apostles, and indeed, with the Church as a whole.

The function of the rock foundation is further defined by Jesus as the power of the keys and the power to bind and loose. In the house where Jesus is the householder, Peter is given authority to rule as representative of the master. The formula also includes authority to teach and to impose doctrine. The metaphor of binding and loosing means to exclude from the community and to re-admit, also to impose an obligation and to release from it, finally, to declare something lawful or prohibited. This triple function is also assigned by Jesus to the other apostles (Mt 18:18), but it is clearly Peter's in a special way which is his alone. The Gospel of Matthew does not explain what the primacy of Peter consists of. But the two-fold conferring of authority does not make sense unless a single function is meant, though shared at various levels.

According to Lk 22:27-32, a quarrel among the disciples inspired by ambition and desire for power gave Jesus the occasion of proclaiming the law of the kingdom of God, readiness to serve the brethren. And here Jesus gave a special task to Peter, promising him his prayer to enable him to fulfil it. According to the words of Jesus, Satan was to bring the disciples into a situation of severe trial for their faith. This took place in fact at Jesus' death. And even Peter was not to be spared this crisis of faith (cf. Lk 22:33f.). But the prayer of Jesus, offered for Peter in particular, was to help him to recover, and it would then be his task to provide support for his "brothers," that is, for the whole community. Peter is to be a stronghold of the faith.

According to Jn, Jesus fulfils his promises and completes his transmission of authority after the resurrection. It is understandable that the confirmation of the authority should be after the resurrection, since the existence and life of the Church are linked to the resurrection of the Lord. Peter is made shepherd of the flock. This metaphor, common in the OT and NT, comes from an agrarian culture and is based on the notion that the shepherd has to find pastures and watering-places for the flock, to defend it against attack and to preserve due order within the flock. What is meant therefore is that the Lord who will no longer be visibly and historically present appoints a representative who has to mediate Christ's salvation, the life of salvation, by preaching the word and establishing salvific symbols. He must also protect this life from all threats from within and from without.

In the Acts of the Apostles, Peter appears as the head of the young Church, conscious of his responsibility and full of the power of the Spirit. He is the successful, enterprising and courageous preacher of the gospel. He is equipped with authority to combat anything unholy within the Christian community. It is he who breaks through the bounds of Judaism into the universality of the message of salvation. He is the pace-maker for the mission to the world. This is all described without any effort to glorify him or to gloss over his weaknesses (cf., for instance, Acts 1:15-26; 2:14-40; 3:1-26; 4:8; 5:1-11; 5:29; 8:14-17; 8:18-25; 9:32-43; 10:15). The importance and the limits of Peter's authority are shown in the dispute between him and Paul at Antioch when the question of the persistence of the ritual law of the OT arose (Acts 15:7-12; Gal 2:11-21). And in general, it was only normal, in view of the simple, rudimentary and hence undeveloped organization of the primitive Church, that the exercise of the Petrine functions should have been on a modest scale. Further, according to the words of Jesus, the authorities were to see themselves and to behave as the servants of the rest and not as their lords (Mt 20:26 ff.; Lk 22:25 ff.; Jn 13:1-20). The primacy of Peter was not in any way diminished by the fact that he exercised his function of head by keeping in touch with the consensus of the Church and remaining in loving fellowship with it. He remained head of the Church when he left Jerusalem and went to Rome (cf. Acts 12:17; 1 Pet 2:11; 5:13; Heb 11:13).

C. Historical Development

Jesus himself did not appoint successors either to Peter or to the other apostles. The succession follows from the nature of Peter's mission (Mt 28:18 ff.), which is to the ends of the earth and the end of time. The succession to Peter is not on the same lines as succession to the other apostles, since he can have only one successor at a time. According to the faith of the Church, this is the Bishop of Rome, since Peter was in Rome and suffered a martyr's death there. Sufficient proof for this is given in Ignatius of Antioch (*Ad Romanos,* 4, 3), Dionysius of Corinth, the Roman presbyter Gaius and Irenaeus of Lyons. Peter's going to Rome must be ascribed to the impulse of the Spirit pervading the Church as well as to Peter's own decision. And it is not impossible that the link between Rome and succession to

Peter was based on a decision of the Church towards the end of the apostolic age. The Roman papacy passed from a rudimentary to a fully-developed stage. Under the stress of circumstances, in the course of history, many alien tasks accrued to the Popes, including the government of the Papal States. Then as political, cultural and social conditions changed, the Popes freed themselves once more from such tasks, though only slowly, hesitantly and often unwillingly, fearing that the loss of worldly power might involve restrictions on their spiritual mission. The changing shape of papal power corresponds to the changes in the whole Church. It is determined by political and cultural shifts in the course of history, though also by the personal character of any given Pope.

In the early centuries, there are many proofs that the Church was conscious of the primacy of the Roman Pontiff, but the testimonies are in germ, so to speak, and not fully explicit. The first is provided by a letter of Bishop Clement of Rome to the Church in Corinth at the end of the 1st century. Quarrels have broken out in Corinth, and Clement acts as peacemaker. He does not intervene authoritatively, but displays a deep sense of responsibility for the whole Church. It is this sense of responsibility which inspires his initiative. The spirit, the force and the claim of the Roman Pontiff are heralded in the letter, which was held in extraordinarily high esteem throughout the Church in the 2nd century.

Ignatius of Antioch says that the Roman Church is "president of love," that is, first in the realization of the new principle introduced by Christ into history. He goes on to say that the Roman Church teaches others but does not itself receive instruction. He begs it to take care of the Church in Syria. The reason for Rome's precedence, as explained by Ignatius, is that Peter and Paul lived in the Roman Church and preached the gospel there.

Irenaeus of Lyons defends tradition against Gnosticism. To establish what the tradition is, the local Churches founded by the apostles are the competent witnesses. The apostolic succession guarantees the truth of the doctrine. In such a matter sufficient proof has been given when it is shown that in the greatest and most ancient Church, one universally known and founded by the glorious apostles Peter and Paul, its line of bishops goes back to the apostles and that its doctrine is therefore apostolic. "With this Church, on account of its more primordial authority (or: more effective priority, "propter potentiorem principalitatem") all other Churches in every place cannot but agree, since in it the Christians of all places have preserved the apostolic tradition" (*Adversus Haereses,* III, 3, 3).

Tertullian and Hippolytus regard Peter as the first in the line of Roman bishops. Cyprian sees the unity of the Church as founded on Peter. The link with Peter provided by succession to the episcopal office is, according to Cyprian, the fundamental justification of all episcopal power and likewise determines the unity of the Church universal. When Peter settled in Rome, the primitive Church embodied in Peter also settled there. Hence the

Roman Church is the *ecclesia principalis*. Optatus of Milevis (d. before 400) held that communion with the Roman Church guaranteed the legitimacy and divine authority of the other Churches. Ambrose (on Ps 40:30) says: "Where Peter is, there is the Church." Augustine in his struggle against Pelagianism strove with growing vigour to gain the support of Rome, because, as he said, only the verdict of the Apostolic See could give the proper emphasis to the decision of the African bishops (*Epistle,* 172, 29).

From the 2nd century on, the Bishop of Rome was asked to decide in questions of controversy, e.g., the date of Easter (see the accounts of the numerous journeys to Rome in Eusebius's *History of the Church*). From the 4th century on there is the fact that bishops look to Rome for protection of their rights, and that Rome is the court of appeal in matters of law, while appeals against its decisions were held to be inadmissible. The Roman baptismal Creed came to be authoritative. Rome played an essential role in the fixing of the canon of Scripture, as also in the struggle against Gnostics, Marcionites and Montanists.

In the Middle Ages, the papacy was discussed only incidentally, in connection with other problems such as the manner of ordination of priests, the analysis of faith and especially in solving the questions raised by the founding of new religious orders in the 13th century. These orders wished to be dependent only on the Pope, and not the bishops, especially in financial matters. Religious thus became in a special way the "sons of the Pope." A tendency in the opposite direction has only set in recently. In late scholasticism, the pressure of historical cirumstances, i.e., the occupation of the papal throne by rival Popes, gave rise to the "conciliar theory," which made the Council and not the Pope the supreme authority in the Church (see *Conciliarism, Schism* IV). The conflict between Conciliarism and the doctrine of papal primacy went on for centuries, in spite of the condemnation of the theory at the Council of Florence, till the First Vatican Council, at which the question was decided in favour of the papal primacy (see *Gallicanism*). But at the Second Vatican Council a certain synthesis was arrived at, without prejudice to the primacy of the Pope.

Thomas Aquinas used ancient Greek notions of monarchy rather than biblical ones to justify the papal primacy as the most perfect form of government. It guaranteed the unity and peace of the Church. According to Bonaventure, there is a first and supreme principle in every realm, to which all particulars can be reduced, and from which in turn all particulars derive. The Pope is the summit of the whole hierarchical structure of the Church. All duly constituted power in the Church stems from him. This was a consideration inspired by neo-Platonist thinking, and led Bonaventure to a view of the primacy which differed considerably by its exaggerations from what was later defined as Church doctrine. Peter John Olivi came in the course of his defence of the Spirituals against the Curia to hold the view that the Pope was Antichrist. Here he anticipated one of the theses of the

Reformers. In theology after the Council of Trent, as the concept of the ecclesiastical hierarchy, especially that of the magisterium, was worked out in opposition to the Reformation, the doctrine of the primacy was given a more and more systematic form till it finally reached the stage in which it was adopted by the First Vatican Council.

The way in which the Bishops of Rome understood their universal mandate is instructive. To some extent, such self-interpretations were included in the declarations of the First Vatican Council. This is true, for instance, of the declaration of the papal legates at the General Council of Ephesus (431; cf. *DS* 3056), which was acclaimed unanimously by all the fathers present. So too the profession of faith of Pope Hormisdas, which was subscribed to by some 250 Eastern bishops and thus ended the Acacian Schism (484-519; cf. *DS* 3066, 363). It was also accepted by the eighth General Council, Constantinople IV (869; *DS* 128). So too finally the profession of faith of the Emperor Michael Palaeologus, which he made as representative of the Eastern Church and swore to through his legates at the Council of Florence. Mention may also be made of a pronouncement of Pope Siricius (384-98; *DS* 181), which says that it is the task of his office to bear the burdens of all, since "the blessed Apostle Peter bears them in us" (*DS* 181) and thus protects his heritage. Innocent I (401-17), in the course of a letter written at the instigation of Augustine to the bishops of Africa during the Pelagian conroversy, wrote as follows: "In your search for the things of God . . . you have followed the examples of ancient tradition . . . and confirmed the strength of your faith in true insight, since you affirmed that the matter in dispute among you should be referred to our judgment, knowing as you did what was due to the Apostolic See. For from this See comes all episcopacy, and all the authority which goes with this title" (*DS* 217). In 1302 Boniface VIII declared in the bull *Unam Sanctam:* "Therefore this one and only Church has not two heads like a monster, but only one body and one head, Christ and his vicar Peter and the successor of Peter. . . For all men, it is absolutely necessary for salvation to submit to the Roman Pontiff. This we declare, affirm and proclaim" (*DS* 872; *D* 469). Wycliffe's spiritualizing image of the Church and the views of Huss, who was theologically dependent on Wycliffe in many respects gave rise to a number of papal condemnations of theses in which the papacy was rejected or underestimated (*D* 633, 635-9, 646-50, 652, 655; *DS* 1207,1209-13, 1220-3; 1226, 1229). Other important affirmations of the primacy include that of the Council of Florence (17th General Council, 1438-45), the Lateran (18th General Council, 1512-17), the bull *Exsurge Domine* of 5 July 1520 and the rejection of Gallicanism and Febronianism, two movements in which the Conciliarism rejected by Florence lived on.

A distinction must be made between the dogmatic statement of the primacy, i.e., explicit faith, and the actual exercise of the office, though there is a close connection between affirmation and action. In the first thousand years the exercise of papal primacy took the form of arbitration. Later the Popes themselves took the initiative more and more in making decisions. For a long time they exercised their authority by means of fraternal admonitions. But as early as the 2nd century, it also took the form of juridically binding precepts. Pope Victor (189-98) gave forceful expression to the primacy. The Churches in Asia Minor had refused to accept the Roman dating of Easter. In face of the resulting disunity, Victor excommunicated them, not just by breaking off his own communion with them but by expressly excluding them from the fellowship of the whole Church. In doing so he appealed to the fact that the graves of the Apostles Peter and Paul were in Rome. Pope Stephen I, the first, as far as we can see, to appeal to Mt 16:18 ff., demanded of all the acceptance of his doctrine on the baptism of heretics and threatened those who opposed it with excommunication, appealing to the authority conferred on the Apostle Peter, which he claimed had been transmitted to Peter's successors. From the 4th century on the Roman Pontiffs, Siricius (384-98), Innocent I (402-17) and Zozimus (417-18) in particular, claimed the primacy in more and more explicit terms. Leo the Great was especially clear and definite on the matter. Human and subjective elements may have played a part, but their action was primarily inspired by the conviction that as successors of Peter they had a task to fulfil which was committed to them by the Lord of the Church. That the claim of Rome was fully in keeping with the mind of the whole Church was clearly manifested at the General Council of Chalcedon, to take one example. When the letter of Pope Leo was read to the Council, the fathers cried out: "This is the faith of the Fathers. This is the faith of the apostles. Peter has spoken through Leo." The letter sent by the Council to Leo describes the Pope as the interpreter of the voice of the Apostle Peter. Gelasius (492-6) laid down the basis of the theory of the two powers which led in the Middle Ages to the subordination of the temporal to the spiritual power (Innocent III, Innocent IV, Boniface VIII).

If the affirmations and exercise of the primacy in Christian antiquity are compared with the doctrine of the First Vatican Council and subsequent practice, the extent of the development cannot but be apparent. Nonetheless, there is an undeniable continuity between apostolic times and the present day. In action and reaction, both the Bishops of Rome and the Church universal became more and more clearly conscious of the primatial position of Rome. For the organization of the wide-ranging Church provinces, the patriarchate structure was historically characteristic. This form was undoubtedly affected by the development of papal authority, but it was not eliminated. For in general, this structure only came into play in its function of supreme judicial authority, even in matters of faith. In later history, since the beginning of the Eastern Schism (1054), patriarchal authority in the West was absorbed into the primatial. Bishops are appointed directly by Rome and are directly subject to the Bishop of Rome, without the intermediate authority of a metropolitan.

The First Vatican Council determined the full extent and also the limits of papal authority, against episcopalist tendencies on the one hand and integralist tendencies on the other. The Council aimed at stating its faith in such a way that the total self-understanding of the Church could find expression in it. By reason of external circumstances and also of the immaturity of ecclesiology, only part of the problem could be dealt with, that of the papal primacy. As regards the bishops, the Council was content to put in a saving clause, which was meant to ensure that no detriment should be done to the ordinary power of the bishops, given them by Christ. The strong emphasis on the primacy launched a line of development which took the concrete form of Roman centralization and which now prompts a search for a form of exercise of the primacy which will allow the bishops, not merely in theory but also in practice, the freedom of movement which properly belongs to them. The most important text of Vatican I is as follows:

"We teach and declare that the Roman Church has the primacy in ordinary authority, by the disposition of the Lord, over all other Churches. This jurisdictional power of the Roman Pontiff, which is truly episcopal, is direct. Towards this authority the pastors and faithful of every rite and rank, both individually and collectively, are bound by the duty of hierarchical subordination and true obedience, not only in matters of faith and morals but also in matters of discipline and government in the Church throughout the whole world. By maintaining the unity of fellowship as well as of the same faith with the Roman Pontiff, the Church of Christ is thus one flock under one supreme pastor . . . The authority of the Supreme Pontiff does no detriment to the ordinary and direct power of jurisdiction by which the bishops, the successors of the apostles, appointed by the Holy Spirit, are truly pastors of the flocks assigned to each of them to rule and feed. It is, on the contrary, acknowledged, strengthened and defended by the supreme and universal pastor, as was affirmed by St. Gregory the Great when he said: 'My honour is the honour of the universal Church. My honour is the vigorous strength of my brothers. I am only truly honoured when due honour is paid to each of them . . .' Because the Roman Pontiff is, by divine right of the apostolic primacy, head of the whole Church, we also teach and declare that he is the supreme judge of all the faithful, to whose judgment appeal can be made in all matters which come under ecclesiastical examination. But the verdict of the Apostolic See may be rejected by no one, since there is no higher authority, and no one may pass judgment on its judgment. Hence they stray from the right path of truth who affirm that it is permissible to appeal to a General Council against the judgments of the Roman Pontiffs, as if the General Council were a higher authority than the Roman Pontiff.

"If anyone therefore says that the Roman Pontiff has only the office of supervision and guidance, but not full and supreme power of jurisdiction over the whole Church, not merely in matters of faith and morals but also in matters of discipline and government in the Church throughout the whole world; or if he says that the Pope has only the major share but not the whole fullness of this supreme power; or that this power is not ordinary and direct over both the Churches individually and collectively and the pastors and faithful individually and collectively: let him be excluded" (*D* 1827-31; *DS* 3060-64).

Other statements about the papal primacy are to be found in the encyclical of Pius XII *Mystici Corporis,* 29 June 1943, and in many texts of the Second Vatican Council.

The primacy of the Pope defined by Vatican I refers not to the power of orders *(potestas ordinis)* but to the pastoral power *(potestas jurisdictionis).* The teaching authority, the magisterium, which is often, though incorrectly, regarded as a distinct type of authority, should be ranged under the pastoral or jurisdictional power. (See *Ecclesiastical Authority; Magisterium.)* As regards the power of orders, the Pope is not superior to the bishops. Nonetheless, power of jurisdiction and power of orders are linked very closely to the Pope, since his supreme pastoral power is based on the fact that as Bishop of Rome he is the successor of the Apostle Peter. Even though a baptized person when elected Pope at once possesses papal power when he accepts the election, episcopal consecration, by virtue of the link between power of orders and power of jurisdiction, is essential to the taking up of supreme power in the Church. The two powers form an organic unity, though they need not come at the same time.

In the realm of jurisdiction, the Pope possesses supreme, full and universal power in the Church. It is truly episcopal and takes in every member of the Church. Its extent is determined by the revelation which took place in Jesus Christ. The Pope has no authority in purely worldly matters. Claims of such a nature put forward in the Middle Ages were due to historical circumstances and did not derive from the primacy proper to the Pope. According to the teaching of Vatican I, the papacy is to be regarded as instituted by Jesus Christ and not as the result of historical developments or even as the outcome of intrinsic necessities in the Church. The Pope is not given his mandate by the Church, and he is not the delegate of the bishops, even though he acts in the name of the whole Church and of the bishops representing the whole Church—as he does, even when acting on his own initiative. The election, which has gone through many changes of form in the course of history, though now long since stabilized, serves to designate the holder of the office. But the papacy itself is based on the commissioning of the Apostle Peter, though the Pope is not the Apostle Peter, any more than the bishops are apostles. The main difference is that the apostles were at once the (direct) bringers and witnesses of revelation, while the bishops are (indirect) transmitters of revelation.

Vatican I gave no formal explanation of how the succession to Peter actually came about in the course of Church history. The Christological perspective in which the Pope was placed is of particular importance. The Church does not have two heads, but only one, inasmuch as the invisible head, Christ, is represented by the Pope as the visible head. The emphasis on the relation to Christ, so far from excluding, rather presupposes the spontaneity, freedom and individual qualities of each wielder of the primacy. In the activities of the primacy, Christ comes to the fore precisely in the fragility of men. The personal character of each Supreme Pontiff is fraught with consequences, in spite of his call to be the instrument of Christ. Nonetheless, the authority of the Pope is ultimately the authority of Christ. When the Pope exercises his power of jurisdiction, his pastoral office, he is owed internal and external obedience. Since it is Christ who acts in the primatial actions of the Pope, the papal power is rooted in the sacramental character of the universal Church (cf., for example, Jn 20:21-23). Normally, only those united with Christ in the Spirit are called to transmit to others the salvation given by Christ. According to Jn 21:15ff., Peter's love of Christ is the presupposition of his being charged to feed the flock of Christ. The wielders of spiritual authority are to live in peace with God and with the brethren. The Church had indeed to learn by experience in the course of history that union of heart with Jesus Christ can be lacking, but that this does not mean the loss of papal authority (against Wycliffe, Huss and Luther). The primacy would in fact be null and void if it were dependent for its value on something which could never be definitely ascertained, like the mind and heart of the holder of the office. Nonetheless, the normal situation is that the representative of Jesus Christ lives in union with Jesus Christ. Otherwise not only would the salvation of the Pontiff himself but that of the whole messianic community be endangered. Hence too it has always been the conviction of the Church that a Pope who fell into heresy would lose his office. But the question has yet to be solved as to who should determine the fact of heresy in such a case. In any case, a sinful holder of the primacy is a grave scandal. The intrinsic bond between power of orders and of jurisdiction shows that the actions of the Pope, even in juridical matters, are concerned with salvation and sanctification. The reason why Christ combined the full and supreme pastoral power in one member of the Church, the Bishop of Rome, seems to be that the continuity and unity of the Church are guaranteed and displayed in this office. Communion with the Pope brings out the full membership of the saving community, the *communio sanctorum* as communion of saints and communion in the holy, in the most visible and reliable way. Hence the institution of the primacy appears as a manifestation of Christ's concern for the inner unity and the reliable proclamation of the message of salvation both within and without the people of God.

The universal episcopate of the Pope naturally brings up its relationship to the episcopate. The question is all the more important because Vatican I affirmed that papal power was truly episcopal. In spite of the division into local Churches under the personal rule of a bishop, the Pope is universal bishop, so that the whole Church appears as comprised within one diocese. Though the pope is not superior to his fellow-bishops by virtue of the power of orders, he is, in this view, by virtue of his power of jurisdiction and its primacy, bishop over all members of the Church, both bishops and faithful. And he can make use of this episcopal power in any part of the Church. Nonetheless, there are not two bishops in each diocese, the local ordinary and the universal Pontiff. In spite of the direct episcopal power of the Pope, the local bishop remains the immediate pastor of the flock entrusted to him. It seems impossible to reduce the relationship between the universal episcopal authority of the Pope and the local episcopal authority to a satisfactory juridical formula. But it is certain, at any rate, that the universal episcopal authority of the Pope does not entitle him to intervene at will. In particular, he could not abolish episcopal rule in the Church. "The right of the Pope to intervene in the government of a diocese rests therefore not on an authority of like nature to that of the local ordinary, and one which would be in competition with it in every way, but on a higher right which is prevented by the principle of subsidiarity from intervening except when the ordinary competent organ fails" (K. Mörsdorf). But here again it is for the Pope to judge when such a situation has arisen. The primacy lays in fact grave obligations on the holder. He is not free to remain silent when he ought to speak, and again, he may not speak out of turn. There is much in all this which remains and must remain the decision of the Supreme Pontiff himself, but he is nonetheless inexorably bound to the charge given by Jesus Christ. This charge means service of the people of God and hence of the salvation of the individuals. The Pope is appointed as member of the Church on behalf of the Church. His actions, by virtue of Christ's dispositions, stem from the Church and in turn serve the Church. Pope and Church do not face each other like strangers who come from different parts. On the contrary, the Pope speaks as a member of the Church to the other members, though as one equipped with special and indeed supreme authority. And the Church in turn is a brotherly fellowship within which the Pope lives as brother and father. Highly as a member of the Church may be placed by the primacy, he is just as profoundly at the service of all. Thus the primacy may mean supreme authority, but its truest meaning is the most intensive service (*servus servorum*). The Pope has to answer to Christ for the way in which he serves the salvation of all (1 Pet 5:1-4). Thus the primacy is itself also a form for the expression of love, placing itself at the service of men in obedience to God's eternal plan of salvation (1 Cor 13:13). But the love of which we speak here is of such a type that it cannot connive at or confirm man's self-assurance or selfish ease, his worldly longings or his enslavement to the world. It has to tell the arrogant and self-centered to go out of themselves and find the liberty of the children of God, freedom from anguish and freedom in joy. For man, this often means disquiet and disturbance. He shrinks from taking the step across the abyss to God and hence finds the challenge to do so an imposition. Hence an institution which binds him formally by law to go out of himself and give himself to Christ, is for him a scandal. While it is true that all the efforts of the Church can become a scandal, the character of scandal is concentrated in the papacy as in a focus, because from it comes the supreme statement of the obligations which are intended for man's well-being but can nonetheless be felt as threats to earthly self-assurance and appear furthermore at times in forms which are not consistently understandable, since they have to pay the tribute of human frailty. At the same time, these considerations show that the exercise of the primacy is determined as to its necessity, its proportions and its limits, by the approach of the reign of God and by the salvation of men. It cannot be used to train men in obedience for the sake of obedience. Hence it must respect human freedom, which is man's highest natural good and takes priority in doubtful cases, since man in his freedom is analogously the image of God. Hence the primacy cannot restrict man's freedom except to the extent that such restriction is necessary for his salvation.

Vatican I left the question open as to how the relationship between primacy and episcopacy should be determined. The solution given by Vatican II was the affirmation of the collegiality of the bishops. It was not the intention of Vatican II to limit the primacy, but to complete the affirmations of Vatican I and supply what was omitted there. The collegiality of the bishops is to be understood in a broad sense. Vatican II used great emphasis and piled up formulations to point out that the college of bishops essentially includes the Bishop of Rome, the Pope, and that as head of the college he is so much part of it that without the Pope there is no college of bishops, and that the college only possesses spiritual authority inasmuch as the Bishop of Rome is a member of the college and is over it as its head. Without his membership, the college would be reduced to a sum total of individual bishops. An exceptional situation occurs when a Pope becomes incapable of acting as Pope, as for instance when he is mentally ill or falls into heresy or has died. In such an exceptional case, the college of bishops would not cease to exist as a college. It would not disintegrate into a number of individual bishops, because important factors of unity remain effective—unity in confession of Christ, unity in the Spirit, in love, in the celebration of the memorial sacrifice. These factors are also effective and play a decisive role in normal times, when the Pope presides over the college of bishops as its head. And these factors make it clear that the unity of the college is not just an external juridical bond. Its basis must be understood as sacramental. That the Pope is essential to the constitution of the college is the visible manifestation of a unity which is ultimately based on the sacramental element. For the rest, in an abnormal and exceptional case the Church is obliged to give itself a head once more. This is done by the election of a new Pope.

The collegiality of the bishops in the context of the primacy presents theology with a difficult problem. Vatican II declared that the Bishop of Rome, by virtue of his office as vicar of Christ and as pastor of the Church universal, has full, supreme and universal authority, which he can exercise always and everywhere without needing the consent of the bishops. This affirmation corresponded to Vatican I. But Vatican II supplemented it to the effect that the college of bishops, in common with the Bishop of Rome as its head, is also *(quoque)* holder of full and supreme power over the Church universal. The Council thus affirmed with regard to the college of bishops a doctrine which had already been universal in the Church with regard to the General Councils. The statement on papal power includes the word "universal," which is not used in the Council's statement on the power of the college of bishops. But this does not change matters in any way. Though the relationship between the holder of the primacy and the college of bishops (with the Pope as its head) is made quite clear in the texts of the Council, the "Nota Praevia Explicativa" added to *Lumen Gentium* (cf. H. Vorgrimler, ed., *Commentary on the Documents of Vatican II,* vol. I [1967], pp. 297 ff.) put the matter beyond all possible doubt by saying that the distinction is not "between the Roman Pontiff and the bishops taken collectively, but between the Roman Pontiff by himself and the Roman Pontiff together with the bishops. Since the Supreme Pontiff is *head* of the college, he alone can perform certain acts which in no wise belong to the bishops, for example, convoking and directing the college, approving the norms of action, etc." But it is worth noting that the introductory explanation says that the Pope can use various methods in making these decisions, as the circumstances of the times demand. He need not confine himself to a form laid down once and for all. The Pope being entrusted with the care of the whole flock of Christ, it is for him to judge, as the needs of the Church change in the course of time, the manner in which he will exercise this charge, either personally or collegially. Though the final text of the Council does not say so, it may be assumed that even when the Pope acts on his own initiative, without the suggestions of the bishops and without their co-operation, exercising his authority for the whole Church, he then acts as head of the college. For he always speaks in the name of the Church as well as for the Church. When he acts as Pope, he never acts as a private person, but always as successor of the Apostle Peter, whose task it is to give effect to what has been handed down in the people of God. The college of bishops possesses full and supreme power not because this has been given it or conceded to it by the Pope, but by virtue of its own competence, in consequence of Christ's institution. But since the Pope, his characteristic membership, is essential to the constitution and effectiveness of the college, the consent of the Pope is required for every decree of the college of bishops. This consent is to be taken in the strict sense. It is not a subsequent confirmation, but an element intrinsic to the decree from the start and indeed a vital element.

This is so even if the consent of the Pope only comes in the external form of a subsequent approbation. The same conclusion may also be drawn from the formulas used in the publication of the decrees of Vatican II since the holding of the Council.

But the manner in which the Pope exercises his function as chief member of the episcopal college can vary very widely. Here the actual situation can be of extreme importance. The participation of the Pope can range from a voluntary or even silent acceptance of a decree of the bishops to a solemn promulgation. And the Pope can decide which form he chooses. In view of the historical facts, especially the proceedings of the ancient Councils, we are justified in assuming that the way in which the Pope exerts the rights or authority which are his by divine institution, is dependent on human factors and historical circumstances—so much so, that the observer who does not view the processes in the light of faith may be able to see only the human and historical factor.

The fact that the Pope with the college (or the college with the Pope as its president) possesses full and supreme authority in the Church, while the Pope alone also does so without the college, leads to a question which seems to be insoluble and indeed to contain an inner contradiction. The question is: are there two supreme powers in the Church, in rivalry with one another? Or: is not the college of bishops once more stripped of its power by the fact that the Pope exercises supreme power, even without the bishops? The Council itself left the question open. The traditional answer is that there are two inadequately distinct organs of supreme ecclesiastical power: inadequately distinct, inasmuch as the Pope is himself a member of the college of bishops. Another view is that there is only one wielder of supreme authority in the Church, the college as constituted under the Pope, the holder of the primacy. To avoid prejudicing the primacy of the Pope, the supporters of this thesis add that even when the holder of the supreme authority is so defined, a distinction must be made between actions which the Pope alone performs, without the college, even though in the name of the college, and actions which have a strictly collegiate character by virtue of authoritative papal participation.

To proceed according to the strict logic of law, it would perhaps be more correct to say that the Pope is the one organ of supreme authority, and then add that he can exercise this authority either alone or along with the bishops in a collegiate act. This thesis would appear most suitable to ensure the unity of the Church insofar as it stems from the supreme living authority within it. But the unity is also assured by the supposition of two inadequately distinct organs, since the two organs are combined together in unity by the fact that the Pope is head of the college. Parallel to this is the truth that the primacy suffers no detriment or danger when the supreme authority of the college of bishops is affirmed, with the due precautions. It may well be that in deciding for one or the other solution, psychological and jurisprudential factors may be more strongly at work than strictly theological ones.

What is always true is that the Pope is never alone, but is always in essential union with the bishops. Even if it is undeniable that he can always exercise freely his supreme authority, nonetheless, by virtue of his responsibility for the unity of the Church, he is perpetually being thrown back upon his unity with the bishops. Rather than being a "free" agent, the Pope, like the college of the bishops, has to adhere to divine revelation, as attested in Scripture and tradition, as handed on incorrupt through the apostolic succession and in particular through the concern of the Bishop of Rome, and as preserved in its purity and faithfully interpreted in the light of the Spirit of truth in the Church (Vatican II, *Lumen Gentium,* art. 25). The activity of the Bishop of Rome must be directed to the well-being of the Church (*ibid.,* Introductory Explanation, art. 3). Hence not only the bishops but also the Supreme Pontiffs are bound to take adequate steps, by appealing, for instance, for help to theological science, by exploring the faith of believers, to strive to ascertain correctly the revelation attested in Scripture and also to find the way to present it in adequate terms. This effort is an intrinsic element of the power of jurisdiction belonging to the Pope. He has not therefore just a formal authority, but one which is also determined as to its content. If it is to be exercised in accordance with the will of Christ, it must, like the exercise of the freedom which is man's right, always submit itself to the true message which comes from God, that is, to what is attested in Scripture. But then, it is the Holy Spirit who is at work in the Church universal. It is he who links the faithful who discharges a spiritual office with the faithful who has not such an office, binding them together in a unity which is often full of tension.

Case 5

The Removal of the Pope

During a meeting of the 1989 Synod of Bishops, Pope Carlos suffered a stroke. The Pope was hospitalized a month. When he was released, however, he was paralyzed on the left side and his speech was impaired. The doctors said he would probably never walk again and his speech would be slurred and difficult to understand, even after extended therapy. The Pope would only be able to do a minimal amount of work followed by long periods of rest. Pope Carlos believed it was contrary to Church tradition to resign the papal office. His work fell far behind schedule. One group of church leaders believed that if the Pope did not resign in a short time, the cardinals should declare an emergency, meet in conclave, and elect a new pope. Others said there is no legal authority for such action and believed it would set a bad precedent. Pope Carlos died unexpectedly.

Exercise

1. Give the arguments for and against the Church having legislation which provides for the removal of a pope who is seriously ill, insane, senile, or in heresy.

2. Draft legislation that would provide for the removal of a pope, including the reasons for removal and the procedure for removal.

References

United States Constitution, Amendment 25.

Izbicki, T. M., "Infallibility and the Erring Pope: Guido Terrini and Johannes de Turrecremata," *Law, Church and Society,* K. Pennington and R. Somerville, eds. (Philadelphia: University of Pennsylvania Press, 1977), 97-111.

Mirus, J. A., "On the Deposition of the Pope for Heresy," *Archivum Historicae Pontificiae* (Rome: Pontificia Universitas Gregoriana, Facultas Historicae Ecclesiasticae, 1975), 231-48.

Council

Hans Küng

THEOLOGY

1. Concept

Councils or Synods are assemblies (σύνοδοι, *concilia)* of representatives of the universal Church or local Churches for mutual consultations and for reaching decisions on Church affairs. A distinction must be drawn between Ecumenical Councils representing the universal Church and the various kinds of particular councils (general, patriarchal, plenary, primatial, imperial and provincial synods).

2. Historical Sketch

The forms taken even by the Ecumenical Councils have been of diverse kinds. According to existing canon law, no Ecumenical Council can take place unless it be convened by the Pope. The rights of the Pope also include the chairmanship (either in person or through his delegates) of the Council, the fixing of subjects for discussion and the rules of procedure, the location, adjournment and dissolution of a Council, and the confirmation of the decisions reached (*CIC,* can. 222; cf. can. 227). All cardinals, patriarchs, archbishops and bishops, abbots and prelates with an area of jurisdiction of their own, the abbot primate, the superiors of religious congregations and the superiors-general of exempt orders, and also the titular bishops have the right to vote, provided nothing to the contrary had been laid down in the terms of convocation. The theologians and canonists summoned to the Council possess only an advisory vote (can. 223; on representation and premature departure cf. can. 224-5). Council Fathers can also propose questions for treatment at their own initiative, but such proposals are subject to the approval of the president (can. 226). The Ecumenical Council possesses the highest jurisdiction over the universal Church; appeal from the Pope to the Council is excluded; in the event of the death of the Pope the Council is suspended (can. 228-9).

These stipulations codify, in all essential points, the procedure followed at Trent and at the First Vatican Council. Among them there is hardly a point which was not disregarded at one or many or perhaps even at most of the Ecumenical Councils. In particular, it is historically untenable that the "Ecumenical Councils" of the first century were generally convened, presided over and confirmed by the Pope. What all these questions primarily involve are stipulations of canon law, insofar as the constitution bestowed on the Church by the gospel is not embodied in them.

The Petrine office must be effectively represented at an Ecumenical Council, since it is of the essence of the constitution of the Church, of which the Council must be representative. However, this representation was verified in very different ways at the Councils, sometimes merely through subsequent approbation. And it cannot be denied that conflicts have occurred in the past between Church and Pope, or that they may occur in the future—as in the possible case of a heretical or schismatical Pope and his "deposition."

Direct representation of the laity at the Councils (and not merely indirect, through the clergy) is not only dogmatically possible, but also desirable from the theological viewpoint of the universal priesthood. The laity's direct knowledge of and responsibility for the world also make it desirable; under some circumstances it is absolutely necessary. On the other hand, a Council directed against the authorities of the Church would conflict with the order of the Church and, in particular, with the nature of the Ecumenical Council, which is intended as a representation of the universal Church, for such representation is not possible without the bishops.

Considerable differences are to be found in every respect between the provincial Councils of the 2nd and 3rd centuries (out of which the Ecumenical Councils developed), the eight ancient Ecumenical Councils of the Byzantine East convened by the Emperor, the papal General Synods of the Latin Middle Ages, the late medieval reform Councils of Christendom, the purely ecclesiastical Tridentine Council of Catholic reform and Counter-Reformation, and the First Vatican Council which was dominated by the Pope.

3. Theological Meaning

The Church itself is the comprehensive "assembly" (ἐκκλησία, from καλέω), called together by God himself; it is a "con-cilium" (con-kalium, from *concalare,* i.e., to call together; Greek: καλέω) of those who believe. Thus in a deep theological sense the Church itself can be called an "Ecumenical Council of divine convocation." The universal Church, as a fellowship of the faithful, has a conciliar, synodal (collegial) structure throughout; this is true of the local (parish), particular (diocese), provincial and universal Church.

In this perspective the Ecumenical Council in the usual sense (i.e., Ecumenical Council of human convocation) can be described as a comprehensive representation (not merely in the sense of delegation, but as portrayal and as realization) of the Ecumenical Council of divine convocation (of the universal Church), very suitable for consultations and reaching decisions, ordering and shaping the universal Church, but not essential. (The Church is also assembled in a true and very intense manner in liturgical worship, especially at Mass.) The first Christian account of Church Councils expresses this meaning of the Council: "Aguntur praeterea per Graecias illa certis in locis concilia ex universis ecclesiis, per quae et altiora quaeque in commune tractantur, et ipsa repraesentatio totius nominis Christiani magna veneratione celebratur." (Tertullian, *De Paenitentia,* 13, 6-7; *Corpus Christianorum,* II, 1272.)

The idea of representation—whatever form it took—has always been fundamental to an understanding of the Ecumenical Council. The Ecumenical Council is or ought to be an authentic representation of the *ecclesia una* (in concord and moral unanimity of the decisions), *sancta* (the external framework, basic attitude and conciliar decisions should be determined by the gospel), *catholica* (the obligation of individual Churches to recognize the council), *apostolica* (the apostolic spirit, the apostolic witness and—serving these—the apostolic office are decisive for the Council). Insofar as the Holy Spirit operates in the Church according to the promise of Jesus, he also operates in the special event of its representation, in the Ecumenical Council of human convocation. Therefore, the Ecumenical Council can claim a special, binding authority, even if its decrees and definitions are imperfect, fragmentary human words (cf. 1 Cor 13:9-12). Its documents—the doctrinal decrees should be distinguished from the disciplinary ones—only possess the binding character which the Council concerned itself bestows on them. Every Council and every conciliar decree should be understood historically and interpreted in its historical context.

Case 6

Pope and General Council: Who Is Supreme?

In 1377 Pope Gregory XI transferred the curia of the papacy from Avignon, France, back to Rome. Thus ended the "Avignon Papacy," but the "Western Schism" soon occurred. Fourteen months after his arrival in Rome, Gregory XI died.

Sixteen cardinals, who were without exception wealthy and worldly prelates, were in Rome. Four were Italians, one Spanish, and the rest French. They were surrounded and at times mobbed by Romans who demanded a Roman, or at least an Italian, pope. The cardinals elected Bartolomeo Prignano, who took the name Urban VI. A tactless man, who was overbearing, sadistic, yet a reformist, he soon had the hostility of all the cardinals. The French cardinals departed, soon followed by the Italians. The cardinals declared their choice void because it was dictated by mob violence, and they proceeded to elect Robert of Geneva as Pope Clement VII. Europe divided allegiance.

Urban VI was succeeded by Boniface IX and he by Innocent VII, who was followed by Gregory XII. Clement VII at Avignon was succeeded by Benedict XIII.

Negotiations for resignation of either or both pontiffs continued and failed. Canonists such as Hostiensis, John of Paris, Marsilius of Padua, and Ockham, developed the theory of the supremacy of a council over a pope. Necessity seemed to lead to such axioms as the Church universal is superior to pope and cardinals and what concerned all should be dealt with by all.

Finally, the cardinals of both obediences announced a general council at Pisa for March 25, 1409. Neither of the rival pontiffs attended. Nevertheless, the council deposed both of them, Benedict XIII of Avignon and Gregory XII of Rome, and elected Alexander V, who died one year later and was succeeded by John XXIII.

John XXIII ultimately was persuaded to convoke the Council of Constance in 1414. The council, without intervention of any pontiff, decided that it had full authority to continue in existence, and in the decree *Sacrosancta* the council decreed that it had authority from Christ and claimed the obedience of all, including the pope. The council then deposed John XXIII. A few days later the Roman Gregory XIII resigned. In 1417 Benedict XIII was deposed.

After debating a method of election, the Council of Constance agreed that the cardinals, plus six representatives from each nation, would be electors. The electors chose Oddone Colonna as Martin V. Martin V was succeeded in 1431 by Eugene IV who accepted the decrees of the Council of Constance with the expressed reservation of any diminution of the rights, dignities, and preeminence of the See of Rome.

Exercise

1. Research the theory of conciliarism. Is such a theory acceptable in light of modern understandings of the Church?

2. Describe various models of the Church and the role of the papal office therein.

3. Discuss who is the final arbiter within the Church in such conflicts as the Western Schism.

References

Dulles, A., *Models of the Church* (Garden City, New York: Doubleday and Company, Inc., 1974).

Izbicki, T. M., "Infallibility and the Erring Pope: Guido Terrini and Johannes de Turrecremata," *Law, Church and Society,* K. Pennington and R. Somerville, eds., (Philadelphia: University of Pennsylvania Press, 1977), 97-111.

McNeill, J. T. "The Relevance of Conciliarism," *The Jurist* 31 (1971), 81-112.

Mirus, J. A., "On the Desposition of the Pope for Heresy," *Archivum Historicae Pontificiae* (Rome: Pontificia Universitas Gregoriana, Facultas Historicae Ecclesiasticae, 1975), 231-48.

Tierney, B., *Foundations of the Conciliar Theory* (London: Cambridge University Press), 1968.

Synod of Bishops

D. R. Foley

The Synod of Bishops came into existence on Sept. 15, 1965, with the publication of *Apostolica Sollicitudo* by Pope Paul VI. This motu proprio described the Synod as a permanently constituted body of bishops charged with advising the pope on matters of importance to the whole Church. However the papal initiative was merely anticipating what had come to be the obvious intent of the members of Vatican Council II. The world's episcopate, newly aware of collegial responsibility, wanted to share more closely in the central governing activities of the Church. The formation of the concept of the Synod of Bishops followed the same difficult conciliar course as the formulation of the principle of collegiality.

After almost 100 years' experience of living with the defined power of the papal office which was decided in Vatican Council I, the Church of the second half of the 20th century displayed an avid interest in a balancing statement on the authority of the episcopate. Such a preoccupation was evident in the *vota* submitted by the bishops and prelates, the university faculties, and the curial departments in preparation for Vatican Council II. But the first official teaching of the Church which analyzed the power of the episcopate inevitably alarmed churchmen who saw a need to defend the papacy in what they took to be an attack on that office. Predictably, the give-and-take of the collegiality debate resulted in a compromise statement on the power of the body of bishops. Some important and controverted questions about the divine origin of episcopal authority and its exact relationship to the authority of the pope remained unsettled. So, the college of bishops, as number 22 of *Lumen Gentium* asserted, has full and supreme authority over the universal Church. In union with the pope as head of the college, the body of bishops can exercise its authority solemnly, in an ecumenical council or in ordinary ways determinable by the pope. Thus the statement on the supreme authority of the episcopate emphasized the preservation of papal power. The collegial principle thus enunciated in *Lumen Gentium* affirmed the vital importance of the episcopate and at the same time made it possible for that importance to be neutralized, to be reduced to the level of moral suasion.

The conciliar statement on the bishops' pastoral office was colored with the same shading between rights and their exercise. Section 4 of *Christus Dominus* ascribed to the office of bishops a share in the governance of the whole Church. But, in the practical application of that principle, in numbers 5, 6, and 7, the right to govern universally was reduced to a duty to be concerned about all the Church's problems. In this context, the Synod of Bishops, conceived by its first proponents among the conciliar fathers as a way in which the college could govern the Church effectively, appeared more as an instrument for the pope to employ in the exercise of the primatial office. *Apostolica Sollicitudo* preceded by a matter of weeks the solemn vote on *Christus Dominus,* which took place on Oct. 28, 1965.

NATURE AND PROCEDURES

The note of papal control, evident in the manner of the announcement of the Synod, is echoed in the two documents that gave the Synod its structure. *Apostolica Sollicitudo* referred to the Synod as the acting force of the world's episcopate. But neither this document nor the *Ordo* regulating the Synod's activity mentioned the principle of collegiality. In its constitution and its procedures the Synod is placed under the care of the pope.

In the prefatory remarks of his motu proprio, Pope Paul VI afforded the episcopate the opportunity to share the burden of the apostolic office. But the overtures were to be his alone. He brought the Synod into being to serve the universal Church under his direct and immediate authority. Pope Paul foresaw the possibility of growth by the new institute. But any development was to be within the boundaries of the Synod's general norms as set down in *Apostolica Sollicitudo.* There the nature and purpose of the Synod, its relationship to the pope, and the composition of the Synod in all its forms were determined. The motu proprio defined the Synod as a permanently existing, consultative canonical entity that would function occasionally, at the discretion of the pope. If ever the Synod were accorded deliberative power by the pope, the Synod's decisions would still have to be ratified by him. Other papal prerogatives include authentication of the elections of members of the Synod, designation of topics for discussion, dissemination of related information, the settings of the agenda, and the right to preside over Synod meetings. The same sort of papal control is operative whether the Synod gathers in general, extraordinary, or special assemblies. All three forms of synodal assemblies provide representation for the Oriental churches, episcopal conferences, clerical religious institutes, and curial departments. The pope can name additional members, up to 15 per cent of the eligible membership.

As *Apostolica Sollicitudo* placed the Synod by its very nature under the authority of the pope, the rules for the Synod's operations made it apparent that he would guide its development. The *Ordo* for the procedures to be followed in synodal deliberations was published on Dec. 8, 1966, by Cardinal Amleto G. Cicognani, Secretary of State for Public Affairs. The *Ordo* further delineated the part to be taken by the pope in the Synod. He alone would consider the opinions voiced by Synod members. The pope names and controls the functions of the Synod's presiding officer and secretary general. Commissions for disputed matters and study commissions are to be staffed by papal appointees. Thus the main facets of the procedural life of the Synod are subject to papal approval, if not totally dependent on his initiative.

SYNOD IN PRACTICE

Pope Paul VI convened the first Synod of Bishops, a general assembly, on Sept. 29, 1967. The agenda comprised the revision of the *Code of Canon Law,* dangers to the faith, seminaries, mixed marriages, and the liturgy. The Synod approved broad principles to be followed by the commission for the revision of the Church's general law. Synodal fathers supported the formation of an international theological commission and a pastoral declaration by the Holy See of the major problems concerning the faith. As for seminary policy, the Synod urged involvement of episcopal conferences in all phases of seminary structuring and in the formation of seminary rectors and teachers. On questions relating to mixed marriages, the Synod membership largely favored the existing legislation, but did want more flexibility. By large majority votes, the synodal fathers favored the granting of dispensations from canonical form in mixed marriages at the local level and a great relaxation of the traditional guarantees. Matters of liturgical renewal passed on by the Synod included additional Eucharistic prayers for the Latin liturgy, changes in the words of consecration, and the revamping of the Divine Office. During the 24 meetings held in the first Synod of Bishops, more than 300 speeches were made and more than 100 written interventions were submitted; 42 samplings of opinion were conducted.

In addition to the many suggestions on substantive business, the members of the 1967 Synod also offered proposals about refining the procedures of the Synod itself. Pope Paul VI appointed a commission to correlate the proposals, and a revised *Ordo* was ratified by the Pope on June 24, 1969. One change spelled out more clearly the power of the pope over the Synod's direction and decisions. To him alone belongs the right to transfer, suspend, or dissolve a Synod assembly. Other significant changes restricted the competence of study commissions and lessened the secrecy requirements to allow more communication of information about the Synod.

The second Synod of Bishops opened in an extraordinary assembly on Oct. 11, 1969. Pope Paul VI convoked this meeting in order to provide a forum for the exploration of possible ways to improve collegial practices. As the extraordinary session came to a close, the Pope notified the membership of two more changes. Synod convocations were to be scheduled at 2-year intervals, and a 15-member general secretariat was established to give continuity from one Synod to the next. One of the first recommendations of the enlarged secretariat was to suggest that Synod meetings take place every 3 years, a suggestion that was later adopted by the Pope.

The third general meeting of the Synod of Bishops was in 1971, at which time a less ambitious agenda was set before the membership. The ministerial priesthood and considerations of international justice were the topics considered. After extensive discussions of these difficult subjects, the Synod decided to leave the final drafting of its recommendations to specially appointed commissions. The next scheduled general meeting of the Synod of Bishops will deal with one issue, the evangelization of the nations.

The Roman Curia

I. The Secretariat of State or Papal Secretariat and the Council for the Public Affairs of the Church

The Secretariat of State or Public Secretariat

The Secretariat of State or Papal Secretariat, offers the closest assistance to the Supreme Pontiff both in the care of the universal Church and in dealings with the branches of the Roman Curia.

The Secretariat handles anything the Supreme Pontiff entrusts to it as well as matters of ordinary business which do not fall within the competence of the departments of the Roman Curia. It fosters relations with these departments, with the Bishops, with the Legates of the Holy See, with civil governments and their representatives, and with private persons but without prejudice to the Council for the Public Affairs of the Church and, as occasion requires, in accord with it.

The Council for the Public Affairs of the Church

It pertains to this Council to treat all matters which pertain to civil governments. It also handles subjects submitted to its examination by the Holy Father, particularly where there is some connection with civil law. The Council fosters diplomatic relations with nations and has charge of nunciatures, internunciatures and apostolic delegations, jointly with the Secretariat of State.

II. The Sacred Congregations

The Sacred Congregation for the Doctrine of the Faith

The Sacred Congregation for the Doctrine of the Faith has the task of safeguarding doctrine on faith and morals throughout the entire Catholic world. It examines all questions which touch faith and morals or are connected with the faith itself. It also examines new doctrines and opinions and promotes study on these matters. This Sacred Congregation reproves doctrines opposed to the principles of the faith after the interested Bishops of a region have been heard. It studies the books referred to it and, if necessary, reproves them after the author has been heard and has had an opportunity to defend himself and after the Ordinary has been forewarned. It also examines all that concerns "the privilege of the faith" both in law and in fact. It is competent to pass judgment on errors about the faith according to the norms of an ordinary process. It safeguards the dignity of the sacrament of Penance. The Sacred Congregation proceeds administratively or judicially according to the nature of the question to be treated.

The Sacred Congregation for Bishops

In those places and for those persons not subject to the Congregation for the Oriental Churches or for the Evangelization of Peoples, the Congregation for Bishops establishes new dioceses, provinces and regions and divides, unites and realigns them after consulting the interested Episcopal Conferences and others; it erects military vicariates and, after consulting the Episcopal Conference, prelacies for special pastoral ministries for various regions or social groups. This Congregation provides also for the naming of bishops, apostolic administrators, coadjutors and auxiliaries of bishops, military and other vicars and prelates enjoying personal jurisdiction.

It is competent for all things that have to do with bishops and publishes norms which, through the Episcopal Conference, provide for the more urgent needs of the faithful.

The Sacred Congregation for the Oriental Churches

This Congregation has as many offices as there are rites of Oriental Churches in communion with the Apostolic See. It treats all questions which pertain either to persons, or to discipline, or to the rites of the Oriental Churches, even if they are mixed in that by the nature of the thing or of persons they involve Latins. Territories in which a major part of the Christians belong to Oriental rites are subject only to this Congregation. Even in Latin territories it carefully supervises the faithful of Oriental rites and provides as much as possible for their spiritual needs even by the establishment of their own hierarchy if the number of faithful and circumstances require this.

The Sacred Congregation for the Sacraments and Divine Worship

The Sacred Congregation for the Discipline of the Sacraments oversees all matters which pertain to the discipline of the seven sacraments without prejudice to the other offices of the Holy See which have a special competency. It alone examines the non-consummation of a marriage and the presence of causes for the granting of a dispensation and everything connected with them. It has competence with regard to the obligations connected with major orders and it examines questions about the validity of sacred ordination.

Sacred Congregation for the Causes of Saints

The Sacred Congregation for the Causes of Saints, presided over by a Cardinal with the assistance of a Secretary and an Undersecretary, is competent in all matters which in any way pertain to the Beatification of Servants of God or to the Canonization of the Blessed or to the preservation of Relics.

This Sacred Congregation is divided into three offices.

The Sacred Congregation for the Clergy

The Sacred Congregation for the Clergy is competent in all those things which concern clerics who exercise an apostolate in a diocese, whether it be their persons, their work or pastoral ministry.

1. First Office: the Congregation studies, proposes and urges the means and aids by which priests strive for sanctity. This office also has charge of everything which concerns the work and discipline of the diocesan clergy.

2. Second Office: particularly promotes the preaching of the Word of God and the works of the apostolate and organization of catechesis, evaluates and approves pastoral and catechetical directories, fosters national and international Catechetical Congresses and indicates the opportune norms for religious instruction of children, young people and adults.

3. Third Office: looks to the preservation and administration of the temporal goods of the Church without prejudice to the other Congregations which have temporal goods committed to their vigilance.

The Sacred Congregation for Religious and Secular Institutes

This Sacred Congregation is divided into two sections: one for Religious and the other for Secular Institutes.

1. First Section: is entrusted with the affairs of all religious institutes of the Latin Rite and their members. It is also competent in matters which pertain to societies of common life, whose members live like religious, or to Third Orders as such.

2. Second Section: is competent in the same way, all else being equal, for secular institutes which, although not religious, make a true and complete profession of the evangelical counsels in the world.

The Sacred Congregation for Catholic Education

It is competent for all that pertains to the formation of clerics and the Catholic education both of clerics and of the laity.

1. First Office: is charged with the direction, discipline and temporal administration of seminaries and whatever touches the education of the diocesan clergy and the scientific formation of religious and secular institutes.

2. Second Office: oversees universities, faculties, athenaea and any institute of higher learning which has the name "Catholic" insofar as they depend on the authority of the Church, not excluding those directed by religious or the laity.

3. Third Office: cares for the establishment of parochial and diocesan schools; watches over all Catholic schools below the level of a university and faculty, as well as all institutes of instruction or education dependent on the authority of the Church.

Also within the Congregation is located the Pontifical Work for Vocations, which is charged with coordinating and promoting the work of fostering all ecclesiastical vocations.

The Sacred Congregation for the Evangelization of Peoples or for the Propagation of the Faith

It is competent for those things which pertain to all the missions established for the spread of the kingdom of Christ throughout the world and therefore for whatever is connected with the assignment and transferral of the necessary ministers, for describing ecclesiastical boundaries and proposing those who will govern them. It encourages the development of an indigenous clergy to whom will be gradually entrusted more authority and work. In the places subject to it the Congregation sponsors missionary initiatives and promotes missionary vocations and spirituality. It has charge of all that pertains to the holding of synods and councils, to the establishing of episcopal conferences and to the review of their statutes and decrees. The Congregation has a Supreme Council for the direction of Pontifical Missionary Works, on which depend the general Councils of the Missionary Union of the Clergy, the Society for the Propagation of the Faith, the Society of St. Peter the Apostle, and the Society of the Holy Childhood.

III. Secretariats

The Secretariat for Promoting Christian Unity

The Secretariat is competent for the promotion of Christian unity and has the duty to do so. It has charge of relations with those of other communities; considers the correct interpretation and observance of the principles of ecumenism; promotes Catholic groups and coordinates the efforts at unity both on the national and international levels; institutes colloquies on ecumenical questions and activities with Churches and ecclesial communities separated from the Holy See; deputes Catholic observers for Christian congresses; invites to Catholic gatherings observers of the separated brethren; orders into practice conciliar decrees on ecumenical matters. Furthermore, it is competent for all questions concerning religious relations with Judaism.

Secretariat for Non-Christians

This Secretariat occupies itself with those who, although outside the Christian religion, profess some religion or have a religious sense. It fosters studies and promotes relations with non-Christians to bring about an increase in mutual respect and seeks ways to establish a dialogue with them; it receives and carefully weighs the wishes of the Ordinaries; it provides for the formation of those who participate in dialogue.

Secretariat for Non-Believers

With the approval of the Supreme Pontiff, the Secretariat studies atheism in order to explore more fully its nature and, as far as possible, to establish a dialogue with non-believers who sincerely wish to collaborate.

Council for the Laity

The norms were published in the apostolic letter, "Catholicam Christi Ecclesiam" of 6 January 1967 (A.A.S., LIX, pp. 25-28).

Justice and Peace

IV. TRIBUNALS

Supreme Tribunal of the Apostolic Signatura

First Section: the Tribunal judges the matters assigned to it in the Code of Canon Law; it prorogues the competence of tribunals; it extends the forum for strangers in Rome to cases of matrimonial nullity in extraordinary circumstances and for grave reasons; it supervises the proper administration of justice; it provides for the establishment of regional and interregional tribunals; it enjoys the rights assigned to it in concordats between the Holy See and the various nations.

Second Section: the Signatura settles questions about the exercise of administrative ecclesiastical power which are referred to it. It also passes on conflicts of competence among the departments of the Holy See; it examines administrative matters referred to it by the Congregations of the Roman Curia as well as questions committed to it by the Holy Father.

The Sacred Roman Rota

The Rota is a tribunal of the Holy See which hears appeals from decisions of regional, metropolitan and diocesan tribunals. It is also a court of first instance for cases specified in the law and for others committed to the Rota by the Roman Pontiff. The greater part of its decisions concern the nullity of marriage. In such cases its competence includes marriages between two Catholics, between a Catholic and non-Catholic, and between two non-Catholic parties whether one or both of the baptized parties belongs to a Latin or Oriental rite.

Sacred Apostolic Penitentiary

The jurisdiction of this tribunal includes whatever pertains to the internal forum, even non-sacramental. It is competent in matters pertaining to the granting and use of indulgences.

V. OFFICES

Apostolic Camera

It cares for and administers the temporal goods and rights of the Holy See during a vacancy.

Prefecture for Economic Affairs of the Holy See

This is directed by a commission of three Cardinals and coordinates and watches over the administration of the possessions of the Holy See. It receives the reports on the receipts and disbursements of the Church's goods and the various budgets.

Administration of the Patrimony of the Holy See

Ordinary Section: Performs the tasks of administration committed to it.

Extraordinary Section: Handles the duties committed to it by the Sovereign Pontiff.

Prefecture of the Papal Household

It is in charge of the Apostolic Palace and is at the service of the Holy Father both there and wherever he goes. It arranges audiences with His Holiness and supervises papal ceremonies other than the strictly liturgical.

General Statistics Office of the Church

This office gathers and organizes the data which seems necessary or useful for a better understanding of the state of the Church and for assistance to its Bishops.

VI. Permanent Commissions

Pontifical Commission for Biblical Studies

Pontifical Commission for the Revision of the Code of Canon Law

Pontifical Commission for Revision of the Code of Oriental Canon Law

Pontifical Commission for Social Communications

Pontifical Commission for Latin America

Pontifical Commission for the State of Vatican City

C. THE LOCAL CHURCH

The Bishop as Head of the Local Church and Its Discipline

Eugenio Corecco

I. The Church, Sacrament of the Trinity

The Church, like every Christian mystery, has her origin in the mystery of the unity and plurality of the Trinity, and it is in the Trinity that she has her ultimate explanation.[1] Therefore, it is impossible to explain the Church in terms merely of philosophy or history,[2] for there is a tension in the Church which derives from the fact of many local Churches existing within the one universal Church, and this tension remains insoluble without a religious explanation, since the Church "is the people brought together in the union of the Father, Son and Holy Spirit."[3] This polyvalent nature of the Church has been taken into account from the very beginning of theological reflection. St. Paul, followed by St. Cyprian, gave to the term "church" both a local and a universal meaning.[4] In patristic thought the universal view of the Church seems to have dominated,[5] while in the living structure of the Church there prevailed in early times the local Church, which was directly experienced in practical Christian life. In both East and West, theology and practice developed independently of each other, with little reference from one to the other, and this gave rise to differing ec-

1. M. Philipon, "La santissima Trinità et la Chiesa," in *La Chiesa del Vaticano II* (Florence, 1965), pp. 328-31; E. Zoghby, "Unità e diversità della Chiesa," *ibid.*, pp. 525, 535-37.

2. W. Beinert, "Die Una Catholica und die Partikularkirche," in *Theol. u. Phil.* 42 (1967), pp. 3-5.

3. Vat. Eccl. 4, 2 (Documenti, II Concilio Vaticano, ed. Dehoniane).

4. Cf. K. Rahner, *Episkopat und Primat* (Quaest. Disputatae 11) (Freiburg im Br., 1961), pp. 21-30; G. Dejaifve, "La collegialità nella tradizione latina," in *La Chiesa del Vaticano II, op. cit.*, pp. 838-40; J. Hajjar, "La collegialità nella tradizione orientale," *ibid.*, pp. 816-17.

5. A. Schmemann, "La notion de primauté dans l'ecclésiologie orthodoxe," in *La primauté de Pierre dans l'Eglise Orthodoxe* (Neuchâtel, 1960), p. 141; M.-J. Le Guillou, "L'expérience orientale de la collégialité épiscopale et ses requêtes," in *La collégialité épiscopale* (Unam Sanctam 52) (Paris, 1965), p. 176; Y. Congar, "De la communion des Eglises à une ecclésiologie de l'Eglise universelle," in *L'Episcopat de l'Eglise Universelle* (Unam Sanctam 39) (Paris, 1962), p. 228.

clesiologies and systems of Canon Law, which were to be the fundamental cause in their turn for the final break which came at the great schism.[6]

II. The Theology of the Local Church: Communion

The Idea of the Church

The ecclesiology embodied in the idea of communion, although found elsewhere, is typical of Eastern theology. It approaches the problem of the Church empirically; starting with the datum of the local community, Eastern theology attributes to it a content based on a history and anthropology quite different from the Western view. While Latin theology emphasized rather the characteristics of the Church as in this world, Eastern theology showed an Hellenistic taste for the characteristics of the spiritual side of the Church. The Church is like an icon; she is the sacrament of the heavenly, spiritual, realities. Such an ecclesiology is essentially sacramental and eucharistic, based on the local community, which is always seen as a constant, perfect manifestation of the universal Church. The basic principle governing the relations between local Churches was the concept of realizing in a concrete way the universal alliance in Christ that obtains between the various churches in the οἰκουμενη. This was achieved not merely by norms dictated from above, but rather by the various practices developed by the Churches themselves, whether at the personal level—letters, hospitality and service—or in their liturgical contacts (εὐλογια, the *fermentum* and excommunication), or in the later development of institutional contacts (synods and synodal letters).[7] The role of the bishop of Rome in this inter-Church activity was merely relative. He was considered not so much as an authority with power derived from a divine right higher than the other bishops, but more as the custodian of the Church's unity, with power not *over* the Church but rather *within* the ecclesial communion.[8] And this communion in its turn depended rather on a bond of love in the Holy Spirit *(sobornost)* than on the legal position of a monarchical authority deriving from the possession of an ecclesiastical office.[9]

6. On this whole question, and in particular on sections II and III of this article, cf. Y. Congar, *Neuf cent ans apreès. Notes sur le "Schisme oriental"* (Irenikon) (Chevetogne, 1954), pp. 16-181; *idem,* "De la communion . . . ," *loc. cit.,* pp. 227-60; *idem,* "Notes sur le destin de l'idée de collégialité épiscopale en Occident au Moyen Age (VII—XVI siècles)," in *La collégialité episcopalé, op. cit.,* pp. 99-129.

7. Cf. Y. Congar, "De la communion . . . ," *loc. cit.,* pp. 231-35.

8. Cf. A. Alivisatos, "Les conciles oecuméniques, V, VI, VII, VIII," in *Le Concile et les Conciles* (Unam Sanctam) (Chevetogne, 1960), p. 120; H. Marot, "Conciles anténiceens et conciles oecuméniques," *ibid.,* pp. 42-43.

9. M.-J. Le Guillou, *Mission et Unité. Les exigeances de la communion* (Unam Sanctam 34) (Paris, 1960), pp. 184-200; E. Ivanea, "Sobornost," in *Lex Theol. und Kirche* 9 (Freiburg,[2] 1964), pp. 841-42.

Synods

This ecclesiology was interpreted by the orthodox in terms of an acephalous synodal system.[10] Since the Church ought faithfully to reflect the equality which obtains between the persons of the Trinity, and since also the bishops, by reason of their consecration, are equal among themselves, the structure of the synods was of equals among equals; the ultimate level of authority was never any particular individual, but the body of bishops as a whole.[11] The institution which best reflects this ecclesiology is the synod *endemousa,* by virtue of which the Byzantine Church considers itself as being permanently gathered in synod. In this situation, the position of the patriarch is quite different from that of the pope. The pope governed the Roman synod and also claimed authority over the ecumenical synod, in addition to the power he obtained in later times over the provincial councils. But in the Byzantine Church the synod cannot proceed without the patriarch, nor can he make final decisions without reference to the synod.[12]

The Function of the Bishop

The image of the bishop as a mystical and cultic figure takes precedence over the canonical and juridical idea of his function. The bishop is seen as the type of the Father in the life of the Church; he is the liturgical figure who unites the whole of the local community in a twofold movement: their return to the Father and their bond of communion with all the other Churches.[13] The collegial aspect of the bishop's function was seen as being so important[14] that any higher personal authority of a monarchical nature was quite excluded. The authority of the bishops at the local level was all the stronger for this. The higher bishops (patriarchs and metropolitans) have their various powers only insofar as these are acknowledged as theirs by the whole body of bishops (ecumenical councils and the patriarchal synod).[15]

10. This acephalous arrangement is not necessarily restricted to the synodal regime only. It is also possible within a monarchical system; cf. the medieval Byzantine theologians on the doctrine of "pentarchy"; cf. V. Pospishil, *Der Patriarch in der Serbisch-Orthodoxen Kirche* (Wien, 1966), pp. 63-78. See also *Loi organique de l'Eglise autocéphale de Grèce* (1923) and *Charte constitutionelle de l'Eglise de Grèce*, published in *Istina* 7 (1960), pp. 153-72, 279-300, where it is clear that the Holy Synod is the supreme legislative, administrative and judicial organ of the autocephalous Church of Greece.

11. M-J. Le Guillou, *Mission et Unité II, op. cit.,* p. 189.

12. J. Hajjar, "La collegialità nella tradizione orientale," in *La chiesa del Vaticano II, op. cit.,* pp. 818-31; *idem,* "Synode permanent et collégialité épiscopale dans l'Eglise byzantine au premier millénaire," in *La collégialité épiscopale, op. cit.,* pp. 151-66.

13. Th. Strotmann, "L'evêque dans la tradition orientale," in *l'Episcopat et l'Eglise Universelle, op. cit.,* pp. 309-314. Latin theology usually prefers to compare the bishop to Christ; cf. J. Pascher, "Die Hierarchie in sakramentaler Symbolik," in *Studien über das Bischofsamt* (Regensburg, 1949), p. 292.

14. J. Hajjar, "La collegialità . . . ," *op. cit.,* p. 823.

15. V. Pospishil, *op. cit.,* pp. 64-65. For the discussion over the existence of absolute rights belonging to the person of the patriarch, see especially pp. 69-72.

When translated into juridical terms, this became a system of concessions. However, these were not concessions granted from above, as in the Latin Church, but rather from below, a system which thus eliminated the possibility of any personal interference within the sphere of jurisdiction which belonged to the lower bishop. Thus at the local level, the bishop enjoyed considerable autonomy of action.[16]

III. The Theology of the Universal Church

The Concept of the Church

Because of the West's different eucharistic theology, Latin ecclesiology developed along its own lines. In the East, the idea of transcendence was much to the fore, and in the breaking of bread the bishops are seen as all representing Christ in the same way. In the West, however, there was a more juridical view of the eucharist, seeing it rather as a sacrifice of reconciliation, in keeping with the power of binding and loosing. The redemptive act, which is celebrated by the bishops in the eucharistic sacrifice, is performed in a special way by the successor of Peter (Mt. 16, 19), who therefore enjoys primacy over all the others.[17] The Augustinian view of the eucharist was that the local celebration is a reflection of the unity of the local Church; this idea was taken up in a one-sided way by the Middle Ages. "Church" became synonymous with the whole body, incorporating all believers in a vertical structure.[18] The "Church of Rome," understood at one time as referring to the local Church, became equivalent to the "Catholic Church," reflecting a kind of imperial, universal vision. The decretals, typical of the Latin mentality, incorporated this vision into a system of discipline, tending to reduce all to uniformity. With the Gregorian reform in the West, the Church detached herself from the feudal theocratic structure, and this enabled her to define herself as a perfect society, with her own autonomy and law, as distinct from the secular power[19] and to transform herself into some sort of vast diocese, into which even the new religious orders were directly incorporated.[20] The pope has the *plenitudo potestatis;* he is the *fons et origo* of all ecclesial life and the first

16. Cf. the list of the rights of the patriarchs and metropolitans in N. Milasch, *Das Kirchenrecht der morgenländischen Kirche* (Mostar,[2] 1905), pp. 326-29, 335-38. On the rights of bishops in an "eparchy" (diocese), cf. *ibid.,* pp. 372-86, 456-58.

17. C. Andresen, "Geschichte der abendländischen Konzile des Mittelalters," in *Die ökumenischen Konzile der Christenheit* (Stuttgart, 1961), pp. 79-84.

18. B. Neunheuser, "Chiesa universale et chiesa locale," in *La chiesa del Vaticano II, op. cit.,* pp. 628-30.

19. Y. Congar, "L'ecclesiologie de la Révolution française au Concile du Vatican sous le signe de l'affirmation de l'autorité," in *L'ecclésiologie au XIXe siècle* (Unam Sanctam 34) (Paris, 1960), p. 90.

20. O. Rousseau, "La doctrine du ministère épiscopale et ses vicissitudes dans l'Eglise d'Occident," in *L'Episcopat et l'Eglise Universelle, op. cit.,* pp. 286-87.

bishop of every diocese.[21] The principle underlying his relations with the bishops appears now as the appointment of each pastor *in partem sollicitudinis papae;* consequently, Catholic doctrine reduces the bishop to the position of a mere vicar or legate of the pope.[22]

Synods

This all-embracing pyramid scheme of the Latin Church implies also a different view of councils. General councils appear in the West not so much as assemblies of bishops meeting together; rather, they appear as representatives from all Christianity to offer advice to the supreme pontiff. The pope is the head, the bishops the members. They are not present on an equal footing, nor even as a body, but as individuals.[23] With the Council of Trent, the episcopate recovered *de facto* its collegial responsibilities.[24] However, ecclesiology, under pressure from Protestantism and Gallicanism, became yet more centered on the papacy and the universal Church, thus overshadowing the concept of communion in favor of the "society" aspect as contained in the idea of juridical primacy.[25] This increasingly undermined the autonomy and strength of the particular councils of the local Churches.[26]

21. The quarrel between the seculars and mendicants in the 13th century, which was more than a mere controversy over spirituality, had an influence on ecclesiology; cf. J. Ratzinger, "Der Einfluss des Bettelordensstreites auf die Entwicklung der Lehre vom päpstlichen universalprimat, unter besonderer Berüchsichtigung des heiligen Bonaventura," in *Theol. in der Geschichte und Gegenwart* (Munich, 1957), pp. 697-724; Y. Congar, "Aspects ecclésiologiques de la querelle entre mendiants et séculiers dans la seconde moitié du XIIIe et le début du XIVe siècles," in *Arch. Hist. Doctr. Lit.* (1961), pp. 35-151.

22. Y. Congar, "De la communion . . . ," *loc. cit.*, pp. 238f.; cf. also J. Rivière, "In partem sollecitudinis . . . Evolution d'une formule pontificale," in *Rev. Sc. Relig.* 5 (1925), pp. 210-31.

23. C. Andresen, *loc. cit.*, pp. 75-149; G. Fransen, "L'ecclésiologie des conciles médiévaux," in *Le Concile et les Conciles, op. cit.*, pp. 125-41; H. Jedin, *Struktur-probleme der ökumenischen Konzilien* (Cologne, 1963), pp. 2-27.

24. The conciliarism in the Council of Constance had little true feeling for collegiality in spite of its insisting on an "ecclesiology of the Church"; cf. C. Moeller, "La collégialité au Concile de Constance," in *La collégialité épiscopale, op. cit.*, p. 149.

25. On the ecclesiology of the period, cf. Y. Congar, "Kirche, II Dogmengeschichtlich," in *Handbuch Theologischer Grundbegriffe I* (Munich, 1962), pp. 807-12; cf. also H. Fries, III Systematisch, *ibid.*, pp. 812-22.

26. From the time of Trent until the end of the 19th century, approximately 260 provincial or plenary councils were held in the Latin Church. If we take 90 as the minimum number of ecclesiastical provinces, it looks as if the number of councils during this time was approximately 2% of the number laid down by Church law. Cf. E. Corecco, *La formazione della Chiesa negli Stati Uniti d'America attraverso l'attività sinodale, con particolare riguardo al problem dell' amministrazione dei beni ecclesiastici* (Munich, 1962).

The Function of the Bishop[27]

As a result of the tension in the relations between the local and universal Church, the juridical idea of the bishop has fluctuated considerably in the West. As in the East until the 14th century, the authority of the bishop as head of the local Church is unquestioned *(ein gewaltiger Herr).*[28] His position is based on the possession of a legitimate function, and his judicial and administrative authority is expressed symbolically in the one eucharist which is shared by the whole presbyterate and people.[29] His decisions are taken in the light of the advice given by the presbyterate, the wishes of the people and local tradition. When the Church found herself obliged to adapt to the pressure of the politico-religious unity of a new world, the bishop was changed into the local administrator, representing an omnipresent civil and ecclesiastical government, a development which effectively depersonalized his relations with the local community (cf. the practice of absolute ordination). Progressive centralization by Rome certainly weakened the position of metropolitans (now considered merely as an extension of the papal primacy); it also reduced the status of bishops in the West, who had indeed consolidated their position by establishing both their private (cf. the system of the proper Church) and public rights (feudal functions, *bannus*). But now they resembled more the suffragan bishops who held the suburban sees.[30]

Episcopal authority was also threatened in the internal government of the diocese; from the early Middle Ages the spread of the parochial structure had gradually broken up the presbyterate, transforming the priest into a minister who enjoyed his own proper rights and had lost for the most part any collegial link with his bishop.[31] The late Middle Ages saw the granting of innumerable privileges and exemptions (convents, religious orders, foundations and universities). This, plus the policy of benefices adopted by the Holy See (reservations), backed by the particular law and *consuetudo,* served to exaggerate the position of cathedral chapters, the higher prelates (archdeacons and auxiliary bishops) and the laity (right of patronage).

This twofold weakening of the bishop in his relations both with those below and above him was embodied likewise in Scholastic theology. The

27. For this whole question, cf. W. Plöchl, *Geschichte des Kirchenrechts* I (Vienna,[2] 1960), pp. 332-33, 165-66; II ([2]1962), pp. 141-44; III (1959), pp. 257-58; H. Feine, *Kirchliche Rechtsgeschichte* (Cologne, [4]1964), pp. 124-27, 213-19, 364-79, 533-39.

28. U. Stutz, *Kirchenrecht* (Sonderabzug, 1904), pp. 825-26.

29. In Milan and Carthage at the end of the 4th century, there was only one eucharist for the whole city on Sundays; cf. V. Monachino, *La cura pastorale a Milano, Cartagine e Roma nel secolo IV* (Rome, 1947), pp. 55-56, 188-90.

30. For the three different areas in which the influence of Rome was felt, cf. P. Batiffol, *Cathedra Petri* (Unam Sanctam 4) (Paris, 1938), pp. 41-59.

31. B. Bazatole, "L'eveque et la vie chrétienne au sein de l'Eglise locale," in *L'Episcopat et L'Eglise Universelle, op. cit.,* pp. 342-48. For the history of the development of the parish, cf. A. Blochlinger, *Die heutige Pfarrei als Gemeinschaft* (Einsiedeln, 1962), pp. 57-122.

power of jurisdiction, now seen as independent of the power of orders,[32] was taken as a mere extension of the papal power of orders, while as far as the power of orders was concerned the bishop was not really distinguished from the *simplex sacerdos* (the same power of order, the non-sacramental nature of the episcopate).[33] The medieval universalist culture was able to conceive authority only in the form of a leader in command of a body; thus the bishop was viewed in isolation, a papal representative linked to a locality,[34] bound by an oath of obedience and obliged to an *ad limina* visit. He was underrated, both as guardian of the local Church, because of interference by third parties, and as a link with other Churches and the universal Church, since in spite of intense synodal activity, the Middle Ages had little idea of what episcopal collegiality really was.[35]

The Tridentine reform did understand to an extent that the ecclesial crisis originated in this imbalance which had weakened the episcopal office. Unable to resolve the basic question of the human or divine origin of the bishop's jurisdiction, the Council tried instead to cope with the difficult problem of how to strengthen not only the papal power but also the power of the bishops.[36] This it did by the pragmatic device of *delegatio a jure,* which conferred on bishops—"loaned" to them, as it were—faculties which were considered proper to the position of the pope.[37] To counteract the abuses arising from the innumerable exemptions, the Council restored the right of the ordinary to visit and to supervise (especially with reference to the administration of ecclesiastical property), and recognized his right to legislate in his own territory without papal approval, and to dispense in particular cases from the common law. Obligations were also laid down for the bishop (residence) helping thus to establish a higher image.[38] This was not

32. On this question, cf. K. Mörsdorf, "Die Entwicklung der Zweigliedrigkeit der kirchlichen Hierarchie," in *Münchener Theol. Zeit.* 3 (1952), pp. 1-16; K. Nasilowski, *De distinctione potestatis in ordine in primaeva canonistarum doctrina* (Munich, 1962); E. Corecco, "L'origine del potere di giurisdizione episcopale: aspetti storico-giuridici e metodologico-sistematici della questione," in *La Scuola Cattolica* 96 (1968).

33. O. Rousseau, *loc. cit.,* pp. 279-96.

34. Y. Congar, "Notes sur le destin," *loc. cit.,* pp. 113-27; G. Alberigo, *Lo sviluppo della dottrina sui poteri nella Chiesa universale* (Rome, 1964), pp. 4-7.

35. According to Y. Congar *(ibid.,* pp. 118-27), the idea of episcopal collegiality was "abolished" in the Middle Ages by the doctrine of the divine right of the college of cardinals. Cf. also M. Garcia Miralles "El Cardinalato de institutione divina y el Episcopado en el problema de la succesiòn apostòlica segun Juan de Torquemada," in *XVI Semana Española de Teologia* (Madrid, 1957), pp. 249-74.

36. W. Bertrams, "De quaestione circa originem potestatis iurisdictionis episcoporum in concilio tridentino non resoluta," in *Periodica Rer. Mor. Can. Lit.* 52 (1963), pp. 458-62; G. Alberigo, *op. cit.,* pp. 11-101; H. Grisar, "Die Frage des päpstlichen Primates und des Ursprunges der bischöflichen Gewalten auf dem Tridentinum," in *Zeitschr. f. kath. Theol.* 8 (1884), p. 453-507, 727-84.

37. E. Rösser, *Die gesetzliche Delegation* (Paderborn, 1937), pp. 113-27.

38. H. Jedin, *Das Bischofsideal der katholischen Reformation* (Bruges, 1953).

yet a true restoration of the powers of the bishop, because once again he was considered, as also in the Code of 1917, as being too dependent on the papacy. The whole ecclesiological structure still overemphasized the individual and did not sufficiently take into account the bishop's function and his collegial responsibility.

IV. The Reform of Vatican Council II

The Council's Ecclesiology

The particular value of the local Church was stated in Vatican Council II, as it had been in no other council.[39] However, taken overall in the teaching of the Council, the local Church is still seen in a slightly impersonal way, as the situation by means of which the universal Church is made manifest.[40] The fundamental principle relating to the local Church was introduced very late in the history of the schema of the *Constitution on the Church,* so that it did not exercise the same overall influence as the idea of the universal Church. However, the fact remains that the Council provided full justification for an ecclesiology which centers on the eucharistic community.[41] The temptation was overcome to take the local Church merely as an administrative unit of the universal Church, and in fact its existence is based on dogmatic reasons, and not only on historico-sociological ones. The particular Church does realize in itself the universal Church, insofar as in the bishop's celebration of Word and sacrament there is made present the mystery of the Trinity; it offers at the same time the essential meeting point for men to come into contact with the mystery of salvation,[42] a mystery which indeed is fully represented in the symbol of the universal Church,[43] which is, in Christ, the sacrament of the union both with God and with the whole human race.[44]

Now the unity of the Church is derived not from uniformity but from her plurality,[45] and the local Churches, in their own, proper way, are an essential part in an ascending hierarchy to be found fully explained in the Council (patriarchate, diocese, parish, house church[46] and separated ecclesial communities[47]). The Council did not take up any position with regard to the

39. F. Kantzenbach, "Luthers Konzilstheologie und die Gegenwart," in *Luth. Monatshefte* 5 (1966), p. 169.

40. Cf. W. Beinert, *loc. cit.,* pp. 8-9.

41. K. Rahner, "Das Zweite Vatikanische Konzil, Kommentare I," in *Lex. Theol. und Kirche* (Freiburg, 1966), pp. 242-45.

42. W. Beinert, *loc. cit.,* pp. 10-11.

43. The local Church is the symbol of the whole ecclesial body only by virtue of its communion with the universal Church. Ecclesial communion is a dimension which transcends the merely local Church.

44. Vat. Eccl. 1.

45. Vat. Eccl. 13.

46. Vat. Eccl. 11, 2; Vat. Laic. 11, 4.

47. Vat. Oec. 13.

debated question whether the universal Church was prior to the local Church or vice versa. In fact there exists both the structure belonging to the universal Church (primacy and episcopal college) and the structure characteristic of the local Church (the episcopal office).[48] Christ did not give priority in his institution either to the local Church or to the universal Church;[49] rather, he founded the Church as such, with her own twofold structure, whose parts are complementary.

The Collegial Structure

Beginning with her own concrete experience, the early Church always considered the idea of the college of bishops as secondary to the concept of the local Church. Modern theology has never experienced directly the Church as active in her councils; theology is under the influence of illuminism even yet. Hence the theological approach to this problem has been speculative rather than historical.[50] And so, the Latin theology of the universal Church influenced Vatican Council II more with reference to the Church's structure—collegiality—than at the purely ecclesiological level. In fact the Council did not recognize the true character of collegiality in the strict sense, and rather took as its central points the problem of the relations of the bishop to the papal primacy and the question whether the subject of power was single or twofold.[51]

If the Council did reappraise the shape and form of local councils,[52] with particular reference to the modern form of the episcopal conference,[53] it nevertheless did not apply the idea of collegiality to them, putting aside the hypothesis that they could be a way of sharing in the supreme power of the universal college.[54] In fact, they are a genuine form of collegiality, of a local kind, and differ from universal collegiality in that they do not enjoy power over the whole Church. While the Code of Canon Law had seen in the episcopal conference only an institution which derived from the papal primacy, Vatican Council II recognized the local collegial gathering as an institution whose ultimate justification was the proper, ordinary power of the bishops. In particular, it made the episcopal conference a real in-

48. Y. Congar, "Neuf cent ans après," *op. cit.*, pp. 84-85.

49. This point of view was put forward by Archbishop Veuillot in his *relatio* on the Textus Emendatus, 1964; cf. K. Mörsdorf, "Kommentare II," *op. cit.*, p. 151, n. 4.

50. J. Ratzinger, "La collegialità episcopale: spiegzione teologica," in *La Chiesa del Vaticano II, op. cit.*, pp. 745-47.

51. On this point, cf. W. Bertrams, *Il potere pastorale del papa e del collegio dei vescovi* (Rome, 1967), pp. 62-122; C. Colombo, "Constituzione gerarchica della Chiesa e in particolare dell'episcopato," in *La Costituzione "De Ecclesia"* (Milan, 1965), pp. 237-61; K. Mörsdorf, "Primat und Kollegialität nach dem Konzil," in *Uber das bischöfliche Amt* (Karlsruhe, 1966), pp. 42-45.

52. Vat. Ep. 36.

53. Vat. Ep. 37-38; Eccl. Sanc. I, 41.

54. A distinction should be made between formal and material collegiality. Cf. W. Aymans, *Das synodale Element in der Kirchenverfassung* (Munich, 1967), Chapter 4, Part I.

termediary between the central authority and the local bishop, in a position now to exercise a more general form of authority, and not only in particular cases.[55]

The Function of the Bishop

1. The Local Church as the Criterion of the Bishop's Function

The bishop, from both the theological and juridical point of view, emerged from Vatican Council II with his position radically revised, in his relationship both with higher authority and with the local Church. The doctrine of collegiality has underlined his juridical and moral responsibility to the whole Church. The reconsideration of the position of the local Church has restored the original responsibility of the bishop for the local Church. Now the local Church is an ecclesial body only insofar as it is able to show forth the essential characteristics of the universal Church, and likewise the bishop is only the local Church's legitimate head, insofar as he is a member of the college of bishops. Therefore, the local Church should be taken as the criterion by which the function of the bishop may be defined, since he presides over the local Church and is its representative in the assembly of bishops.[56] Thus we can see that it was not only for reasons of administration that Vatican Council II, for the first time in the history of the councils, was concerned with the definition of the nature of a diocese.[57]

2. The Personal Aspect of the Bishop's Power

Analogously to the universal Church, there is within the diocese a personal principle of unit and a collegial principle.[58] The bishop is the personal principle, insofar as he possesses by divine right the complete power of orders and jurisdiction necessary to carry out his apostolic duties of teaching, sanctifying and ruling.[59] The Council completely reversed the whole approach to the episcopal office by fully restoring the bishop to the position he originally enjoyed—and still enjoys to an extent in the Oriental tradition.

55. On this whole problem, cf. K. Mörsdorf, *Kommentare II, op. cit.,* pp. 228-32, 237-38.

56. K. Rahner, "Bishop und Bistum," in *Handbuch der Pastoraltheologie* I (Freiburg, 1964), pp. 167-79.

57. Vat. Ep. 11, 1; 22-23.

58. On the subordination of the one principle to the other, cf. K. Mörsdorf, "Uber die Zuordnung des Kollegialitätsprinzips zu dem Prinzip der Einheit von Haupt und Leib in der hierarchischen Struktur der Kirchenverfassung," in *Wahrheit und Verkündigung, M. Schmaus zum 70 Geburtstag II* (Munich, 1967), pp. 1435-45.

59. Vat. Eccl. 25-27. *Lumen Gentium* expressly makes a distinction between the office and the power, to avoid any confusion between the doctrine on the triple office of the bishop and his "triple power." For the relationship between the power of orders and jurisdiction and the triple office, cf. K. Mörsdorf, "Heilige Gewalt," in *Sacramentum Mundi* II (Freiburg, 1967ff.).

The power of orders of the bishop was not defined by the Council by referring it to the priestly power of orders, but rather the other way around, and the sacramental fullness of the priesthood was predicted of the bishop.[60] With reference to the power of jurisdiction, on the other hand, the Council eliminated any possibility of seeing such jurisdiction as deriving from the papal primacy by affirming explicitly that the individual bishop has, *per se* and in his own right, all the ordinary powers necessary for his apostolic function.[61]

From the system of the concession of powers by the pope to the bishop, it had been a natural step to the system of questions reserved to the pope. Since the divine right does not exist in the abstract but can only be realized in the process of history by the development of human rights,[62] the problem is how to know in the concrete which powers are necessary for the bishop to be able to look after the discipline of his own local Church, so as to ensure that it is a valid manifestation of the universal Church. There is in fact a fundamental objection to the rigid juridical system of reservations. The office of bishop should indeed have limits laid down as to its content, lest the general legal presumption in favor of the bishop given by Vatican Council II degenerate into something completely arbitrary, but the problem obviously cannot be solved merely by the granting of a general faculty to dispense from the common law;[63] the bishop must also be able, in the revised Code of Canon Law, to influence directly, through his administrative and judicial activity, his own local discipline, taking into account the special characteristics and requirements of his own diocese.[64] Therefore, it is rather a question of restoring to the local Church its own internal autonomy and unity, which will make possible a pastoral policy for the diocese as a whole under the final responsibility of a single individual. This is the tendency, for example, of the norms of the Council which emphasize the global responsibility of the bishop in some sectors[65] and support this in a negative way by

60. Vat. Eccl. 21, 2.

61. Vat. Ep., 8/a.

62. K. Rahner, "Bischof und Bistum," *loc. cit.*, p. 176; *idem*, "Uber den Begriff des 'Ius divinum' im kath. Verständnis," in *Schriften zur Theologie* V (Einsiedeln, 1962), pp. 249-77; *idem*, "Uber Bischofskonferenzen," *ibid.*, VI (Einsiedeln, 1965), pp. 438-42.

63. Vat. Ep. 8/b.

64. On this whole question, cf. K. Mörsdorf, *Kommentare* II, *op. cit.*, pp. 158-61, 166-71; *idem*, Neue Vollmachten und Privilegien der Bischöfe," in *Arch. f. kath. Kirchenrecht* 133 (1964), pp. 82-101.

65. While the Code of Canon Law attributed to the bishop a mainly negative function in supervising the execution of the liturgical norms (cf. Canon 1261), the Council abrogated Canon 1257 and returned to the bishop a general commission to supervise the liturgy in his diocese in keeping with the new law. Cf. Vat. Lit. 22, 1, Instr. Vat. Lit. 22; K. Mörsdorf, *Lehrbuch des Kirchenrechts* II (Paderborn, [11]1967), pp. 365-70.

cancelling out the centrifugal tendency which took the clergy,[66] laity[67] and religious[68] away from the direct authority of the bishop. In a word, it is a question of translating into practical terms of law the picture of the bishop given in the *Decree on the Pastoral Office of Bishops in the Church,* nn. 11-16.[69]

3. *The Power of the Synod*

As pastoral activity develops in our industrial, consumer society which is seeing rapid expansion in every field, there is the risk of overtaxing the abilities of one individual. This consideration, and especially the fundamental theological teaching on the bishop, has led to a rediscovery of the further, lower, dimension of the episcopate. The bishop is rescued from the isolation into which he had fallen by several factors: the theological restoration of the presbyterate, the representation of priests in the shape of the council of priests,[70] and also, though only by analogy, the other councils and commissions on which religious[71] and also the laity have a consultative function. All of this is intended to involve every sector of the diocese and extend responsibility to the whole community. This isolation of the bishop was already known in the Middle Ages, when the idea of a unified pastoral policy was inconceivable, given the absence of any notion of collegiality[72]—a state of affairs which persisted even into recent times, in spite of a considerable missionary effort, under the guise of the partial exclusion of the bishop from the problems of the universal Church. The teaching on collegiality and on the local Church, which ought to reflect in the most authentic way possible the universal Church, was incorporated in the clear directives which came from the Council, with the purpose of preventing any kind of parochialism in the local Church, and rather promoting interecclesial responsibility—for example, a unified policy in pastoral theology,[73] in ecumenism[74] and in mission work.[75]

To sum up: the central teaching of the Council on episcopal collegiality has had the effect of restoring the standing of the bishop in the universal

66. Vat. Ep. 31-32; Eccl. Sanc. 20-21. Cf. H. Schmitz, "Amtsenthebung und Versetzung der Pfarrer im neuen Recht," *Trierer Theol. Zeitschr.* 76 (1967), pp. 357-71.

67. Vat. Ep. 28; Eccl. Sanc. I, 18.

68. Vat. Ep. 34-35; Eccl. Sanc. I, 22-40. A. Scheuermann, "Kommentar zum Ordensdekret des II Vatikanischen Konzils," in *Das Konzil und die Orden* (Cologne, 1967), pp. 105-08; *idem,* "Die Ausführungsbestimmungen zu den Konzilsweisungen für die Ordenzleute," *ibid.,* pp. 122-37.

69. K. Mörsdorf, *Kommentare* II, *op. cit.,* p. 173.

70. Cf. O. Saier, "Die hierarchische Struktur des Presbyteriums," in *Arch. f. kath. Kirchenrecht* 136 (1967), pp. 341-91; L. Weber, "Der Priesterrat," in *Der Seelsorger* 38 (1968), pp. 105-18.

71. Religious are included among the diocesan clergy; cf. Vat. Ep. 34, 1.

72. Y. Congar, "Notes sur le destin . . . ," *loc cit.,* p. 118.

73. Cf., for example, Vat. Ep. 6; Vat. Presb. 10; Vat. Miss. 19, 4; 20, 1; Eccl. Sanc. I, 1-5.

74. Cf., for example, Vat. Oec. 4, 11; 5; 10,1.

75. Cf., for example, Vat. Miss. 20; 38, 1-2.

Church, while also strengthening his position as head of the local Church. Limits have been imposed on his authority—first from above, by incorporating him into an interdiocesan discipline, in the shape of an intermediate collegial institution (the episcopal conference), and second from below, by providing for the advisory function of the priests and laity.

Case 7

The Authority of the Local Bishop

The Ames Diocese, located in the southwestern United States, recently held a synod. Participation in the synod included elected representatives from among the clergy, religious, and laity. Bishop John Ferro of Ames agreed to the following norm:

> The bishop of the Ames Diocese shall have veto power over all items passed by the synod. By a two-thirds majority, the synod may override any veto, and the bishop shall then accept and implement the item unless said item is contrary to the teachings of the magisterium.

By an almost unanimous vote, the synod passed the following law for the diocese regarding reception of the Eucharist:

1. Catholics within the Ames Diocese shall be permitted to receive Communion as often as they participate in the Sacred Liturgy, even if this shall occur more than once a day.
2. Separated Christians may receive Communion during a Catholic liturgy unless grave scandal shall occur. The judgment as to grave scandal shall rest with the chief celebrant of the liturgy.

Bishop Ferro did not approve of either law. He was advised that the first law was contrary to the general law of the Roman Church and the particular law of the United States which had not implemented such a broad norm concerning reception of the Eucharist. The second law he opposed as contrary to general Church discipline and perhaps the teachings of the magisterium. Therefore, Bishop Ferro vetoed both norms.

After lengthy debate, the synod overrode both vetoes. Bishop Ferro, submitting to the governing norms, reluctantly accepted the first law although he doubted his authority to implement such a decree. He refused, however, to acquiesce to the second because it was contrary to the teachings of the magisterium.

Subsequent to the synod, people regarded both laws as official legislation of the diocese and thus operative law. The Congregation for Sacraments and Divine Worship sent an official notice to Bishop Ferro stating, in substance, that he was operating outside the scope of his episcopal power to establish particular local laws concerning frequency of reception of Communion and that the bishop had no authority to establish such a law. The practice therefore must cease. Nothing was mentioned regarding the second law permitting reception of Communion by separated Christians.

Priests of the diocese in accord with the second law began admitting separated Christians to Communion, especially at weddings of mixed religion. The priests reasoned that the override prevented the bishop from forbidding the admission of separated Christians to Communion.

Exercise

1. Theologically, what is the relationship between the bishop of Rome and the bishop of Ames?

2. Canonically, what is the relationship between the bishop of Rome and the bishop of Ames?

3. Can the bishop of Ames act independently or contrary to the Apostolic See in matters other than doctrine?

4. Analyze the validity of each law passed by the synod.

References

Decree on the Pastoral Office of Bishops in the Church, Vatican II, par. 4-10.

Dogmatic Constitution on the Church, Vatican II, Chapter III, par. 18-29.

"Ecclesiae Sanctae" (August 6, 1966) I, 15, *Canon Law Digest* VI, 264.

Collins, P. W., "The Diocesan Synod—An Assembly of the People of God," *The Jurist* 33 (1973), 399.

Coriden, J. A., "The Diocesan Synod: An Instrument for Renewal for the Local Church," *The Jurist* 34 (1974), 68.

Donnelly, F. B., 'The New Diocesan Synod," *The Jurist* 34 (1974), 396.

McBrien, R. P., "Collegiality: State of the Question" *The Once and Future Church.* J. A. Coriden, ed. (New York: Alba House, 1971), 1-24.

Senate of Priests

T. J. Green

The Council or senate of priests is a body intended to give "effective counsel" to the bishop in the governance of the diocese, and thus the bishop is to "hear the priests, consult with them, and enter into discussion with them" in whatever pertains to "the needs of pastoral activity and the good of the diocese" [*Presbyterorum Ordinis* (hereafter PO) 7, *Ecclesiae Sanctae* (ES) 1.15.1] By sacramental ordination a priest is received into the order of presbyters or the presbyterate. The local presbyterate is the corporate union of all priests of a particular church (i.e., a diocese) united among themselves and headed by the bishop [PO 8, *Lumen Gentium* (LG) 28]. This is not merely a social or political structure but a theological reality arising from the nature of ordination. Vatican Council II's rediscovery of this profound priestly bond represents a healthy development in light of the somewhat impoverished sense of diocesan collegiality in recent centuries.

The foundation of the relationship between priest and bishop is not primarily a juridical mission but their mutual sharing in the one priesthood of Christ even though in different degrees. The bishop is the witness and agency of unity within the local Church and in its relationship to the universal Church in conjunction with the presbyterate. In fact the latter enters into the definition of a diocese: ". . . that portion of God's people which is entrusted to a bishop to be shepherded by him with the cooperation of the presbytery" [*Christus Dominus* (CD) 11]. This definition illustrates a return to the patristic tradition of stressing presbyteral collaboration in diocesan government.

The principle of collegiality implies that no particular church can be in good health unless its bishop knows his priests and listens to them, encourages them, and inspires them. The senate of priests is a particularly appropriate vehicle for facilitating on-going communication and collaboration within the presbyterate of a diocese presided over by the bishop.

Nature and Obligation

By instituting the senate of priests, Vatican II attempted to revitalize existing collegial bodies, such as cathedral chapters and diocesan consultors, whose purpose has been to assist the bishop as his council according to Canon Law, to administer the diocese during a vacancy (PO 7; CD 27; CIC c. 391, 427), and to stimulate bishop-priest collaboration in diocesan government.

The motu proprio of Paul VI, *Ecclesiae Sanctae* of Aug. 6, 1966, brought the clarity and force of law to the conciliar insights. It stressed the necessity of such a senate as a significant vehicle of bishop-priest pastoral collaboration despite the reluctance of some bishops to institute such a body (ES 1.15.1).

Finally the circular letter of the Congregation of the Clergy of April 11, 1970, confirmed the obligatory character and commented on the positive benefits of such bishop-priest collaboration: more frequent contact and sharing of pastoral experiences, more perceptive awareness of diocesan needs, updating of pastoral approaches amid changing circumstances, etc. (ActApS 5).

Representation and Competence

The representative character of the priests' senate differentiates it from similar organisms such as the diocesan consultors or the cathedral chapter, which have functioned as the bishop's senate without necessarily being representative of the presbyterate. The senate represents the presbyterate including priests who are members of religious institutes, at least to the extent that they are engaged in the diocesan ministry and apostolate (ES 1.15.2). The implications of this representative character are spelled out in the above-mentioned circular letter, which calls for the involvement of priests in different ministries and regions and from different age groups (ActApS 6). While the senate may have ex officio members and participants designated by the bishop, it seems appropriate that the majority be elected by their peers in order to have real credibility and accountability (ActApS 7). A corollary of this is the need for on-going communication between the members of the senate and the rest of the presbyterate, e.g., open meetings, nonsenate members on senate commissions.

The senate of priests is to offer on-going and comprehensive counsel to the bishop in view of more effective diocesan government while facilitating better bishop-priest and priest-priest relationships (PO 7, ES 1.15.1). The 1971 Synod of Bishops identifies the following senate tasks: ". . . to seek out clear and distinctly defined aims, to suggest priorities, to indicate methods of acting, to assist whatever the Spirit frequently stirs up through individuals or groups, and to foster the spiritual life, whence the necessary unity may more easily be attained" [*Osservatore Romano,* Eng. ed. (OssRom) 2.2.1]. The senate is not confined to specifically priest-oriented issues but rather should concern itself with a broad range of pastoral concerns, e.g., sanctification of the faithful, doctrinal teaching, diocesan government. Yet it should not deal with matters requiring a more discreet procedure, e.g. personnel assignments (ActApS 8).

On occasions the bishop must consult or even obtain the consent of the diocesan consultors or the cathedral chapter (deliberative vote). However at present the vote of the senate is consultative despite its description as a special or preeminent consultative organ. In other words its decisions do not bind the bishop unless the universal law of the Church or he provide otherwise (ES 1.15.3, OssRom 9). Nevertheless one should not underestimate the importance of consultation in the Church's canonical tradition. Furthermore Vatican II has embodied a new appreciation of participatory activity [*Gaudium et spes* (GS) 75] while giving the Church a new thrust toward representative governance, a significant departure from the policy of recent centuries. Consultation is neither a concession nor a privilege but rather is rooted in the nature of the Church as a community of believers endowed with distinctive gifts of the Spirit. It is true that the senate's counsel is specifically required only in matters of parish modifications (ES 1.8, 21.2-3). Yet the preceding comments on the broad pastoral role of the senate emphasize the desirability of consultation not only when strictly obligatory but as a general policy, as well as the bishops' grave moral responsibility to exercise authority collegially.

Relationship to Other Bodies

While the senate of priests has replaced the diocesan consultors or cathedral chapter as the principal diocesan consultative organ (ActApS 9), the latter bodies retain their role, for the present, in cases requiring their counsel or consent (ES 1.17.2, ActApS 10). The senate at present ceases to exist during the vacancy of a diocese while the consultors-chapter remain in existence to govern the diocese and elect a vicar or administrator (ES 1.15.4; ActApS 10; CIC cc.431.1, 432.1). In order to avoid needless conflict some have suggested constituting the membership of the senate of priests in whole or in part as the diocesan consultors.

Another means proposed by the Council to promote shared responsibility was the establishment of a diocesan pastoral council composed of selected clergy, religious and laity to "investigate, evaluate and formulate practical conclusions" in view of promoting conformity of the whole people of God to the Gospel (CD 27; ES 1.16.2). Although the senate of priests is obligatory, the pastoral council, while important and helpful, is not absolutely required at present; and the bishop along with the presbyterate is to evaluate the opportuneness of its establishment and foster those circumstances required for its institution and efficient operation [ES 1.16.2; circular letter of the Congregation for the Clergy (Jan. 25, 1973) 6]. While both the senate of priests and the pastoral council are consultative organs concerned with the pastoral issues, the senate deals with them specifically in terms of its ministerial charism for ecclesiastical leadership.

The presence of priests at the meetings of certain episcopal conferences testifies to a growing cognizance of the supradiocesan dimension of the presbyterate (PO 10). There is ample historical precedent for such supradiocesan involvement, especially priest-bishop interaction in the

Church's conciliar life at various levels. In light of the interdependence of various local churches and the growing significance of episcopal conferences in the life of the Church, it seems appropriate that new ways be found to institutionalize bishop-priest collaboration at the national and regional level (OssRom 2.2.1).

Another manifestation of the supradiocesan character of the presbyterate has been the National Federation of Priests' Councils. Organized in 1968, its stated purposes have been to give priests' councils and associations a representative voice in various issues, to improve communications among priests, and to make recommendations to bishops, priests, and others after appropriate research. While its representational character has been questioned, it has contributed to priestly development in such areas as continuing education, personnel policies, priestly spirituality, and grievance procedures. While such a group might be regarded as a body apart from the bishops, thus threatening ministerial unity, one should note both the conciliar stress on the right of priests to associate (PO 8, OssRom 2.2.1) and the positive benefits of such common endeavors. Progress in structuring forms of genuine bishop-priest collaboration should obviate possible dangers to ecclesial communion.

In the present transitional period conflicts between the senate of priests and other newly constituted or previously existing structures are inevitable. Hopefully pastoral experience will suggest guidelines clarifying the competence and functioning of the various organs (ES 1.17). Gradually the Church will develop practices responding to the renewed vision of shared responsibility. New juridical expressions of the fundamental ministerial unity of bishop and priests will undoubtedly require a change in mentality on the part of both. Hopefully such movement toward genuinely collaborative diocesan decision-making will respond to the aspirations of many for an ecclesiastical leadership characterized by consultation and consensus.

Structural Arrangements of the Parish

William J. LaDue

A Brief History

1. The Structure of the Parish in the First Centuries

It has been incontrovertibly established that the development of Christianity in the first two or three generations was located principally in the cities and the towns of the Roman Empire. It was out of these urban centers that the missionary movement was extended into the rural areas in the second century. The development of the Christian communities in the cities and towns took many forms, so that, as a result, it is almost impossible to give any kind of generic description of Christian life on the level of the urban worshiping community in the first two centuries.[1] For the most part it can be said that the hierarchical leaders, i.e. the bishops, the priests, and the deacons, constituted a community of some sort, and frequently led a common life. In the larger centers there must normally have been some sort of partitioning of the whole body of believers into smaller groups for the purpose of weekly worship. This we know happened in places like Rome and Antioch, and this undoubtedly occurred in the other cities where Christianity took significant roots.

In second century Rome there were about a half dozen *tituli* or local worshiping communities. These were served by members of the Roman *presbyterium,* who continued to live and function, to a notable extent, as a unit. The *tituli,* although dispersed throughout the city of Rome, did not seem to have any territorial jurisdiction. They seemed rather to consist of spontaneous groupings of people who came together in order to worship with their friends and relatives. It is interesting to note that the division of Rome by Pope Fabian into seven ecclesial districts in the middle of the third century, for the purpose of better serving the poor, was realized along territorial lines, but this in no way affected the non-territorial division of the Christian population of the city into the various *tituli.*

With the movement of Christianity into the country, new forms of Church life and Church policy began to evolve. As soon as a rural church attained a certain size and significance, a bishop was commonly installed there; he was normally considered a subordinate of the nearby urban

1. Cf. K. Baus, *Handbook of Church History,* Vol. I, New York: Herder and Herder, 1964, pp. 346-355.

bishop. These rural bishops or *chorepiscopi* were gradually eliminated in the third and fourth centuries and replaced by priests. After the liberation of the Church under Constantine, rural parishes in the West were ruled by priests from the *presbyterium* of the nearby urban church, while in the cities priests were in charge of the various titular churches. At the beginning of the fourth century, the number of such *tituli* in Rome had grown to twenty-five.[2] At the end of the fourth century and during the fifth century, the priests in charge of the rural churches took up residence in the country and received more and more jurisdiction over their parishioners from the bishops. In the fifth century, prior to the disintegration of the Roman Empire, the property of the Church both in the cities and in the country was held in patrimony by the community and administered by the bishop.[3] It was he who appointed presbyters and deacons to the various communities within his jurisdiction, and it was he who provided for their material well-being. He bore the principal responsibility for the management and maintenance of Church property and buildings. From all that we are able to discern, the priests serving in the cities lived something of a common life, while those in the country, for the most part, did not. The authority of the bishop, however, was clearly recognized, not only in terms of the apportionment of clerical personnel, but also in the management of ecclesial property and in the distribution of revenues from that property. This seems to have been the situation in the churches of the West prior to the decomposition of Roman law and Roman order in the sixth and seventh centuries.

2. *The Modification of Parish Life and Structure Under the Gallic and Germanic Influences*

The upheavals of the sixth, seventh, and eighth centuries, which brought about a whole new social, economic, and political order for Western Europe, also had an enormous effect upon parish life and parish structures.[4] Beginning with the Merovingians, and particularly with Charles Martel (714-741), Church property was secularized and removed from the control of the bishops. The rural churches, which were public ecclesiastical property under Roman law, now became privately owned, and, to an ever greater extent, privately controlled. The transfer of parish churches, first in the country and then in the towns, into the hands of private land owners between 650 and 850, transformed the entire fabric of Church life in Europe and the British Isles. The popes and local bishops fought vigorously against this development, but the trend could not be reversed. The evils that came out of this system of privately owned churches were profound and almost incalculable. As a matter of fact, we are suffering even today from some of

2. J. Gaudemet, *L'Eglise dans l'empire romain,* Sirey, 1957, p. 372.

3. *Ibid.*, pp. 299-311.

4. Cf. W. Croce, in *The Parish, From Theology to Practice,* Hugo Rahner, ed., Westminster, Md.: Newman, 1958, pp. 13-16.

the dire effects of this modification. The parish churches became, as a result, subjected to the authority of the local lords or property owners. After all, they were the ones who owned the lands and the buildings, and consequently they assumed the authority to select and provide for the candidates for pastoral offices. The churches were run, to a great extent, according to their wishes. The local bishops had less and less power over the conduct of the parishes and over the parish priests. They were no longer nominated and paid by the bishop, they were chosen and salaried by the local lay lord or property holder.

It would take too long and, indeed, be much too painful to recount all of the ills that have resulted from the system of the *eigenkirchen*. The selection of clerical office holders on the part of the lay lords was done, in many if not in most cases, according to their own aims and purposes, rather than according to the pastoral needs of the people. The custom of common life broke down with the introduction of the benefice system, which was one of the emergents of the secularization of the Church property. The conferral of a pastoral office was accompanied by the giving of a right to receive a fixed revenue from the property owner. The pastor's prerogatives and his income were then tied to the land. The territorial principle prevailed in the determination of the jurisdiction and the prerogatives of the parochial office holder. The bishop's control over the selection of ministerial candidates was reduced to the point where almost indescribable abuses could grow up all over Europe. Men who were not able, must less prepared, to serve the Christian needs of others in a ministerial capacity became more the rule than the exception. This whole new pattern of Church life and Church organization brought about a general disintegration of pastoral care and responsibility. Countless efforts were made, particularly during the ninth century, to cope with these abuses, but to very little avail. It was not until the instigation of the Gregorian Reform in the second half of the eleventh century that powerful influence from Rome could be brought to bear upon the deteriorating situation.[5] It was Alexander III (1159-1181) who attempted to change the juridical ground of the right of patronage of the lay lords. He determined that the *jus patronatus* was a *jus spirituali annexum,* and consequently it fell within the ambit of Church law. Therefore the Church's norms regarding the selection and training of candidates for the ministry and the articulation of ministerial responsibilities on the level of the parish had to be obeyed and respected by the lay property owners, since these matters constituted a large part of their obligations as members of the Christian society.

In spite of the canonical modifications instigated by Gratian and completed by Alexander III, the difficulties continued. Under the private church

5. Cf. Fliche, *La Réforme grégorienne (Histoire de l'Eglise,* vol. VIII) Paris: Bloud & Gay, 1950, pp. 95-106.

system, the *bannus parochialis* prevailed.[6] The pastor of any given territory had exclusive rights over his subjects. It was necessary for them to worship in the parish church, to confess before the parish priest, to receive their Easter Communion from his hands, and to be married and buried by him. In most cases, if one went to another church he was not admitted into the worshiping community. When shifts in population enlarged the numbers in a given parish, the pastor was loathe to take an assistant since this would normally mean that his already meager income would have to be shared by another.

These unfortunate conditions were much more prevalent in the rural areas and the small towns than in the growing cities. In the ninth and tenth centuries, a good number of cathedral and collegiate chapters were formed in the larger urban centers of Western Europe. The members of these chapters lived celibate communal lives, whereas the priests stationed in the rural districts and the small villages were very often married.

During the Middle Ages and, indeed, up to relatively recent times, it was the parish priest who had the right to appoint assistants and to dismiss them. It was he who determined their income and the conditions under which they lived. One need hardly note that the plight of these assistant pastors was often miserable at best.[7]

The rise of the mendicant communities in the thirteenth and fourteenth centuries created no end of tension, since their pastoral efforts brought them into conflict with the exclusive jurisdiction of the parish priests. The popes continued to give more and more jurisdiction to the mendicants in order that they might teach and administer the sacraments to the needy, the ignorant, and the deprived, but this intrusion into their authority was not accepted by the local priests, especially in the light of their traditionally exclusive parochial prerogatives.

The changes which the parochial system underwent under the Frankish and the Germanic influences resulted in great harm for the faithful. Almost all these developments briefly referred to were gravely disadvantageous in terms of sound and healthy parochial life. It is no wonder that after the high Middle Ages Christendom was ripe for revolution.

3. The Reformation of Parish Life—Trent to the Present

One of the primary disciplinary objectives of the Council of Trent was the strengthening of the Ordinary's shepherding power within his diocese. The lines of communication between the bishop and his parish priests were to be improved and expanded in order that true pastoral care could be restored. Each diocese was to be divided into parishes in such a way that every parish

6. Cf. A. Blochlinger, *The Modern Parish Community,* New York: Kenedy, 1965, pp. 73-75.

7. *Ibid.,* pp. 80-82.

priest would be able to get to know his people. There was to be but one pastor in each parish, and no one was to hold the title to more than one parish at one time. It was not clearly established by Trent, however, that parish membership should be determined exclusively on the basis of the territorial principle. Territorial parishes were certainly preferred, but other kinds of parochial units were also envisioned as possibilities.

The celebrated *bannus parochialis* was weakened somewhat by Trent, but was generally left intact. In the seventeenth century, Clement X (1670-76) watered down somewhat the exclusive parochial prerogatives by acknowledging the rights of the faithful to receive the sacraments, in certain circumstances, from someone other than their parish priest.[8] It should also be mentioned that the Council of Trent did not substantially alleviate the plight of the assistant priests. They remained under the almost absolute control of their pastors. It must be said nonetheless that, as a result of the legislation of Trent, there was a great deal of improvement in parochial life in the West. Many of the atrocious abuses of the late Middle Ages were eliminated, and the teaching and sanctifying functions of ministry were performed with considerably greater effectiveness.

The vitality of the pastoral mission, however, was not able to develop, in the centuries after Trent, to the point where it could cope with the thundering social and cultural changes brought about in the nineteenth century by the industrial revolution. It is difficult to underestimate the degree to which the Western world was transformed by the economic revolution of that century. After 1830, the migration into the towns and cities increased at an almost unchartable rate. The large cities grew even larger, while the number and structure of the parishes did not change appreciably. In European cities like Paris, Brussels, Essen, Vienna, and Milan, it was not uncommon between 1850 and 1900 for parishes to average between 25,000 and 35,000 parishioners each.[9] A condition was created which made the ordinary pastoral care of souls simply impossible. In spite of these population shifts, there were no significant changes in the structures of the parish.

The 1917 Code set forth legislative patterns for parish life that can now be judged to have been inadequate. There is in the Code a further movement away from the traditionally exclusive parochial prerogatives.[10] Although it is true that according to canon 94, §1-3, a Catholic acquires his parish by virtue of his place of residence, it must be noted that canon 467, §2, leaves people relatively free to attend Mass, receive the Eucharist, to confess, and receive their instructions somewhere else.

Hence, insofar as Canon law itself authorizes the admonition of the faithful to

8. *Ibid.*, p. 90.

9. *Ibid.*, pp. 99-105. In the United States, a similar development has taken place within the past two generations. Cf. J. T. Ellis, *American Catholicism*, Chicago: University of Chicago Press, 1969, pp. 124-130.

10. S. Sipos, *Enchiridion Juris Canonici*, Rome: Herder, 1954, pp. 265-6

> take part in the parochial life, this admonition can concern only a 'frequent' participation . . . and may be given only if the parishioner does not thereby experience any additional inconvenience.[11]

The Second Vatican Council did not address itself to the matter of the parish principle. It did, however, broaden the possibilities for more frequent exceptions to the territorial principle which was so strongly emphasized in the 1917 Code. In paragraph 23 of the Decree on the Pastoral Office of Bishops in the Church, bishops are given the right to provide a distinctive parochial atmosphere for different nationalities and language groups. Nothing was said, however, about the possibility of gathering together parochial communities on the basis of any other criteria than territory, rite, or language. In the light of the changing patterns of human life, especially in the cities, the strong emphasis in present law upon the territorial principle as the basis of the formation of parishes no longer seems viable.

A similar judgment can be rendered with regard to canons 464, §1, and 467, §1, which outline the basic tasks of the parish ministry. The parish can no longer be looked upon as being responsible for the whole gamut of the *cura animarum.* Ministerial service in our time has become entirely too sophisticated for the parish priests to be able to handle any more than a small segment of it. To continue to live with the presumption that the local parish should still constitute the ordinary source of the full range of ministerial service for the great numbers of our Catholic people, especially those living in the urban areas, is foolhardy and unreal. It is true that the development of various forms of diocesan ministerial service in the United States since the 1917 Code in the areas of social action and education have lifted a number of responsibilities from the parish. Nonetheless, too many of us continue to live with the idea that the ordinary source of pastoral care, of whatever variety, is the parish priest or priests. This, I submit, is no longer a valid presupposition.

Finally, the relationship between the pastors and the assistant pastors, as outlined in the 1917 Code, is patronizing and seriously detrimental to their functional efficiency and mutual personal growth. The prescriptions of canon 476 place the *vicarius cooperator* literally under the thumb of the pastor. It is true that the assistant pastor is assigned by the bishop and that his status is guaranteed in the common law more clearly than before. But his situation in law remains basically that of a minor, in spite of the fact that the norms of the Code require him to be a professional. Canon 476, §7, directs that he should be treated *paterne* by the pastor. This directive might have been acceptable more than a generation ago, but it can only be looked upon as obsolete in our day.

By virtue of paragraph 21, §3, of *Ecclesiae Sanctae,* the regulation of canon 460, §2 (requiring no more than one pastor in any parish) can be put aside in favor of a collegial organization of the parish ministry. According

11. K. Rahner, *Theological Investigations,* Vol. II, Baltimore: Helicon, 1963, p. 293.

to this *motu proprio* of August 6, 1966, local Ordinaries have full authority to modify substantially the canon law on parishes if the need should be present. The paragraph cited above reads as follows:

> The bishop of the diocese on his own authority can establish or suppress parishes or *change them in any way* after consultation with the council of priests, in such a way, however, that, if there be agreement between the Apostolic See and the civil government, or rights acquired by other physical or moral persons, the matter be suitably settled with them by the competent authority.

The power of the local bishop to set aside the common law governing parishes and the rights and duties of pastors is now available in cases of proved need. The only requirement is that the bishop consult first with his council of priests. The wording of the paragraph of *Ecclesiae Sanctae* obviously provides that the bishop can change *on his own authority* the laws regarding parishes *in any way*. For example, if he should decide that it is necessary for him to constitute all of his parishes served by more than one priest as team parishes in the full sense, he could, by virtue of this new norm, disregard the prescriptions of canon 460, §2, as long as an established pastoral need can be demonstrated.

Proposals for the Reform of Parish Structures

In the light of this background, historical and legal, I would like to present the following proposals for the modification of the structures of the parochial ministry. These proposals represent only a partial response to the present needs for parish reorganization. Practically nothing is said here regarding the function and shape of parish councils and the role of the layman in parish life. These are also matters of extreme concern, but not everything can be done at once.

1. It is necessary that the entire diocesan shepherding commitment be thought out again and reorganized in a thorough fashion. This, it seems to me, is the proper role of the diocesan senate of priests. At the present time, certain ministerial services are being provided on a diocesan basis, while the majority of them remain the responsibility of the parishes. This balance should be changed radically. The shepherding responsibilities in the areas of secondary religious education, adult education, therapeutic counseling, marriage counseling, and vocational counseling should be constituted as an integral part of the diocesan ministerial commitment. These services can no longer be provided adequately in every parish because they require particular talents and specialized training. These services should be provided on a regional basis within the diocese, rather than on a parochial basis.

The services which can be rendered adequately on the level of the parish should be cared for there. The primary responsibility of the parochial ministry should be the ordinary preaching and elementary catechesis, liturgical celebrations of sufficient variety and vitality, and the organization of the local works of Christian charity. A more definite delineation of shepherding responsibilities would not only contribute to the efficiency of the overall ministerial mission within the diocese but would do much to eliminate what is perhaps the basic reason for the growing identity crisis among our diocesan priests. We cannot expect them to be masters of everything, and as long as we do in fact presume that they can do practically everything, they will be frustrated in the living out of their roles and in the determination of their functions.

Briefly then, let me recommend that the entire shepherding commitment of the diocese be spelled out by the priests' senate in such a way that those services which are to be the responsibility of the diocese as such be more sharply distinguished from those services which are to fall upon the individual parishes. In the light of my recommendations above, the diocesan services should be expanded, while the parochial services should be reduced.

2. After the reapportionment of the shepherding functions on the level of the diocese has been accomplished, the principle of collegiality, so magnificently extended into all sectors of Church life by Cardinal Suenens in his recent book, *Coresponsibility in the Church,* should be applied to all of these various ranges of priestly mission. Whenever a given service—be it on the level of the diocese, a region of the diocese, or within the local parish—requires or involves a number of priests, the organization of this apostolate should have a collegial character. This is particularly crucial regarding organization on the level of the parish. Cardinal Suenens has stated the following with regard to the present relationship between the pastors and associate pastors:

> Canonically speaking, the pastor is everything, and the curates are meant to help carry out his plan: there is no true coresponsibility. In our existing legislation, curates have no status and no direct responsibility. This is a situation which opposes the awakening and the development of their personality as much as it blocks the realization of any efficacious pastoral activity.[12]

One of the strongest mandates of the *Decree on the Ministry and Life of Priests* concerns the need for priests, especially those engaged in the parochial ministry, to work in an atmosphere of mutual trust, acceptance, understanding, and fraternity. Only in this fashion will the responsibilities of the ministry be fulfilled with reasonable adequacy. With growing awareness that there is all too often tension and a lack of cooperation where there should be harmony and teamwork, the following observations are set forth in order that the relationships on the parochial level may be more maturely determined and more profitably lived.

I submit that both the pastor and the associate pastor be given the same formal authority on the level of shepherding responsibility by virtue of their

12. L. J. Suenens, *Coresponsibility in the Church,* New York: Herder and Herder, 1968, p. 131.

appointment by the Ordinary. The pastor would possess, in addition, administrative authority by virtue of his appointment by the local bishop.[13] By shepherding authority is meant here the power to teach, to perform the actions of sacrament and worship, and to direct the Church people in their individual and communal exercise of the corporal and spiritual works of mercy. In these areas, there should be no formal distinction between the power of the pastor and the power of the associate pastor. The administrative authority of the pastor, on the other hand, would be really only a service function for the shepherding authority. The one having the power of administration would be expected to serve the others in the sense that it would be his responsibility to coordinate the exercise of the shepherding functions for the members of the ministry serving that parish. Once that service has been performed, and until such time as some sort of disharmony arises in the exercise of the various shepherding prerogatives, the administrative authority would not be operative.

> The fundamental role of the leader is to make collegiality possible. He is its guarantee. He is there primarily so that each member may be part of a whole, and thus assume full responsibility within and toward a common effort. The role of the one in charge is not that of making a 'personal' decision after having taken the advice of others into account. For in that case it would still be 'his' decision. His role is rather to make it possible, insofar as this depends upon him, for there to be a common decision which commits each member to the decision, in such a way that they are solidly behind it and willing to accept all the consequences of what has been decided together.[14]

The total shepherding responsibility should be assessed by the pastor and the assistant pastor, and then divided specifically by mutual agreement with the clear understanding that full shepherding authority is possessed by each, commensurate with his respective areas of responsibility. The character of the relational climate between pastor and associate pastor would, I submit, be far more healthy and productive if it were established according to the above guidelines. Such an approach would more effectively insure that each and every member of the ministerial team serving in a given parish would come to see himself as an adult professional, dedicated, along with his brothers, to the service of the Church people of the latter twentieth century.

3. The final proposal for the reform of parochial structures arises out of the increasing obsolescence of the territorial principle as the norm for the determination of parish affiliation. There is no doubt that the strict application of the territorial principle makes for good order. However, the needs of the modern urban Christian have become so varied, and the spectrum of the styles of Christian commitment has broadened so much in the past decade or two, that a new approach is imperative.

13. Let it be noted here that this distinction between shepherding authority and administrative authority has at present neither an incontrovertible canonical nor theological foundation.

14. L. J. Suenens, *op. cit.*, p. 132.

The fact that a person (or a family) lives in a certain area in no way insures that his (or their) needs regarding basic catechesis, worship, and the direction of the exercise of charity are similar to those of their neighbors. There was a day when this was pretty much the case, but not so today, especially in our urban centers. As Colin Williams has said, ". . . people no longer live where they live."

> By an accelerating centrifugal motion, more and more aspects of life have been separated from the community of residence—most of government has gone, with advanced education, health institutions, business, communications media, leisure activities. To a great extent our decisions are made, our energies expended and our anxieties are formed, away from home. The Church, however, is still centered on residence, and has this time apparently failed to change its shape to meet the changing patterns of secular life.[15]

Strictly territorial groupings of the faithful are frequently artificial and deadening. For how many of our younger people in urban America is the local parish the center and the wellspring of rich and dynamic faith-life? Some years ago, Father Greeley spoke, in this connection, of the rise of the "new communities" in our country and praised them because without these new groupings, countless young, educated Catholics would be deprived of the opportunity to express forcefully and to experience the corporate dimension of their Christian faith.[16]

The underground parishes and the floating parishes are facts of our time which have been the products of real needs. Most of these communities are composed of good, intelligent, responsible people for whom the local parish no longer has much meaning. These facts should not be disregarded. The Church has operated too frequently, down through the years, oblivious of the exigencies of the real situation, and these mistakes have been costly indeed.

The experience of the past five years has proved, I believe, that the underground parish movement will never affect more than a very small percentage of our Catholic people. At the same time, the shift away from strictly territorial parochial groupings has to be achieved on a far broader scale to answer our real contemporary needs. The solution, I feel, lies in allowing for, and even encouraging, the development of various styles of parochial life within the larger regions of a diocese. No parish should attempt to respond to the needs of all of the people living within its territorial limits, catechetically, liturgically, or through its social action programs. If it does, it will end up with no discernible corporate identity. Each parish, within a larger region of a diocese, should be allowed to develop its own style which would appeal to a certain segment of the people living in that

15. C. Williams, *Where in the World?*, New York: National Council of Churches, 1963, pp. 7-8.

16. A. Greeley, "The New Community," *The Critic*, June-July, 1966, pp. 32-37.

general region. One parish, for example, could appeal to those who strongly feel the need for innovation and new approaches in liturgy and catechesis. Another parish could attempt to respond to and serve those who are more inclined to the traditional patterns of worship and proclamation. A third parish in the same region could place a strong emphasis in its programs on the social implications of the Gospel and so forth.

This arrangement must not be imposed from above in some wooden fashion. It will grow and flower by itself if people are left to affiliate with the parish whose programs best respond to their Christian needs in the areas of catechesis, liturgy, and charitable service. This is not a new idea. A pastoral approach such as this has been employed by a number of Christian denominations in our country for some time, especially in the shaping of the urban ministry. There are dangers involved in moving away from our strong Catholic commitment to uniformity, but these are minimal, I believe, when compared to the enormous risks emerging from a rigid, unbending attachment to a policy of "morphological fundamentalism" (Hans Schmidt). We should have learned by this time that uniformity does not necessarily bring about unity. As a matter of fact, uniformity normally deadens, while unity demands vitality and richness of life as an indispensable predisposition. Thomas O'Dea, in his fine book, *The Catholic Crisis,* makes the following observations regarding the new surge of structural evolution which has been precipitated by Vatican II:

> A long period of realignment, of deinstitutionalization and reinstitutionalization, of conflict lies ahead. Yet that in itself is not to be deplored. At worst it but represents the continuation in an open, more healthy form of the condition that has long existed beneath the repression and surface calm of an authoritarian atmosphere and structure. More hopefully viewed, it may be said to represent the coming of life and vitality to renew the body of the old Church. What is most significant is that the *aggiornamento* forces have won legitimation in the Council and that they maintain that status. It is doubtful whether all the attempts of the frightened or desperate can stop this long process once it has started. Next, it is very important that the unity of the Church be preserved; conflict should remain a form of dialogue and assume a condition in which freer and more profound dialogue can develop. What is sometimes called the 'old Church' and the 'new Church' must remain one Church so that in facing these great problems all the resources of the many-sided Catholic tradition will be involved.[17]

17. T. O'Dea, *The Catholic Crisis,* Boston: Beacon Press, 1968, p. 1958.

Case 8

Pastors

On January 1, 1979, the reigning Roman pontiff issued the encyclical *Christus Vir,* which declared that homosexual relationships which included sexual expression were contrary to Roman Catholic moral teaching. The issue of homosexuality had been debated for a number of years. A special papal commission had been appointed to study the issue. The secret report of the majority, which had leaked to the press, favored the recognition of the goodness of permanent homosexual unions and the possible blessing and recognition of such unions. The pontiff sided with the minority's absolute condemnation and so issued his encyclical.

Comments around the world varied. The bishops of the United States issued a joint communique declaring adherence to *Christus Vir.* Nonetheless, numerous theologians, clergy, religious, and laity, including a group of priests in the Ames Diocese, publicly spoke against the encyclical. The Ames' group issued a public statement disagreeing with *Christus Vir.* Among them was diocesan Fr. James Mallone, pastor of St. Mary's Church in Ames.

In response to the statement, the bishop informed the group, including Father Mallone, that they must retract their statement within ten days and cease speaking against *Christus Vir.* Further, the priests would be suspended of all faculties within the diocese until a public retraction was made. When the group refused, the bishop suspended the priests' faculties, including Father Malone's, to preach, celebrate the Eucharist publicly, and minister the sacrament of reconciliation, except in urgent cases. No other canonical action was taken by the bishop.

Father Mallone, as pastor, is determined to establish his right of dissent within the Church. He joined other members of the group in appealing the bishop's decision. He has asked you to be his ecclesiastical advocate.

Exercise

As advocate you must decide the canonical effect of the suspension on Father Mallone, clearly establish the canonical procedure for appeal, and prepare a brief in defense. However, the brief must anticipate the bishop's argument against Father Mallone. Finally after weighing the merits of the case, you must decide the case.

References

Code of Canon Law, canons 145, 451, 461-70, 1344, 2157-67, 2186-91, 2278-84.

Decree on the Ministry and Life of Priests, Vatican II, par. 2.

Decree on the Pastoral Office of Bishops in the Church, Vatican II, par. 31.

"Ecclesiae Sanctae" (August 6, 1966) I, 20, *Canon Law Digest,* VI, 264.

New Catholic Encyclopedia. 2nd ed., s. v. "Pastors."

Episcopal Conferences

Frederick R. McManus

Conferences of bishops, principally national episcopal conferences, were given definitive canonical status in the Church only in 1965 by Vatican Council II (decree on the pastoral office of bishops, *Christus Dominus*). Conferences had been recognized, however, for several generations, and some had canonical statutes approved by the respective conference and the Apostolic See. Such assemblies of bishops, as distinct from more formal particular councils, appear to have originated in Belgium in 1830, in Germany in 1848, in Austria in 1849, in Italy (regional rather than national meetings) from the same year. Their importance was recognized, but only at the level of ecclesiastical provinces, in the 1917 Code of Canon Law (c. 292).

The first such assembly of bishops in the United States took place in September 1919, although there had been annual meetings of the metropolitan archbishops in the preceding decades. (Subsequently the American episcopate met in annual conference but transacted business chiefly under the formality of the National Catholic Welfare Conference, Inc.; after Vatican Council II the episcopal conference was reorganized under the title, National Conference of Catholic Bishops, and the NCWC was succeeded by the United States Catholic Conference.)

PRECEDENTS

The theological and canonical precedents of the modern episcopal conference are found in the collegial (conciliar or synodal) exercise of church authority by the bishops of a region or country, especially in the assemblies of bishops of the patriarchates and provinces; the development is also related to the more personal responsibility of patriarchs, primates, and metropolitans for the several local churches or dioceses. The basis for the conference of bishops as a mode of collegial exercise of episcopal responsibility was described in the conciliar constitution on the Church: "By divine Providence it has come about that various Churches established in different places have in the course of time coalesced into several groups, organically united. These groups, while preserving the unity of faith and the unique divine constitution of the universal Church, have their own discipline, their own liturgical usage, and their own theological and spiritual heritage. Some of these churches, notably the ancient patriarchal churches, like parent stems of the faith, have begotten other, daughter churches. . . . In like manner the episcopal conferences of today are able to render a manifold and fruitful assistance, so that the collegial sense may be concretely applied'' (*Lumen Gentium,* no. 23).

The origin of the canonical authority of conferences, whether in the action of a general council or pope conferring such authority or in the innate constitution of the local churches in their regional groupings and relationships, was deliberately left open. Historically such bodies as particular synods of bishops arose from the communion that is of the essence of the Church, thus having a sure theological basis. As canonical institutes, episcopal conferences have a responsibility that is determined from time to time by the written law and by custom.

The contemporary determination of episcopal conferences—as continuing moral and canonical entities and not as mere meetings—is found in the conciliar decree *Christus Dominus* (nos. 37-38, somewhat further specified by the apostolic letter of Pope Paul VI, *Ecclesiae sanctae,* of Aug. 5, 1966, I, 41). The function of the conferences is described as the collegial exercise of the pastoral office for the good of the Church in the whole nation or territory and for the good of the individual churches. All bishops who excercise the ministry in the territory are members as are other local ordinaries except vicars general; titular bishops who do not have an office and papal legates are not members. More important, each conference determines whether bishops other than local ordinaries and coadjutors are to have voting rights. Other provisions describe the enactment of statutes for the government of conferences (which require the confirmation of the Apostolic See); the need for a permanent, central council or committee, episcopal commissions, and a secretary general; the possibility of a union of conferences of several nations (either bringing together conferences which retain their autonomy or, in the case of smaller countries, substituting for individual conferences).

The conciliar decree encouraged similar developments for collaboration among bishops of various Eastern Churches in the same territory; the bishops of Eastern Churches in full communion with the Catholic Church are members of the respective national conference itself. Postconciliar Roman decrees ordinarily mention that the patriarchal synod of each Eastern Church has a responsibility parallel to that of the Western episcopal conferences. The conciliar decree also encouraged relations among conferences of various nations, but these relations were restricted in *Ecclesiae sanctae* so that common action requires prior notice to the Apostolic See.

Competence and Limitations

The competence of episcopal conferences extends to the entire common good of the local churches which constitute it, and its most effective apostolic effectiveness may be achieved by the moral consensus of the members, through pastoral or disciplinary agreements and through statements of a doctrinal or pastoral character. A special question arises, however, concerning the decisions of an episcopal conference which have juridically binding force; these may be legislative enactments and thus be a part of the particular canon law, or they may be juridically binding decisions of an administrative or even judicial nature. Closely related to this question is the requirement, for all juridically binding decisions, of a two-thirds majority vote of all the members who have a deliberative (as opposed to a merely consultative) vote, rather than the usual canonical norm of decisions by a majority of those present and voting; coupled with this is the requirement that such decisions be confirmed by the Apostolic See. This latter provision does not alter the nature of such decrees which remain the decisions of the conference and not papal law, but confirmation is a necessary condition. (In some postconciliar papal documents, national adaptations of such disciplinary matters as penitential days and procedures for mixed marriages are said to require only subsequent notification of the Apostolic See rather than any formal confirmation.)

Both national or regional councils, also called plenary councils, and episcopal conferences may consider any matter and issue decisions, statements, guidelines, and the like. Episcopal conferences, however, are unlike councils in that they may not issue decisions with juridical force binding upon the faithful and hierarchy (clergy) of their territory except in specified matters. This limitation upon the legislative and other related canonical authority was imposed because of fear that the authority of conferences (whether innate authority or that conferred by a general council or pope) might be an encroachment upon the integrity of the local church and especially upon the individual bishop's pastoral office; the limitation also reflects a fear of encroachment upon papal authority.

Nevertheless, the areas of church discipline where conferences may, under conditions mentioned above, make laws and other binding decisions are very large. They are frequently mentioned in the decrees of Vatican Council II and in almost every postconciliar papal document on church discipline.

The principle is explicitly enunciated in *Christus Dominus,* no. 38, 4: the force of canonical obligation extends to those cases "in which (a) it is prescribed by the common law or (b) it is established by special mandate of the Apostolic See on its own initiative or (c) it is established by the Apostolic See upon petition of the conference itself." Thus, while the scope of canonical decision-making authority was strictly limited to the enumerated cases, no limitations are placed upon the increase of such cases, which may come about either in the common law (which means in this instance the legislation of the general council and the postconciliar papal legislation) or by special decision of the Apostolic See (if, for example, a conference receives the faculty to enact its own procedural legislation, subject to Roman confirmation).

In the conciliar legislation, liturgical discipline is frequently assigned to the authority of the episcopal conferences, since the 1963 constitution on the liturgy (no. 22) anticipated the later determination of *Christus Dominus*. The episcopal conferences may thus make laws concerning liturgical adaptations (*Sacrosanctum Concilium,* nos. 37-40), including the creation of new national rituals (*ibid.,* 63 b). Although the conciliar decrees do not mention the role of the conferences in making regulations about the distribution of ordained ministers, *Ecclesiae sanctae* of 1966 states that "to enact ordinances and to publish norms for the bishops" in this matter (1, 2); they are also competent "to enact appropriate ordinances" to impose subsidies on dioceses in favor of the apostolate of charity or of churches in need (1, 5). These, however, are only instances of a constantly growing scope of competence of episcopal conferences, and it may be expected that in the redaction or revision of each part of the canon law, more cases will be assigned to their legislative and other jurisdictional authority. Even those canonists who would prefer to remove the limitations upon the competence of conferences insist that their legislative role is completely secondary to their pastoral responsibility, which may be exercised in most circumstances without resorting to the enactment of juridically binding norms.

Case 9

The Authority of the Episcopal Conference

On May 29, 1969, the Sacred Congregation for Divine Worship issued the decree *Memoriale Domini,* which stated that each episcopal conference could seek approval from the Apostolic See for the reception of Communion in the hand. The decree required a two-thirds majority to pass a resolution to seek approval from the Apostolic See.

In many areas of the United States, persons were already receiving Communion in the hand. Many bishops favored formalizing this manner of reception of Communion, especially because it seemed to be emerging as an area of conflict among various groups within the local churches. However, each time the resolution to seek approval of Communion in the hand came before the United States bishops, it failed to receive the requisite two-thirds vote, although a majority of bishops voted in its favor each time.

Bishop Thomas Smith, whose diocese bordered Canada, had been asked by various priests to approve Communion in the hand within the diocese. Such practice was already approved in Canada, which caused particular problems for the border communities. Further, the students at the Catholic student centers within the diocese had been receiving Communion in such a manner for over five years. Finally, if the practice were approved, people would have the option to receive in the traditional manner or in the hand. This, hopefully, would calm the "obedience argument" brewing among certain members of the clergy and laity.

Bishop Smith favors the idea, but realizes that the National Conference of Catholic Bishops has not approved the option.

Exercise

1. Advise Bishop Smith concerning the authority of the Episcopal Conference and his relationship thereto.

2. Advise Bishop Smith concerning his authority to approve the practice within his diocese without the approval of the Episcopal Conference and/or the Apostolic See.

References

"De Episcoporum Muneribus" (June 15, 1966), *Canon Law Digest* VI, 394.

Decree on the Pastoral Office of Bishops in the Church, Vatican II, "Christus Dominus," pars, 8-10, 36-38.

"Memoriale Domini" (May 29, 1969), *Canon Law Digest* VII, 652.

D. INSTITUTES OF CONSECRATED LIFE

The Spirit of the Proposed New Law for Institutes of Consecrated Life*

Francis G. Morrisey

It is now some twelve years since Pope John XXIII established the Pontifical Commission for the Revision of the Code of Canon Law.[1] During this time the members of the Commission and the consultors appointed to assist them in the preparation of the new law have worked diligently to carry out the task assigned to them by Popes John and Paul VI. In the last few years, Episcopal Conferences have begun to see the first results of the work carried out by the Commission. To date, some four texts have been distributed to the bishops for comments, and many other documents are now in the final drafting process. Canonists have already examined texts relating to the Fundamental Law of the Church, Administrative Procedure, Delicts and Sanctions, and Sacramental Law. The contents of some of the other schemas are found, at least indirectly, in accounts published in the Commission's review, *Communicationes,*[2] and in various scientific journals.

The proposed new law on Institutes of Consecrated Life fits into this last category at the present time. In spite of the fact that a first definitive text has not yet been distributed to the Episcopal Conferences and to other organisms for comment, we are able to discern with a good deal of certainty, the orientations already accepted by the Commission and incorporated into the preliminary drafts. I would refer above all to the writings in *Communicationes,*[3] and to studies published in *Periodica,*[4] *Studia Canonica,*[5]

*Paper presented at a session on the law for institutes of consecrated life, under the auspices of the Canadian Religious Conference, Ottawa, May 5-7, 1975.

1. Cf. *Communicationes,* 1 (1969), p. 35.
2. Pontifica Commissio Codici Juris Canonici Recognoscendo, *Communicationes,* Romae, Typis polyglottis Vaticanis, 1969.
3. Cf. *ibid.,* 2 (1970), p. 168-181; 5 (1973), p. 47-69; 7 (1975), p. 63-92.
4. Jean Beyer, S.J., "De Institutorum vitae consecratae novo jure", in *Periodica,* 63 (1974), p. 145-168, 179-222; 64 (1975), p. 363-392.
5. Mark Said, O.P., "The Present State of the Reform of the Code Concerning the Section 'De Institutis Perfectionis' ", in *Studia Canonica,* 8 (1974), p. 213-235.

Review for Religious,[6] The Way,[7] and elsewhere. These reports, prepared by members of the sub-commission and by other canonists, show us the amount of work that has been carried out to date.

The draft document on the institutes of perfection will be unique in its category. Instead of proceeding in a somewhat patchwork fashion, as was the case for some of the other sub-commissions,[8] an entirely new text was prepared, based on the inspiration of the Council and of the post-conciliar legislation. The end result will raise a number of interesting questions since the new inspiration of this particular document will have to be felt in the other sectors of the law, or else we will have legislation in one area that will be quite out of touch with legislation in other parts of the Code. An example of this is to be found in *Communicationes* when referring to the canons on sacred worship.[9] It is stated there that theological principles are not to be retained in the new law unless they are necessary for a proper understanding of the text, while, in the section on institutes of consecrated life, a number of introductory "theological" canons are to be incorporated, giving a new thrust to all the law as we now have it.

In the following pages it is our purpose to comment on these proposed changes as they now stand. To some extent, this will be premature; yet, in other ways, because of the concordant writings of the commentators, we feel on secure ground. Any changes to be made in the draft, as it now stands, before it is to be distributed to the Conferences for comments would be minimal, since no further meetings of this sub-commission are scheduled for the immediate future.[10]

Our remarks will be divided into three sections. In the first part of this study, we shall examine the text itself, without reference to detailed contents; we shall then examine the proposed law, and, subsequently, give some comments on the work as it now stands. It is hoped that these remarks will enable us to appreciate more the work that went into the preparation of this document, and understand the impact of this new law, which, in the words of Father M. Said, is "a gift from God".[11]

I. The Text of the Proposed New Law for Institutes of Consecrated Life

A study of the text of the proposed new law could encompass the following perspectives: the preparation of the text, the various plans or divisions adopted, the principles to be applied in the drafting of the individual

6. Kevin D. O'Rourke, O.P., "The New Law for Religious: Principles, Content, Evaluation", in *Review for Religious,* 34 (1975), p. 23-49.

7. Jean Beyer, S.J., "Institutes of Perfection in the New Law of the Church", in *The Way, Supplement,* No. 13, 1971, p. 87-115.

8. Cf., for instance, *Schema documenti pontificii quo disciplina canonica de Sacramentis recognoscitur,* Romae, Typis polyglottis Vaticanis, 1975, 96 p.

9. Cf. *Communicationes,* 5 (1973), p. 43.

10. Cf. J. Beyer, "De Institutorum. . .", *loc. cit.,* p. 146; M. Said, *loc, cit.,* p. 221.

11. M. Said, *loc. cit.,* p. 235.

canons. Let us examine each of these points in order.

a. The Preparation of the Text

In the beginning, the sub-commission was known as the study group on the law for "religious"; the name was later changed to "institutes of perfection", in order to be applicable to those institutes which were not known as "religious", such as secular institutes, and others.[12] It was then proposed to change the name once more, so that it is now known as the sub-commission for the institutes of consecrated life.[13]

The sub-commission first began its discussions in 1966, and met on some fifteen occasions, for a total of 87 days of work.[14] Some 25 consultators have been designated to date to work on the preparation of the draft.[15] These simple facts are enough to show us the amount of work that went into the new document.

b. The Division of the Text

The plan that was to be followed in preparing the new text was first published in *Communicationes* in 1970.[16] At that time, it was proposed to have a number of introductory canons, then a general part providing those norms which were to be common to all institutes of consecrated life. This was to be followed by a second part containing prescriptions peculiar to certain forms of consecrated life. In 1971, the plan of the second section of the law was changed, and it is this revised division that has been adopted.

As it now stands, there would be six preliminary or introductory canons. The first section of the norms would contain some seven chapters: 1) constitution of institutes and their parts, 2) dependence of institutes upon ecclesiastical authority 3) government of institutes, 4) temporal goods and their administration, 5) admission into an institute, 6) the obligations of institutes and of their members, and 7) separation from an institute.

The second part of the law is to be divided into three chapters: 1) religious institutes, 2) institutes of united apostolic life, and 3) secular institutes.

As can be easily seen, there are both advantages and disadvantages to a division of this type. One of the most significant advantages is that the general canons, applicable to all institutes, may be simpler in form since they do not state to which category they are applicable. Indeed, after the recognition of secular institutes by Pope Pius XII in 1947,[17] the task of drafting general norms became even more complicated, because exceptions had to be made in each case for these new institutes. One disadvantage of the new division is that the norms governing a particular institute are going to

12. Cf. J. Beyer, "De Institutorum. . .", *loc. cit.*, p. 145.

13. M. Said, *loc. cit.*, p. 219.

14. J. Beyer, "De Institutorum. . .", *loc. cit.*, p. 146.

15. *Communicationes,* 1 (1969), p. 31; 5 (1973), p. 190-191.

16. *Ibid.*, 2 (1970), p. 175-176.

17. Pius XII, Constitution "Provida Mater Ecclesia", February 2, 1947, in *A.A.S.*, 39 (1947), p. 114-124.

be found in three places: the general canons, the special ones, and the particular law of the institute itself. Another disadvantage, which will be easily overcome in time, is the necessity of introducing an entirely new canonical vocabulary applicable to all forms of consecrated life; one example of this is the term "moderator" to replace "superior"; other cases would be the use of the word "member" for "religious", "candidate" for "novice", "incorporation" for "profession", and so forth.[18] A further disadvantage, and probably a more serious one, is that the flow of the law itself is impeded. For instance, after the canons on admission to the institute, one would expect to find those on profession. However, since the notion of profession is not equally applicable to all, these canons are to be found in the special norms, and, in their place, we find legislation referring simply to incorporation.

c. *The Principles to Be Applied in the New Law for Institutes of Consecrated Life*

In addition to the general principles accepted by the Synod of Bishops in 1967 and applicable to all the new law,[19] a number of additional guidelines were to be taken into consideration in drafting the new canons. Some of these could be considered to be fundamental, others of lesser importance.

i. *Fundamental Principles*

In his studies on the proposed draft, Father J. Beyer lists the following fundamental principles, expressed in the *Relatio* published in *Communicationes*:[20] the gift of consecrated life is to be aptly expressed, the proper spirit of each institute is to be fostered, the new law is to be flexible, allowing for adaptations, and, finally, the principles accepted by the second Vatican Council are to be observed and respected in the new law.

The purpose of the canons, in this perspective, is to foster the growth of the vocation given by God as a gift, to assist the workings of grace so that the perfection of charity will be more easily attained, and, once attained, preserved and protected. Thus, the theological elements must be combined with the juridical ones, and the pastoral aspects not neglected since juridical norms, though they do not contain the gifts and graces proper to the consecrated life, ought nevertheless to foster the growth of this divine vocation.[21]

The spirit of the Founder must be recognized in each institute, and this spirit sustained through praiseworthy traditions of the group. Thus, the common law will necessarily be limited to very broad or general principles, and sufficient latitude will have to be given in the particular law to express more clearly the special charism which will distinguish one community from

18. Cf. K. O'Rourke, *loc. cit.*, p. 29.
19. Cf. *Communicationes*, 1 (1969), p. 77-85.
20. Cf. J. Beyer, "De Institutorum. . .", *loc. cit.*, p. 153 sqq.
21. Cf. J. Beyer, "Institutes of Perfection. . .", *loc. cit.*, p. 92

another. The acceptance of this principle will help overcome a rather serious consequence of the 1901 *Normae* and the subsequent rules of 1921[22] whereby all constitutions were expected to follow a somewhat standard pattern, with the eventual result that the Constitutions and Rules of one community were almost identical with those of another institute having the same general purpose.

Constitutive principles, as proper to all institutes striving to obtain the perfection of the evangelical counsels, would have to be stated. Disciplinary norms, which follow upon these as a consequence, would have to take into account the principle of subsidiarity accepted by the 1967 Synod of Bishops.[23] If the norms remain general, the particular law will eventually override in importance the common law as it is now understood. This would mean that it would be considerably easier to incorporate any necessary changes in legislation without having recourse each time to the Holy See, and flexibility would be assured.

In the second Vatican Council, the principles of representation and participation of members in the affairs of the institute were approved by the Fathers. We have all lived through the application of these principles during the past ten years! Nevertheless, in spite of some disenchantment with this new form of participatory responsibility, it would have been a retrograde step to revert in the new law to the modes of application prevalent before the Council. As a result of this principle, power is not to be concentrated for too long a period in the hands of one individual; obedience is to be active and responsible; all the members are to cooperate together to promote the work of the Church. Each institute will have to define its own modes of participation and representation in accordance with a minimum number of general principles.

The application of these four fundamental principles will ensure that the law will be able to provide apt and appropriate means whereby the particular gift of the Spirit to each institute will be preserved and fostered.

ii. Additional Principles to Be Applied

Father Beyer[24] lists five additional principles that the Commission took into account as it proceeded with its work: 1) the diversity of the institutes and their specific form of life were to be maintained; 2) there must exist the greatest possible harmony between the common law and the particular law of each institute so that the common law would only prescribe that which is strictly necessary; 3) there must exist equality between masculine and feminine institutes with no distinction in law based on a differentiation of the sexes; 4) "the greatest possible respect should be accorded to the dignity

22. Cf. *A.A.S.*, 13 (1921), p. 312-319.

23. Cf. *Communicationes*, 1 (1969), p. 80-81.

24. "De Institutorum. . .", *loc. cit.*, p. 157 sqq.; "Institutes of Perfection. . .", *loc. cit.*, p. 92.

of the human person, his rights, his personal responsibilities, and his normal development, to enable him to achieve physical and psychological maturity";[25] and, finally, 5) "provision should be made in the general law for a just application of the principle of subsidiarity, leaving to each institute its own responsibility".[26]

Without unduly criticizing the text of the present canons on religious, since they were written for a different period of time, we can easily recognize that they did not meet with all of the criteria expressed in these principles. Some of the guidelines, such as the protection of the rights of individuals, are certainly found in the 1917 Code, and it would be ridiculous to state that they were *totally* absent. Nevertheless, the emphasis has now shifted, as times change, and it would indeed be rather difficult to find fault with the new principles as they are expressed.

Having examined the basic philosophy underlying the new text, we can now proceed to consider some of the principle prescriptions which it contains. This will be the object of the second part of this study.

II. The Contents of the Proposed New Law for Institutes of Consecrated Life

The contents of the proposed new law may be examined under three headings: the preliminary canons, the common norms, the particular legislation.

a. The Preliminary Canons

The purpose of the six preliminary canons is to describe and define the consecrated life, "a life devoted to a closer following of Christ through commitment to the evangelical counsels".[27] These canons are primarily theological in nature and contain a rich teaching that not only incorporates the conciliar thrust, but also provides a basis upon which the legislation is to be built.

The consecrated life is a stable form of life, by which the faithful, under the guidance of the Holy Spirit, through the profession of the evangelical counsels seek the perfection of charity in the service of the Kingdom of God, and become clear signs in the Church foretelling heavenly glory. The importance of the profession of the counsels is such that without them, there is no form of consecrated life recognized as such by the Church. The dominant characteristic, then, of consecrated life will not be life in common or any other factor, since these are not common to secular institutes, but the profession of the counsels, either explicitly or implicitly according to the Constitutions.[28]

The second canon refers to the charismatic state of those who are living

25. *Ibid.*, p. 92.
26. *Ibid.*
27. K. O'Rourke, *loc. cit.*, p. 29.
28. Cf. J. Beyer, "De Institutorum. . .", *loc. cit.*, p. 164.

the consecrated life. The state of consecrated life does not pertain by nature to the hierarchical structure of the Church; however, it is related to the life and holiness of the Church, and is to be held in esteem by all.

The third introductory canon concerns the evangelical counsels themselves. They are founded on the doctrine and example of Christ and constitute a divine gift which the Church has received from the Lord and which she forever preserves through His grace.

The fourth canon, based on the teachings of *Lumen Gentium,* No. 46, states the value of the profession of the counsels and the contribution that this form of life makes to the development of the human person. Those who profess the evangelical counsels do not become, by their consecration, strangers to their fellow men; rather, they cooperate spiritually with all of mankind through prayer, sacrifice and the spreading of the Gospel message.

In the fifth canon, the distinction between clerical and lay institutes, and between pontifical and diocesan ones is spelled out. Clerical institutes henceforth will be those which assume the exercise of sacred orders and have been recognized as such by the competent legislator.

Finally, the last canon refers to the equality that is to exist in law between masculine and feminine institutes, unless the context or nature of the case indicates otherwise.

These preliminary norms provide us with a number of elements that would have to be taken into account in developing any revitalized theology of the religious life. Father O'Rourke[29] lists some of these: the consecrated life is a *stable form* of life; it *dedicates* people to God who is loved above all things; it *orders* them by a new and special title to the honour of God, the salvation of the world, and the building up of the Church; it *enables* its members to seek the perfection of charity in service of the Kingdom of God and witness heavenly glory in the Church; it is *constituted* by the inspiration of the Holy Spirit; is canonically *erected* by competent ecclesiastical authority; is *accepted* by professing the evangelical counsels; and *unites* the faithful to the mystery of the Church in a special manner through charity to which the counsels lead.

It can be easily recognized, then, that these elements, to be incorporated into the general legislation of the Church, are not found as clearly expressed in the present law for religious.

b. Those Elements Common to Institutes of Perfection

It would not be possible, nor necessary, to comment in detail on the proposed new canons in this section. Fathers Beyer and O'Rourke have already done so in a succinct and clear manner. The best manner of proceeding would be, it seems, to signal out some of the principal trends to be found in each chapter to provide an overview of the major changes in spirit to be introduced.

29. *Loc. cit.,* p. 30.

The first chapter, on the constitution of institutes and their parts, contains a number of new prescriptions. One important change will be a recognition given to the Episcopal Conferences to approve the erection of new institutes, provided all unnecessary duplication is avoided. The particular law would determine the way in which an institute is to be divided into parts, either residences or larger administrative units. Changes in institutes which affect matters determined by the Holy See require the permission of the same Holy See. Suppression of an institute would belong to the Holy See, and not to the authority which first established it. Likewise, and most importantly, the Holy See would have the right to dispose of the property of a suppressed institute. This new prescription expresses more clearly the norms found in the present canons 498 and 1501. Property of the suppressed house should be distributed according to particular law and justice, the intentions of the donors being observed.

The characteristics of this first chapter are the application of the principle of subsidiarity, and an effort to decentralize institutions. Very few matters, for instance, require the consent of the Holy See; the particular law will determine the way in which many of the norms applicable to the erection of institutes and their parts are to be applied.

The second chapter on the dependence of institutes upon ecclesiastical authority, is one of two general chapters on government. It must be remembered that an institute of consecrated life is constituted for the service of the whole Church.[30] This explains why Church authorities have a right, in specified instances, to intervene to ensure the common good.

However, as a most important counterpart to this principle, another statement is made to the effect that institutes have the autonomy of internal government and of particular legislation, and this autonomy must be respected by all. This autonomy would extend, according to Father Beyer, to the right to preserve one's particular charism, to carry out one's work according to the approved statutes, and to be protected against undue intervention from outside sources.[31] This is not an infringement on the rights of the Church since the Constitutions, in virtue of which this apostolate is to be carried out, would have been approved by the competent ecclesiastical authorities.

In virtue of the new law, religious are subject to the Holy Father by their vow of obedience; this is the same as in the present law; they are also subject to the bishop according to the norms of law. Consent of the bishop would thus be required to transfer the motherhouse of the institute from one diocese to another. Pontifical institutes would remain subject to the local Ordinary in those matters pertaining to public worship and to the external and public works of the apostolate. The possibility of exemption is also mentioned in this section.

30. *Ibid.*, p. 32.

31. J. Beyer, "De Institutorum. . .", *loc. cit.*, p. 185.

The third chapter on the government of institutes concerns the authority given to moderators to govern individuals and groups within the community, carrying out their pastoral mission according to the particular laws of the institute.[32] Power will be defined in the context of service (Mt., 20, 26); moderators must strive to promote the human and Christian dignity of the members. Coupled with obedience, both moderators and members will be able to grow to the perfection of charity in trust and confidence.

The spiritual duties of the moderator are being clearly spelled out. "Besides being solicitous about their duties, moderators are to help members seek and love God, foster fraternal communion, promote the growth of the Church and the love of fellow man, and help members draw closer to Christ through the practice of the evangelical counsels".[33]

In the fourth chapter on the temporal goods of the institute and their administration, a number of principles have been accepted. In the present Code, administrators must refer to canons 531-537 and to those on administration, for instance, canons 1530-1532, etc. Lately, it has become apparent that these canons are insufficient to meet the needs of contemporary society. A number of principles have been approved for the general legislation, but they will necessarily have to be applied by particular law and the determination of the Episcopal Conferences. Father Beyer presents a number of these principles:[34] the temporal goods of the institute are ecclesiastical goods, and thus subject to the vigilance of the Church. The capacity of institutes to acquire, possess and administer these goods is to be determined by the particular law; it may be restricted or even totally excluded as in the case of certain Orders.[35] Norms for the use and administration of goods are to be defined by each Institute, and the practical administration is to be entrusted to a treasurer. The rules for ordinary administration, as opposed to extraordinary administration, are again to be determined by the particular law. Norms regarding conveyance or alienation are to be determined according to the prescriptions of the new patrimonial law of the Church.[36] Communities are exhorted to make gifts to the needy and to live according to a spirit of poverty.

One principle that is found in the new law and which does not seem as clearly defined in the present Code, is the principle of accountability. Indeed, it seems quite incongruous today that major superiors, and even local Ordinaries, are rather limited as far as accountability is concerned. To overcome any possible deficiency in this regard, administrators would be called upon to render an account of their work, according to the norms of the particular law.

32. K. O'Rourke, *loc. cit.*, p. 32.
33. *Ibid.*, p. 34.
34. J. Beyer, "De Institutorum. . .",*loc. cit.*, p. 193 sqq.
35. For instance, the Franciscan Order.
36. Cf. *Communicationes,* 5 (1973), p. 100, nos. 33-34.

Probably the most important part in this first section, as far as the individual members of the institute are concerned, is the fifth chapter on admission into the institute. Here, the canons would be divided into four articles referring to the preparation of those who are to be received, their formation, their incorporation into the institute, and, finally, the formation of incorporated members.

It is in this section that the Commission goes to great pains, it seems, to retain only those prescriptions that would apply to all members of institutes of consecrated life. No reference, for instance, is to be made to the "novitiate" or to "profession"; instead, more general terms are used, such as "probation" and "incorporation". We have already referred above to this modification.

No person may be incorporated into an institute, unless in the manner prescribed by particular law, such as by vows or promises. Incorporation carries with it the rights and obligations defined in particular statutes; through incorporation the institute assumes the responsibility, under a new title, of leading the member to his goal according to the statutes of the institute.[37]

Most of the new norms already found in the instruction "Renovationis causam" of January 6, 1969[38] are being incorporated into the text, with the exception of the rules referring to the possibility of dividing the probation year into two or more periods. The conditions for the validity of admission to probation are simplified: a person must be at least 17 years of age; not be married or bound by vows in another institute of consecrated life; not have concealed admission into another institute, substantial indebtedness, or the need to render an account to legally constituted authority.

For the validity of the temporary incorporation, it is simply required that the person be at least 18 years of age, have completed the valid canonical probation, be judged worthy according to the requirements of the particular law, and be admitted by the competent superior.

In the sixth chapter on the obligations of institutes and their members, we see that "the principal responsibility of each institute is to understand its vocation in Christ and in the Church, to preserve faithfully its particular nature according to the spirit of the founder, and to strive sedulously to achieve the goals of the community, being attentive to the signs of the times".[39] In this chapter we find listed the obligations of members in both spiritual and community matters. The spiritual exercises have been reduced to a minimum, to enable the members to show forth the gentleness and kindness of Christ in their lives.

37. Cf. K. O'Rourke, *loc. cit.*, p. 37.

38. S.C. Religious and Secular Institutes, Instruction "Renovationis causam", January 6, 1969, in *A.A.S.*, 61 (1969), p. 103-120.

39. K. O'Rourke, *loc. cit.*, p. 38.

The final chapter of the first part refers to separation from the institute. It was evident to anyone who had tried to apply the norms of the present Code, even as updated by recent legislation, that they were most difficult to use. Recent changes in the law have authorized the exempt Orders to apply the more simplified norms for dismissal used in congregations.[40] In spite of this change, much remained to be done. The new law proposes to leave many of the actions in this section to the institute itself, without the necessity of having recourse to the Holy See, except in cases of appeal.

The matter of this chapter is distributed in four articles: transfer to another institute, departure from the institute, dismissal, and the juridical condition of those who are separated.

Members could be authorized to live outside the community for up to three years; a member in this state would lack active and passive voice for the duration of the period.

In the review of this first section of the law, the common norms, it was not our intention to examine each prescription, but rather to show certain trends that are to be found: accountability, promotion of personal development, respect of subsidiarity, fostering of coresponsibility, and evident flexibility. These trends are definitely in line with the principles studied in the first part of this paper. The general law, as it is to be presented, must be situated in this perspective and not viewed as a "rigid series of injunctions".[41]

c. Specific Elements

The second part of the proposed new law contains a number of preliminary canons, followed by three chapters on religious institutes, institutes united for apostolic life, and secular institutes.

The preliminary canons envisage the various charisms of the Spirit manifested in all institutes, and determine rules for the preparation of particular law; these norms should not be multiplied without reason—the same principle as was applied in the first part of the law regarding norms to be found in the Code itself.

A general canon would then follow on the eremetical or anachoritic life by which the faithful, through withdrawal from the world, consecrate their lives to the praise of God and the salvation of others.

In the canons on religious institutes, the public vows are coupled with a common life according to the norms of particular law. The common religious life is lived either in monastic institutes or in those dedicated to apostolic works, such as institutes of Canons regular, conventuals, and apostolic institutes.

The second and third titles of this part concern institutes united for

40. S.C. Religious and Secular Institutes, Decree, March 2, 1974, in *A.A.S.*, 66 (1974), p. 215-216.

41. Pope Paul VI, Address of September 17, 1973, in *Origins,* 3 (1973-1974), p. 272.

apostolic life and secular institutes. The law would state that these latter, by assuming the practice of the three evangelical counsels strengthened by a sacred bond, constitute a true and proper form of the consecrated life.[42] A person who is already definitely incorporated into a secular institute and receives sacred orders, may be incardinated into a diocese or not, depending upon the norms of the individual institute.

The specific canons, since they will extend to all the recognized categories of institutes must, again, be general in tone, even though referring to a particular group of persons. The particular law will also play a very important role in this section, enabling each body to organize its own life within a broadly defined framework.

Having completed this brief overview of the proposed new law, we could now make a number of comments on the text that would help us evaluate, at a distance, the work to date of this particular sub-commission.

III. Observations on the Proposed New Law

A number of observations, some general, some more particular, come to mind upon reading the various articles published to date. We will divide these remarks into two: a number of positive comments, and then some points which might require additional perfecting.

a. Positive Comments

One can not help in reading the commentaries to detect a note of optimism. Instead of proceeding in a patchwork manner, as mentioned above, the law has been completely renewed. This being the case, the law will serve as a model for other sectors of the Code that are still being revised.

1) Among the general positive comments that seem to arise, we could mention that the new law has as its purpose to foster the renewal and rejuvenation of spirit and meaning for individuals in the consecrated life.[43] This becomes manifest especially when the preliminary canons are studied.

2) The document, with its theological formulation and pastoral outlook will respond more readily to the needs and the mentality of today. Instead of being a strictly juridical text, it has a life-giving flow from within that increases the hope and desire to live this consecrated life more fully. Because of this formulation, the text does not appear at first sight to be restrictive, and thus enables the reader to approach it with a more open and less suspicious mind.

3) The responsibility given to each institute to determine its own direction and orientation is very positive. This option taken by the Code Commission provides for a needed recognition of charisms and a necessary decentralization.

4) Another important characteristic is the recognition of equality before

42. Cf. K. O'Rourke, *loc. cit.*, p. 46.
43. Cf. *ibid.*, p. 47.

the law of masculine and feminine institutes. This, of course, was rather overdue and will be welcomed by all.

5) A feature that will also be appreciated is the relative brevity of the general law, since it will not enter into unnecessary details. Combined with this will be the flexibility of the law, since each community will be able to have more leeway.

6) The simplification of dismissal procedures is certainly necessary to avoid harm to both the institute and to the member.

7) The reduction of the number of cases where recourse to the Holy See is required will also be of significance.

8) The incorporation of the principle of accountability is something that was most necessary, especially in the area of administration of ecclesiastical goods.

9) The respect to be shown to the dignity of the person is another characteristic of importance, indeed a primary facet of any just law.

This simple enumeration of qualities is sufficient to show us that the proposed new law for institutes of consecrated life will be a great improvement over the present legislation. What will be needed now is a desire to live this new law in such a way that it may produce the intended effects, and as a life-giving law of the Spirit will set us free (cf. Rom., 8, 2).

b. Some Elements That Could Require Further Clarification

In spite of its numerous qualities, as is the case with any human achievement, there are some general elements in the proposed new law which might make it difficult to accept.

1) The first comment, which might be very subjective in nature, is that since there were no women on the sub-commission, the feminine dimension is missing in a law that will be lived to a great extent by women. Certain ideas and insights would probably have been added had the composition of the committee been different.

2) The preparation of codes of particular law will certainly tax smaller institutes. However, with the preparation they received during recent general chapters, this difficulty might be easily overcome.

3) Greater emphasis could be placed on service to one's fellow man so that the purpose of consecrated life will not only be interior, but, through the practice of the counsels, will lead the members to even greater desire to serve others in the name of the Lord.[44]

4) While, by principle, the law does not define, there does not seem to be reference to many descriptive definitions of terms in the new law. This might lead to some confusion since we are dealing with a new vocabulary that must necessarily be technical. Some of the terms even appear to be artificial or too general, such as "moderator", "incorporation", and so forth.

44. Cf. *ibid.*, p. 49.

5) Reference was made to the exemption of communities. It could be asked whether this institution truly has a place in the Church today.

6). One of the most evident obstacles is that the second part of the law will appear to be repetitious. Indeed, it could be asked whether it is truly appropriate to have a division of this nature which could tend to be artificial at times. It is probably necessary, though, if the commission intends to be logical with its desire to protect the dignity of persons and foster the charism of each particular institute and its special mode of life.

7) Since the bishops have already received the draft text of the proposed administrative procedure, should not some mention be made in the text of the possibility of using this procedure for the resolution of misunderstandings that might arise within an institute, or between communities, or between the societies and the local Ordinaries. In this area, too, we must not lose sight of the perspective of protecting the rights of individuals and of juridical persons.

8) There are a few instances where recourse to the Holy See is still necessary; it would seem, though, that in some of these cases it becomes necessary to have recourse to a higher authority than to the one who first performed the act, for instance, for the suppression of a diocesan institute. The application of the principle of subsidiarity might be further extended in this direction, although there are certainly situations where it would be preferable to have recourse to an outside arbiter.

CONCLUSION

At the end of this lengthy study, it is rather easy to summarize the spirit of the proposed new law.

It constitutes a sign of hope. This hope is to apply not only to the individuals, but also to the institutes themselves. Many smaller communities might simply not be able to cope with the new norms, and might disappear; others will rediscover their original momentum and will blossom to new life. There will also be hope for the Church since this vocation is lived *in* the Church and *for* the Church of Christ. When people devote their existence with enthusiasm and life-giving joy to a cause such as this, their influence extends to so many other persons.

In addition to being a sign of hope, the new legislation is also a sign of adaptation to our times. Having lived through certain periods when other values were stressed, it is now time to live the values of justice, respect and equality which so characterize our age. The Church must also be a leader in this field. The new law provides a sufficient challenge to respect these values; if they are disregarded, it will not be the fault of the law, or of the lawmakers, but the consequence of our human condition whereby we are always in need of purification, although we have been redeemed in the blood of Christ.[45]

45. S.C. Divine Worship, *Ordo Paenitentiae,* December 2, 1973, No. 3, p. 10.

May this new law, when it is promulgated, lead all of us to a greater desire to live its principles and have them applied in our lives so that the message of Christ may be heard to the very ends of the world and the following of Christ proposed in the Gospel become the supreme rule of our lives.

Case 10

Religious: Local Church and the Roman See

St. Benedict's Abbey, located within the Ames Diocese, is governed by Abbot Boniface Schmidt, O.S.B. The Benedictine abbey operates a college preparatory school for day and boarding students. The abbey is considered progressive as compared to the diocese. Abbot Boniface receives a letter from Bishop Norman Carter of Ames addressed to all Catholic high schools. It requires that textbooks for high school religion courses must be the series *Faith as Catholics.* Any other textbook is forbidden and exceptions will be made only rarely and on a case-by-case basis. The theology classes at St. Benedict's use no set series of textbooks since course offerings vary. However, the Dutch Catechism, unabridged, is used in the theology sequence "Christian Faith," which each student must take at least one quarter each year.

Abbot Boniface and his monks reject the requirement of the bishop as an interference with academic freedom and with the historic autonomy accorded Benedictine monasteries and their schools. Abbot Boniface gently but emphatically writes Bishop Carter stating the abbey's position. He informs the bishop that St. Benedict's therefore will not initiate the use of *Faith as Catholics* in its school.

Bishop Carter replies to Abbot Boniface that all Catholic schools are under his authority, that the autonomy of a religious institute only involves internal matters relating to the religious, that the principle of academic freedom does not exist regarding the teaching of Catholic doctrine, that unless St. Benedict's submits to his regulations it must close the prep school, and that no matter what previous law existed, Vatican II recognized the bishop's complete authority within his diocese.

Further, Bishop Carter orders Abbot Boniface to faithfully observe the liturgical norms of the New Order of the Mass and to cease such practices as spontaneous presidential prayers and distribution of the consecrated wine by merely placing the chalice on the altar without a minister distributing it.

Abbot Boniface again rejects the educational requirement. Further, he maintains that the abbot of the monastery is the proper ordinary regarding monastic liturgies. As long as the liturgies are monastic, the abbot is the competent ordinary. A monastic liturgy, which includes celebration of the Eucharist, is part of the monastic *horarium* and is attended only by monks, students of the school, and guests of the monastery. At St. Benedict's only the monks and students attend the Eucharist, although occasionally some guests are present. Abbot Boniface so informs Bishop Carter.

Needless to say, Abbot Boniface and Bishop Carter have reached an impasse. Bishop Carter threatens public exposure and the imposition of an interdict. Abbot Boniface implies that he will appeal to the Sacred Congregation for Religious and Secular Institutes. Bishop Carter issues an interdict. Abbot Boniface appeals to the Sacred Congregation for Religious and Secular Institutes. The latter responds, stating that Abbot Boniface's position is correct in both instances and that Bishop Carter cannot interpose such an interdict. Bishop Carter responds by appealing to the Sacred Congregation for Bishops which has authority in all cases relating to bishops. That congregation responds by stating that it, not the Sacred Congregation for Religious and Secular Institutes, has jurisdiction in this matter, that the bishop is the proper ordinary for determination of liturgical law and for the safeguarding of the Sacred Liturgy, and that all educational institutions, other than a seminary operated and maintained for the exclusive use of a religious institute, are under the local ordinary.

Abbot Boniface rejects the response of the Sacred Congregation for Bishops, and stands by the response of the Sacred Congregation for Religious and Secular Institutes. Another impasse has been reached. Both parties therefore appeal to the Apostolic Signatura.

Exercise

As a research assistant for a judge of the Apostolic Signatura, you are to formulate the issues in this case and analyze each issue according to the law. Particular concern should be given to the issue of jurisdiction.

References

Constitution on the Sacred Liturgy, Vatican II, par. 22, 26.

Decree on the Up-to-Date Renewal of Religious Life, Vatican II.

Decree on the Pastoral Office of Bishops in the Church, Vatican II, par. 33-35.

"Directives for the Mutual Relations Between Bishops and Religious in the Church," (May 14, 1978), *Origins* 8, 161-75.

"Ecclesiae Sanctae" (August 6, 1966) I, 22.

"Liturgicae Instaurationes" (September 5, 1970), *Canon Law Digest* VII, 40.

Gallen, S.J., J. F., "Canon Law for Religious After Vatican II," *Review for Religious* 31 (1972), 949-66, and annually thereafter.

Orsy, L., "Hierarchy and Religious: Responsibilities, Rights and Duties," *Canon Law Society of America Proceedings, 1977,* 19-29.

Seasoltz, R. K., "Monastic Autonomy and Exemption: Charism and Institution," *The Jurist* 34 (1974), 316.

Case 11

Diocesan Priest Plans to Enter a Religious Order

During his thanksgiving after Mass, Fr. Tom Alder recalled the more important stages on his way to ordination. Gently but firmly, it appeared to him, the Lord had led him on.

That afternoon he met with Bishop Henry Bond, his ordinary, to discuss his plans to become a Cistercian at Merton Abbey. Though he labored enthusiastically and effectively as an associate pastor and a high school instructor, the young priest felt irresistibly drawn to a deeper prayer life. He had discussed with others his attraction to a contemplative life in his seminary days and often during his six years in the priestly ministry. "Get better acquainted with the Cistercians and pray for guidance," his spiritual advisers had suggested. He had read the Cistercian rule, made retreats at the Cistercian abbey in Bangor, and discussed his "vocation" with the master of postulants. He had even been interviewed by the acceptance committee of the abbey and was encouraged by their positive evaluation. He came to Bishop Bond to inform him of his decision to become a monk.

As he listened to Father Tom, the bishop appeared cold and distant. "I'll have to think the matter over," he said. "Our diocese is not glutted with vocations, you know. We can use every priest we can get a hold of. However, you should remember that it's been my policy not to accept ex-religious into our diocese. What if you should decide to leave the Cistercians? Let's think this thing through."

Tom tried to hide his disappointment. He thanked the bishop for his concern. As he left for home, he mused "What should I do next? Apparently Bishop Bond is not in favor of my plan. What are my obligations toward him and the diocese?"

Exercise

1. Trace the development of the Church's discipline concerning transferring from a diocese to a religious institute, e.g. excardination, incardination, profession of vows.

2. Outline the procedures to be followed in Father Tom's case.

3. What are the legal obligations of the diocese and Merton Abbey to Father Tom during the period of transfer?

4. What arrangements should be made between Father Tom, the diocese, and Merton Abbey?

References

Ellis, A. C., "Reception of Seminarians into Religious Institutes," *Review for Religious* 5 (1946), 260-63.

Koesler, L. *Entrance into the Novitiate by Clerics in Major Orders,* Canon Law Studies, no. 327 (Washington: The Catholic University of America, 1953).

E. THE LAITY

The Right of the Church People to Participate in Ecclesial Decision-Making*

William J. LaDue

One of the essential features of Catholic ecclesiology is its insistence upon the essential distinction between the ministerial and the baptized priesthoods.

> Though they differ from one another in essence and not only in degree, the common priesthood of the faithful and the ministerial or hierarchical priesthood are nonetheless interrelated. Each of them in its own special way is a participation in the one priesthood of Christ.[1]

In spite of this essential difference, the Second Vatican Council placed considerable stress upon the basic equality of all believers,[2] the importance of the general priesthood,[3] and the need for true collaboration between the ministers and the rest of the faithful.[4] This represents a marked change of emphasis compared with the 1917 Code of Canon Law. We have indeed come a long way in the past half century or more, but we have a long way to go before the ideals of the recent council concerning the active cooperation of both priesthoods in the realization of the Church's mission are achieved.

* Paper presented at the eighth annual general meeting of the Canadian Canon Law Society, held in Quebec City, October 1-4, 1973.

1. *Lumen gentium,* No. 10. English version from W. Abbott, ed., *The Documents of Vatican II,* New York, Herder & Herder, 1966, p. 27.

2. *Ibid.,* No. 32 ". . .if by the will of Christ some are made teachers, dispensers of mysteries, and shepherds on behalf of others, yet all share a true equality with regard to the dignity and to the activity common to all the faithful for the building up of the body of Christ". W. Abbott, *loc. cit.,* p. 58.

3. *Apostolicam actuositatem,* No. 1. ". . .this most holy Synod earnestly addresses itself to the laity whose proper and indispensable role in the mission of the Church it has already called to mind in other documents. The layman's apostolate derives from his Christian vocation, and the Church can never be without it". W. Abbott, *loc. cit.,* p. 489.

4. *Lumen gentium,* No. 32. "For the distinction which the Lord made between sacred ministers and the rest of the People of God entails a unifying purpose, since pastors and their faithful are bound to each other by a mutual need". W. Abbott, *loc. cit.,* p. 58.

A good many studies have been published since 1965 on the subject of the rights and prerogatives of all the faithful,[5] but there is very little presently available in the area of our special concern, namely, the right of the Church people to participate effectively in the decision-making process. By this I mean a significant role in those ecclesiastical governmental processes which articulate the presence and mission of the Church in the world.

This understanding of participation seems somewhat contrary to current trends in Church government at least at the highest level. For example, the recent circular letter on pastoral councils, sent to the bishops of the world from the Congregation for the Clergy and dated January 25, 1973, confines the role of such bodies within very narrow limits:

> . . .this participation of the faithful in the mission of the Church is not the same as participation in the exercise of political power. . .Accordingly, the pastoral work, namely of teaching, sanctifying and ruling, and the power necessary for it are not bestowed by the Lord on the entire community of the faithful, but are conferred on sacred pastors by a special consecration and a canonical mission. . .
>
> The pastoral council enjoys only a consultative voice (*Eccl. Sanctae,* N. 16, 2). The recommendations and suggestions of the faithful which they propose within the confines of their ecclesiastical communion and in the spirit of unity are of great value for the formation of decisions. . .
>
> Therefore, the bishop should greatly esteem its proposals and suggestions and seriously consider the judgments on which they agree, preserving the freedom and authority which are his by divine law. . .[6]

There is no reference in the first paragraph quoted to the teaching, sanctifying and shepherding functions of the baptized priesthood, affirmed, among other places, in paragraph 31 of *Lumen gentium.* Each of these functions, according to the Constitution, is to be exercised by the faithful in their own way, both in the Church and in the world.[7] In the last two passages cited, there seems to be no effective sharing on the part of the members of a pastoral council in the decision-making activity, since that activity is described as being the sole responsibility of the Ordinary.

With this in mind, let us examine our tradition concerning the nature of the relationship between the hierarchical priesthood and the common priesthood in the area of ecclesial decision-making.

* * *

5. See P. Lombardia, "Lay People in Church Law", in *The Irish Ecclesiastical Record,* 109 (1968), pp. 281-312; A. Del Portillo, *Faithful and Laity,* Shannon, Ireland, Ecclesia Press, 1972.

6. *Origins,* September 13, 1973 (Vol. III, No. 12), pp. 187-188.

7. ". . .et de munere Christi sacerdotali, prophetico et regali suo modo participes facti, pro parte sua missionem totius populi Christiani in Ecclesia et in mundo exercent". *Lumen gentium,* No. 31, in *Sacrosanctum Oecumenicum Concilium Vaticanum II: Constitutiones, Decreta, Declarationes,* Rome, Typis Polyglottis Vaticanis, 1966, p. 152. The Latin text is cited here because the Abbott translation is faulty at this point.

The New Testament evidence reflects quite a different spirit from that which animates the above quoted circular letter. For example, from chapter fifteen of the *Acts of the Apostles,* describing the so-called 'council' of Jerusalem, scholars feel justified in distilling from the narrative the working conclusions that significant pastoral decisions in the apostolic period were to involve the apostles, the presbyters and the whole Church.[8] Community collaboration in important decision-making is also reflected in the selection of Judas' replacement in chapter one, and in the institution of the Seven in chapter six of *Acts.* St. Paul, particularly in chapter twelve of *I Corinthians,* seems to underline as grounds for such coresponsible action the possession of the Spirit on the part of all the doctrine of the Body.[9] The German writer, Rudolf Schnackenburg, is even more emphatic than most of his Catholic colleagues in pointing out the indications of effective collaboration in policy-making in the New Testament. As a matter of fact, he sees such traces not only in *Acts,* the Matthean material, and in Paul, but also in the Johannine literature because of the very strong emphasis upon the brotherhood of all believers found there.[10]

* * *

There is also important patristic evidence, beginning from the *First Letter of Clement* to the Corinthians (c. 96), and running through the second and third centuries, which indicates that although the distinction between the ministers and the laity is traceable to the sub-apostolic period, both groups through these generations were quite aware of the fact that they possessed distinct, inalienable and complementary functions.[11] In the middle of the third century there is the extremely valuable testimony of Bishop Cyprian of Carthage whose letters give us the clearest picture of the episcopate of his period. Cyprian phrased his overriding principle of operation as follows:

> . . .from the beginning of my episcopate, I decided to do nothing of my own opinion privately without your advice (i.e. the presbyters) and the consent of the people.[12]

His letters indicate an abiding commitment to deliberate with his people and a disposition of responsiveness to all, as is evidenced in this passage:

8. See M. Bourke, "Collegial Decision-Making in the New Testament", in *The Jurist,* 31 (1971), pp. 9-13.

9. See G. MacRae, "Shared Responsibility. Some New Testament Perspectives", in C. Curran & G. Dyer, ed., *Shared Responsibility in the Local Church,* Chicago; reprinted by *Chicago Studies,* 9 (1970), pp. 11-15.

10. R. Schnackenburg, "Community Cooperation in the New Testament", in *Concilium,* New York, Herder & Herder, 1972, No. 77, pp. 17-19.

11. M. Jourjon, "Les premiers emplois du mot laic dans la littérature patristique", in *Lumière et vie,* 12 (1963), No. 65, pp. 41-42.

12. *Epistle,* 14. 4.

> I think that I alone ought not give a decision in this matter since many of the clergy are still absent. . ., and since this examination (i.e. candidates for orders) must be discussed and investigated more fully, not only with my colleagues, but with the whole people themselves.[13]

With the conversion of Constantine and his later accession to sole power over the whole Roman Empire, many profound structural changes began to take shape in the Church.[14] Bishops came to share in the privileged status of civil officials, and thus they were drawn away from their people.[15] The disintegration of the *presbyteria* in the fourth century also contributed heavily to the evolution of a much more monarchical episcopate. Nonetheless, the laity continued to participate in the selection of their bishops at least until the sixth century.[16] It must be noted that this right included much more than a share in the selection of the candidate; it also involved the prerogative of deposing or expelling a bishop who proved unworthy of his charge.[17]

* * *

Another extremely vital area of cooperation in decision-making is revealed in the history of the ecclesiastical councils. Hilaire Marot has stated that from the very beginning of the conciliar development, i.e. from the latter part of the second century, lay people were participants in a great number of those assemblies.[18] It appears that they were involved at least to some extent in the deliberations through their observations and advice especially regarding those matters which more immediately affected them, but they did not vote, nor did they sign the conciliar enactments. Then too, we must not forget the fact that the Roman emperors, beginning with Constantine, had very focal roles to play in the general councils which did so much to shape the life of Christendom during the first millenium.[19]

Yves Congar notes that laity participated actively and frequently in the local councils of Spain, Gaul and England from the sixth through the eighth centuries.[20] During this period, there were many such "national" assemblies which contributed enormously to the growth of the Church in Western Europe.[21] Regarding this lay activity Congar says the following:

> A study of the Frankish and German councils, which from the fourth century

13. *Epistle,* 34, 4.
14. See Massey Shepherd, "Before and After Constantine", in *The Impact of the Church upon its Culture,* J. Brauer, ed., Chicago, U. of Chicago Press, 1968, pp. 17-38.
15. *Ibid.,* p. 35.
16. J. Lynch, "Co-responsibility in the First Centuries", in *The Jurist,* 31 (1971), p. 41.
17. *Ibid.,* p. 41.
18. H. Marot, "Conciles antenicéens et conciles oecuméniques", in Y. Congar, ed., *Le concile et les conciles,* Paris, Cerf, 1960, p. 25.
19. H. Küng, *Structures of the Church,* New York, Thomas Nelson, 1964, pp. 78-79.
20. *Lay People in the Church,* 1st ed., London, Geoffrey Chapman, 1959, p. 236.
21. Y. Congar, *L'Ecclésiologie du haut moyen âge,* Paris, Cerf, 1968, pp. 132-133.

functioned as regular organs of church government, shows that the laity assisted standing up and did not take part in the discussions; they made complaints, supplied information, and gave evidence; and when the canons were read they together responded Amen at the end.[22]

This conciliar activity waned in the ninth and tenth centuries; and as the influence of the people became less noteworthy, the Church became more and more a clerical affair. For example, Pope John VIII (872-82) declared that although the Church could be described as the *populus fidelis,* it was principally the clergy whom he designated by the term, *ecclesia.*[23] The faithful came to be nothing more than the *elementum passivum,* to be taught, sanctified and shepherded.[24]

* * *

With the reform movements of the eleventh century, and the Gregorian reform in particular, there was a resurgence of synodal activity. These developments were initiated and abetted by the German emperors.

> After a renewed decline of the papacy under Benedict IX, in 1046 Henry III put an end to the chaos surrounding papal succession at the epoch-making synods of Sutri and Rome. . .
>
> Under the subsequent German popes (especially Leo IX and Victor II) a large number of reform synods were held in and outside of Italy, marked by a strong participation of secular person. . .Lay persons also played an important role at the synods of the subsequent popes, Nicolas II and Alexander II. . .Gregory VII was the first to formulate the idea of a synod at which both the clerical and secular social estates were to be represented.[25]

Another product of the Gregorian reform was the re-discovery and revival of Roman law, especially the law of Justinian. One of the Roman legal principles which found great favor and eventually wide acceptance in the Middle Ages was the norm—*quod omnes tangit, ab omnibus approbari debet.* Its employment in Roman imperial law was quite restricted, but it came to be accepted in the twelfth and thirteenth centuries as a pivotal constitutional principle in the Church and in western polity generally.[26] Yves Congar contends that from Innocent III (1198-1216) on, the maxim was used in the ecclesiastical sphere not only as a procedural rule in private law cases, but as a sort of general directive requiring the consultation of in-

22. *Lay People in the Church,* pp. 236-237.
23. Y. Congar, *L'Ecclésiologie. . .,* pp. 239-240.
24. This mentality is well captured in the famous canon of Gratian's *Decretum,* "Duo sunt genera" (C. 12, q. 1, c. 7).
25. H. Küng, *Structures of the Church,* pp. 81-82.
26. See Y. Congar, "Ouod omnes tangit, ab omnibus tractari et approbari debet", in *Revue historique de droit francais et étranger,* 35 (1958), pp. 210-259.

terested parties before certain actions were taken in a community.[27] The norm had entered into the realm of public or constitutional law.

In conformity with the notion which was gaining currency since Gregory VII (1073-85), Innocent III's announcement of the Fourth Lateran Council in 1213 indicated that all those who were concerned, and whose conduct the agenda would affect, should somehow be involved and directly represented.[28] For the most part, the synods and councils of the thirteenth century, including the general councils of Lyons in 1245 and 1274, were conceived of as representative assemblies to which the laity were invited. The reason which was frequently explicitly alleged was that the matters to be discussed affected all, and *quod omnes tangit, ab omnibus tractari et approbari debet.*[29] It was especially during the course of the thirteenth century that the hierarchical structure was complemented by a wide implementation of the principle of consultation and consent on the part of the faithful. The final power of decision, however, belonged to the bishops alone. They were the only persons who signed the conciliar documents.[30] But lay influence was at least as great in the synods of this period as it was in the assemblies in Spain, Gaul and England centuries before.

Because the climate of congregational responsibility had taken such deep roots in the Western Church of the thirteenth century, it is not at all surprising that the absolutist pretensions of Boniface VIII (1294-1303) at the end of the century met with such resistance.[31] From the early thirteen hundreds, ecclesiological treatises began to appear; some of them embodying constitutional limitations upon the papacy, e.g. John of Paris' *De Potestate regia et papali,* while others, e.g. Giles of Rome's *De ecclesiastica potestate,* exalted and defended the absolute power of the Petrine office.[32] John of Paris presented an acceptable version of constitutionalism for the Church, whereas some of those who came down the road after him, e.g. Marsilio of Padua and William of Ockham, most assuredly did not. After 1450 or so, the absolutist direction in ecclesiological writings prevailed, suffering few setbacks until the present century. Note, for instance, the absolutist mentality of Pius X in his encyclical, *Vehementer nos,* of February,1906:

> The Church is by its very nature an unequal society. There are within it two different classes of persons: the members of the various orders of the hierarchy, and the multitude of believers. These two classes are so distinct that it can be said that with the hierarchy alone rests the right and the authority to move and

27. *Ibid.,* pp. 211-212.

28. *Ibid.,* p. 215.

29. *Ibid.,* p. 216.

30. *Ibid.,* p. 243. For a valuable summary of this intriguing medieval development, see B. Tierney, "Medieval Canon Law and Western Constitutionalism", in *The Catholic Historical Review,* 52 (1966), pp. 1-18.

31. *Ibid.,* p. 244.

32. See B. Tierney, *The Crisis of Church and State,* Englewood Cliffs, N.J., Prentice-Hall, A Spectrum Book, 1964, pp. 180-210.

> direct members toward the goals of the society. The office of the multitude, on the other hand, is to permit themselves to be ruled and to follow obediently the directives of the office-holders.[33]

This seems far away, indeed, from the constitutional spirit of the thirteenth century, and it must be affirmed that it was this absolutist atmosphere which pervaded in the 1917 Code.

* * *

Without attempting even a brief description of the recent renewal of interest in the Council of Constance (1414-18) and the status of its decree, *Haec sancta,* in particular, let it at least be asserted that this council was, in the admission of all, simply crucial to the life and unity of the Church. Whether one argues with Paul de Vooght and Hans Küng that *Haec sancta* is a valid ecumenical pronoucement expressing a viable doctrinal position concerning the overriding competence of general councils in matters concerning the faith, the rooting out of schism and the general reform of the Church *in capite et in membris;*[34] or, whether one holds with Joseph Gill that the decree has been rightly considered for centuries as invalid or inoperative,[35] all have to admit that the Council of Constance did unify the shattered Church. In connection with our argument, it is important to emphasize that at this council there were great numbers of representatives of the laity, e.g. the emperors, princes, ambassadors of the kings, etc. many of whom enjoyed full voting rights.

> It is of extraordinary importance, however, that at this ecumenical council, which was the only one to succeed in restoring Church unity, full voting rights were had not only by theologians and canonists, but by important lay personages.[36]

The mentality of Pius X's *Vehementer nos* would have seemed rather heterodox to the lay delegates at Constance who had come to participate actively in the deliberations that they hoped would heal the divisions tearing the fourteenth century Church asunder.

* * *

The absolutism of the centuries after Trent which reduced the faithful to a completely passive status began to dissolve away between the two World

33. P. Gasparri, ed., *Codicis Iuris Canonici Fontes,* Rome, Typis Polyglottis Vaticanis, 1925, Vol. III, p. 664.

34. F. Oakley, *Council Over Pope?,* New York, Herder & Herder, 1969, pp. 106-107. See also A. Fransen's splendid résumé: "The Council of Constance: State of the Problem", in *Concilium,* New York, Paulist Press, 1965, Vol. 7, No. 1, pp. 17-37.

35. J. Gill, S.J., "The Fifth Session of the Council of Constance", in *The Heythrop Journal,* 5 (1964), pp. 131-143.

36. H. Küng, *Structures. . .,* p. 87.

Wars of this century. Pius XI's *Actio Catholica* had much to do with precipitating a thaw. Then there was Pius XII's *Mystici Corporis* (1943) and his momentous allocution to the newly created cardinals on February 26, 1946. On that occasion he said the following:

> . . .the Church can be considered as the society of those who, under the influence of grace, in the course of perfecting their personal dignity as sons of God and in the development of all their human gifts, build up the formidable fortress of the human community. It is in this capacity, Venerable Brothers, that the laity find themselves in the front line of the Church's life. For them, the Church is the vital principle of human society. Therefore, they, especially they, should have an ever deepening awareness that they do not just belong to the Church, but rather are the Church, that is, the community of the faithful, under the guidance of the pope and the bishops in communion with him.[37]

After World War II, there was a surge of scholarly interest in the ecclesial role of the laity. No doubt the most outstanding and influential study of this period was Yves Congar's *Jalons pour une théologie du laïcat,* published in 1953. It is entirely likely that no other work had as much effect upon Vatican II's deliberations regarding the position and responsibilities of the laity as did this masterpiece.

* * *

The most significant event during the recent council enhancing the status of all the baptized was the decision made by the Fathers in October of 1963 to bring together all the general materials concerning the people of God in order to build a new chapter on this topic, to be located before the treatment of the hierarchy and immediately after the chapter on the mystery of the Church.[38] This arrangement allows for and, indeed, posits the need for a theology of the common priesthood. As a matter of fact, it is only against this sort of theological background that the essentially ministerial character of the hierarchical priesthood can be adequately comprehended. Chapter four of *Lumen gentium* takes up the question of the identity of those faithful who are neither office-holders nor members of religious communities. Paragraph 31 gives a kind of definition of the laity which Ferdinand Klöstermann summarizes as follows:

> In the first place, like all the faithful, laymen are incorporated in Christ by baptism, thus becoming members of the People of God and sharing in Christ's office as priest, prophet and king; furthermore, and specifically, they share in that

37. *A.A.S.*, 38 (1946), p. 149.

38. G. Philips, "History of the Constitution on the Church", in H. Vorgrimler, ed., *Commentary on the Documents of Vatican II,* 5 vols., New York, Herder & Herder, 1966-1969, Vol. I, p. 110.

> office in a particular manner *(suo modo)* and carry out the mission of the whole Christian people in the Church and the world in their own way *(pro parte sua)*.[39]

In spite of the ample attention given to the regal function of the laity in the world, the council had very little to say about their shepherding role in the Church. It did assert that the assimilation of Christ's sacrificial attitude on the part of the laity is a crucial regal function for the maturation of the Body of believers.[40] Also, on a number of occasions the documents encourage consultation with the laity by the hierarchical priesthood at all levels of the Church's life, and there are recommendations that suitable structures be created to facilitate this sort of dialogue.[41] If, however, these bodies, such as diocesan pastoral councils, are to be considered as strictly advisory in character, with no policy-making prerogatives whatsoever, are we doing full justice to our traditions and our history? Can more be said, should more be said about the right of the faithful to participate in the Church's deliberative processes, especially in the light of the New Testament and our synodal experience, particularly the experience of the Council of Constance?

I submit that more should be said and that there is ample ground for affirming more in the Vatican II teaching itself. *Lumen gentium* spells out quite clearly the Pauline doctrine of the charismatic structure of the Church.

> It is not only through the sacraments and Church ministry that the same Holy Spirit sanctifies and leads the People of God and enriches it with virtues. Allotting His gift "to everyone according as He will" (I Cor. 12:11), He distributes special graces among the faithful of every rank. By these gifts He makes them fit and ready to undertake the various tasks or offices advantageous for the renewal and upbringing of the Church, according to the words of the Apostle: "The manifestation of the Spirit is given to everyone for profit" (I Cor. 12:7). These charismatic gifts, whether they be the most outstanding or the most simple and widely diffused, are to be received with thanksgiving and consolation, for they are exceedingly suitable and useful for the needs of the Church.[42]

Charisms are aptly defined by Hans Küng as, "God's call to the individual person in view of a specific service within the community, including the ability to perform this service".[43] It would be very difficult to deny that many of these gifts of the faithful relate to the shaping of the presence and mission of the Church at all levels. If then, these *charismata* are not effectively brought to bear on the decision-making process, if they

39. "Constitution on the Church — Chapter IV", in H. Vorgrimler, ed., *loc. cit.*, Vol. I, p. 237.

40. *Lumen gentium*, No. 36.

41. *Ibid.*, No. 37; *Christus Dominus*, No. 27.

42. *Lumen gentium*, No. 12, W. Abbott, *loc. cit.*, p. 30.

43. Hans Küng, "The Charismatic Structure of the Church", in *Concilium*, New York, Paulist Press, 4 (1965), No. 1, p. 31

do not constitute an integral part of the deliberations generating policies and priorities, such decision-making will not be operating with all of its constituent ingredients. Unless all of the charismatic endowments relating to the forging of the Church's apostolate at any given level are inserted into the deliberative blend, at least in some sort of representative fashion, that process will be defective. The only way in which we can be assured that these gifts will be present to and operative in the policy-making procedure is to structure representative institutions, such as pastoral councils, endowed with decision-making prerogatives. The inalienable rights of the hierarchical priesthood, within our Catholic understanding of Church, need not in any way be jeopardized thereby. The hierarchical right of discernment can and must include the emergency power to block those policies which it judges to be clearly detrimental to the believing people and their growth in gospel life. But to leave these charisms outside of the deliberative process is to leave the Spirit, at least in part, out of the policy-making within the Church.

* * *

In addition to theological reasons, there are also canonical grounds for declaring the right of the faithful to be involved in ecclesial decision-making, and even in the legislative process. A fascinating argument, growing out of the decretalists' understanding of the efficient cause of customary law, was suggested not long ago by R. Philippot of the University of Louvain.[44] Philippot leans very heavily upon Alphonse Van Hove's treatment of custom in his celebrated commentary on the first book of the 1917 Code.[45] Canon 25, which opens the *titulus* on customary law, states quite unqualifiedly that custom of any sort obtains the force of law only (i.e. *unice*) from the consent of the lawgiver. Van Hove points out that this position was not the prevailing one until after the Council of Trent. Although the consent of the lawgiver has always been considered as essential, the nature of its causality has been diversely interpreted. The decretalists (e.g. Joannes Andrea, Antonius de Butrio, Panormitanus) taught that a community by means of its consent could, with no more than the general permission of the legislator, generate customary law; and hence, could be considered as being endowed with some sort of true legislative potential.[46]

However, the writers after Trent, such as Suarez, were of another mind. They taught that it was only the approbation of the lawgiver which gave the force of law to the mores of a community; and therefore, the people were not to be considered as possessing legislative potential of any sort.[47] Van Hove notes that Suarez made it quite clear that the laity were unable to

44. "Le droit d'initiative dans l'Eglise", in *L'Annee canonique*, 17 (1973), pp. 733-756.
45. *De consuetudine et temporis supputatione*, Rome, Dessain, 1933, pp. 1-237.
46. *Ibid.*, p. 41; pp. 68-72.
47. *Ibid.*, pp. 72-75.

receive this sort of law-making power.[48] This mentality is the one which has prevailed since Trent, and it most assuredly animates the Code of 1917. If, however, we accept the viability of the other position, and we have every right in the world to do so in the light of our tradition, then we can rightly assume that there is some legislative potential residing in the community itself. This potential becomes operative, according to the consistent teaching of the decretalists, in the creation of customary law. But there is no reason why the community's law-making capacity cannot be activated in other ways. If the faithful possess that potential, it would be rather difficult to demonstrate that it allows for but one expression.

I submit that the legislative capacity of the community could very well be activated through a representative council presided over by the local bishop. As long as the ordinary's prerogatives as described above are adequately safeguarded, such a body of priests, religious and laity would be more than an aggregate of consultors. Their power would not be merely consultative, but deliberative, and in a very true sense, legislative.

* * *

In summary then, the charismatic endowment of all believers affirmed by Vatican II, the right of all the baptized to share in the regal or shepherding function not only in the world but also in the Church (also taught by the recent council), and the consistent position of the decretalists concerning the legislative prerogatives of the community ground a just claim on the part of the lay people to share effectively in the process of ecclesial decision-making. Although their participation in the regional and general councils of the patristic era and the Middle Ages was for the most part restricted to a merely consultative voice, there seem to be adequate theological and canonical reasons to affirm for all the faithful a much wider prerogative, that is, a real capacity to enter into the shaping of community policies and norms of action. We are convinced that such collaboration will contribute greatly to a more effective articulation and realization of the presence and mission of the Church.

48. *Ibid.*, p. 41; p. 72.

Case 12

Shared Responsibility in the Church

While Fr. Jack Whittle was pastor at Holy Cross, the parish gained the reputation of being a far-out, progressive parish. The parish council exercised a great deal of power; the laity were enthusiastic in their support of the church and its flourishing school; a sense of community was developing. Some parishioners, however, were startled by some of the liturgical changes and began to make things unpleasant for the easy-going pastor. Wishing to avoid a hassle, Father Jack asked to be assigned to Immaculate Conception Church as an associate pastor.

Bishop Alfred Cornell replaced Whittle with Fr. Ralph Crowe, "a no-nonsense priest, who wanted things done right." Immediately the new pastor forbade girls to serve Mass, suspended the services of women distributors of Communion, and insisted that the congregation kneel for the Eucharistic prayers. When the parish council members complained about his abrupt manner and insisted that they be involved in decisions affecting parish life and practices, Crowe retorted that he was the pastor and that he would not relinquish his right and obligation to manage the affairs of the parish.

After several women, encouraged by the parish council, tried to distribute Communion at Mass, Father Crowe dissolved the council. Emotions ran high. The parish was divided.

The council sought relief from Bishop Cornell, who mulled over the matter and then wrote: "This is an issue of whether a parish council is advisory to the pastor or whether it runs the parish. I encourage you to talk things over and to work with your pastor."

To this the council, requesting Crowe's removal, responded: "The issue involves your appointment of a priest who is unable to cope in a renewed Catholic community. It also touches the role of the laity as 'sharers of responsibility' in the Church."

Exercise

1. Explain the canonical principle regulating consultative and deliberative proceedings.

2. Develop the theme: "The Role of the Laity in the Church."

3. Explain the relationship between the pastor and the parish council.

4. Delineate the responsibilities of a pastor towards his parish and towards his bishop.

References

"Basic Bylaws for Parish Councils," *The Jurist* 28 (1960), 352-61.

Bastnagel, C. "The Requirement of Consultation for Valid Action," *The Jurist* 9 (1949), 365-95.

Bligh, B., "Parish Consultative Councils," *The Clergy Review* 55 (1970), 258-64.

Boyle, J. P., "Presbyters, Pastors, the Laity and Decision-Making in the Church," *American Ecclesiastical Review* 169 (1975), 592-609.

Leckey, D., "Ministry and the Role of the Laity," *Origins* 8 (1978), 97, 99-101.

PART III: *Canonical Norms and Select Procedures*

A. GENERAL PRINCIPLES OF CHURCH LAW

The Church Society and the Organization of Its Powers

William H. Onclin

The Church of Christ is at the same time the Mystical Body and an organized hierarchical society; it is simultaneously the Church enriched with heavenly blessings and the terrestrial Church. Such is the teaching of the Second Vatican Council in the dogmatic Constitution *Lumen Gentium,*[1] where we also read: "This Church, constituted and organized in the world as a society, subsists in the Catholic Church, which is governed by the successor of Peter and by the bishops in union with that successor" (No. 8).

* * *

The organization of a society is determined by the form of its government, that is, by the composition and functioning of the organs which are entrusted with the assuring of its direction. In the Church, as a society in this world, the office of direction for the realization of the supernatural common good of the faithful is called by the Council the *munus pascendi seu regendi,* and this office is distinct from the other offices proper to the Church, the *munus docendi* and the *munus sanctificandi.* The exercise of an office necessarily demands the power required for its accomplishment; hence the *munus pascendi seu regendi* demands the power of direction which can be called the *potestas pascendi seu regendi*—traditionally called the *potestas jurisdictionis,* the power of jurisdiction, or the power of government. It is, then, the composition and the functioning of the organs of the power of jurisdiction or government which determine the organization of the Church.

Relative to the composition and the functioning of the organs of govern-

1. *AAS,* 57 (1965), 5-112.

ment in the Church, it would appear that three characteristics can be put in relief:

1) first, the Church is at the same time a monarchical and an oligarchical society; its government is monarchical and collegial;
2) second, the Church is a unified society, but decentralized as well;
3) third, the Church's power of governing, a power fundamentally one and indivisible, has several functions which must be distinguished; the Church does not, however, recognize—as do many modern states—the separation of powers.

I. The Church as a Monarchical and Oligarchical Society

In civil societies, since no one form of government is of absolute necessity, a wide range of possible forms is open to the choice of the people who constitute these societies. These forms are multiple and vary according to circumstances, each country, at present or in the past, having its own. According to the classical theory, these forms of government can be reduced to three type-forms, pure or mixed, among which this option may be exercised: namely, the monarchy, which is government by one person alone; oligarchy or aristocracy, which is government by some of the people; and democracy, which is government of the people, that is, government by the community of people who constitute the society.[2]

In the Church, on the contrary, the form of government having been defined by its divine Founder, this form does not depend on the free choice of the community of the faithful who constitute the ecclesiastical society. It is to the pastors entrusted by Christ with the direction of His Church—and, in principle, exclusively to them—that the public power, the power of governing in the Church, pertains. And, also in virtue of the will of Christ, the power of supreme and full government in the Church belongs on the one hand to the supreme pontiff, and, on the other, to the college of bishops in union with him. In the Church the supreme pontiff is invested with the plenitude of power, unlimited in space, unconditional in form. The Code of Canon Law, resuming the definition of the First Vatican Council,[3] affirms this formally in canon 218. In the terms of § 1 of this canon, the Roman pontiff, successor of Peter in the primacy, has not only the primacy of honor, but also the full and supreme power of jurisdiction, *supremam et plenam potestatem iurisdictionis in universam Ecclesiam,* both in matters of faith and morals as well as in those which concern discipline and the government of the Church spread throughout the entire world. The Second Vatican Council, in the dogmatic constitution *Lumen Gentium,* promulgated on November 21, 1964, confirms this, declaring: "In virtue of his office, that is, as vicar of Christ and pastor of the whole Church, the

2. Cf. J. Dabin, *Doctrine générale de l'Etat* (Bruxelles-Paris, 1939), pp. 180 ss.

3. Constitutio dogmatica 1 *de Ecclesia Christi,* cap. 3: cf. H. Denzinger, *Enchiridion symbolorum et definitionum,* n. 1826-1827.

Roman pontiff has full, supreme, and universal power over the Church. And he can always excercise this power freely'' (No. 22). The government of the Church is, then, monarchical.

At the same time, however, this government is collegial and thus oligarchic. For, in fact, the college of bishops, in union with its leader, the supreme pontiff, also holds supreme and full power in the Church. This is also stated by the Second Vatican Council in the same Constitution on the Church:

> The order of bishops is the successor to the college of the apostles in teaching authority and pastoral rule; or, rather, in the episcopal order the apostolic body continues without a break. Together with its head, the Roman pontiff, and never without this head, the episcopal order is the subject of supreme and full power over the universal Church. But this power can be exercised only with the consent of the Roman pontiff (No. 22).

To be sure, other institutions can, by the mandate of the pope or of the college of bishops, obtain a participation in the exercise of this governing power. So it is that, in fact, in the legislation in force in the Church, the sacred Roman congregations have today a part in the exercise of the governing power. They exercise an administrative function in giving instructions and in issuing decrees concerning the application of laws. In virtue of the motu proprio *Cum iuris canonici Codicem* of September 15, 1917, they are even invested with a certain right of initiative in the legislative domain, and can, each within the limits of its competence, when the good of the Church urgently requires it, draw up general decrees which, approved by the Pope, are truly universal ecclesiastical laws. But these institutions, or others, whatever they be, participate in the exercise of the power of government only in virtue of the mandate given them by the supreme pontiff or the college of bishops, to whom alone, by divine law, pertains the assuring of the direction of the Church as a society in this world.

II. The Church, a Decentralized Society

A society is called centralized or decentralized according as its public power, the power which it uses for the realization of the common good, is centralized or decentralized.

The public power is *centralized* when the authority in charge of the society monopolizes directive and commanding power and determines, either directly or indirectly, everywhere and in every matter, the various activities or functions necessary for attaining the common good of the society. In the centralized society, the so-called central authority retains all powers; the institutions or persons charged with the exercise of these powers receive their competence from this central authority of which they are either the delegates or the organs.

Public power is *decentralized* when, to a certain extent, inferior authorities, presiding over certain groups constituted within the society, possess on their own certain public powers, which they exercise for the common good of the group for which they are responsible, under the higher control of the central authority. In a decentralized society, the existence of a common good proper to certain partial communities within the society is recognized, a common good which does not necessarily coincide with that of the society as a whole. The authorities presiding over these partial communities are not, then, the representatives or agents of the society's central authority, but rather they possess a part of the public power on their own, determined by the exigencies of the common good of the communities whose government they must assure. Nevertheless, the common good of the partial communities being subordinate to that of the society as a whole, it belongs to the society's central authority to direct and supervise the exercise of the power held by the inferior authorities.

The Church of Christ in this world is a decentralized society. It is so by reason of the existence of various Churches, each of which, according to the designs of Providence, enjoys a certain autonomy and has its own organization and governing body. As the Council declares in the constitution *Lumen Gentium:*

> Within the Church particular Churches hold a rightful place. These Churches retain their own traditions without in any way lessening the primacy of the chair of Peter. This chair presides over the whole assembly of charity and protects legitimate differences, while at the same time it sees that such differences do not hinder unity but rather contribute toward it (No. 13).

First of all, in the one Church of Christ there are various Churches distinct according to rite, which can be called *Ecclesiae peculiares ratione ritus.* They enjoy a certain autonomy and are governed by pastors who have a proper power of government. "By Divine Providence," as the Constitution *Lumen Gentium* says,

> it has come about that various Churches established in diverse places by the apostles and their successors have in the course of time coalesced into several groups, organically united, which, preserving the unity of faith and the unique divine constitution of the universal Church, enjoy their own discipline, their own liturgical usage, and their own theological and spiritual heritage.

So speaks the Council in the dogmatic constitution *Lumen Gentium* (No. 23) and in the decree *Ecclesia Catholica* (No. 3). And the Council solemnly declares that these Churches, "the Churches of the East, as much as those of the West, fully enjoy the right, and are in duty bound, to rule themselves. Each should do so according to its proper and individual procedures" (Decree *Ecclesia Catholica,* No. 5). These Churches are then autonomous, and those who govern them have a proper power of government, a power which they exercise under the direction of the sovereign pontiff.

Next, there are those particular Churches called diocesan. These as well constitute decentralized groupings within the universal Church. In fact, according to the definition which the Council enunciates in the decree *Christus Dominus:*

> A diocese is that portion of God's people which is entrusted to a bishop to be shepherded by him with the cooperation of the presbytery. . . . The individual bishops, to each of whom the care of a particular Church has been entrusted, are, under the authority of the supreme pontiff, the proper, ordinary, and immediate pastors of these Churches. They feed their sheep in the name of the Lord, and exercise in their regard the office of teaching, sanctifying, and governing (No. 11).

The Code of Canon Law affirms that the power of the bishops in their dioceses is an ordinary and immediate power, but the Code does not call it a proper power, *potestas propria.* According to canon 329, § 1, the bishops, successors of the apostles, are appointed to the particular Churches which they govern in virtue of an ordinary power under the authority of the Roman pontiff. In the terms of canon 334, § 1, residential bishops are the ordinary and immediate pastors of the dioceses confided to them; and, according to canon 335, § 1, they have the right and the duty to govern their diocese, in both spiritual and temporal affairs, with legislative, judicial, and coercive power, to be exercised according to the rules of the holy canons.

In none of these canons defining the power of the bishop is mention made of a proper power. In fact, since the eleventh century, the question of the immediate origin of the bishop's governing power within his diocese has been contested. This question was posed in the Middle Ages under the influence of the so-called *Curialist* current which, to accentuate the primacy of the See of Rome, defended the thesis of the immediate communication of episcopal jurisdiction by the pope. In the preparatory discussions for the Council of Trent, the question was posed very precisely, but the theologians were divided: some of them—Jacques Laynez and Alphonse Salmeron, for example—defended the thesis of the direct communication of episcopal power by the pope; while others, such as Alphonse de Castro and François de Vitoria, favored the opposite thesis, holding that the bishops' power of jurisdiction derives immediately from Christ. The Council of Trent did not wish to settle the dispute: the declarations concerning the power of the bishops of Session XXIII, Chapter 4, decide nothing in favor of either thesis.[4]

After the Council of Trent, the discussion continues. Among those favoring the immediate communication of power by the Pope can be cited F. Suarez, Benedict XIV, D. Bouix, F. X. Wernz, S. Aichner,[5] and, more

4. Cf. F. Claeys Bouuaert, "Evêques," *DDC*, t. V, col. 572.

5. F. Suarez, *Tractatus de legibus ac Deo legislatore,* L. VI, cap. 14, n. 6, in ed. C. Berton, t.

recently, F. X. Wernz-Vidal and R. Naz.[6] Among the partisans of the opposite opinion are G. Vasquez, H. de Tournély,[7] and, more recently, R. Scherer, and F. Claeys Bouuaert.[8]

The First Vatican Council did not formally pose the question. But now, after the Second Vatican Council, the question has been resolved.

According to the dogmatic constitution *Lumen Gentium,* all the pastoral duties of the bishops are bound to the episcopacy and are rooted in episcopal consecration:

> Episcopal consecration, together with the office of sanctifying, also confers the offices of teaching and of governing. (These, however, of their very nature, can be exercised only in hierarchical communion with the head and the members of the college) (No. 21).

And in the decree *Christus Dominus,* concerning the pastoral work of the bishops, the Council calls the governing power which the bishops possess in their dioceses a proper power:

> The individual bishops, to each of whom the care of a particular Church has been entrusted, are, under the authority of the supreme pontiff, the proper, ordinary, and immediate pastors of these Churches. They feed their sheep in the name of the Lord, and exercise in their regard the office of teaching, sanctifying, and governing (No. 11).

Therefore the *commissio*—that is, the act of confiding a diocese to a bishop—does not confer on its recipient the episcopal powers of teaching, sanctifying, and governing, but rather only assigns him a portion of the people of God for whom he will exercise these powers, which are inherent in his duties as their ordinary, immediate, and proper pastor. The powers themselves are conferred on him by episcopal consecration and thus by God. The *commissio* by the competent authority renders these powers apt for efficacious exercise by entrusting to the bishop that portion of people of God for whom he will have to exercise his duty as their proper pastor.

It follows that the particular Churches to which diocesan bishops are appointed are decentralized provinces whose government is assured by the bishop not as a representative of the sovereign pontiff, but in the name of God himself.

6 (Paris, 1856), pp. 67-68; Benedictus XIV, *De Synodo dioecesana,* L. I, cap. 4, in ed. Louvain (1763), t. 1, pp. 28-33; D. Bouix *De Episcopo* (Paris, 1873), t. pp. 54-81; F. X. Wernz, *Ius decretalium,* t. 2 (Rome, 1899), n. 737, pp. 880-885; S. Aichner, *Compendium iuris ecclesiastici* (Brixinae, 1900), § 115, p. 394.

6. F. X. Wernz-P. Vidal, *Ius canonicum,* t. 2 (Romae), n. 579-580, pp. 725-731; R. Naz, *Traite de droit canonique,* t. 1 (Paris, 1955), n. 621, p. 439.

7. Cf. D. Bouix, *op. cit.,* t. p. 61.

8. R. Scherer, *Handbuch des Kirchenrechtes,* t. 1 (Graz, 1886), pp. 557-559; F. Claeys Bouuaert, "Evêques," *DDC,* t. V, col. 571-573.

III. THE VARIOUS FUNCTIONS OF POWER

Properly speaking, the Church's power of government, like the governing power of the temporal society, is a power which is fundamentally one and indivisible. The reason for this is that this power has but one end, namely, the common spiritual good—or more exactly, the common religious good—of the faithful who constitute the Church. This governmental power, this *potestas pascendi seu regendi,* which Christ has bequeathed to the pastors whom he has put in charge of his Church, includes all the activities which are necessary for the direction of the faithful, of whatever nature they might be. For, if the power of government is one and indivisible in its end, it is not so in the forms of activity which it must undertake in view of this end. One in its essence but multiple in its various aspects, this power is divided into various functions which correspond to the various activities necessary for the realization of the common good. And, in turn, for the realization of these diverse functions, various persons and institutions called constituted powers are established.

The terms *functions* and *powers* are not synonymous. By functions are meant the various social activities necessary for the realization of the end of the society, the common good. Constituted powers, on the other hand, are the persons or institutions which are entrusted with the work of fulfilling these functions; and these institutions, these powers, use one or more vehicles or organs to assure their concrete realization.[9]

That the governmental mission confided to the Church requires various activities, that it thus demands diverse functions, is unanimously affirmed by canonical teaching. But concerning the definition and the limits of the various principal functions, unanimity among canonists is far from complete.

The medieval doctrine of the commentators of Roman law and of the canonists, as well as the canonical teaching of our own time, generally distinguish only a double function of the power of government. Referring to a fragment of the Digest of Justinian (D., I, 16, 2), they distinguish, according to its mode of exercise, voluntary and contentious jurisdiction. *Contentious* jurisdiction, according to the definition of these commentators, is that which of itself is exercised against the will of the subjects, *quae per se loquendo exercetur in invitos.*[10] This jurisdiction includes the decisions and decrees of tribunals and acts in which the affected party intervenes. *Voluntary* jurisdiction, on the contrary, is that which is exercised with the consent of the subjects, *quae exercetur in volentes,*[11] and concerns

9. Cf. W. Onclin. "L'organisation des pouvoirs dans l'Eglise," *Actes du Congrès de droit canonique, Paris 22-26 avril 1947* (Paris, 1950), pp. 370 ss.

10. Cf., for example, Pl. Böckhn, *Commentarius in ius canonicum universum* (Salisburgi, 1776), L. I, tit. 29, n. 7; A Reiffenstuel, *Ius canonicum universum* (Venetiis, 1735), L. I, tit. 20, n. 8; L. Ferraris, *Prompta Bibliotheca canonica. . . , v° Iurisdictio,* n. 4; and others.

11. So Pl. Bockhn, A Reiffenstuel, L. Ferraris, *loc. cit.*

the exercise of public power which is effected without litigation and without accusation.[12] As examples of voluntary jurisdiction, the authors cite the concession of dispensations and privileges, absolution from censures, the granting of benefices or dignities, etc.

Regarding *legislative activity* or the function of legislation, the commentators disagree as to whether this pertains to contentious or voluntary jurisdiction. Most agree that law-making is an exercise of contentious jurisdiction,[13] while others such as F. X. Wernz and J. D'Annibale[14] are of the opinion that it flows from voluntary jurisdiction. In fact, legislative activity, as it is conceived and defined in both civil and canonical teaching, is neither contentious nor voluntary jurisdiction. There is apparently only one commentator of the Middle Ages who appreciated this. One of the outstanding disciples of Bartolo de Sassoferrato, Baldo degli Ubaldi (*Baldus de Ubaldis,* 1327-1400), was a doctor of both civil and canon law, and a celebrated professor of Perugia as well as of several Italian universities. It was he who wrote: "triplex est iurisdictio: quaedam contentiosa, fori contentiosi; quaedam voluntaria, fori voluntarii; quaedam statutaria, faciendi leges et statuta."[15]

The triple division of governmental power—namely, into legislative, executive, and judicial power—has been commonly admitted by civil law and employed in the organization of civil governments ever since it was proposed by J. Locke (1632-1704) and especially by Montesquieu (1689-1755). Along with this division, democratic states have applied as well the principle of the separation of powers which Montesquieu proposed as the means of preventing the abuse of power and safeguarding the liberty of the citizens.[16] The separation of powers consists in having the various functions of government each under the exclusive competence of certain persons or institutions, distinct and separate from one another. This division of competences among several distinct institutions is, according to Montesquieu, a guarantee against the abuse of power, so natural to those who hold it. As Montesquieu wrote:

> Eternal experience teaches that every man who holds power is tempted to abuse it; he pushes until he can push no further! Who would dare say it: even virtue needs limits! That no one might abuse power it is required, by the very disposition of things, that power stop power.

12. So V. Pichler, *Summa iurisprudentiae sacrae universae seu Ius canonicum* (Augustae Vindelicorum, 1733), L. I, tit. 29, n. 5.

13. So P. Laymann, *Theologia moralis* (Patavii, 1733), L. I, Tract. IV, *De legibus,* cap. 5, n. 3; E. Pirhing, *Ius canonicum in quinque Libros Decretalium* (Dilingae, 1674), L. I, tit. 31, sect. 1, § 1, II, n. 2; V. Pichler, *op. cit.,* L. I, tit. 29, n. 5.

14. F. X. Wernz, *Ius decretalium,* t. 2, n. 3, p. 9; I. D'Annibale, *Summula theologiae moralis,* t. 1 (Romae, 1896), n. 72.

15. Baldus de Ubaldis, *In Codicem commentaria* (Venetiis, 1586), L. VIII, tit. *de emancipationibus,* 48 (49), 1, n. 1.

16. *De l'esprit des lois,* Livre XI, chap. 4.

The Church at least at the highest level does not recognize the separation of powers, as do most democratic states, and she cannot. The pastors whom Christ has set over his Church have title to the plenitude of governmental powers: they are at once legislators, executives, administrators, and judges. At the same time, since the fulfillment of the mission entrusted to these pastors cannot be effectively assured by them alone, the exercise of certain functions of government must be assigned to other persons or institutions whose duty it is to assure these functions under the authority of the pastors whom God has set over his Church. But at this level a separation of powers can be admitted. It is, therefore, important to carefully distinguish the various functions of government and to fix the proper object of each.

Up to the present time, canonical legislation and doctrine have lacked well determined concepts concerning the functions of governmental power. On the one hand, in effect, the Code of Canon Law, in canon 201, § 3, retaining the division formerly admitted, distinguishes between the power of judicial jurisdiction and that of non-judicial or voluntary jurisdiction; and many commentators of the Code propose only this one division of governmental functions.[17] These same commentators teach that legislation belongs to non-judicial jurisdiction.

On the other hand, the first schema of the First Vatican Council, in chapter 10, *de Ecclesiae potestate,* declares that the Church possesses full and absolute power—namely, legislative, judicial, and coercive power (Coll. Lac., VII, 570); and the Code of Canon Law, under the influence of this schema, affirms in canon 335, § 1, that bishops have legislative, judicial, and coercive power in their dioceses. It is also from this division that certain canonists conclude to the necessity of including among the acts of legislative power not only ecclesiastical laws, but also precepts given to various individuals, the *praecepta singulis data,* and even matters relating to the administration of goods.

The uncertainty of canonical doctrine and legislation regarding the functions of governmental power has led a good many commentators to adopt the threefold division so long familiar to national constitutions. Before the Code, S. Aichner taught that the power of jurisdiction includes the legislative, judicial, and coercive powers as well as that power known as "administrative";[18] M. Lega affirms that jurisdiction includes all the power necessary to govern the Church—namely, legislative, executive, and judicial power.[19] Similar is the teaching of F. Cavagnis and F. M. Cappello.[20] After

17. So N. Hilling, *Das Personenrecht des Codex Iuris Canonici* (Paderborn, 1924), p. 94; Ph. Maroto, *Institutiones Iuris canonici* (Matriti, 1919), n. 724, pp. 862-865; A. Toso, *Ad Codicem Iuris Canonici Commentaria minora,* L. I (Taurini-Romae, 1921), p. 171; F. X. Wernz-P. Vidal, *Ius canonicum,* t. 2, n. 375; M. Conte a Coronata, *Institutiones iuris canonici,* t. 1 (Taurini, 1948), n. 277, p. 324.

18. S. Aichner, *Compendium iuris ecclesiastici,* p. 70.

19. M. Lega, *Praelectiones de iudiciis ecclesiasticis,* t. 1 (Romae, 1905), p. 59.

20. F. Cavagnis, *Institutiones iuris publici ecclesiastici,* t. 1 (Romae, 1906), p. 66; F. M. Cappello, *Institutiones iuris publici ecclesiastici* (Augustae Taurinorum, 1913), p. 18.

the Code, the same division was proposed by many authors, such as V. Del Giudice, H. I. Cicognani-D. Staffa, and L. Rodrigo.[21]

In our opinion, the revised Code should adopt this three-part division: it best corresponds to the various activities required by the government of the Church; it will better permit the defining of the powers of persons entrusted with the exercise of certain competences by the Church's pastors; and it will contribute to giving the Church a clearer and simpler legislation.

The Church in the world is a society and as such she is charged with directing, with governing, those who are incorporated into her. Now, this governing involves activities of various kinds which, in virtue of their proper object, can be reduced to three types. These constitute the three functions of governmental power.

The Legislative Function

The governing of the Church and the directing of the faithful demand, first of all, that general prescriptions be enacted, applicable to all the faithful living in *de facto* given conditions. These prescriptions, which directly assure collaboration among the faithful in obtaining the common spiritual good, are the object of the legislative function. This function is, therefore, characterized by the general nature of its prescriptions, imposed for the common good. Its object is the creation, modification, or suppression of a general juridical condition, a common statute, and it includes all regulations of a general order, whether they be called *laws, common precepts,* or approved *canonical customs.*

The Administrative Function

The common good also demands an ensemble of concrete measures to assure the application of the laws and to furnish the faithful with the services or institutions necessary or useful for their spiritual good. To assure the certain and equitable application of laws, *instructions* are needed to explain their real import, and *particular decrees* to determine their concrete execution. These instructions and decrees are the object of the administrative function. However, this function is not limited solely to the domain of executive acts properly so-called; it is far vaster and includes, in general, all individual measures and concrete acts useful to the end of the society, be these of a juridical nature or of a material character. The principal object of juridical administrative acts is either the application of a pre-established general canonical statute to a determined case—for example, the erection of a diocese or parish or the appointment of a pastor—or the establishing of an individual canonical statute: for example, in the granting of a privilege by way of rescript.

21. V. Del Giudice, *Istituzioni di diritto canonico* (Milano, 1936), p. 70; H. I. Cicognani D. Staffa, *Commentarium in Librum Primum Codicis Iuris Canonici,* t. 1 (Romae, 1939), p. 132; L. Rodrigo, *Tractatus de legibus* (Santander, 1944), n. 35, p. 23.

The Judicial Function

The common good demands, finally, that controversies regarding rights in particular instances be settled by a certain and authoritative judgment. It demands as well that the violation of laws imposing punishments be authentically established. These sentences or judgments constitute the proper object of the judicial function.

The carrying out of these functions belongs by right to the pastors to whom Christ has confided the direction of his Church and the particular Churches of which she is composed. By right, then, these functions are carried out by the college of bishops in union with the sovereign pontiff, as well as by the head of this college, the sovereign pontiff, for the universal Church; they are carried out, according to the modes and methods determined by the supreme authority of the Church, by the bishops—each for the particular Church under his care, or several conjointly for various particular Churches together. At the same time, the fulfilling of these functions—or one or another of them—can also be accomplished through institutions or persons to whom these pastors, within the limits of their competence, confide the *exercise* of these functions. In the universal Church, the Roman pontiff establishes some departments of the Roman Curia especially for administrative functions and others for judicial ones. In the diocese, the vicar general is in charge of administrative functions and the officialis has the exercise of the judicial function.

The introduction of this three-part division of governmental power into the legislation of the Church will, as we have said, add more clarity, more precision to this legislation. One or two examples will suffice to demonstrate this.

We have just mentioned the vicar general. According to canon 368, § 1, of the Code of Canon Law, the vicar general, in virtue of his office, *vi officii,* holds the same powers of jurisdiction in the diocese as the diocesan bishop by his ordinary power, except those which the bishop reserves to himself or for which the law demands a special mandate of the bishop. The rule is absolute: it is too absolute. Really, as a matter of fact, the vicar general does not hold the power of legislation in the diocese. This is not stated as such in the Code, but is deduced from canons 362 and 2220: the former states that the bishop alone is synodal legislator; the latter declares on the one hand that those who have the power to make laws or impose precepts can attach penalties to them and, on the other hand, that the vicar general cannot, without special mandate, impose penalties. Nor does the vicar general hold judicial power since, according to canon 1573, § 1, of the Code, the judicial power belongs in principle to the officialis whom the bishop is obliged to appoint.[22] It follows then that the vicar general

22. Cf. Kl. Mörsdorf, *Rechtsprechung und Verwaltung im kanonischen Recht* (Freiburg i. B., 1941), p. 118; *Lehrbuch des katholischen Kirchenrechts,* t. 1 (München-Paderborn-Wien, 1964), p. 430.

possesses in principle only an administrative competence; that, in principle, he is entrusted solely with the exercise of administrative work. Legislation which would so state matters would certainly be simpler and more precise.

We also mentioned privileges. In regard to the nature of privileges and the legislation regulating them, the teaching is very divided.

According to the Code of Canon Law, privileges can be acquired not only by direct concession of the competent authority and by communication, but also by law, by legitimate custom, and by prescription.

What is the nature of the privilege? The Code gives no generic definition. The definition used by commentators before the Code is that which is given, following Isidore of Seville, by the Decree of Gratian: "Privilegia sunt leges privatorum, quasi privatae leges" (D. III, c. 3). This definition, in turn, completes that of Innocent III, according to which "Privilegium est lex privata, . . . aliquid specialiter indulgens" (C. 25, X, V, *de significatione verborum,* 40). However, this definition of privilege is certainly not applicable to privileges accorded by law or introduced by custom: neither laws nor customs can be called *privatae,* since by definition they contain a *praeceptum commune* and are given to a community *legis recipiendae capax.* Nor is it applicable to a privilege granted to a particular person by rescript since, not being given to a community, this privilege cannot be called a law. Again, the definition is not applicable to a privilege acquired by prescription, since by its very nature the privilege is a means of acquiring subjective rights, and it cannot establish an objective right, as does law.

The legislation of the Code should, then, make the distinctions necessary to define the proper nature of these privileges. *Materially* considered, the privilege is a favor, a favorable statute, granted to or acquired by a person or a community. *Formally* considered, the privilege is either a law, a custom, a prescription, or a particular act, a rescript. But as a particular act, an administrative act, the privilege has an individual character since it establishes in favor of one or more persons a special objective right.

Also, in the present legislation concerning privileges, most of the provisions can be applied only to privileges granted by particular acts. Other privileges should be regulated by the legislation relative to laws, customs, or prescriptions. However, the Code does not state this and so lends itself to confusion. Introducing a distinction between acts of a legislative nature and those of an administrative one would surely bring about a clarity and certitude much to be desired.

To sum up: in the revised Code, acts of a legislative nature, such as laws and common precepts, must be clearly distinguished from acts of an administrative nature, such as precepts given to particular persons, rescripts and privileges granted by particular acts. The clear distinction among the various functions of power can unquestionably help to give Church legislation the certitude and precision required by the common good.

The Canons on Ecclesiastical Laws Revisited: *Glossae* on Canons 8-24

Ladislas Orsy

On the feast of Pentecost in 1977, we celebrate the sixtieth anniversary of the promulgation of the Code of Canon Law. Sixty years used to be reckoned as time enough for two generations to come and to go, a long span by any measure.

They were sixty productive years for canon law; who can count the commentaries that appeared in so many places, in so many languages! One should think that the work of commenting on the text of the Code is by now completed. After all, canons are not supernatural mysteries. There must come a time when all that can be said about their meaning has been said; the mission of the commentator has been accomplished.

Therefore, sixty years after their publication, someone may well ask, is it wise to revisit them all over again? Is it not presumptuous to look for some kind of hidden meanings in the words and sentences; for meanings that would have escaped so many learned and industrious *iurisprudentes* of two generations? Rather, we should take the *consensus* of respected authors, and thus assured, go about our daily task of administering justice in the Church.

Such objection to revisit the canons were well grounded if our law consisted of precise sentences composed of immutable concepts, all enclosed in a sterile case where there is no pulse of life. *There* change would be inconceivable, as there was none in the tomb of Tutankamon, after it was sealed by Egyptian officials in 1350 B.C. until it was opened again by Howard Carter in 1922 A.D.

But if law is something else than inanimate treasure hidden in the ground, if it is more like living seed planted in good soil, then the situation is different! The seed strikes roots, grows into a tree, and for a generation or two it brings fruit hundredfold. The metaphor is fitting. After all what else is legislation than the communication of intelligent norms of action by the legislator to the rest of the community? The words of the laws are signs and symbols; they carry meanings from those in authority to other citizens. Meanings, indeed, are not precious carvings on a stone to guard and respect. They are living creatures. Once conceived in the mind and given birth through human speech, they exist and grow on their own, feeding from their own environment.

Any language is a historical phenomenon, subject to evolution through subtle shifts and changes. Meanings follow the rhythm of those mutations; they, too, develop, change slightly or radically; in short, behave as historical beings. In sixty years new meanings emerge, old meanings fade away.

Moreover, there are intelligent persons on both sides of the law: those who make it and those who receive it. Persons change too, externally and internally. They can put the same text into a broader horizon, they can look at it from different standpoints, they can explain it, using the categories of a new cultural context. Throughout it all, the old law is made anew —without many adverting to what is happening.

To sum it up: it makes sense to revisit the canons. The sentences and the words have not changed; they are the very same that were printed sixty years ago. But their meanings may have shifted. Above all, we have a new generation around. Their horizon has been broadened by Vatican Council II; their vantage point is a different one. Also, in their speech there is evidence of a new philosophical approach to the old truth.

Hence our attempt to read the old canons with new eyes, and be a *glossator* of modern times. We shall not repeat what has been said by others unless it is necessary as a starting point for our reflections. Where nothing new appears, we rather bypass the text. Where new questions emerge, we pause to reflect.

To help the interested reader to follow our comments whenever it is useful, we give a literal translation of the canon in question; otherwise we simply refer to the legal issue that is the subject-matter or the starting point of our comments.[1]

CANON 8, § 1: LAWS ARE INSTITUTED WHEN THEY ARE PROMULGATED

In 1917 this was an epoch-making sentence. It determined with precision the point of time when laws come into being. Also, it expressed the cool attitude of the new Code toward a mainly customary law. Of course, the Code never foreclosed the development of customs, but it set the conditions so stringently that sixty years later we wonder if any custom, at any place, has ever been recognized as valid.[2]

The legislator obviously looked into the future and laid foundations for a new legal system. He believed firmly that the main instrument of good order

1. The footnotes to this article are not only references to sources and authorities; they play another role as well. They expand on the theological and philosophical background of our reflections; also, they provide concrete examples and illustrations for the more abstract propositions in the main text. Further, they play the role of connecting links between the themes of the different canons. Thus our notes form an integral unity with the main text: our thoughts are in both the text and the notes.

2. Canon 28 is the classical example of how difficult the Code made the recognition of a legally valid custom. Canon 28 refers to a new custom *praeter legem;* a custom that is usually the simplest and potentially the least disruptive for the community. Before such a custom could be recognized by the competent authority, the community must practice it for forty uninter-

will be statutory legislation composed with care and precision. Nor did he expect that the meaning of the text will ever change, once it has been promulgated. It is not farfetched to say that behind the text there is a quiet reaffirmation of that scholastic philosophy which operates with clear and unchangeable concepts that are signs of perpetually identical essences, a philosophy found more in some manuals than in Saint Thomas.

Promulgation, in legal terminology, is a solemn act. If no law comes into being without promulgation, no significant change in the law can come about without the same solemnity since substantially it would be a new law.

Canon 17, §2, confirms this view, as we shall see later. The community of faithful is not expected to shape the law. The old adage, *mutatio legis odiosa: to change the law is odious,* was probably lingering in the mind of the legislator. He was not thinking in the terms of an evolutionary and steadily progressing society as *ours* is; he was catering for a well ordered and settled society as *his own* was. Since he did not anticipate a rapidly moving and developing community, he did not build into the Code permanent instruments to help and to check the natural development of the legal system, as courts do in many civil systems. Change can come through the legislator only; he will promulgate it. Such an approach is not mitigated by canon 29 which states that the best interpreter of our laws is the customs of our people.

Behind such approach to canon law there was an understanding of the Church that has been deficient under some aspects. Great importance was given to the power of jurisdiction which is vested in the ecclesiastical superior, as the ultimate source of law. Less importance was attributed to the power of the Spirit which is diffused in the whole Church, as influencing the mind and the actions of the community. The vision of the Church expressed in *Lumen gentium,* stressing the powerful presence of the Spirit throughout the whole social body, is now having an increasing impact on our conception of canon law.

Be this as it may, the first moment in the life of the law, the act of promulgation, remains important for every interpreter, including the most recent ones, no matter what happened over sixty years ago. Once I heard the late Father Creusen say that his friend and colleague, Father Vermeersch, used to remark right after the promulgation of the Code that an adequate interpretation of the canons will be possible in the future without much reference to history. Soon Father Vermeersch realized that he was wrong. In

rupted years with full knowledge of what they are doing, *scienter;* and with the intention of binding themselves, *cum animo se obligandi.* No real flesh and blood community will ever act in such a way.

The nature of custom is (although not according to canon 28) that it develops gradually, with hesitations, probably alternating between periods of fervor and remission. To require an intention from the beginning *on the part of the community* to bind themselves is absurd; it would require a collegial action! Canon 28 presupposes well-planned action for a long period of time; it does not understand the sociological fact of evolving usages. The conditions for other types of customs such as customs against existing laws are even more stringent; see canons 25-30.

a similar way, a latter-day interpreter of the law may be tempted to bypass history and to speak of new meanings only, arising (perhaps legitimately enough) from a new theology. Yet, any interpretation without history is unsatisfactory and unreliable. Even when there is an evolution, its starting point should be stated, and the reason for new meanings explained. The historical dimension must be explored; the original meaning that was communicated at the time of the promulgation must be reconstructed. Every commentator should start from there, but no one should stop there. Too much has happened in sixty years. Primacy and episcopacy underwent an evolution; so did many of the sacraments. In the Code a non-Catholic Christian is not our brother, he is a separated heretic! And so forth. There are new understandings and new meanings around. The commentator should show the whole span of the evolution that has taken place.

It follows that anyone writing a commentary to the Code today cannot be unfamiliar with historical methods. Comments that would take the words abstracted from time and space would be without grounding; such explanations would be vitiated from the beginning.

* * *

Canon 8 can be looked at from a procedural point of view, too. Then it clearly says that the proof for the coming into being of a law (not necessarily for its present existence) is in the act of promulgation.

There is a legal philosophy behind this approach, evident in other parts of the Code as well, especially in laws concerning marriage. It appreciates clarity nearly above all other qualities in the law.[3] It would be interesting to investigate the hierarchy of values pursued by the legislator of the Code. The result would probably show that he tried to build a system that excelled above all in clear concepts that eliminated ill-shaped and potentially obscure norms. From then on, he acted logically when he gave less importance to judicial decisions. If the law is clear, the courts should follow it; they should

3. This pursuit of clarity has been often attributed to Cardinal Gasparri, especially concerning the canons on the sacrament of marriage. The attribution may not be without foundation. One may wonder if he was influenced in his teaching years at the *Institut Catholique* by the philosophy *des idées claires et distinctes.* At any rate a typical example of the pursuit of legal clarity even against common sense is in the general rule that a marriage null and void in the beginning remains invalid forever unless explicitly convalidated. For instance, if a woman agrees to marry under fear so great that she just simulates consent, the marriage remains invalid even if the source of undue pressure ceases and she chooses to remain with her partner, out of newly conceived love and dedication. For a long time the old law of the Church was that when the source of pressure ceases, e.g., the threatening father dies, the woman must walk out of the marriage in six months or else the law presumes that in the new circumstances she freely agrees to be the lawful wife of her partner.

The law of the Code is clear and can be easily handled by tribunals. The old law could present the judges with obscure situations, but how much closer it was to common sense and human conditions.

not clarify it. The system uses the courts to apply the law to cases, not to pronounce about legal obscurities.

A commendable philosophy, but a price had to be paid for its advantages. The Church did not have, and still does not have (not officially anyway), a constitutional instrument for the steady and peaceful development of its own legal system. Fortunately, the needs of life have overcome the rigidity of the norms. The jurisprudence of the Rota has been made public regularly; in fact it has become the most important reference book for the guidance of other tribunals. Through judicial decisions the canons of the Code were given a new meaning that its drafters would be astonished to read. It all happened without promulgation.

We know today what the drafters of the Code may have not known: evolution is a fact of life. It happens whether we want it or not; the wise legislator will provide instruments not only for the promulgation but also for the evolution of the laws.

To build such provisions into our legal system may be the greatest challenge for our future legislation. It may even be the key to its success or failure. Let us warn the reader: the question is not simply that of accepting or rejecting a new theory, that of evolution. The issue is in building a legal system that is realistically adjusted to the world in which evolution is a fact of life. Unless there are built-in factors or agencies in our legal system to keep it moving ahead with a developing world that we intend to serve, our laws will become inanimate monuments and not instruments of life.

This problem is not merely that of canon law. All civil systems struggle with the same issue. To a greater or lesser extent they created agencies that help and control the continuous evolution of the laws. Congress or parliament is steadily making new laws, courts are adjusting them to new situations, from time to time the nation revises or amends its constitutions.

CANON 8, § 2: PRAESUMPTIO

We reflect on one concept only: *praesumptio*. See also canon 16, § 2.

Praesumptio is a fundamental concept in procedural law; therefore it may be worth our while to spend some time examining its meaning and role critically. Such investigation may also give us the opportunity to raise some fundamental questions about the language, nature, and operation of canon law.

The usual definition of presumption is *rei incertae probabilis coniectura*. This is true in ordinary parlance; the common sense meaning of presumption is "a conjecture of something that remains uncertain."

Does the same definition hold in the technical science of canon law? Hardly so. More often than not, when a presumption is made, nothing is conjectured, no speculation is involved; if anything it is avoided. The law simply takes a stance concerning an event, or a person, and holds to it irrespective of the real state of things. The result is that all procedures are speeded up; there is no need for long investigations.

At times the law allows proofs to the contrary, the praesumptio is then called *iuris*. Thus, law is presumed to be territorial until there is proof to the contrary. The possessor is presumed to be owner unless there is evidence that the *dominus* is someone else. The accused is presumed to be innocent until his culpability is demonstrated. The law, however, is not particularly anxious to get to the heart of the matter and to discover the truth; mostly it leaves to an *actor* to come forth with proofs if he so desires. It is more important to go on with the business of living than to lose ourselves in endless inquiries.

At times, the law does not allow proofs to the contrary, no matter what. Then there is *praesumptio iuris et de iure*. Every subject of the legislator is presumed to know the law; that is, the legislator treats everyone as equally knowledgeable about the law. There is no point in pleading ignorance; no proofs are admitted. The system is definitely not interested in the truth of the matter, still less tries to conjecture it!

But if presumption is not *rei incertae probabilis coniectura,* what is it?

It is a technical legal device. The law singles out certain signs in the life of the society, such as age, profession, promulgation of the law, etc., and handles them as signals for certain legal effects or processes to come into play to resolve dubious situations. The device speeds up the administration of justice. Its structure is based either on what occurs ordinarily (the possessor is more often than not the owner), or what is obviously an advantage for the community (no one should be allowed to escape the burden imposed by the law through pleading ignorance).

Some Thoughts on the Language of the Law

This leads us directly into another problem: the nature of legal language. Canon law today is a sophisticated scientific system that developed its own language, grammar, even sentence structure; it did so in common with other modern legal systems. It is not written for the uninitiated; to understand it, special and extended training is necessary. It *is* true that lawyers speak a language that no one else can understand.

We take such differentiation between ordinary language, the vehicle of common sense, and technical language, the instrument of science, for granted in other fields while we resent it in the field of law. No one expects the doctor to write his prescription in such a way that a layman could understand it; nor do doctors bother to communicate among themselves without technical terms, using interminable descriptions so that people around could understand them. Yet, we often want the lawyer to speak the language of the man on the street.

The science of canon law has a long history, it goes back to Gratian, at least. He was its first great systematician. Ever since, the language of canon law has become more and more refined, nuanced, and difficult to understand without the necessary foundations and background. Such a process of specialization should not be pursued for the sake of obscurantism, but it should not be curtailed either for the sake of popularity because the renouncement of scientific language would only impoverish our science.

Law needs precise tools to handle well widely differing cases in real life.

Much of this is obvious on reflection. But the problem had to be mentioned because there is a trend that wants the law of the Church to speak to the ordinary man in ordinary language, and there is a resentment against technical speech. Our contention is that in the sophisticated culture of the twentieth century the Church cannot avoid a scientific approach to complex problems. In due course, we may use Italian or English or, who knows, Chinese as the special instrument of canon law, or perhaps all three as authentic tools of the legislator, but still the Church will have to legislate for a sophisticated world in a scientific way, in a technical language, as all civilized states do.

From Language to Substance

The issue of language, however, cannot be fully understood and appreciated, without looking at a problem of substance hidden behind it. To put it bluntly for the sake of clarity: the language of canon law does not refer to the whole of reality but only to a part of it, precisely because the science of canon law does not deal with the whole of reality but only with a part of it. It is concerned with social relations. Any mistake about this will lead at best to confusion, at worst to disaster. Such a statement cries for clarification.

Explanation given by contrast may work better and may even be more convincing than a precise chain of reasoning. Let us contrast the science of theology with that of canon law.

Theology is concerned with reflection on the whole reality of Christian mysteries as far as they can be understood by human intelligence. It wants to know as much about them and as completely as it is possible for mortal men.

Not so with canon law. Like all legal systems, it is interested in social relations and in good norms to make them workable. It does not want to penetrate into the depth of mysteries.

To put the same in another way: questions originating in theological reflection want to embrace the totality of mysteries, all and each of them in their breadth and length and height and depth. Questions originating in canon law (to be made, to be applied, or to be interpreted), originate in the needs of social life and are concerned with social structures and relationships. . . .

Theology and Canon Law

We firmly believe in both the respective autonomy and the harmonious unity of the two sciences, theology and canon law. Theology in some way is the matrix from which law grows in the Church. If it does not we are no better than legal positivists working around some religious objects. An increasing understanding of the mysteries of faith must feed and nourish the law throughout Christian centuries.

But law is concerned with that small portion of reality that is the world of ascertainable social relationships. We need intelligent and clear norms of action, we need easily ascertainable signs for the existence of structures and institutions. If canon law were asked to define the mysteries, legalism would strangle the community to death; if theology were asked to give legal norms of action, the community would collapse in confusion. . . .

The distinction between the field of theological reflection and the field of decision where norms of action belong is grounded in the theory that distinguishes in a human person a capacity to understand and to surrender to truth and a capacity to recognize some value and appropriate what is concretely good for him. To surrender to truth means to acknowledge that something *is* in the real world, it is there independently from us; when we acknowledge its existence we transcend our own little world. To appropriate what is concretely good for us means decision and action that shapes and builds not only our character but the universe around us. Therefore the distinction between the object of theological reflection and the object of moral decision is not merely nominal; it flows quite naturally from the nature of man who can transcend himself in two different ways.[8]

In other terms, to confuse theological reflection with decision for values is to manifest openly a confusion in our perception of the internal structure of a human person.

Wisdom, therefore, is necessary in the revision of our law. Reform must be based on theology, but theology should not become law.[9] Nor should law

. . . 8. For further explanation and inspiration to continue philosophizing on this subject, see Bernard Lonergan, *Method in Theology* (New York: Herder and Herder, 1972). Among the reviewers of this book Bishop C. C. Butler, O.S.B., brought out clearly the distinction between intellectual inquiry and the ethical imperative in Lonergan's method. Butler writes:

"*Method* . . . recognizes that just as understanding is an operation that represents a higher viewpoint than sensing and imagination, and just as judgment represents a higher viewpoint than the understanding which it nevertheless presupposes, so *the quest and affirmation of value represent a higher viewpoint, supervening upon and 'sublating' that of judgment.*" B. C. Butler, "Method in Theology," *The Clergy Review* 57 (1972):585. (italics added).

9. For the same reason we cannot favor the inclusion of dogmatic statements in any new Code or new corpus of laws of the Church. A dogmatic statement, in the form of a canon is like a tender tree transplanted into a soil and under a climate where it cannot flourish. It refers to mysteries, and mysteries do not bear legal analysis. It has a hidden strength in itself that presses for the expansion of the original meaning for an on-going deeper understanding. A legal text has a claim to stability.

Methodologically the best way of giving a theological foundation to the new legislation is to write good theological introductions to legal decrees, letting each one be interpreted and grow in its own way. The apostolic constitution *Poenitemini,* on penance (AAS 58 [1966]: 177-198), is an excellent model of such a complex piece of theological instruction and statutory legislation. The theological introduction remains inspiring to this day; in fact, it gained a new invade the field of theology. Fortunately the *latter* is not the problem of our post-Vatican II age. Each generation has it own virtues and vices, even in cultivating the sacred sciences.

Our comments that began with the concept of *praesumptio* led to reflections on the nature of legal language, and finally on to the nature of legal science itself. We sought unity and harmony in our theory because, if those qualities are there, they create a presumption that we are close to reality. After all God has made this world one and harmonious.

CANON 9: PROMULGATION TAKES PLACE IN THE ACTA APOSTOLICAE SEDIS OR IN SOME OTHER LEGALLY DETERMINED WAY

There is no need to quote canon 9 at length. It is enough to remark that while theoretically the method of promulgation prescribed there is clear and neat, in practice the Holy See itself recurs to other means with increasing frequency. Recent laws were mostly promulgated independently of the *Acta* although they were eventually published there. They had special provision for the time of *vacancy,* and the date of first application. Indeed, with delays that inevitably occur today in printing presses, with all the vagaries of transportation through mail to countries all over the world, promulgation through the *Acta* has become cumbersome and unreliable. Reasonably enough, the Holy See used other means of communication for the promulgation of laws such as the publication of a new law by the Vatican Press, official announcements through all available media of communication about the date the law is meant to enter into vigor, etc.

From the point of view of procedure, canon 9 tells us about the evidence that proves promulgation in ordinary circumstances: it is in the *Acta Apostolicae Sedis.*

CANON 10: LAWS REGARD THE FUTURE NOT THE PAST, UNLESS OTHERWISE STATED

This canon has stood up well to the test of time. Its meaning remains, especially in matters concerning the solemnity of acts, inabilities, penalties, and similar cases.

Yet this canon gives us an opportunity to recall that, even if our laws regard the future, they have their roots in the past, that is, in the body of laws that the Church used before the promulgation of the Code.

Under some aspects the Code was a break with our traditions but for the better part the new Code was an expression of continuity with the old *corpus.* Most canons have some relationship with the past either directly or dialectically. Directly, when they consolidate an earlier tradition, as many of the canons on ecclesiastical properties do; dialectically, when they break with tradition and prescribe a new approach as happens on many points in matrimonial legislation (engagement, canonical form, fear, etc.). In neither

relevance through the introduction to the new Order of Penance. In *Poenitemini* the legal dispositions are distinctly and separately given in a clear way.

case can a canon be understood in its proper context unless its historical antecedents are known. Often enough, to find the meaning of a text at the time of the promulgation of the Code, it is necessary to investigate the law of the Decretals.

The Code may well regard the future, but it cannot be properly understood without the past. Nor will our future legislation be a complete break with tradition. When the new law of the Church comes, it will apply to future events and situations but it will have to be rooted in the old law—as direct continuation of it or as dialectical response to it.

CANON 11: ONLY THOSE LAWS SHOULD BE TAKEN AS INVALIDATING OR INCAPACITATING WHICH SAY EXPRESSLY OR EQUIVALENTLY THAT AN ACT IS NOW NULL AND VOID OR A PERSON IS INCAPACITATED

A great foundational rule that can be stated quite simply in positive terms: the legal system of the Church stands for the validity of the acts and for the capacity of the persons. The burden of proof is always on those who deny that an act was properly performed or that a person was not qualified to act. If the validity or capacity is contested on the basis of law and not on some contingent fact, the adversary must show that the law itself declares beyond any reasonable doubt invalidity or incapacity.

Since there are many ambivalent expressions in the Code regarding the validity of an act or the capacity of a person, in spite of the craving of its drafters for clarity, this canon fulfills an important purpose. Presumption is always on the side of validity, of capacity. It is definitely a positive outlook.[10]

Anglo-Saxon common law does not know such a sweeping provision. There, if an expression is doubtful, it is left to the courts to determine its meaning and to declare validity or invalidity accordingly. When this happens at the highest level of the judiciary, it is virtually mandatory for all other courts to follow the decision.

CANON 12: MERE ECCLESIASTICAL LAWS DO NOT BIND THOSE WHO ARE NOT BAPTIZED; NOR THOSE WHO ARE BAPTIZED BUT DO NOT ENJOY SUFFICIENT USE OF REASON; NOR THOSE WHO HAVE REACHED BUT HAVE NOT COMPLETED THEIR SEVENTH YEAR OF AGE, UNLESS THE LAW EXPRESSLY ORDERS OTHERWISE

The Binding Force of Ecclesiastical Laws on Non-Catholics

When we speak of the binding force of laws we are speaking of the right of the legislator to bind his subjects. Equally we are speaking about the duty

10. For a virtually comprehensive list of terms indicating expressly or equivalently invalidity or incapacity, and for a list of ambivalent expressions (too numerous to quote here), see Klaus Mörsdorf, *Die Rechtssprache des Codex Juris Canonici* (Paderborn: Schoeningh, 1967), pp. 93-97.

of the subjects to obey. Right and duty must go together. One cannot exist without the other.

In this canon the legislator states that he has the intention to bind all those who are baptized Christians. Such intention is obviously possible: not only possible but the legislator tells us that he has it. Yet the question should be raised whether or not there is a corresponding duty in the intended subject. If not, the intention of the legislator does not reach the subject; in realilty there is no law.

Duty arises when a human person is able to perceive some real and concrete good, some value that is morally or religiously good for him. From the perception of such value there should follow a realization that the good intended is attainable in the circumstances. Then the person has the duty to reach out for it, to move from theory into action.

But in the case of baptized Christians who are not Catholic, there is simply no perception whatsoever of the value of the Catholic Church in the terms of a spiritual good that is concretely necessary or even useful for them. Since there is no such perception of value, there can be no realization of any duty to observe the Catholic laws. Since there is no awareness of duty, the binding force of law simply does not reach them.

This reasoning implies that the binding force of law cannot be considered abstractly. Either it operates in the concrete world or it does not exist at all.

Nor can the law be defined by its unilateral relationship to the legislator only: if there is no duty in the intended person, there is no law that binds him as a member of the community. Law is an act of communication; the bond cannot arise if there is no communication at all.

* * *

The legal theory that holds that non-Catholic Christians can be bound by the laws of the Catholic community may well have its origin in the exaggerated conception of the *ex opere operato* effect of the sacraments. The legislator is saying that once baptism has taken place, the person belongs to the community and carries the burden of obedience. Yet even the most moderate authors would stress today that no one can become a member of the community unless he completes the gift of baptism with a free option for the community, that is, with an act of faith that embraces the Church among other mysteries.

It should follow then that as long as a person has not professed his faith explicitly in the Catholic Church, he cannot be bound by its law. He is not a full member of the community.[11]

11. Full membership in the community of believers cannot have its origin in the mere fact of baptism alone, although baptism is a sacramental act and has its own effect towards such membership. To reach the fullness of participation in the life of the Church, the baptized person must give himself freely to the community of God's chosen people. It is then that the covenant offered to him through baptism is completed. He becomes a member of Christ's body

Even if someone does not accept the theological reasoning on which our conclusion rests, he could hardly deny its respectability and hence its probability. In other terms, to say the least, there is doubt that non-Catholic Christians can be bound by the Catholic Church. Since there is doubt, in virtue of our own legal principles, they are not bound by our laws.

Behind it all, there is the epistemological issue that sweeps through the field of three sciences in this case: philosophy, theology, and law. Can anyone concretely be bound by a duty that never passed through his mind?

Someone may well be willing to argue that such obligation is possible in the abstract, even if in the concrete it should not be urged. He can point to the attitude of the Church. The Code laid down the obligation in the abstract, but the Church was wise enough not to insist on it in concrete cases. Such an approach, however, avoids the problem rather than solves it. There is again a fundamental question lurking in the background: do moral obligations concern an abstract world, or do choices about values and consequently norms directing such choices refer to the concrete world only?

To disprove the former and to argue the latter is beyond the scope of our study, but we grew convinced that the former stance is critically vulnerable; the latter is much better grounded.[12]

The Age of Reason

The expression *age of reason* is used here according to the scholastic theory, powerfully expressed by Saint Thomas, that the light of reason is given instantly to a human person at a precise point of his life. Before rationality is given, one carries no responsibility; after receiving it, as Saint Thomas says, the person must choose immediately between loving or hating his Creator, either the act of love for God *or* his total rejection.

I have not come across any historical explanation why this "enlightenment" has been placed around the year of seven; presumably because those who reflected on the issue considered significant that around that age a child is able to read and to write and can be introducted into the minor complexities of mathematics. But those thinkers were captives of a metaphysical theory. For them the essence of rationality was either given instantly and then substantially or it was not there at all. They had little notion of personal development that can be perceived only through empirical observation. They could hardly conceive of a human being whose rationality

with all the blessings and burdens, and all the rights and duties that it entails. In stressing freedom, in the community of chosen ones, we reach back to a traditional doctrine that taught that when an infant is baptized, he eventually must give himself by a free act of faith, hope, and love to God. Thus the sacrament of initiation brings fruit and makes the person fully integrated into Christ's body.

12. For further information and discussion see Joseph de Finance, *L'affrontement de l'autre* (Rome: Università Gregoriana, 1973); Bernard Lonergan, *Method in Theology* (New York: Herder and Herder, 1972), especially Chapter 2, "The Human Good," pp. 27-55.

evolves slowly and painfully over many years and comes to maturity only on the threshold of physical adulthood.

The legislator may, of course, need some simple criteria to determine when a subject is bound by the laws. It is interesting to note that, in spite of all metaphysics, common sense prevailed in the Code when it came to practical applications. The Code gives different ages, well above seven when it prescribes the special requirements for entering the novitiates of a community (fifteen), for contracting marriage (sixteen for men, fourteen for women), when it comes to assigning liability for delicts and crimes (fourteen or twenty-one), when it states the necessary age for bishops (thirty) or superiors general of nuns (forty).

As we mentioned in connection with the binding force of the law concerning non-Catholic Christians, the right to legislate goes together with corresponding duty to obey, so that there is law only if both elements, the intention of the legislator and the perception of the subject, are present. The legislator may well want to bind a child of seven but, if the child is not able to perceive the obligation that the authority places on him, how can he be bound? In such circumstances there cannot be law for him.

Practical consequences are especially important in a context where the child would be bound by law "under mortal sin." It is hardly conceivable that a child of seven should be able to grasp the meaning of such a fundamental break with God and responsibly, or rather with deliberate irresponsibility, bring such a break about.

Binding Under Sin

There is no doubt that those who hold the power of the keys can impose a serious obligation on the members of the community. But such disciplinary power except in the case of the office of the pope does not bring with it the charism to pronounce authentically whether or not the breach of the obligation is virtually an infallible sign of a fundamental break with God and the Christian community. That can be a complex theological issue depending much on the nature of the law, the needs of the community, the capacity of the person to respond to a norm of action. Even when the pope himself is the legislator, and he stresses the grave obligation to obey the law, a conscious theologian will ask the question whether or not besides imposing a serious obligation the pope wanted to decide with his whole apostolic authority the doctrinal question of the specific gravity of the breach of law.

As a general rule it is good to recall that, according to the witness of history, popes hardly ever intended to give final answers to a doctrinal question through an act of legislation.

By saying this much, we are stressing a strongly traditional doctrine: the nature of virtue and the nature of sin should be determined on the basis of Christian moral tradition that has its own critical methodology. Our reflections are not meant, of course, to prevent the legislator from insisting on the gravity of obligations; he can certainly do so. But whether or not the breach of duty amounts to a fundamental break with God and the community is a delicate point of doctrine. It cannot be decided accidentally: there is too much at stake, no less than life eternal or exile forever from the Father's house.

The concern of the law is social relations. It can bind consciences, but it should be left to moral theologians to determine the moral fruits of both obedience and disobedience. To pronounce on the quality of virtue or sin is a doctrinal issue. To make laws, to impose them on the community, is disciplinary activity. We are again dealing with two autonomous fields (jurisprudence, moral theology), that ought to be integrated into each other without trespassing into each other's territory.

It follows that in the revision of our laws the legislator may rightly insist on different degrees of obligation but probably he will wisely stop short of making precise statements about the exact gravity of sin involved. Indeed, the new legislation concerning fasting and abstinence and the divine office seems to reflect such an approach on the part of the legislator.

CANONS 15 AND 16: IGNORANCE, DOUBT, AND ERROR

Canons 15 and 16 deal with the question: how the law should handle ignorance, doubt, and error, all fairly frequent occurrences.

But even before the law comes into operation, there are the previous questions: *what is ignorance? what is doubt?* and *what is error?*

These are epistemological questions. Even if strictly legal definitions of the terms are conceivable and feasible, canon law is not interested in formulating them. It just takes some definitions over from philosophy, holds them for true, and then gives the necessary prescription for the situation.

The reason for the restraint of our law is obvious: canonists for centuries have gone through a fairly uniform philosophical training and were given convenient definitions. They realized that all that the law had to do is to say what should be done when a philosophically defined situation arose. Since modern civil lawyers do not benefit from such a common background, their systems tend to determine more closely the meaning of these states of mind.

It follows that there is no canonical definition of ignorance, doubt, and error or for that matter of knowledge, certainty, and truth; the law is merely voicing philosophical and epistemological theories that it has inherited from ages past. But if the justification for the definitions we use comes from outside the law, from philosophy in particular, then there is no need to have *faith* in them. They are as good as their rational basis is, no more and no less. This statement should be stressed because through the assimilation of such theories into the manuals of canon law, and into judicial and administrative decisions on the highest level, the distinction between the two fields, philosophy and canon law, has become blurred, and philosophical definitions are used as if they were canonical prescriptions.

Indeed, it is enough to read canon law manuals and published decisions of our courts to realize that canon lawyers may easily take the wrong direction when they analyze cases involving ignorance or doubt or error. They handle the definitions as if they came from law and they are unaware that the problem at hand is not legal; law is simply using some material taken from the field of another science.

Philosophy and law ought to work together, but they must remain autonomous sciences, each requiring special competence.

. . . To examine the whole Code for its philosophical assumptions and liberate the legal prescriptions from what is not acceptable any longer on epistemological grounds would not be idle work. Probably many of our problems regarding rights and duties included in contracts, or states of life, would benefit from such a purifying operation.

Further, we may ask, how effective the revision of canon law can be, if the philosophical and epistemological foundations of our laws are not revisited and reexamined with all the critical rigor that modern scholarship is able to offer.

Ignorance, Doubt, and Error:
The Need for a New Critical Approach

. . . It is not our intention . . . to follow the well-worn path and give more definitions. We are not proposing finished concepts. Rather, we want to build up a reasonably realistic understanding of them. Law does not postulate that we should have clear and distinct ideas of everything; it asks only for a reasonably clear idea of a few things, in order to recognize situations in which certain procedures must enter into operation.

Ignorance is certainly a *state of mind*. In this we do not differ from classical scholastic philosophy. It is a deficiency at some point of the process of knowing; it can arise at any point of it. There may be no data of information available; then there is ignorance, an easily recognizable situation. Someone who never heard of such a penalty as excommunication is ignorant of it; he is not censured.

Further, a person may not have had any insight into the data actually in his possession; he may not have achieved any understanding of the information received. He is ignorant, he is not able to read behind the surface, he does not understand, *non intel-legit*. Such ignorance is difficult to spot; the breakdown in the process is inside, in the person. His mind does not work, for some reason, be it negligence, laziness, or incapacity. He remains ignorant in spite of some material knowledge. If knowledge is merely a process of looking at an object, then of course no one can be held ignorant once it is proved that he looked at that thing. But if knowledge means understanding as well, clearly there is no true knowledge in the person just described.

Moreover, someone may have all the data and may understand them, but he never goes as far as to accept what he understands as truly existent. A

Protestant or a Muslim may know all about Catholic doctrine of marriage and understand its intricacies (as many do), but has never surrendered to such doctrine as expressing reality. He does not know such doctrine as *true.* Is this condition of his still ignorance? It is; most certainly so. Not to know that something exists in reality even if one understands *what* its elements can be is a radical deficiency in knowledge. It is not enough to know *what* something is, it is equally important to know if it *is,* if it *exists* in reality.

Such ignorance is even more difficult to establish legally since both elements, the data and their understanding, are there. Yet, can anyone ever be bound by the duties of a Christian if he never surrendered to the truth of Christianity?

Ignorance is not a simple concept. And the law as such has no right to decide what ignorance is. The issue is philosophical and epistemological. But the legal consequences of a new epistemological theory are indeed far reaching.[17]

Let us turn to *doubt.* It is a stage in the process of acquiring knowledge. When concerning a thing, person, or situation, there are some but not enough data available, our intelligence is not able to come to an understanding; it can only set up hypotheses with insufficient foundations. Then there is doubt. But the doubt may exist somewhere further ahead in the process, just as ignorance can, such as when too many meanings are compatible with the data, none of them fully satisfactory. Even more, a doubt may concern the existing reality itself: after critical inquiry a person may doubt whether there are enough reasons to surrender to the value that his intelligence appreciates as good for him. Whenever a person is in any of these predicaments, he is in doubt.

The doubt can originate in the signs and symbols themselves through which the legislator attempts to communicate with his subjects or through

. . . 17. To show the importance and the role of foundational questions that originate outside of the law, let us take the epistemological hypothesis that for any decision, to be human at all, previous knowledge and acceptance of the values involved is necessary. Let us see its legal consequences. That is, let us assume that the extent of knowledge about the values desired determines the extent of responsibility. This is not the classical scholastic theory that *some* knowledge is necessary to assume responsibility for a decision; it goes beyond it. It assumes that one is responsible for a decision as far as he knew the concrete value that he wanted to appropriate for himself. Neither more or less. It excludes the theory that through the operation of the will, a person can assume duties not known to the mind.

If this hypothesis is true, the following steps are required to contract a Christian marriage:

(a) the knowledge and understanding of the Church's teaching on the sacrament of marriage, including all the qualities attached to the sacrament as such;

(b) the acceptance of the teaching as true; this can be done with an act of faith only;

(c) the perception of this particular marriage as concretely good for the person who wants to enter into it;

(d) the decision to appropriate that value through taking the necessary legal action.

If our initial hypothesis is right (which is a philosophical and not legal question), there is no sacramental marriage unless the fullness of the process described is completed. If it is impaired, the covenant falls short of sacramentality.

which a fact is apprehended. Classically this is called objective doubt, anything else is subjective doubt. But again, the issue is more complex. When someone does not have the innate capacity to pull together the data and to understand what kind of intelligent meaning is hiding behind them, his incapacity is objective enough. When he refuses to consider the data or uses them selectively because of a bias, he is more likely to suffer from subjective doubt. This distinction should be enough to warn us that the difference between objective and subjective doubt may not be so clear as our classical philosophy claimed it to be.

Error is some kind of an illusion, expressed in judgment. A judgment is proposed as rationally grounded when it is not. Someone surrenders to something that *is* not. How can this happen? Again, there is a breakdown in the cognitional process at some point or other. Maybe the evidence was not carefully gathered, hence the process became vitiated at the source. Or a person handles the factual information selectively, giving more importance to some elements than was due to them and less to others; somehow he misdirected the process while in progress. Or a person surrendered to a judgment that he never critically examined as to its truth. Such attitudes are possible, and they are all real sources of errors.

. . . In the case of *error in persona* concerning a marriage contract (see canon 1083), the classical theory is that when the error is *substantialis* it invalidates the marriage; when it is not, it does not do so. The theory is logical, but it is built on a metaphysical theory that has nothing to do with the law. A human person primarily consists of a substance and true knowledge is in perceiving the substance. To want a person means to want what is essential in him: his substance. Therefore, mistaken knowledge of his or her personal accidents will not, cannot, invalidate the marriage. Hence if Titius wanted to marry Caia whom he believed to be a learned and pious virgin but who turned out after the wedding to be an ignorant and irreligious prostitute, the marriage is still valid. Titius will have to live with the substance of Caia and be satisfied with it—no matter how totally repulsive her accidental qualities are. The law tells him that he obtained what he intended to have; his protests would be in vain. Our law takes its stance from philosophy. There is something radically inhuman in this solution, even if it is logical according to its premises.

If we approach the same issue by analyzing the conscious intention of Titius, we probably find that he never thought about substance and accidents, or distinguished any such things in Caia. He simply gradually built up a knowledge of Caia, of her whole person, but somehow the process has gone astray, somewhere it has broken down: *he* really did not come to know her. Hence Titius never even once intended to take the real Caia; he never once surrendered to the true Caia as a value for him; he surrendered to a false image. He never thought of making the supposed qualities of Caia into an absolute condition either; it simply did not occur to him to act in that way. Take away the theory of substance and accidents and build the conclusion on the conscious intention of Titius; then it is clear that he had no intentión at any point of time to marry Caia. He never undertook the obligation to spend his life with the ignorant and irreligious prostitute.

Better still, let us take the example of *error simplex* (see canon 1084). The classical approach springs from a metaphysical system again. The mind and will are distinct, therefore it is logical that the will can accept an obligation no matter how heavy and long-lasting it is, even if the mind does not know about it. Hence, the Lutheran who always thought marriage was soluble and never knew in any other way is bound forever by an indissoluble union. Further, he may have known about the doctrine but never accepted it as true, yet he would be bound forever. Really such a person is caught in the net of an obligation unaware and unwilling, since he never knew about the duty that is suddenly imposed on him.

Let us try to forget again the metaphysical foundations, and turn to an analysis of the internal operations. We find that, to be human at all, there must be a continuity from knowledge to decision. Or, to say it negatively, no decision can be human unless the value wanted was seen beforehand. If an obligation was not known, it was not assumed. The person never surrendered to the value that it represents. Indissolubility does represent a value.[18]

We took our examples from the law of marriage, but obviously the application of intentionality analysis in place of metaphysical theories neither begins nor ends there. An analagous issue is first mentioned in the Code in canon 12 that speaks of the binding force of the laws for non-Catholic Christians, if not explicitly, certainly by implication.

True, in classical theology the moral obligation to obey the laws of the Church arises from the metaphysical or theological reality of baptism no matter what a person may or may not know, but in our analysis even on the level of faith there must be an awareness of the value to be pursued, of the good to be obtained. Without such awareness the person cannot surrender

18. However one may judge the legal wisdom contained in canons 1083 and 1084, the canons manifest also a philosophical or more precisely ethical thinking that deserves critical analysis.

It is a far reaching and harsh statement to say that *error circa qualitatem etsi det causam contractui,* an error even if it is the very reason for contracting the marriage, *non vitiat consensum,* is really irrelevant when it comes to the question of validity. Is it ethical to bind a person for life partnership on the basis of a decision inspired by an error?

If the marriage is upheld for the sake of the common good, the question still arises how far the good of a person should be sacrificed to the interest of the community? We should not be deterred from asking the question: How far would God hold someone responsible in conscience for the consequences of a consent that was given because of (that is, prompted by) a mistaken judgment.

Similar legal doctrine should be quite acceptable in minor legal matters such as *emptio-venditio.* But the sacrament of matrimony is different: all the complex demands of human dignity and integrity, all the delicate balances of personal good and common good come into play. We think the doctrine contained in these two canons definitely needs critical examination and clarification from deeper sources than law can provide.

to an obligation. And if there is no surrender, there is no duty either.

The same is of course true in the case of children; awareness of a duty in the intelligence is an absolute condition for responsible decision. No duty can exist without such consciousness of an obligation.

There are other fields where the doctrine explained can be fruitfully applied, such as in cases of rights and duties connected with sacred orders, with religious vows, with various offices in the Church.

* * *

More often than not our legal system is blamed for what appears to be inhumanity when in reality the problem is not with the law but with the continuing acceptance of a philosophical system that was a giant step forward in one age but which has been found wanting on a number of points when critically examined in the light of new knowledge given to a later age.[19]

Experts in the law may go into long investigations to find ways to humanize our laws as there seems to be an urgent need for it. They may try to bring about changes by searching for loopholes, perhaps through the manipulation of the law, at times manipulation even beyond recognition. Virtually all interpreters today are attempting to make the old law respond better to our needs. As yet, few canon lawyers think of questioning certain philosophical or epistemological assumptions in the law. Not many are aware of the hermeneutical problem either that is with us whether we like it or not! Many attempts to correct the law through the law are really *magnus passus extra viam:* a movement in the wrong direction.

CANON 17, §1: LAWS ARE AUTHENTICALLY INTERPRETED BY THE LEGISLATOR AND HIS SUCCESSOR; ALSO BY SOMEONE TO WHOM THE POWER TO INTERPRET THE LAWS WAS GRANTED BY THE LEGISLATOR OR HIS SUCCESSOR

§2: AUTHENTIC INTERPRETATION GIVEN BY WAY OF LAW HAS THE SAME BINDING FORCE AS THE LAW ITSELF; AND IF IT DOES NO MORE THAN TO DECLARE THE TEXT OF LAW THAT HAS BEEN CERTAIN, IT DOES NOT NEED PROMULGATION AND IS RETROACTIVE; IF IT RESTRICTS OR EXTENDS THE MEANING OF THE LAW OR CLARIFIES A DOUBTFUL

19. Behind our reasoning there is a contrast between two cognitional theories. One is based on the theory of universal concepts, acquired by looking at the world around us, and perceiving the universal essences in things. Such universal concepts can be stored in the mind and can remain unchanged, forever. A legal text construed through such concepts will remain always the same. The only authentic interpretation will be an authentic declaration whether the law is clear or obscure. In the other theory, the meaning of the law is subject to evolution as our language, understanding, and judgment develops. But ultimately the meaning of the law is really our mind perceiving, understanding and judging the norms given to guide our actions. We are painfully aware how inadequate such a short note is, even to hint at cognitional theories, but there is a remarkably clear explanation of the contrast between the two theories: see Joseph Flanagan "Knowing and Language in the Thought of Bernard Lonergan," in *Language, Truth and Meaning,* edited by Philip McShane (Dublin: Gill and Macmillan, 1972), pp. 49-78. It is a highly recommended introduction into this complex issue.

Meaning It Is Not Retroactive and Must Be Promulgated

When canon 17 § 2 is examined critically, two meanings of "authentic interpretation" arise:

(a) interpretation of a text of which the meaning was always clear;

(b) interpretation of a text of which the meaning was doubtful.

In the first case the interpretation by the legislator consists in declaring again what has been clear in the first place and ever since. Such interpretation needs no promulgation and binds retroactively.

Since what is declared has been clear throughout, the declaration cannot be called interpretation in the ordinary meaning of that word; it is simply an instruction to those who for one reason or another, be it for ignorance or negligence, did not perceive the meaning that was manifestly there.

In the second case a new meaning is given that initially was not there. Consequently to make it law, it needs to be promulgated. Also it must affect the future; it cannot be retroactive.

But such process is not interpretation either, according to the ordinary meaning of the term: it is simply a new piece of legislation.

If neither of these two cases are interpretation, except in a technical and unusual sense contained in this canon, the question emerges: What is interpretation?

Also, can there be an authentic interpretation which fits neither of these cases? In other terms, is the source of authentic interpretation the legislator himself and no one else? Should we conclude that all other interpretations *in* the community or *by* community are not authentic?

Canon 17 follows the epistemological theory on which so much of our legal system has been built. It understands everything in static universal concepts and has no notion of evolution.

But laws cannot stand still in the midst of a living community. First of all, they cannot stand still because they are not made from permanent unchangeable universal concepts that can be frozen into a text and remain so forever. The words are mere signs that carry a meaning; the words themselves are alive and evolve.

Then a community consists of persons, be they legislators, be they receivers of the law. The law lives in their minds and not in books. Communities and persons also evolve all the time. Hence, from the moment the law has been made it is subject to an evolutionary change, be it in the mind of the legislator or of his successor, be it in the mind of those who receive the law.

In other terms, there is no such thing as a static law exhibiting the same clarity or obscurity (as the case may be) that was its primary quality at the moment of its birth. There is only a community of persons with living minds. They make and receive the law; they understand it progressively; in them a process of development is going on. Such development is an ongoing interpretation. It has its roots in the text; it receives its dynamism from the mind.

Facts bear out this approach, the same facts that decry the approach of canon 17. It would be idle to pretend that today all canons in the Code are understood in the same way as they were at the time of its promulgation. There have been many decisions by Roman Congregations, many judgments by the Sacred Roman Rota. They have been published. They are not simple applications of static concepts contained in eternally permanent propositions; rather they witness that our law is alive, its meaning evolves, develops, and changes. It cannot be any other way.

Evolutionary interpretation is always creative work; whether it happens consciously or subconsciously. To a meaning intended or perceived, slight new shades are added, and thus the meaning of the law is expanded. The same process may go the other way too: shades of meaning are taken away, and thus the law is gradually restricted.

Such a process of evolution must not be ignored by the legislator and by jurisprudence. It takes place anyway, but if it is not recognized it cannot be channeled, directed, and used for the healthy progress of the community. In an analogous sense, it *is* authentic interpretation recognized somewhat timidly by canon 29.

In the Anglo-American common law system there is a device to help such an evolution. It is the right of the courts to interpret the law authentically. Any judge would deny that he is a legislator; but a reflective judge would confirm that he makes a contribution to the development of the law.

In the Church we have no such agency. Hence evolution is not officially recognized as authentic.

CANON 18: ECCLESIASTICAL LAWS MUST BE UNDERSTOOD ACCORDING TO THE PROPER SIGNIFICANCE OF THEIR TERMS CONSIDERED IN THE TEXT AND IN THE CONTEXT. IF AFTER INVESTIGATION THEY REMAIN DOUBTFUL AND OBSCURE, THE INTERPRETER SHOULD REFER TO PARALLEL TEXTS IN THE CODE, IF ANY; TO THE PURPOSE AND THE CIRCUMSTANCES OF THE LAW AND TO THE MIND OF THE LEGISLATOR

Interpretation

Good interpretation is a work of art, not a mechanical process. Ordinarily it must be done by specialists for reasons that will become obvious as we progress in our reflections.

(1) A myth should be dispelled right from the beginning. Interpretation is not simply the matter of finding the definition of the terms. There are no human words, there are no texts written by human beings that exist in a vacuum or in some ideal abstract world. If that were possible, all that the legislator would have to do is to store the words and the sentences in an ideal environment where the interpreter can find them. This is a simplistic

conception often at the origin of uncritical and literal interpretations. The reality is far more complex. There is no human word once spoken or written that can stand untouched by the flow of our history.

(2) Every text deals with a topic: it focuses on an object. The legal texts on Christian initiation speak of *baptism*. They do not say what baptism is. They are concerned with practical attitudes and actions surrounding the administration of baptism. Therefore, it is necessary for the interpreter to have a good understanding of the subject matter of the texts, that is, of baptism, before he can start commenting on them. Moreover, he must know if his own perception of baptism is in harmony with that of the legislator; otherwise they may well be talking at cross-purposes. Ordinarily the legislator assumes a great deal of this kind of common understanding between himself and the community before he makes and promulgates the law.

(3) The words and the sentences in the text carry meanings. But words are often ambivalent; they are capable of including slightly or greatly different significations. The interpreter must quite definitely struggle with many possible meanings in the text and ascertain the *one* meaning the legislator intended to put there which is not necessarily the obvious one.

Nor is the right meaning always the one that comes spontaneously into the mind of the interpreter. The greater the difference in time, space, and culture between the legislator and his commentator, the more carefully the interpreter must proceed. We *do* have hermeneutical problems in canon law.

(4) The cultural context of the legislator must be taken into account. He cannot help but use the terms, the categories, of his own particular culture or civilization; he cannot see further than his own horizon. It may happen that the interpreter does not understand this and is naively looking for perfect expressions not affected by external circumstances.

Such a desire is born from an illusion. It supposes that someone, in this case the legislator, could divest himself of his own human condition and speak in a way that is beyond the limits of time, space, and culture. Such inhuman privilege is not given to any one. It follows that no one can appreciate the legal rules taken from the Decree of Gratian unless he has reconstructed the historical circumstances in which they were written. Nor is anyone able to find the right meaning in a legal text coming from the Holy See unless he has a good working knowledge of the highly developed and sophisticated Italian culture. But the process does not end there.

(5) Intelligent interpretation can be done only by a human person blessed with a capacity for critical reflection. No matter how objective the interpreter wants to be, he is projecting something of his own mentality, of his own perception of values, into the interpretation. No one can be a hundred percent objective. If that were possible or desirable, we could use computers for interpretation; they can work with uniform and universal concepts. Human beings cannot and do not. Their mind works on the data offered to

them, on the signs and signals coming from the legislator through space, time, and cultural borders. The interpreter must use his own mental categories to understand such communication; he must use his own cultural background to explicate the full meaning of a concise and compressed legal text. There is the reason why no two commentators are alike, why different schools of interpretation do emerge and do not merge. There is a difference between *Capello* and *Van Hove*; each brings his own personality and culture into the interpretation.

(6) We see now why the task of interpreting laws can look deceptively simple and is infinitely complex. Often the law uses terms that have a meaning in ordinary language. Therefore a person with common sense is able to put a reasonable construction on the legal text out of his own background and believe that it is the meaning of the law. He may not be aware that his mind never achieved a harmony with the mind of the legislator. He may not be aware that the same words may carry different meanings in different civilizations; he does not realize that the legislator himself used (as all human beings do) the mental categories of his own culture and in general was preconditioned by his own civilization. Also, the less than learned interpreter may not be aware that his own mental categories, his own civilization preconditioned him and prejudged the meaning of the text and its explanation. Finally, he may not be aware that he and the laws are all part of an evolving universe. Truly the interpretation of laws is a highly specialized art.

Christian communities are entitled to the best in the art of intelligent interpretation.[20]

20. Canonists have been accused of lack of humanity borne from a narrow legalism. Concerning the past, the accusation was not always without foundation. Concerning the future, the same danger exists for the canonist who does not know the historical roots of his legal system.

Indeed, one of the best remedies against narrow legalism is to acquire broad historical horizons. This means more than to know the past history of some canons; it means to enter into another way of conceiving a legal system, to know other methods of using its principles and reaching conclusions. In practice it means to become familiar with the mind and the method of operation of Gratian, and further back, to be reasonably at home in the world of classical Roman law.

A canonist whose knowledge is confined to the present law only may well be able to find a loophole in the system, to resolve a hard case by the application of canonical equity or epikeia. His solution may bring praise for his Christian spirit, but in the long run he will not build a good reputation for our laws. To the impartial observer he will often give the impression that he is using the old formalism for new ends.

Someone who has historical perspectives is able to place the present law into a much broader context; his horizons include the dimensions of the living Church throughout centuries. The *regulae iuris* of Boniface VIII, even if most of them are not formally incorporated into the Code, are by no means dead; they remain guiding lights for the interpretation of the spirit and the letter of our laws. The dialectical method of Gratian based on the critical play of affirmation and denial, *sic et non,* is still a valuable tool to make us aware of the relative value of each canonical norm. The guiding ideas of Roman law that Fritz Schultz brought so tellingly in his *Principles of Roman Law* (Oxford: Clarendon Press, 1936), can serve as inspiration for canon law that has its roots in Roman Law. *Nihil humanum a me alienum esse puto:* nothing that is

Canon 19: Laws That Impose Penalties or Restrict the Free Use of Rights or Introduce an Exception to the Law Must be Interpreted Strictly

The *laws that impose penalty* should not be confused with laws that impose disabilities on individual persons for the sake of the community, even if the origin of the disability is not the fault of the person concerned.

A disability is often imposed for the sake of the community, for the common good. Since the aim of such laws is to promote the welfare of the community, the interpretation should be in favor of the health and progress of the community. For example, irregularities are imposed on a person not as penalty but as disqualification for an office in the Church. They protect the community by disqualifying some persons for certain offices. The interpretation of such laws should be in favor of the community; that is, the meaning of disqualification should be rather extended than restricted so that even doubtfully qualified persons are restrained from entering an office in the service of the community. It would be incorrect to consider such laws from the point of view of personal rights only.

Free exercise of rights refers probably to fundamental human rights only. The canon should not be approached by saying that in some way all laws restrict the free exercise of rights. The purpose of many laws is precisely to determine the proper field of exercise for rights; if they impose any restrictions, it is for the sake of freedom.

Exception from the law remains an obscure expression. All universal laws are part of one single system that forms a *whole;* one law should not be considered an exception to another. Of course, one law may well restrict or qualify the application of another in certain cases, but that is how every legal system operates.

Perhaps a particular law could introduce an exception from universal law, assuming that the necessary approval has been obtained. In that case, such particular law would be of strict interpretation.

Canon 20: If Concerning a Case, There is No Express Provision By a General or a Particular Law, the Norm Must Be Taken From Laws Made For Analogous Situations (unless it is a Case of Imposing a Penalty), From General Legal Principles Applied With Canonical Equity, From the Style and Praxis of the Roman Curia, From the Common and Steady Teaching of Doctors

The Meaning of Lacuna Iuris

Lacuna means that there is no provision of law for a given situation when

human should be alien to our canonical law. The Romans' love for simplicity, their fidelity to their traditions, their respect for freedom, their attachment to the common laws of our humanity, and above all their famous *bona fides* should be integral parts of our legal world.

there should be one.

The canon is not opening the door for the fabrication of new laws. It does not encourage the multiplication of laws either. It deals specifically with an unusual situation where the good of the community demands the legal resolution of a case but there is no law to be invoked. There is no law in the books; no legally valid custom exists; yet legal action is necessary for the sake of the common good. No system of laws is so perfect that it can provide for all contingencies. In real life there will be always unforeseen situations, emergencies to be taken care of.

Who is competent to recognize such *lacuna* and provide for the need?

This canon is primarily addressed to those who administer the law with power of jurisdiction, such as courts, administrative offices, whether of the Holy See or of a diocese. At times they may be faced with a situation where the good of the community or the welfare of an individual postulates nothing less than a legal solution that has validity in the external forum. But there is no law to justify such legal act. It is in such relatively rare cases that persons with jurisdiction are empowered as it were to create a new law and apply it. To give such extraordinary power to them it is necessary to have this canon. It gives legality to an act that otherwise could be or even should be illegal. It is an unusual broadness in a Code which stresses so much the principle that there is no law without promulgation.

The canon is obviously conceived in favor of persons or communities, presumably to redress some wrong. It is explicitly forbidden to extend the canon to a situation where someone could be penalized.

CANON 21: LAWS MADE TO PREVENT SOME GENERAL DANGER ARE TO BE OBSERVED EVEN IF IN A PARTICULAR CASE THERE IS NO DANGER

This is a simple canon of limited application, or so it appears at the first reading. The obvious example often quoted to illustrate its meaning is the prohibition of reading heretical books or participating in non-Catholic religious services. But the range of the canon goes well beyond such cases. Let us consider the key issues and find the questions that are relevant for the understanding of its text.

What Is Common Danger?

Let us begin by asking what is *danger?*

It is a situation where harm or danger is not merely possible but is positively probable; it is threatening or it is imminent. But to what kind of harm or damage does the canon refer? Hardly to physical danger: after all the Church is primarily a spiritual community. Rather, it refers to some spiritual danger to the peace and unity of the group; anything that is likely to disrupt the life or the operation of the Christian community.

The canon, however, does not speak of a particular danger but of a *com-*

mon one. So, one should ask, when does danger become *common?* what kind of community must it threaten? a parish? a diocese? a religious community? the universal Church itself?

As soon as such questions are raised, other problems arise. Danger to be real must be *concrete.* Therefore, the canon is dealing with a situation of fact. It applies when a well-defined concrete danger actually threatens an identifiable community. It does not apply to all kinds of merely possible or imaginable dangers. It refers to a determinable danger which is somehow manifest and if necessary it could be proved before a court. But otherwise who will be the judge of such a factual situation?

Moreover, what happens if a common danger actually exists in most parts of the universal Church but not in one of its regions? Examples are not difficult to find. Participation in non-Catholic worship can be radically disruptive to the Catholic Community in some places while in other lands where Catholics and Protestants have lived in peace for a long time and learned to respect each other, certain types of participation can be very much in order.

A reasonable interpretation of the canon would be that for the danger to exist concretely, unmistakable evidence of threat should be there; of threat that is likely to disrupt the peace and unity of the community if it is not warded off.

How to Recognize Laws Enacted to Guard Against Common Danger?

An unusual proposition: to know whether or not the law applies, the specific purpose of the legislator must be investigated since the canon applies in case of laws enacted to guard against common danger.

But how can that be known? In no other way than through some evidence that the legislator made the law to ward off common danger. Where can such evidence be found? Perhaps in the text of the law or in a long standing tradition based on experience or in some clarification given by the legislator after the promulgation of the law. The evidence, of course, should be strong, ideally strong enough to convince impartial judges about the mind of the legislator.

After all, it is conceivable that some forbidding laws were not necessarily intended to guard the community against common danger but, for instance, were made to contribute to the sanctification of the community, by promoting devout life, edifying actions, and so forth. Then the canon would not apply.

If it cannot be shown beyond reasonable doubt that the intended purpose of the law was to safeguard the community, the canon should not apply. Besides, whenever this piece of law restricts one of the fundamental freedoms of the subject (for example, freedom to obtain legitimate information), it must be interpreted strictly. If doubt arises, freedom should be favored. That is, the prohibition should not stand.

What Is a Particular Case?

The expression *particular case* must be understood in contrast to *common danger.* The case of an individual wanting to perform the forbidden act would be clearly a particular one. Also, one or a few repeated acts of a particuar community would come under the prohibition of the law. Of course whenever danger actually threatening the community cannot be proved, individuals or communities would be free to act.

What Happens If the Common Danger Ceases to Exist but the Law Remains?

The issue of historical change and evolution comes up in connection with this canon too.

Danger is not danger unless it is concrete, actual, and threatening. What happens to the law if it was justified to guard against common danger at the time the law was made but with the passage of time such danger ceases to exist? Thus Christian communities of different denominations in recent decades moved from a climate of antagonism and opposition into a new relationship of mutual respect and understanding. The former situation created danger; the latter does not. But many of the laws remain as they were in the beginning. Are they still binding? We doubt it.

Similar questions arise concerning laws made against Freemasons, at least in some countries.

The right answer is to say that whenever the common danger ceases the present canon is not applicable. If there is no danger, its *raison d'être* has disappeared; if there is no danger, there is nothing to guard people from.

What Is the Binding Force of This Canon?

Is the binding force of this canon the same as that of other canons, or does it go beyond? Does this prohibition go so far as to cancel out the normal and the legitimate use of *epikeia* and equity?

The need of *epikeia* springs from the nature of the legal system itself. Laws, being general, abstract, and impersonal, cannot provide for particular concrete and personal situations in every case; at times adjustment is necessary. Such need really follows from the limitation from which *all* our norms of action suffer. It is hardly conceivable that this canon should be so radical as to exclude the normal corrective that philosophers ever since Aristotle, including Saint Thomas Aquinas, recognized as necessary for the healthy operation of any legal system.

Equity was never so well defined as *epikeia.* But it certainly means to temper the harshness or the strictness of the law through understanding and mercy that originates in Christian faith and charity. Cases may well arise where this particular canon should be so tempered. It would be unreasonable to assume that the legislator with the general formulation of this text would have intended to exclude the application of equity that must penetrate all the operations of all our laws.

Consequently, the binding force of this canon should be described as admitting the use of both *epikeia* and equity. It is not a canon against reason.

CANONS 22 AND 23: DISPOSITIONS CONCERNING LEGISLATION PROMULGATED AFTER THE CODE; THE LAWS OF INTERPRETATION WHEN THE NEW LAW IS CONFRONTED WITH THE OLD

Canons 22 and 23 are interesting not so much for the detailed provisions they contain about how to handle legislation following the promulgation of the Code as for the philosophy they contain concerning development of the whole legal system.

The substance of the dispositions that reveal the philosophy can be divided into three parts:

When Does a New Law Replace the Old?

The old law is replaced by the new when one of the following three conditions is fulfilled.

(a) The new law explicitly says that the old law is cancelled. No comments are needed.

(b) The new law does not say that the old law is cancelled, but the new dispositions are directly contrary to the old ones.

The old law is cancelled on the basis of the principle of contradiction.

(c) The new law does not say that the old one is cancelled; the new law does not directly contradict the old one, but the legislator takes into hand the whole subject matter of the old law and restructures it in such a way that the new order is incompatible with the old one.

If an analogy from Aristotelian philosophy is allowed, perhaps one could speak of giving a new form to the same primary matter; the old form must disappear.

In all three cases the passage from the old law to the new is abrupt; there is not really what could be called a twilight situation; there is a clear change, from one structure to another, from one set of norms to another. It is interesting to note that all these changes are expected to come through new statutes. Nothing else is mentioned. No evolution through customs, no evolution through interpretation, no gradual transition of any kind. In all three cases a clear act of legislation, presumably through promulgation, puts an end to the old and signals the beginning of the new.

What Should Be Done in a Twilight Situation When There Is Doubt Concerning the Transition from the Old to the New Law?

Canon 23 grants that doubt can arise about the impact of the new law on the old one. What happens then? The Code gives working rules for dealing with the situation. To begin with, a new legislative act does not generate any presumption that the old law is going out of existence. On the contrary, the canon implies a presumption for the continuing existence of the old law. The later law must be adjusted to the earlier one. The canon does not say how far such adjustment should go. Should it be confined to the ordinary limits of broad and narrow interpretation of the new law excluding any extensive or restrictive interpretation? The answer must be *yes:* the ordinary meaning of the terms should be respected; otherwise the new law would be changed and forced artificially into the meaning of the old. The new law should be adjusted to the old but never to the extent that the ordinary meaning of its terms is lost. Thus a scope *is* given to the new law and the system can develop.

The Code Upholds Particular Laws

Canon 22 upholds a very old tradition of the Church, a tradition that precedes even the centralization of jurisdictional power in the Middle Ages. General laws do not cancel out particular laws, whether territorial or personal. Particular groups of Christians can grow and develop according to their own tradition and inspiration. The only exception is an explicit cancellation of a particular law by the general one. Clear contradiction between new general law and the old particular one or the general reorganization of the subject matter by general laws would not be enough to put an end to the life of a particular law.

There is a freedom guaranteed by canon 22. It concerns ecclesiastical moral persons of many kinds; among them dioceses and religious communities occupy an important place.

* * *

Canons 22 and 23 are inspired by the principle: *mutatio legis odiosa:* change in the law is odious. When it must be done, it must happen in an unmistakable way; it must be a step consciously taken and stated. An evolution quietly taking place is not contemplated by the canons. If there is a doubt the scale must tilt in favor of the old.

There is a latent conflict there. Why should the legislator bother to bring forth new statutes when the general effort of the courts, administrators, and interpreters should be rather the opposite: to divest the statute recently promulgated from its newness and bring it within the field already covered by the old legislation. Should not the very fact that a new law was made create a presumption that the legislator intended to communicate something new?

Indeed, the presumption advocated in canon 23 was not taken too seriously over the sixty years of the Code; rather it has been quietly turned around. Whenever a new law appeared, the interpreters assumed that the legislator had something new to say. They searched for it and mostly found it. Indeed it would be difficult to quote one single law made after the Code that had been simply adjusted to an old meaning. An evolution, in fact, has been taking place.

Canon 24: Some Remarks on Precept

The canonical meaning of precept has been amply commented on and explained. There is only one point that we like to single out as problematic and in need of clarification.

A precept is normally given to an individual person and as such it has a legitimate place in the legal system. But historically the custom of *common precept* developed, and it became a way of legislating by those who had no legislative power or who, if they had it, did not want to use it formally.

While many canonists built up a theoretical justification for such practice on the basis of common precept, practical experience over long periods of time has shown that it is better to avoid such disguised legislation.

Consequently, if a *desideratum* can be expressed for the future, we suggest that the right to give a precept should be strictly confined to precepts given to individuals. Communities should be governed by laws. Laws not only have more stability but are usually prepared with greater care. It is conceivable of course that for peculiar reasons the same precept could be given to several individuals, but then it should be given distinctly to each.

Our preoccupation is really a simple one: there should be no disguised legislation anywhere in the Church, even under the cover of common precepts. By restricting precepts to individuals, the danger of unconstitutional legislation is eliminated. The community gains not only in clarity and simplicity but also in genuine constitutional government.

Conclusions

In our *glossae* on the canons on ecclesiastical laws, on canons that move from one topic to another, we too moved from one idea to another, at times well beyond the field covered by the text of the law. Can such dispersed comments be brought into a unified body of conclusion?

We think that there is convergence in the questions raised and in the answers given. But the answers are not final by any means: more often than not they are starting points for further reflections.

1. The canons on ecclesiastical laws for the most part retain the character of procedural instructions. They can be best used by judges, administrators, and interpreters. They give directions for the smooth and right operation of the whole legal system. In Title One of Book One, the Code is more concerned with the working of the laws than with substantive rights and duties. In this the Code is very close indeed to classical Roman law. It is close

enough to the origins of Anglo-Saxon common law too.

The weakness of our system is that we have rules in theory but we do not have strong procedural institutions in practice, as the Romans had, as many modern states have. Our legal system needs some strengthening to tilt the balance more toward government by law than government by man; that is, justice given through courts rather than through administrative offices. Although it remains true that in the Church personal government on both levels, universal and particular, will have its role to play. At any rate, the jurisdiction of our courts could be broadened in practice well beyond the adjudication of marriage cases.

2. In the canons examined we find a curious mixture of the practical and procedural bent of classical Roman law and the static character of a certain type of scholastic philosophy coming more from manuals than from Saint Thomas. There is a built-in trend in the canons against growth, development, and natural evolution, especially when this happens unconsciously through the instinctive action of the community. Therefore, there is a tangible gap between real life and our legal system. Such a gap leads to an isolation of canon law not only in the cultural world of ours but within the Christian community. We do not have legal institutions to take care of evolution, institutions that could steadily and peacefully adjust the law to changing circumstances.

3. To this day canon law remains immune to movements that deeply influenced the development of sacred sciences in recent years, to questions concerning issues of epistemology and hermeneutics. There has been hardly any dialogue between theologians working on those problems and canon lawyers. Perhaps canon law is the only ecclesiastical science that still works virtually exclusively with concepts inherited from philosophers who performed an admirable task in their own time, but who have been corrected, completed, superseded under several aspects. We have no hope of being a useful instrument for the Church of the future unless we accept new challenges and questions coming from our fellow philosophers and theologians.

4. Canon law or for that matter canon lawyers can rightly and responsibly operate from a very rich background only. Somewhere in the middle ages canon law became separated from theology. And both sciences paid a high price for it. It was the beginning of a development toward excessive legalism that marked so deeply the life of the Church after the Council of Trent until very recent times. Vice versa, the absence of practical dimensions took away something of the practical even kerygmatic character of theology.

Canon law that does not have its roots in other sacred sciences and humanities, that does not have horizons that embrace other legal systems, can lead only to a new narrowness with a new loss of respect for the law in the Church.

5. While research and discussion should continue concerning individual

legal institutions, we should be concerned increasingly with the foundational questions of the legal system of the Church. Questions and answers of this nature should not be inserted into any new Code nor into any new statutory law. But they should be at the origin of them all.

B. SELECT PROCEDURES

Return to the Lay State: The Meaning, Practice, and Reform of Laicization

Terence E. Tierney

I. INTRODUCTION*

Prophetic voices within and without the Church have for a long time stressed the need for reform in the Catholic Church. Since the second Vatican Council, the necessity of such a reform has also entered the consciousness of broad circles inside the Church and has become a "horizon" of the concept of the Church today.

Yet in the post-conciliar period there has been considerable evidence of resistance to such a movement. Opinions are divided, but not only in regard to the exact nature of individual reform. There are also questions regarding how far reforms can really go, in what way, through what mechanisms, and within what period of time they are to take effect.

The number of priests who have abandoned their ministry in the past years is no longer a Chancery secret. It is a topic widely discussed and deeply perplexing to the hierarchy and people alike.

The words "laicization" and "reduction to the lay state" appear quite frequently in the early sections of this study. They are used for purely historical reasons. Indeed, I strongly feel that they should quickly disappear from common parlance in favor of the more dignified and socially acceptable terminology of either "resignation" or "return to the lay state". The former terms involve theological inaccuracies and the pejorative connotation of moral dereliction. The use of the term "reduction" could also be insulting to the laity, unbecoming the dignity of those baptized into Christ.

II. THE MEANING OF "LAICIZATION" AND ITS OUTLINE IN THE 1917 CODE OF CANON LAW

When considering the "reduction" of clerics to the lay state it must

*Acknowledgement is here made to Mr. Wayne Long for access to his unpublished manuscript of the above topic. I have based much of my article upon his research.

always be understood that this "reduction" is properly an external, canonical and juridical procedure. By the juridical "reduction" to the lay state is meant the act which takes away the licit use of the power of orders, deprives the cleric of his rights, privileges and juridical status and makes him equivalent to a layman.[1] This so-called reduction amounts to a withdrawal of the jurisdiction to use the power inherent and intrinsic to the character of orders. It is essentially a question of the exercise of jurisdiction and not a question of the cancellation of the powers conferred by the sacrament of Orders itself. Or again we are confronted with the delicate problem of the primacy of orders vs. jurisdiction or, more properly, the separation of these two elements into distinct categories which are allowed to slip into a "formal" dichotomy. The power of orders can never be taken away by the Church, only its exercise can be prescribed by the competent ecclesiastical authority.

Since the sacrament of Holy Orders imprints upon the soul an indelible character, it is not within the power of the Church to effect an internal or absolute reduction. That the sacrament imprints the character has been the constant teaching of the infallible Church, and its denial was solemnly anathematized in the Council of Trent.[2]

Since the discussion regarding laicization refers to clerics it seems altogether fitting that we define in what the clerical state consists. The Code of Canon Law states that what was then known as "tonsure" brought a person into the clerical state; however, canon 107 presents us with a curious problem relative to the former tonsure and minor orders. It states that "there are in the Church, by divine institution clerics distinct from laymen, although not all clerics are of divine institution".[3] The question herewith presented can be stated thus: "Which clerics are of divine institution?" The answer is forthrightly answered in the second and third paragraphs of canon 108. In the canon, bishops, priests and ministers are listed as having received orders "ex divina institutione", and they are presented in the order of primacy and subordination. In just what the word ministers consists is hazy to be sure, but it would seem it does not include tonsure and, therefore, explains the provision of canon 107.[4]

1. Cf. Stephanus Sipos, *Enchiridion Juris Canonici,* Rome, Herder, 1960, No. 34, p. 143.

2. Sess. XXIII: Decr. de Sacramento Ordinis, Cap. 4, Can. 4. Cf. H. Denzinger and A. Schonmetzer, S.J., *Enchiridion Symbolorum,* Baricome; Herder, 1963, Nos. 1767 and 1774, pp. 413-414, Cf. S. Sipos, *Enchiridion, loc. cit.,* No. 34, 1, p. 143: *"Theologica reductio clericorum ad statum laicalem non datur. Neque quoad ordines iuris divini, neque quoad ordines iuris humani. Non quoad ordines iuris divini. Potestas enim horum iure divino est constituta et a charactere indelebili dependet, ideo est inamissibilis, nec ab ulla poteste auferri potest".*

3. *CIC,* Canon 107: *"Ex divina institutione sunt in ecclesia clerici a laicis distincti, licet non omnes clerici sint divinae institutionis, utrique autem possent esse religiosi".*

4. *CIC,* Canon 108, § 2: *"Non sunt omnes in eodem gradu, sed inter eos sacra hierarchia est in qua alii aliis subordinantur".* § 3: *"Ex divina institutione sacra hierarchia ratione ordinis constat Episcopis, presbyteris et ministris. . .*

The theological difficulty which has been inherent in the above mentioned canon, namely, that some clerics are not of divine institution, appears to have been resolved by the Second Vatican Council and in particular by the Motu Proprios *Ministeria quaedam* and *Ad pascendum* of Pope Paul VI, August 15, 1972.

As a result of these two Apostolic letters, first tonsure (which previously conferred the clerical state, canon 108, § 1)[5] was suppressed as of January 1, 1973. Whence entrance into the clerical state and incardination into a diocese are brought about by ordination to the diaconate.[6]

The provisions of the Code of Canon Law, regarding entrance to the clerical state, hitherto in force were abrogated and the norms of *Ad pascendum* promulgated in their stead. Henceforth all ordained clerics are distinct from laymen since they are clerics by virtue of the diaconate which is an order of divine institution.[7]

The 1917 Code of Canon Law explicitly indicates three methods for the reduction of major clerics to the lay state. This may occur by means of a rescript of the Holy See, in virtue of a decree or sentence according to the norm of Canon 214, or by way of the penalty of degradation.[8] To these three, another method not excluded by the Code may be added: this consists in the granting to a major cleric of a dispensation to contract marriage.

A. Reduction by a Rescript of the Holy See

The sole reference in the Code to the above mentioned means of reduction to the lay state is found in canon 211, § 1.[9] The canon itself is quite clear as to its exact meaning and it is likewise treated concisely by the commen-

5. *CIC,* Canon 108 § 1: *"Qui divinis ministeriis per primam saltem tonsuram mancipati sunt, clerici dicuntur".*

6. Pope Paul VI, *Motu Proprio, Ad Pascendum,* August 15, 1972, IX, in *A.A.S.,* 64 (1972), p. 540. Cf. ID., *Motu Proprio Ministeria Quaedam,* August 15, 1972, No. 1, in *A.A.S.,* 64 (1972), p. 531. The English text of these documents is found in *The Pope Speaks,* 17 (1972-1973), pp. 234-240, 257-261.

7. It must be noted that the Second Vatican Council is at pains to point out, in its dogmatic constitution *Lumen Gentium,* that sacred orders include the deacon, the priest and bishop, the bishop being the pre-eminent possessor of the fullness of orders and both the priest and deacon sharing in that fullness in varying degrees. The clergy, *Lumen Gentium* points out, are not separate from laity so as to form a dichotomous order but rather distinct and set apart for a specific ministry while retaining a unique and intrinsic relationship to the community. Since all Christians are by baptism members of a royal priesthood, the ministerial priesthood is to be viewed as one of many ministries within the Church. Both the clergy and laity are constitutive elements in the formation of one Christian priesthood. Cf. the document "Ultimis temporibus" issued by the Synod of Bishops on the ministerial priesthood, November 30, 1971, in *The Pope Speaks,* 16 (1972-1973), pp. 359-376.

8. Francis Sweeney, C.Ss. R., *The Reduction of Clerics to the Lay State,* Washington, D.C., The Catholic University Press, 1945, Canon Law Studies, No, 223, p. 121.

9. *CIC,* Canon 211, § 1: *"Etsi sacra ordinatio, semel valide recepta, nunquam irrita fiat, clericus tamen major ad statum laicalem redigitur rescripto Sanctae Sedis, decreto vel sententia ad normam can. 214, demum paena degradationis".*

tators most of whom content themselves with a restatement of this canon.[10]

B. Reduction by Way of the Penalty of Degradation

Perhaps the best known in the past and most traditional form of reduction of clerics is that which *per se* is effected through the penalty of degradation. This particular method of reduction is expressly covered in canon 211, § 1.[11] Canon 2305, § 1, clearly states that degradation includes deposition, the perpetual deprivation of the ecclesiastical garb, and the reduction of the cleric to the lay state. Degradation can be inflicted only for a delict mentioned in the law, or if a cleric deposed and deprived of the right to wear the ecclesiastical garb, continues to give grave scandal for a year. The canon states that the degradation may be verbal, or edictal as it is also called. It is effected simply by means of the condemnatory sentence itself, so that all the judicial effects are present immediately upon the passing of the sentence, without the need of its further execution. The other form of degradation, as contrasted to verbal, is real.

According to the law of the Code, the sole method of reducing a major cleric to the lay state by way of penalty is that which employs the penalty of degradation. The Code is quite explicit in determining the instances in which the penalty of degradation is to be inflicted. It defines quite clearly and specifies quite precisely the delicts and the circumstances in which the penalty of degradation may be employed. For example: all apostates from the Christian faith and all heretics and schismatics; clerics who lay violent hands on the person of the Roman Pontiff; any priest who commits the crime of solicitation; violation of the sacramental seal of confession; and finally, any major cleric who presumes to contract a marriage, even if only a civil marriage. (Cf. canons 2314, 2342, 2354, 2368, 2369, 2388.) However, it could be mentioned in passing that the proposed draft text of "De delictis et poenis" for the new Code incorporates substantial changes in this regard.

The penalty of degradation may in and of itself be applied also to minor clerics. But in view of the greater facility granted by the Code for the reduction of minor clerics to the lay state, this penalty is not enumerated among the methods listed for the reduction of minor clerics to the lay state.[12]

10. Cf. Stanislaus Woywod, O.F.M., and Callistus Smith, O.F.M., *A Practical Commentary on the Code of Canon Law,* New York, Joseph F. Wagner, Inc., 1957, Vol. 1, p. 95.

T. Lincoln Bouscaren, S.J. et al., *Canon Law A Text and Commentary,* Milwaukee, Bruce, 1966, p. 148.

F. Sweeney, *op. cit.,* p. 121.

11. *CIC,* Canon 211, § 2: *"Clericus minor ad statum laicalem regreditur, non solum ipso facto ob causas in iure descriptas, sed etiam sua ipsius voluntate, praemonito loci Ordinario, aut eiusdem Ordinarii decreto iusta de causa lato, si nempe Ordinarius, omnibus perpensis, prudenter iudicaverit clericum non posse cum decore status clericalis ad ordines sacros promoveri".*

12. F. Sweeney, *op. cit.,* p.131.

C. Reduction by a Dispensation for Marriage

Major orders constitute a diriment impediment to marriage. Consequently, according to the Code, no subdeacon, deacon, priest or bishop, unless ordained through grave fear or who is in the condition of invincible ignorance or in substantial error regarding the nature of the obligation of celibacy,[13] can validly contract marriage without a dispensation from the law of celibacy.[14] Canon 213, § 2, states that a cleric in major orders who has been reduced to the lay state is still bound by the obligation of celibacy.[15]

The above imputes by way of implication the intrinsic nexus between sacred orders and celibacy, supported by the fact that not even a juridical reduction to the lay state destroys this aforesaid connection unless a dispensation is obtained from the Holy See expressly covering the obligation of celibacy arising from major orders. While it appears that theologically and scripturally, an *intrinsic* linking between orders and celibacy is untenable (yet the force of tradition cannot be lightly dismissed), still, the very fact that the Church requires two separate dispensatory actions intimates that perhaps this debatable intrinsic relationship is in fact questionable. For if the two said obligations were *"de facto"* indispensable and intrinsic elements giving rise to a metaphysical wholeness relative to sacred orders, then it would hardly be possible to separate them into dichotomous obligations.

D. Reduction of Clerics Ordained Under Duress or Grave Fear

In Canon 214 there appears for the first time a positive enactment regarding a case of reduction which the Church has recognized for centuries. The canon states that a cleric who has been forced in consequence of grave fear to receive Sacred Orders, and who did not afterwards, when the fear had been removed, ratify that ordination, not even tacitly, by exercising his orders and by wishing at the same time to subject himself to the clerical obligations by such an act, may be reduced to the lay state by the sentence of a judge with the effect that no obligation of celibacy or of the canonical hours remains, provided of course that the coercion and lack of ratification

13. *Ibid.*, p. 156. It may be objected that this case can hardly be imagined nowadays in view of the instruction of the Sacred Congregation of the Sacraments, December 27, 1930, regarding secular clerics (*A.A.S.*, 23 (1931), pp. 120-129) and the Instruction of the Sacred Congregation of Religious, December 1, 1931, regarding religious clerics (*A.A.S.*, 24 (1932), pp. 74-81). Both of these instructions require the candidate for major orders to take an oath that he is fully cognizant of what the obligation of celibacy entails. Certainly this sworn declaration makes it extremely difficult for the cleric to prove his ignorance. Yet it does not entirely eliminate the possibility although it certainly does exclude the probability of a cleric being so ordained.

14. *Ibid.*, p. 135.

15. *CIC*, Canon 213, § 2: *"Clericus tamen major obligatione caelibatus tenetur, salvo praescripto can. 214"*.

have been legitimately proven. These must be proven according to the norms outlined in canons 1993-1998.[16]

III. Present Procedure of the Return to the Lay State

The fact that recent Popes have provided a canonical process for the release of men from the obligations of the priestly ministry in particular cases indicates a growing sensitivity in the Church to the seriousness of this responsibility. In the spirit of dialogue urged by Pope Paul in his first encyclical, *Ecclesiam Suam,* it is appropriate for the faithful to voice their Christian concern and offer the proper ecclesiastical authorities their own recommendations. Considerations of the best interests of the persons involved and of the good of the faithful suggest that there be established a generally known, dignified and honorable procedure of resignation. No one should be constrained to remain in the clerical life against his will or out of fear of being disgraced for following what he conscientiously believes to be the will of God in his regard.

The following will be an attempt to examine the present procedure regarding the process of laicization. But first, a few preliminary remarks.

Clearly, ordination is a public event, involving the free acceptance of a deep personal commitment to the People of God. In the present order, this commitment cannot prescind from the disciplinary structures of the priesthood. In receiving Orders, a man takes upon himself very serious obligations and responsibilities for the service of the Church precisely as the Church itself has determined that that service should be exercised. Thus it is only fitting that the Church as a whole share in the decision and responsibility for both ordination and resignation from the obligations incurred therein. It is not an authentic Christian response to take into consideration only the individual priest and his particular needs, nor is it acceptable either humanly or from a Christian point of view for a priest simply to abandon his ministry. Both the priest and the community of the faithful function within the context of reciprocal rights and duties. Resignation from the obligations of the priesthood, therefore, can never be simply automatic or without serious consequences for the Church.

The essential elements of the procedure to be followed where dispensations are sought from the Holy See are to be found in two letters and accompanying norms, the first issued by the S.C. of the Holy Office on February 2, 1964, and the second by the Sacred Congregation for the Doctrine of Faith, January 13, 1971. The documents are thoroughly pastoral in tone and intent; the first, however, was never officially published in the *Acta Apostolicae Sedis* but was sent to all diocesan bishops.[17] The doctrine behind the practice is also clearly explained in the encyclical letter *Sacer-*

16. F. Sweeney, *op. cit.,* p. 139.

17. Pope Paul VI, Encyclical Letter, "Sacerdotalis coelibatus", in *The Pope Speaks,* 12 (1967), pp. 291-319.

dotalis Caelibatus of June 24, 1967.[18]

The procedure is basically administrative, i.e., it is a fact-finding procedure (as opposed to a full judicial process) designed to gather the information which the Sacred Congregation has requested as grounds upon which to base a decision for dispensation. Thus, even though grave doubts may arise concerning the validity of ordination, the procedure does not entail the judicial formalities of a trial to determine the nullity or validity of orders.

The instruction provides examples of the kinds of questions that may be used to obtain information sought from the petitioner and various witnesses that might be interviewed. It also provides that the case be concluded with the opinion (*votum*) of the bishop (indeed, without the bishop's positive recommendation there is little hope of obtaining the dispensation). Recent experience among the clergy testifies that, generally, the bishop's *votum* is absolutely crucial to the issuance of the sought-after dispensation.

Though evidently there are differences among the various dioceses and religious communities in the degree of formality with which these cases are handled, the following is generally agreed upon as adequate.

The case is initiated by preparing a petition to the Holy Father, stating the relevant facts and reasons for which a dispensation is sought. This is given either to the priest's Ordinary or to his major superior depending on the case. The bishop or superior then appoints a priest as auditor to talk with the petitioner and take his deposition according to the norms (*investigatio spectat praesertim ad ea quae sequuntur*). The auditor will interview the petitioner to clarify as much as possible the circumstances of the case. In this interview (*interrogatory*) he may freely omit any irrelevant questions or add others which he considers to be significant. The purpose of the inquiry is to determine if the motives expressed in the petition are justified and correspond to truth. The petitioner's background and situation are studied as well as the circumstances leading up to the petition. The bishop or major superior then forwards the acts to the Sacred Congregation for the Doctrine of the Faith, together with a letter of his own in which he mentions what had been done previously to help the priest overcome his difficulties and the question of possible scandal if the request is granted. In this letter he also includes his own reflections upon the merits of the petition.

Upon submission of the petition, the priest is to cease his priestly activities for precautionary purposes (*orator est ad cautelam ab exercitio ordinum prohibendus*). The bishop will probably give him permission to live and dress as a layman, with commutation of the obligation of the Divine

18. Sacra Cong. pro Doctrina Fidei, *Normae ad apparandas. . .*, January 13, 1971, in *A.A.S.*, 63 (1971), pp. 303-312. English text in *The Jurist*, 31 (1971), pp. 672-680. Revised norms were also issued on December 3, 1969, concerning the preparation of the acts of these cases.

Office, even though there has yet been no dispensation from the obligation of celibacy.

The proper Ordinary is responsible for conducting the inquiry, and not the Ordinary of the place where the priest is actually living. In certain circumstances and under certain conditions, the Ordinary of the place of residence may conduct the inquiry if the deposition according to the norms is not forwarded with the petition; then a request is generally made for this from the Ordinary of the petitioner's residence.

The rescript of dispensation embraces inseparably return to the lay state and dispensation from the obligations flowing from Sacred Orders.[19] It takes effect immediately upon notification by the competent Prelate to the petitioner that the dispensation has been granted. The rescript is sent to the bishop or major superior, the contents of which are then to be communicated to the petitioner.[20]

The rescript of dispensation is usually granted on the condition that the priest live elsewhere than in those localities in which his former priestly status was known—usually interpreted as his former diocese (*abesse debet a locis in quibus notus est eius status sacerdotalis*). However, the bishop of the place where he is living may dispense from this provision. The further condition that the marriage of the priest be performed without any special pomp or circumstance, and even somewhat privately is also included. Again, the bishop may dispense from some of these restrictions. Where the ceremony involves a validation, the ceremony is conducted in the presence of a priest appointed by the bishop with the usual confidentiality that normally accompanies such validation.[21] Where witnesses are required by civil law for entering marriage initially, these may be appointed by the bishop or chosen by the couple.

The rescript containing the dispensation ordinarily follows a standardized format, now making no distinction between cases where it is sought to contract marriage and cases where the dispensation will entail permission to convalidate an already existing union.

The instruction closes with a listing of those things which are now forbidden every priest reduced to the lay state and dispensed from his obligation.[22] More will be said concerning some of the conditions at a later point in this study.

19. S.C.D.F., *Normae*, 1971, No. V, 1: *"Rescriptum complectitur inseparabiliter reductionem ad statum laicalem et dispensationem ab oneribus ex sacris ordinibus manantibus"*, in *A.A.S.*, 63 (1971), p. 306.

20. *Ibid.*, No. V, 2: *"Rescriptum mittitur ad Praelatum proprium oratoris, videlicet ad Ordinarium dioecesanum pro sacerdotibus saecularibus, ad Superiorem maiorem pro religiosis, ut cum oratore communicetur, excepto casu de quo n. III, 4°"*, *ibid.*, pp. 306-307.

21. Cf. J. H. Provost, "The Involvement of Dispensed Priests in the Official Ministry of the Church", in *The Jurist*, 34 (1974), pp. 143-153.

22. *Ibid.*, VI, 4: (a) *Ullam ordinis sacri functionem peragat, salvis iis quae habentur Can. 882 et 892*, § 2: (b) *ullam partem liturgicam agat in celebrationibus cum populo, ubi eius condicio est nota, neve umquam homiliam habeat;* (c) *ullum officium pastorale gerat;* (d) *munere*

On June 26, 1972, the Congregation for the Doctrine of the Faith issued an authentic declaration in an attempt to answer questions and resolve a number of difficulties which arose concerning the "interpretation of the norms which govern this serious and particularly difficult matter".[23]

According to the document, it is the Sacred Congregation's duty to weigh the reasons put forward and to make a judgment on each of them, giving due consideration not only to the petitioner's spiritual good, but also to the good of the Universal Church, with faithful observance of the law of celibacy.

For this reason not all causes presented are to be judged sufficient or valid for obtaining the favor sought. Thus the following are *not* to be regarded as sufficient: "a) the simple desire to marry; b) contempt for the law of celibacy; c) attempted civil marriage, or a day scheduled for marriage in the hope of more easily obtaining the dispensation".[24]

In the final section of the document (V) the Congregation attempts to explicitate the meaning of "similar institutes" (*Normae,* n. VI, 4d) in which the petitioner may not participate.[25]

IV. Reflections on the Procedure

Clearly the practice of "laicization" is *prima facie* administrative, that is, largely discretionary. It appears to be relatively simple at least with regard to the aforesaid letters and norms from the Congregations of the Holy Office in 1964 and for the Doctrine of the Faith in 1971. A priest with a valid and just reason for seeking a dispensation can be reasonably assured that the dispensation will indeed be granted, although this is by no means absolutely certain. The fact of the matter is that the way in which the petitions for laicization are handled varies greatly from diocese to diocese and

Rectoris (vel alio munere directivo), Directoris spiritualis et Docentis fungatur in Seminariis, Facultatibus Theologicis et similibus Institutis; (e) *itemque ne munere Directoris scholae catholicae neve munere magistri religionis in quibuslibet scholis, catholicis aut secus, fungatur. Attamen Ordinarius loci, pro suo prudenti iudicio, potest in casibus particularibus permittere ut sacerdos ad statum laicalem reductus et ab oneribus cum sacra ordinatione conexis dispensatus, religionem doceat in scholis publicis, ex exceptione etiam in scholis catholicis, dummodo ne scandalum aut admiratio sit timendum",* in *A.A.S.,* 63 (1971), p. 308.

23. Sacra Cong. pro Doctrina Fidei, *Declaratio. . .,* June 26, 1972, in *A.A.S.,* 64 (1972), pp. 641-643; English translation in *The Jurist,* 33 (1973), pp. 49-51.

24. *Ibid.,* II, p. 642.

25. *Ibid.,* V, p. 643: the words *"similibus institutis"* similar institutes. . ., are to be understood as follows: (a) "Faculties, institutes, schools, etc., of ecclesiastical studies (e.g., faculties of canon law, missiology, church history, philosophy; pastoral and catechetical institutes, and institutes of religious pedagogy, etc.). . . (b) Other centers of advanced studies, even if not strictly dependent upon ecclesiastical authority, in which theological or religious studies are taught". The instruction goes on to say that "where there is doubt concerning discipline relative to theology, the doubt or question will be resolved by the Congregation for the Doctrine of the Faith in consultation with the Congregation for Catholic Education" (*The Jurist, loc. cit.,* p. 51).

religious community to religious community. It is likely, therefore, that a priest seeking such a dispensation would be mistaken to assume that his petition will necessarily be handled as expeditiously and judiciously as possible. It would be extremely difficult to form a reasonable expectation either that the dispensation will be granted or how long the process may take. Moreover, some have suggested that the Holy See is delaying the processing of these petitions in view of the theory that in the course of such delay the petitioner sometimes changes his mind. Whether this particular supposition is true or not is an open question, to be sure. However, one thing is quite clear, if in fact such procedures were used, one would be hard pressed to ascertain their merits. It seems to be a well established fact,however, that many priests do change their minds in the meantime and it may be presumed that the Holy See also wishes to protect them.

The second and perhaps most uncomfortable element in the laicization procedure is its markedly secret nature. Secrecy in its very being is anathema to the Anglo-American mind set. It smacks of dictatorship and provokes a decidedly suspicious response. Let there be no misunderstanding: the Holy See in no way is a totalitarian regime, sniping as it were, from the sidelines. However, the secrecy which so characterized many facets of the work of the S. Congregation for the Doctrine of the Faith is viewed with grave suspicion and distrust in many places and this, to some extent, neutralizes good will towards the Holy See in this delicate matter.

Unless an official announcement is made to the contrary by appropriate diocesan officials (and it is the Order of priesthood properly so called which is the focal point for the overwhelming majority of those seeking to return to the lay state, albeit, the perspective is not limited to the priesthood), the man who receives this dispensation would simply vanish from the scene of his priestly activities with no concurrent explanation which would meet with his satisfaction nor enable other clergy to explain it to the satisfactory understanding of the parishioners. The open farewell of some priests to the people whom they have served (and the practice is indeed growing) notwithstanding, it is generally the policy of both priest and his superior that such practice not be employed. The priest is reluctant to do so, owing to the fact that he feels uncomfortable addressing such a fine group of persons who are not given the whole truth of the matter in question and, therefore, find the entire scenario quite vexing. On many other occasions, the priest would not be willing to make public all his reasons for leaving.

It is not uncommon that the leaving of the ministry seriously injures the priest's reputation and surrounds him in an air of moral dereliction. It is, however, rather important to point out that on occasion, secrecy is a necessity, even to the extent of its being preferred. Still, one must admit that generally only an honest and open approach to the matter enables the faithful to understand the problem and even join together to facilitate the priest's transition to lay life. Clearly, this has not generally been the case to date.

A third element to be considered is the fact the decision to grant the dispensation is made by members of the Sacred Congregation in Rome. Translated into reality, this simply means that the ultimate decision regarding a particular priest's life is effected by persons with no immediate personal knowledge of, or acquaintance with, the petitioner. While this does not render the system unjust nor argue to its illegitimacy, it only says that perhaps the person in the best possible position to render a complete and healing decision might be the priest's immediate superior. It has been suggested that the S. C. for the Doctrine of the Faith appoint consultors residing in each country who, after examination of the acts, would present their recommendation to the Congregation for final processing.

Unfortunately, at present, there are very few facilities available to enable a priest to prepare for a different type of Christian priesthood and occupation. Quite simply, there is no easy transition from priesthood to lay life. The road is indeed winding and rough and it often takes a priest over some incredibly arduous and dangerous terrain. Many never complete the journey, ending up disheartened, distraught, discouraged and confused. Some are even crushed beyond recognition. Many priests who leave the ministry in order to "save their souls" end up losing their faith in God and man, owing to the inability to find adequate resources of mind and body to facilitate their most difficult transition to lay life with some semblance of ease. In no way should bad faith be imputed to Rome in this regard for truly the authorities are not "out to get" the laicized priest. They seem to be, however, a bit unrealistic at times relative to the contribution these men could be making and to affording the priest who leaves, a recognition of his viable contribution to the People of God. Usually the priest leaves his post without adequate counselling, advice or re-education. He has gone through a harrowing and debilitating psychological experience and is ill-prepared for any major life decision.[26]

The Holy See advances several valid and reasonable objections and hesitations regarding the entire process of laicization. One such question revolves around its displeasure and disappointment over the unfortunate unfaithfulness of dispensed priests to their marriage vows. Indeed this is quite regrettable and must be viewed with a certain sense of pity. Still, the fact remains that the exception must not become normative for the rendering of certain key decisions. Law must always take into consideration the unique and exceptional case but must never circumscribe its rule by the exception. All of us must be saddened by any dispensed priest's failure in marriage, but this must never determine how we are to understand laicization, nor affect the manner in which the Church must act in the future regarding dispensation from priestly obligations.

26. Cf. William W. Bassett, "When A Priest Leaves the Ministry", in *America,* vol. 120, March 1, 1969, p. 242. Cf. also Richard A. McCormick, S.J., "Canonical Reflections on Priestly Life and Ministry", in *American Ecclesiastical Review,* 166 (1972), pp. 363-392.

Another point which greatly distresses Church leaders is the fact that many priests come to their superiors to be dispensed with the marriage license already obtained or at least with a wedding date set. This can be poignant to a superior and can evoke a certain backlash. The priest in this case should take the time to find out who he is, where he hopes to be going and just how he plans to get there. While marriage is a major consideration in his decision to leave (in some cases *the* consideration) he should seek to balance himself before he makes yet another commitment for life. Clearly, this is most important for all concerned; moreover, one should always act with a view to those who are to follow him. Life's exigencies demand that human beings plan their future but the arresting question remains. If transition to lay life is so difficult (and if one thinks otherwise he is sadly mistaken) then how can another life commitment be so quickly enjoyed? The long term results of deliberation, preparation and prayer cannot be blithely disregarded.

The letter and norms from the Sacred Congregation for the Doctrine of the Faith, of January 13, 1972, make it clear that with respect to teaching positions at Catholic institutions held by a priest seeking dispensation, he must relieve himself of this ministry before a dispensation is granted. This arresting question arises especially with regard to tenured professors. While the priest in such a position should possibly be required to renegotiate his professorship at another school (any school, Catholic or otherwise), as soon as possible, he nevertheless in justice can demand that he be permitted to stay on at the present institution until he can make the necessary transition. On balance, however, neither the school nor the student must be penalized on behalf of a priest's vocational difficulties.

In general, the lack of respect on the part of many Church leaders, and especially the seeming insensitivity by the authors of the above mentioned norms to the question of human dignity and personality adjustment seem to run counter to all the positive things which the Holy See said in the *Directory for the Pastoral Ministry of Bishops* about priestly fraternity and the solicitude we all must express toward all peoples, but most especially to our brothers in the faith (Gal. 6, 10).[27]

Finally, the authentic interpretation of 1972 appears to be more concerned with the element of scandal relative to a priest's leaving the ministry. It should be noted here that this posture of Rome is in no wise new nor unique to the dispensation of priests. The church authorities have always been most concerned with the consuming question of scandal, as is quite evident in the 1917 Code of Canon Law. Rightly, or wrongly, this question of scandal inheres in the laicization process at the parish level. The hard fact in this matter of scandal is that quite simply and *generally,* people do take scandal from a priest's leaving. While not everyone is so affected, the number of

27. Cf. Sacred Congregation for Bishops, *Directory on the Pastoral Ministry of Bishops,* May 31, 1973, Nos. 106, sqq.

people that are is significant enough to warrant a careful and prudent approach to the leaving of priests. Of course, most, if not all of the scandal could be avoided in many instances if the question were openly and honestly communicated to the People of God. Be that as it may, a distinction must be drawn between "scandal given" and "scandal taken". Some of the laity will be caught up in scandal no matter how exposed and communicated the process becomes. The people with whom we are most concerned are those who will legitimately take scandal because of preconditioning, historical prejudice and non-responsible ignorance. It is to these questions that the Church must address itself.

The distinction, lest it slip into dichotomy, must be pursued. Just as scandal taken is not always valid nor justified, scandal given is not necessarily true scandal properly so called. Few priests seek to be scandalous. But many are imprudent in this regard and people are genuinely horrified at this. The greater majority, however, are good and decent men, who wouldn't think of doing anything to hurt the People of God nor endanger or shake their faith in His Church. It is the human side of the Church with which one is confronted in dealing with the topic of laicization. Just as it is this same dimension at work in the broken marriage syndrome. The Church has always been "sinful" yet holy, that is, it has always lived with the burden of original sin and people will necessarily fail at love and life, often even daily. The scandal comes into play when the priest who is supposed to embody holiness fails to live up to the expectation of the Church in his regard and falls like any other human being. A man's decision to leave the ministry is not in itself a sinful act (although it would perhaps be so in some cases) but it does point up the sinful or failing dimension of life. Perhaps it is the unrealistic approach to religion and God that has landed us in such a state. Perhaps if we had heeded the words of St. Paul more closely we could have avoided so many of our troubles (cf. Romans 7, 18-20). But life contains the forces of un-love as surely as it contains the breath divine of grace, and it is with the forces of un-love that we must contend, but the grace of God will enable us to accommodate and ultimately conquer.

V. Thoughts for the Future

It has been suggested by many that the procedure which should be followed in the future regarding the dispensation of priests from all obligations arising from Sacred Orders be founded upon the concept of resignation. That is a process of the tendering and acceptance of a resignation from a position of public trust and dedicated service to the Church. It seems that the title "resignation" is much more apt and to the point of the issue of dispensation from the ministry and to that extent is to be preferred over, say, "laicization" or more still, "reduction to the lay state". However, to leave the active ministry is not so simple a matter as mere resignation, for there is much more at stake than just the particular desire or need of a priest. While I believe all priests who find it necessary to move elsewhere should be able to be dispensed and aided in their difficult time of transition, I likewise feel that a certain accountability is essential. The sacred commitment to orders cannot be lightly set aside and it seems almost certain that most of those leaving do not treat it lightly. Yet for reasons of accountability it becomes imperative and behooves the Church to retain at least the essential fact-finding characteristic of the dispensation or resignation procedure. It would appear that all those involved would benefit from such a profound move and, hopefully, humane procedure. The Church at this point is in a most efficacious position to render and exercise its ministry of reconciliation.

If the minister of the Gospel cannot be reconciled to his ministry, at least he should be accorded the mercy of Jesus and enabled to share in the reconciliation with his superior and brother and, most importantly, the People of God at the local level. For instance, the marriage of a priest who has been properly dispensed and honorably released from the ministry could well be as public an event as that accorded any other member of the faith community. In this mode of reconciliation, the Church publicly attests to this person's good standing within the People of God. Since he has been dispensed legitimately from the obligation of his Orders he is *de facto* considered by the highest authorities in the Church to be in good faith and good standing, and this fact may be celebrated. But those who choose the less edifying route, namely to act out of disregard for the Church and her laws are rightly viewed as less sincere and solicitous regarding the People of God. Their leaving should be, if anything, deeply lamented but never celebrated.

This process of resignation and reconciliation should follow a standardized, uniform, socially acceptable, and generally known pattern and format. The process must be simple yet complete, responsible and healing, and, above all, atomized with respectfulness of the dignity of the persons involved and of the welfare of the Church. The procedure should result not only in a complete release from the obligation of the priestly life and ministry, but also in the honorable integration of the person into the community of the Church in another capacity.[28]

The carrying out of the resignation process should be as concise and terse as justice and reconciliation demand. This generally should not exceed a six months' period. Moreover, the filing of the petition to resign need not mean automatic cessation of priestly activities, nor should it precipitate such cessation of ministerial activities, save when it would pose serious and potential danger to either the faithful or to the priest himself. However, the priest's own good judgment should be a weighty measure in this regard, but not the only one. Subjectivism must be tempered with objective insight. The priest must be willing to respect the prudent judgment of the Ordinary in

28. Cf. W. W. Bassett, *loc, cit.*,p. 244.

this matter and the Ordinary should seek the sagacious counsel of his advisors and the priest's own peers, especially the pastor, associate pastor and deacon (if a deacon is presently serving) of the parish where the petitioning priest is functioning.

The above mentioned approach to the resignation of a priest would afford him the opportunity to leave with grace and dignity and facilitate his transition into a new area of Christian living. The Church can ill-afford disregard in this most necessary administration of healing activity. What a man about to re-pattern his entire life does not need is to be put out into the street, as it were, until the dispensation is processed. The people could very well aid the priest while coming to a practical understanding of this most thoroughly delicate and intricate transition.

Clearly, this procedure depends ultimately upon the lifting of the secrecy now surrounding resignation. This could take place more easily now than it could have some five or ten years ago since the element of surprise is now greatly diminished in the minds of most people. It could be stated, likewise, that there should not, and must not be, a general norm of secrecy for this spawns fear and distrust. It must, however, be noted that there will be cases where a certain measure of secrecy would be prudent and essential, especially if the priest has incurred a censure (incidentally, the notion of censure in Canon Law is in need of revision).[29]

The more vexing and uncomfortable question pertains to those priests who have attained a considerable degree of education and are professionals and scholars of the first order. Their ability to continue teaching, etc., needs immediate addressing. This subject poses no easy solution. These men have earned a right to be heard (providing they have remained loyal to the mind of Jesus on matters of faith; this does not exclude scholarly speculation) and could be of inestimable value to the Church community. Their past contribution cannot be lightly ignored nor dismissed out of hand. While certain difficulties are apparent, they are by no means insoluble. The Church might even consider calling these "select" few to give counsel on the problem of ministry, celibacy, authority.

Since the contribution of such priests who have returned to the lay state has been enormous and recognized by others in the field of the ecclesiastical sciences, can the Church afford to act as if their contribution is minimal or their research unrecorded? It seems altogether fitting that the Church set up a council of priests who have left the ministry, for the purpose of entertaining suggestions as to where the causes for many priests leaving might lie and establish some sort of ecclesiastical machinery to deal adequately with these perplexing questions. Only with the approved and competent assistance of those who have seen fit to resign their ministry can the Church proceed to an enlightened resolution of at least part of the problem. Certainly those who have left can communicate more of the visceral elements involved in

29. Cf. *ibid.*, p. 245.

resignation and perhaps add immeasurably to the effective handling of priests on a healing plane. Not all who have left would be equally qualified to serve the Church in such a counseling capacity, some I dare say, could hardly serve at all. However, many priests who have chosen to leave possess a most impressive list of credentials, not the least of which is their exemplary Christian life. From the best of the ranks would be drawn an eminent group of Christian laymen who understand the problem of resignation in a way that anyone who has not so resigned could never fully understand.

The rudiments for tackling all of the reforms requisite in the Church today are already present to us. The fielding of such an important problem is an involved process which must occur throughout the organism of the entire Church. Every member of the Church must be able to make his contribution; everyone must fulfill his appropriate function.[30]

30. Cf. Alois Müller, *Pratical Theology of Church Reform,* in *Concilium,* Vol. 3, No. 8, 1972 (US Edition, Vol. 73), p. 77.

Case 13

Steps to Religious Profession, Ordination, and Laicization

John Coates was ordained a priest at age 28. After two restless years in the apostolate of the Society of St. Michael, an exempt religious institute, he began to wonder whether he had done the right thing in becoming a religious and being ordained a priest. He remembered how he had promised his dying mother that he would become a priest, and he recalled his feeling of pride and accomplishment in proving to his peers and superiors that "he could make it to the priesthood." Now he doubted his motives and felt trapped.

"To sort things out for himself," he sought and obtained a leave of absence. He took a job in the Baltimore School System and soon won the respect and admiration of his colleagues. The school nurse fell in love with him. Wishing to marry Alice, he petitioned for laicization, but was turned down. "I have a natural right to marry," he protested to Alice. They planned a June wedding and were married before a justice of the peace in Baltimore.

Exercise

1. Identify the stages of formation required by particular and universal law for admission to religious life and to ordination.

2. List the documents generally required by institutes of consecrated life at each successive stage of a member's formation.

3. List the documents required of candidates for ordination to sacred orders.

4. Describe the laicization process.

5. What is John Coates' canonical status after his attempted marriage? Has the Society of St. Michael any obligations towards him?

References

Sacred Congregation for the Doctrine of the Faith, "Norms for the Preparation, in Diocesan and Religious Curias, of Cases of Reduction to the Lay State with Dispensation from the Obligation Attached to Sacred Ordination," *The Jurist* 31 (1971), 672-80.

Sacred Congregation for Religious and Secular Institutes, "Assisting Those Who Leave Religious Institutes," *Review for Religious* 33 (1974), 769-71.

———, "Leave of Absence or Exclaustration," *Consecrated Life* 2 (1977), 164-69.

Carr, A. M., "Canonical Status of Married Priests" (Reply), *Homiletic and Pastoral Review* 68 (1968), 705-6.

Gallen, J. F., "Is Exclaustration Often Used Now?" *Review for Religious* 33 (1974), 1204.

McCann, M., "The Process of Exclaustration," *Sisters Today* 49 (1977-78), 532-38.

Report of the Canon Law Society of America to the National Conference of Catholic Bishops on the Subject of Due Process

PREAMBLE

In accordance with the authentic teaching of the Catholic Church, the members of this Society express their conviction that all persons in the Church are fundamentally equal in regard to their common rights and freedoms,[1] among which are:

> The right and freedom to hear the Word of God and to participate in the sacramental and liturgical life of the Church;[2]
> The right and freedom to exercise the apostolate and share in the mission of the Church;[3]
> The right and freedom to speak and be heard and to receive objective information regarding the pastoral needs and affairs of the Church;[4]
> The right to education, to freedom of inquiry and to freedom of expression in the sacred sciences;[5]
> The right to free assembly and association in the Church;[6] and such inviolable and universal rights of the human person as the right to the protection of one's reputation, to respect of one's person, to activity in accord with the upright norm of one's conscience, to protection of privacy.[7]

The dignity of the human person, the principles of fundamental fairness, and the universally applicable presumption of freedom[8] require that no member of the Church arbitrarily be deprived of the exercise of any right or office.

NOTION OF DUE PROCESS

The adequate protection of human rights and freedoms is a matter of concern to all men of good will; the adequate protection of specifically ecclesial rights and freedoms has become a matter of increasing concern to all members of the Church.

Rights are protected in many ways. Indirectly, they are protected by education, growth of moral consciousness, development of character; directly, they are protected by law. Rights without legal safeguards, both preventive and by way of effective recourse, are often meaningless. It is the noblest service of law to afford effective safeguards for the protection of rights, and, where rights have been violated, to afford effective means for their prompt restoration.

Phrased in abstract terms, the question whether there ought to be "due process" in the Church answers itself since everyone is obviously entitled to whatever process is "due." In all governmental procedures respect should be paid to the rights of all persons involved, whatever this may require. The question becomes real only when specific content is given to the expression "due process" so that what is asked is whether certain specific substantive and procedural protections are due, in given sets of circumstances, in order that the rights of persons involved be adequately safeguarded.

Most of the current discussion and writing about "due process" in the Church is conditioned by Anglo-American common law tradition which requires, substantively, that no fundamental right or freedom shall be denied without adequate justification; and procedurally, that every individual be accorded certain specific protections in administrative and judicial procedures. Among such procedural protections are, for example: the right to be informed of proposed actions which might prejudicially affect one's rights, the right to be heard in defense of one's rights, the right, in the face of accusation which could result in the imposition of a penalty, to confront one's accusers, and those who testify in support of the accusation, the right

5

not to be judged by one's accusers. Any nuanced statement of due process will have to make distinctions between many different types of situations; the notion of due process is not univocal but analogous. It is a principle of justice rather than a specific rule of law.

Ecclesiological Implications

a. Unity of Authority in the Bishop

It is questioned at times whether this very notion of due process has any proper place in the Catholic Church which we understand to be, by divine institution, a hierarchical society in which the fullness of governmental power is vested in the episcopate.

> Bishops govern the particular churches, entrusted to them as the vicars and ambassadors of Christ . . . This power, which they personally exercise in Christ's name, is proper, ordinary, and immediate, although its exercise is ultimately regulated by the supreme authority of the Church, and can be circumscribed by certain limits, for the advantage of the Church or of the faithful. In virtue of this power, bishops have the sacred right and duty before the Lord to make certain laws for their subjects, to pass judgment on them, and to moderate everything pertaining to the ordering of worship and the apostolate.
>
> The pastoral office or the habitual and daily care of their sheep is entrusted to them completely. . .[9]

It is the opinion of some that there cannot be in the Church any such separation of powers as exists, for example, in the American form of government, in which authority is divided among legislative, executive and judicial branches of government.

> The unity of authority is a necessary element of the hierarchical structure of the Church and a juridical expression of the oneness of the spiritual authority derived from Christ.[10]

If the bishop has the fullness of governmental power—legislative, executive, and judicial—it is argued that no one could enforce specific requirements of the American concept of "due process" against the bishop; he would (in person or through his delegate), by reason of the unity of

6

authority centered in himself, be legislator, administrator, law-enforcer, prosecutor, judge, and jury.

In response to this approach, three considerations seem to be pertinent. First: a constitutionally dictated separation of powers, as realized, for example, in the United States, is a special doctrine of government whose particular features are not to be identified with the requirements of "due process." Many of the requirements of "due process," both substantive and procedural, are relevant to all forms of government, even the most centralized. The right to be heard in defense of one's rights, for example, is not limited to those who live in a government characterized by separation of powers. The particular way in which authority is distributed, or not distributed, in a given society differs according to the nature and traditions of the society itself; guaranteeing fundamental fairness against abuse of authority should be the concern of every society regardless of the particular arrangement of legislative, executive, and judicial powers in the governmental structure of the society.

Secondly: the approach, if valid, would argue against protections from abuse of authority already provided in the Church by the present Code of Canon Law. Elaborate procedures are prescribed which a bishop must follow in the removal of pastors;[11] detailed rules concerning the competence of courts, right to counsel, admissibility of evidence, burden of proof, number of judges, and availability of appeal, surround the exercise of judicial power;[12] and a bishop is required regularly to enact diocesan legislation "in synod."[13] All of these are in the nature of procedural limitations upon the bishop, and yet they have been thought to be consistent with the centralization of all governmental authority in the local bishop.

Thirdly: the approach seems to presume that securing the protection of basic human rights to members of the ecclesial society is equivalent to undermining the authority of the bishop. "Due process" does place limitations on a bishop's exercise of power, but, so far from undermining his authority, it does much to win respect for it, and so enables him to govern more effectively. The declaration and protection of fundamental rights by guaranteeing proper substantive and procedural safeguards is one of the most important exercises of governmental authority by the bishop. If they are genuine rights, the bishop loses nothing by being required to respect them.

7

b. Vatican II Development

It seems to the members of this Society that the present moment in the history of mankind imperatively calls for further development in the recognition of fundamental fairness in the governmental life of the Church. We believe this position to be solidly founded in the teaching of the Second Vatican Council:

> A sense of the dignity of the human person has been impressing itself more and more deeply on the consciousness of contemporary man. And the demand is increasingly made that men should act on their own judgment, enjoying and making use of responsible freedom, not driven by coercion but motivated by a sense of duty. The demand is also made that constitutional limits be set to the powers of government, in order that there may be no encroachment on the rightful freedom of the person and of associations.[14]
>
> If conscientious cooperation between citizens is to achieve its happy effect in the normal course of public affairs, a positive system of law is required. In it should be established a division of governmental roles and institutions, and, at the same time, an effective and independent system for the protection of rights. Let the rights of all persons, families, and associations, along with the exercise of those rights, be recognized, honored and fostered.[15]

Each of these statements refers directly not to the Church but to civil society. But they have obvious implications for the Church, since the Church is and must ever be "a sign and a safeguard of the transcendence of the human person."[16] It would be unfortunate if, while civil societies labored to build "an effective and independent system for the protection of rights," the Church allowed itself to remain at a lower stage in the development of adequate safeguards for the protection of human rights. The ferment of the gospel, which is especially active in the Church of our time, is arousing in the hearts of Christians an irresistible demand that the human dignity of each member of the faithful should be recognized and protected by suitable legal guarantees.[17]

That the Church must develop adequate institutions to keep pace with modern society is implicit in the whole program of aggiornamento which inspired the Second Vatican Council. The Council fathers declared that the

8

Church must always remain in harmony with the temporal order "so that the mission of the Church may correspond more adequately to the special conditions of the world today."[18] In this regard, the ecclesiology of Vatican II developed earlier ecclesiologies in a manner consonant with secular developments in the field of human rights, particularly in the new emphasis placed on the rights and dignity of each member of the laity.

> Let sacred pastors recognize and promote the dignity as well as the responsibility of the layman in the Church. . . .Let them confidently assign duties to him in the service of the Church, allowing him freedom and room for action. Further, let them encourage the layman so that he may undertake tasks on his own initiative. . .Furthermore, let pastors respectfully acknowledge that just freedom which belongs to everyone in this earthly city.[19]

The characteristics of a free man are precisely that he has rights, that he is not dependent for the enjoyment of his rights upon the good will of his superiors, and that his rights are effectively protected so as to be legally inviolable. The aim of "due process" is precisely to give such inviolability. For men of our time, the legal protection of inviolable rights in the Church would be an especially persuasive sign of that just freedom proclaimed by the gospel as belonging to all men. To the extent that authorities in the Church are able to secure the fundamental rights of Christians they are fulfilling an important part of their service as pastors.

c. Disciplinary Matters

It may be asked how resort to the protective procedures of "due process"is to be reconciled with the virtue of obedience to one's bishop. It seems to the members of this Society that the obedience a bishop legitimately expects when he seeks the unity of the diocesan apostolate never requires a person unwillingly to give up his Christian rights. Moreover, obedience may take on new significance as God's People accept not only the decisions of their bishop but the consensus of their fellow Christians and the Christian community at large which explicitly concurs in and supports those decisions. "Due process" is simply one of the effective ways in which authority is exercised and obedience realized.

A more precise question may be asked whether in cases where the local ordinary is himself a party to the dispute he can be bound to accept, or

9

responsibly can bind himself to accept, a decision made by members of his own diocese.

In purely disciplinary matters it would seem evident that there is no theological obstacle to a bishop agreeing, with regard to particular cases and even with regard to whole classes of cases, to abide by decisions of boards or courts over which he has no direct control, just as at present he is bounded by canon law to refer disputes involving his own rights, or temporal goods, or those of the diocesan curia to tribunals for decision.[20] By freely submitting to the determinations of impartial boards or tribunals in matters to which he is a party, a local ordinary would win greater respect for his own integrity and thus govern more effectively.

d. Doctrinal Area

The more difficult question concerns disputes arising in the doctrinal area. Here the bishop cannot abdicate his responsibility as teacher; he must retain his traditional function of giving official expression to Catholic doctrine. But it is the opinion of the members of this Society that he must exercise that responsibility with due regard to the total theological situation. A local ordinary may not make an absolute norm out of his own personal theological interpretations and arbitrarily forbid the dissemination of views which are tolerated elsewhere in the Church.

The bishops of a region or of the nation should be mutually solicitous for the welfare of the Church in every diocese.[21] Should a serious question arise as to whether a given bishop is excessively strict or excessively permissive, there would be nothing inconsistent with his episcopal office if he were to allow the matter to be referred to a panel of his brother bishops for their judgment. Nor, in the opinion of the members of this Society, would it be at all inconsistent with his office as bishop if he were to allow a like referral to a panel of theologians who have a reputation among their colleagues for theological competence. Such a panel, on the national level, would be comparable to the international theological commission recently established to advise the Congregation for the Doctrine of the Faith. The members of this Society recommend to the American hierarchy the establishment of such a national theological commission.

In view of the great complexity of doctrinal questions at the present moment and the increasingly acute sensitivity of the faithful to the right of free

10

inquiry and expression in the Church, it is the opinion of this Society that bishops will best maintain their authority by involving experts of different theological tendencies and thus taking advantage of the full resources of the theological community. In this way they will increase, rather than undercut, confidence in their own authority as official teachers.

Thus, "due process" should be viewed as a means to an end. It is useful and important as an instrument to help the Church realize itself as a community of freedom and truth. Those securing it, in positions of authority in the Church, show their love for the People of God, their trust in the working of the Spirit, and their personal disinterestedness by effectively safeguarding the rights of those entrusted to their care.

GOVERNMENTAL CONTEXT

Assessment of the adequacy of present structures in the Church for the protection of rights and resolution of disputes entails a study of the entire legislative, judicial, and administrative structure of the Church.

In the area of legislation, such a study reveals, on the one hand, underutilization of the diocesan synod in the practice of most dioceses,[22] and on the other, recent experimentation with a type of legislative "synod" or "diocesan council" which goes beyond the Code provisions for synods especially in regard to frequency of sessions and participation by religious and laity. In regard to pro-synodal legislation by the bishop, recent development of priests' senates and pastoral councils as consultative and collaborative bodies has opened new opportunities for effective participation in law-making and in the consequent resolution of conflicting interests in the Church through the medium of legislation.

In regard to adjudication, Church law affirms the availability of a judicial remedy for the protection of every right,[23] but practice has revealed understaffed tribunals and the consequent unavailability of tribunal processes for all but marriage conflicts. Moreover, the law recognizes no right to judicial review of administrative decisions of ecclesiastical authorities.

Administrative decisions of bishops are reviewable only by one or another of the Sacred Congregations at Rome, a process which experience

11

often has shown to be unsatisfactory because of distance, requirements of secrecy, unavailability of evidence and witnesses, decisions rendered without accompanying findings and reasoned opinions, and other failures in regard to contemporary standards of fundamental procedural fairness.

The contemplated revision of the Code of Canon Law envisions a broader use of courts for the judicial resolution of conflicts of all kinds, and, in particular, envisions the creation of administrative tribunals in the Church.[24] The Synod of Bishops, meeting in Rome on October 7, 1967, voted unanimously for the establishment of courts to provide review of administrative decisions. Such courts will fit easily into the legal climate of this nation in which the process of review traditionally has sought to provide effective protection against arbitrary administrative action. It is expected that the new Code will delineate the forms such tribunals will take, their competence, and rules of procedure applicable to them. The value of judicial precedent and the interpretation of law afforded by the adjudication of concrete cases will enrich the societal life of the faithful.

It is in the administrative area of government that the Church is experiencing the fastest rate of growth, with the creation of increasing numbers of administrative boards, departments, and agencies to supplement the bishop's personal administrative activities. Personnel boards, liturgical commissions, parish councils, and other administrative bodies are emerging in nearly every diocese. The proliferation of administrative powers necessarily entails an increase in the number of persons entitled to exercise the discretion proper to administrative authority, and hence, an increase in the dangers to human rights and freedom that are inherent in uncontrolled and unchecked discretionary power.

The Code of Canon Law is not without concern for limiting administrative discretion, but such checks as it establishes (e.g. synodal examiners, diocesan consultors, councils of temporalities) have been minimal and are, in many ways, unsuited to the forms of administrative entity coming into existence today.

Procedural fairness in all aspects of the administrative life of the Church is one of the pressing needs of our time; indeed, it is the conviction of the members of this Society that the greatest promise for removing causes of conflict in the Church lies in the elimination of unnecessary discretionary

power in ecclesiastical administrators, and in the development of effective guidelines, controls, and checks upon necessary discretionary power.

It is, consequently, to the resolution of conflicts involving the exercise of administrative authority in the Church that this report principally directs itself; it is in this area that present-day conflicts are most numerous, and it is in this area that grievances most often are based on the denial of fundamental Christian rights.

PROCESS FOR CONCILIATION

> Love your enemies, do good to those who hate you, bless those who curse you, pray for those who treat you badly. To the man who slaps you on one cheek, present the other cheek too; to the man who takes your cloak from you, do not refuse your tunic. Give to everyone who asks you, and do not ask for your property back from the man who robs you. Treat others as you would like them to treat you.[25]

It is not the litigious, but the poor in spirit who are called blessed by Jesus;[26] not judges, but peacemakers who are promised a special reward in the kingdom.[27] Forgiveness from the Father is asked as "we have forgiven those who are in debt to us."[28]

The teaching of Christ on love of enemies, peace-making, and forgiveness is specifically applied by St. Paul to litigation. Christians are rebuked by him for litigating with one another before unbelievers.[29] Christians are told that "it is bad enough for you to have law suits at all against one another; oughtn't you to let yourselves be wronged, and let yourselves be cheated?"[30]

In secular situations, litigation is a last resort. Few controversies capable of judicial resolution are judicially resolved. Conflicts so acute that the parties to them seek the counsel of lawyers are normally resolved by the lawyers through a negotiated settlement. Even in the administration of the criminal law, compromise is the usual procedure. Courts function chiefly to set the outer limits within which compromise will be made. They could not possibly adjudicate all conflicts which lawyers could put before them. Without lawyers to resolve most conflicts the courts could not work at all.

Litigation as a way of reaching a just result requires some sort of equality between the parties, an equality which courts try to insure by isolating the judicial procedure from factors extraneous to the issue, but which no court can insure if the parties are unequal in their resources and ability to engage in protracted litigation. Few persons have the resources and ability to engage in protracted litigation with an institution.

The Code of Canon Law itself discourages litigation as a method of resolving disputes, and urges, in its stead, a process of conciliation:

> Since it is highly desirable that litigation be avoided among the faithful, the judge shall admonish the parties between whom some civil controversy about their own private affairs has arisen and which they have taken to court to have settled by judicial trial, to come to a compromise, if there appears to be some hope of a friendly settlement. The judge can satisfy this duty either before the parties are summoned to court or when they are for the first time in court or finally at any time that he deems most opportune and effective for proposing a compromise.[31]

For these several and convergent reasons, the members of this Society believe that in the Church, which should not only study secular example but also provide example for the world, the primary process for the resolution of disputes should not be a process for the assertion of legal rights but a process for the conciliation of human persons.

It is the opinion of the Society that the following elements are essential to any process for conciliation:

1. Each participant must have the opportunity of a face-to-face dialogue with the person with whom he is in conflict. To be treated as a human person is to be given not only a hearing, but a response. There is no substitute for the dialogue of persons.
2. Unmediated dialogue may become debate; each participant, therefore, must have the opportunity of stating his side of the conflict to a conciliator who will attempt to lead the participants to be reconciled with one another. The conciliator should be informed of the facts and feelings of each participant so that

he may understand what each participant believes to be "the real reason" for the dispute.

3. Dialogue and mediation will fail if either side is convinced that abstract principles such as "the right of conscience" or "the rights of authority" be vindicated at any cost. There are few imperatives of conscience that make only one course of action mandatory, and few rights of authority which can be asserted in only one specific way.
4. Delay and concealment of relevant information have no place in a process of conciliation. Wounds should be healed quickly. Persons should not be left in suspense about their status for protracted periods. The candor of brothers, not the paternalistic assumption that the truth cannot be borne, must characterize exchange designed to heal.

5. The obligation rests with each person in authority or guided by authority to teach by his example that he belongs to a religion whose essence is love.

. . . PROCESS FOR ARBITRATION

Hopefully the vast majority of controversies will be settled through the Process for Conciliation. But because this will not always be possible, it is the opinion of the Society that there should be established a Process for Arbitration for the resolution of disputes not resolved by conciliation.

Arbitration is defined as the reference of a dispute, by voluntary agreement of the parties, to an impartial person or persons for determination on the basis of evidence and arguments presented by such parties, who agree in advance to accept the decision of the arbitrator or arbitrators as final and binding.

In referring a matter to arbitration, parties are presumed to have explored every avenue of negotiation and settlement. It is as a last resort that they call

upon impartial persons for a definitive decision and agree to abide by the result. There is a note of formality in arbitration proceedings, commensurate with the seriousness and importance which should characterize issues brought for resolution to such a process, and there should be some form of recording the proceedings. The time element involved in the various steps of arbitration should be enforced since undue delay prolongs injustice, and so is itself unjust.

An arbitrator must personally be neutral; he must be objective, a person with judicial temperament, able to listen well, to ask good questions, to understand each party's point of view. The principle of subsidiarity would call for a decision being made on a local level whenever sufficient competence is available; on the other hand, the principle of impartiality would indicate that a panel of arbitrators should be selected on a broader basis than the merely diocesan. A regional panel of arbitrators would be highly desirable.

As with the Process for Conciliation, so in regard to Arbitration, the proposals of this Society do not represent a radical innovation in the governmental life of the Church. The Code of Canon Law, in discouraging judicial litigation as a means of resolving disputes, urges in its stead a process for arbitration:

> In order to avoid judicial litigation, the parties may also make an agreement by which the controversy is committed to the judgment of one or several persons who shall decide the dispute according to law, or deal with the affair according to the rules of equity. If they are to follow the rules of law, they are called *arbitri;* if they are to follow the dictates of equity, they are called *arbitratores.*[32]

16

. . . JUDICIAL PROCESS

Notwithstanding the Christian preference for resolving disputes through a process of conciliation of persons rather than through a process for the assertion of legal rights, there remain values indigenous to the judicial process which should not be unavailable to the societal life of the Church. Judicial interpretation of law, judicial delineation of rights, increasingly more precise from case to case, and judicial precedent, especially in the area of defining and protecting Christian rights, are values which the members of this Society would regard as fundamental to an enriching of the governmental life of the Church.

It is the recommendation of the Society, therefore, that pending the establishment of administrative tribunals as part of the revision of the Code of Canon Law, Ordinaries delegate jurisdiction either to existing diocesan tribunals, or to newly created experimental tribunals, for the resolution of disputes between persons in the Church and administrative authorities or bodies within the diocese. It would be hoped that the experience of such judicial processes would provide the Church with a valuable source of direction in the ongoing studies of the Commission for the Revision of Canon Law.

STRUCTURING ADMINISTRATIVE DISCRETION

Not only is it important for ecclesial society to provide mechanisms for the peaceful and orderly conciliation, arbitration, and judicial resolution of disputes when they arise, but also to create, as far as is possible, an atmosphere of Christian living in which disputes are less likely to occur. As indicated earlier in this report, disputes between individual members of the Church and persons in positions of authority in service to the Church arise from a variety of situations in which individuals consider themselves aggrieved by administrative action on the part of authority.

Administrative action usually involves the exercise of a large amount of discretion on the part of administrators; and to the extent that such discretion is uncontrolled and unchecked there exist wide possibilities not only for administrative actions which are in fact arbitrary and unjust, but, more significantly for the rise of disputes in the ecclesial community, manifold

17

possibilities for widespread supposition on the part of those affected that the actions were arbitrary and unjust. Whence arise a proliferation of complaints against authority, of accusations and counter-accusations, and of long and bitter conflicts.

No governmental system in history has been without significant discretionary power; none can be, and the Church's governing authority should be no exception. Discretion is indispensable for tailoring decisions to unique facts and circumstances in particular cases, and for creative solutions to new problems. Total elimination of discretionary power would cripple authority's service to the people by depriving that service of all flexibility.

The conceded need for necessary discretionary power in Church administrators, however, must not be allowed to becloud one's vision either of the large opportunities for abuse of such powers or of the co-existence of much unnecessary discretionary power which has been allowed to grow up in the Church. . . .

NOTES

1. " . . . the chosen People of God is one . . . As members, they share a common dignity from their rebirth in Christ. They have the same filial grace and the same vocation to perfection. They possess in common one salvation, one hope, and one undivided charity. Hence, there is in Christ and in the Church no inequality on the basis of race or nationality, social condition or sex . . . all share a true equality with regard to the dignity and to the activity common to all the faithful for the building up of the Body of Christ." Vat. Conc. II, *Lumen Gentium,* #32.

"Since all men possess a rational soul and are created in God's likeness, since they have the same nature and origin, have been redeemed by Christ, and enjoy the same divine calling and destiny, the basic equality of all must receive increasingly greater recognition. True, all men are not alike from the point of view of varying physical power and the diversity of intellectual and moral resources. Nevertheless, with respect to the fundamental rights of the person, every type of discrimination, whether social or cultural, whether based on sex, race, color, social condition, language, or religion, is to be overcome and eradicated as contrary to God's intent." Vat. Conc. II, *Gaudium et Spes,* #29.

"Futhermore, let pastors respectfully acknowledge that just freedom which belongs to everyone in this earthly city." Vat. Conc, II, *Lumen Gentium,* #37.

2. "The laity have the right, as do all Christians, to receive in abundance from their sacred pastors the spiritual goods of the Church, especially the assistance of the Word of God and the sacraments." Vat. Conc. II, *Lumen Gentium,* #37.

"Mother Church earnestly desires that all the faithful be led to that full, conscious, and active participation in liturgical celebrations which is demanded by the very nature of the liturgy. Such participation by the Christian people . . . is their right and duty by reason of their baptism." Vat. Conc. II, *Sacrosanctum Concilium,* #14.

3. ". . . the laity . . . share in the priestly, prophetic, and royal office of Christ and therefore have their own role to play in the mission of the whole People of God in the Church and in the world. They exercise a genuine apostolate by their activity on behalf of bringing the gospel and holiness to men, and on behalf of penetrating and perfecting the temporal sphere of things through the spirit of the gospel . . . The laity derive the right and duty with respect to the apostolate from their union with Christ their Head." Vat. Conc. II, *Apostolicam Actuositatem,* #2, 3.

"Upon all the laity, therefore, rests the noble duty of working to extend the divine plan of salvation ever increasingly to all men of each epoch and in every land. Consequently, let every opportunity be given them so that, according to their abilities and the needs of the times, they may zealously participate in the saving work of the Church." Vat. Conc. II, *Lumen Gentium,* #33.

"Bishops, pastors of parishes and other priests of both branches of the clergy should keep in mind that the right and duty to exercise the apostolate is common to all the faithful, both clergy and laity, and that the laity also have their own proper roles in building up the Church." Vat. Conc. II, *Apostolicam Actuositatem,* #25.

"Let sacred pastors recognize and promote the dignity as well as the responsibility of the layman in the Church. Let them willingly make use of his prudent advice. Let them confidently assign duties to him in the service of the Church, allowing him freedom and room for action. Further, let them encourage the layman so that he may undertake tasks on his own initiative." Vat. Conc. II, *Lumen Gentium,* #37.

4. "Every layman should openly reveal to (his sacred pastors) his needs and desires with that freedom and confidence which befits a son of God and a brother in Christ. An individual layman by reason of the knowledge, competence, or outstanding ability which he may enjoy, is permitted and sometimes even obliged to express his opinion on things which concern the good of the Church. When occasions arise, let this be done through the agencies set up by the Church for the purpose. Let it always be done in truth, in courage, and in prudence, with reverence and charity toward those who by reason of their sacred office represent the person of Christ . . . Let sacred pastors . . . consider with fatherly love the projects, suggestions, and desires proposed by the laity." Vat. Conc. II, *Lumen Gentium,* #37.

". . . by reason of the gift of the Holy Spirit which is given to priests in sacred ordination, bishops should regard them as necessary helpers and counselors . . . as . . . brothers and friends . . . (the bishop) should gladly listen to them, indeed, consult them, and have discussions with them about those matters which concern the necessities of pastoral work and the welfare of the diocese. In order to put these ideals into effect, a group or senate of priests representing the presbytery should be established." Vat. Conc. II, *Presbyterorum Ordinis,* #7.

"In dioceses, as far as possible, there should be councils which assist the apostolic work of the Church either in the field of making the gospel known and men holy, or in the charitable, social, or other spheres. To this end, clergy and religious should appropriately cooperate with

the laity . . . Councils of this type should be established as far as possible also on the parochial, interparochial and interdiocesan level as well as in the national or international sphere." Vat. Conc. II, *Apostolicam Actuositatem,* #26.

". . . there must be made available to all men everything necessary for leading a life truly human, such as . . . the right . . . to appropriate information." Vat. Conc. II, *Gaudium et Spes,* #26.

"By the natural law, every human being has the right . . . to be informed truthfully about public events," John XXIII, *Pacem in Terris,* #12.

"In addition, the use of the media is a testament to the Church's belief in two fundamental principles of communications, namely, the right to information; and the necessity of public opinion within the Church . . . Man's right to be informed is a natural, inherent right. It is given him by God himself. It is not a privilege conferred by any authority . . . If there have been abuses of this right by any authorities in the Church, we members of the people of God can only regretfully acknowledge the fact and at the same time strive to amend our ways . . . The right to information, however, we firmly believe must be stressed today because only a true and complete knowledge will enable society and man as an individual to stand secure in an age of intellectual and moral turmoil. Moreover, the corollary of this right to information is the right to full expression. The distinguished Commission on Freedom of the Press observed twenty years ago that 'public discussion is a necessary condition of a free society and that freedom of expression is a necessary condition of adequate public discussion' . . . History affords us many examples of the fact that freedom suffers the moment man's inherent right to information begins to be curtailed . . . Closely associated with man's right to information is the necessity of both Church and State to cultivate a healthy public opinion . . . Public opinion, as a symbol and factor of social cohesion, is always an important element in every decision that leaders of both Church and State must make. Those will govern most wisely who attempt most assiduously to evaluate decisions in terms of such a public opinion . . . (As) Pope Pius XII enunciated: 'There would be something missing from the Church's life if there were no public opinion within her, a defect for which pastors as well as the faithful would be responsible.'" U.S. Bishops' Committee for Social Communication, *Statement for World Communications Day,* (1967).

5. ". . . while adhering to the methods and requirements proper to theology, theologians are invited to seek continually for more suitable ways of communicating doctrine to the men of their times. For the deposit of faith or revealed truths are one thing; the manner in which they are formulated without violence to their meaning and significance is another . . . Theological inquiry should seek a profound understanding of revealed truth without neglecting close contact with its own times. As a result, it will be able to help those men skilled in various fields of knowledge to gain a better understanding of the faith . . . This common effort will very greatly aid in the formation of priests. It will enable them to present to our contemporaries the doctrine of the Church concerning God, man, and the world in a manner better suited to them with the result that they will receive it more willingly. Furthermore, it is to be hoped that many laymen will receive an appropriate formation in the sacred sciences, and that some will develop and deepen these studies by their own labors. In order that such persons may fulfill their proper function, let it be recognized that all the faithful, clerical and lay, possess a lawful freedom of inquiry and of thought, and the freedom to express their minds humbly and courageously

about those matters in which they enjoy competence." Vat. Conc. II, *Gaudium et Spes, #62.*

"By the natural law, every human being has the right to . . . freedom in searching for the truth and in expressing and communicating his opinions within the limits laid down by the moral order and the common good." John XXIII, *Pacem in Terris, #12.*

6. "There is a great variety of associations in the apostolate . . . As long as the proper relationship is kept to Church authorities, the laity have the right to found and run such associations and to join those already existing." Vat. Conc. II, *Apostolicam Actuositatem, #19.*

"Worthy too of high regard and zealous promotion are those associations whose rules have been examined by competent Church authority, and which foster priestly holiness in the exercise of the ministry through an apt and properly approved rule of life and through brotherly assistance. Thus these associations aim to be of service to the whole priestly order." Vat. Conc. II, *Presbyterorum Ordinis, #8.*

"From the fact that human beings are by nature social, there arises the right of assembly and association. They have also the right to give the societies of which they are members the form they consider most suitable for the aim they have in view, and to act within such societies on their own initiative and on their own responsibility in order to achieve their desired objectives." John XXIII, *Pacem in Terris, #23.*

7. ". . . there is a growing awareness of the exalted dignity proper to the human person, since he stands above all things, and his rights and duties are universal and inviolable. Therefore, there must be made available to all men everything necessary for leading a life truly human, such as . . . the right . . . to a good reputation, to respect . . . to activity in accord with the upright norm of one's own conscience, to protection of privacy and to rightful freedom in matters religious too." Vat. Conc. II, *Gaudium et Spes, #26.*

"By the natural law, every human being has the right to respect for his person, to his good reputation . . ." John XXIII, *Pacem in Terris, #12.* "Every human being has the right to honor God according to the dictates of an upright conscience, and therefore, the right to worship God privately and publicly. " John XXIII, *Pacem in Terris,* #14.

8. "In the use of all freedoms, the moral principle of personal and social responsibility is to be observed. In the exercise of their rights, individual men and social groups are bound by the moral law to have respect both for the rights of others and for their own duties toward others and for the common welfare of all . . . For the rest, the usages of society are to be the usages of freedom in their full range. These require that the freedom of man be respected as far as possible, and curtailed only when and in so far as necessary." Vat. Conc. II, *Dignitatis Humanae,* #7.

9. Vat. Conc. II, *Lumen Gentium,* #27.

10. 8 *New Catholic Encyclopedia* 61 (McGraw-Hill, 1967).

11. C.I.C., cc. 2147-2167.

12. C.I.C., cc. 1552-1924; 1933-1959. Cf. Krol, *The Defendant in Contentious Trials* (C.U., 1942).

13. C.I.C., cc. 356-362.

37

14. Vat. Conc. II, *Dignitatis Humanae,* #1.

15. Vat. Conc. II, *Gaudium et Spes,* #75.

16. Vat. Conc. II, *Gaudium et Spes,* #76.

17. Vat. Conc. II, *Gaudium et Spes,* #26.

18. Vat. Conc. II, *Lumen Gentium,* #36.

19. Vat. Conc. II, *Lumen Gentium,* #37.

20. C.I.C., c. 1572.

21. "As lawful successors of the apostles and as members of the episcopal college, bishops should always realize that they are linked one to the other, and should show concern for all the churches. For by divine institution and the requirement of their apostolic office, each one in concert with his fellow bishops is responsible for the Church." Vat. Conc. II, *Christus Dominus,* #6.

"From the very first centuries of the Church the bishops who were placed over individual churches were deeply influenced by the fellowship of fraternal charity and by zeal for the universal mission entrusted to the apostles. And so they pooled their resources and unified their plans for the common good and for that of the individual churches." Vat. Conc. II, *Christus Dominus,* #36.

22. Canon 356 requires a diocesan synod every ten years. Although such synods were frequent in the pre-Code Church in America, few dioceses have adhered to the law in this regard in recent decades.

23. C.I.C., c. 1667.

24. The reorganization of the Roman Curia, accomplished by the Apostolic Constitution *Regimini Ecclesiae Universae* (1967), pointed the way to the establishment of administrative courts elsewhere in the Church. The Constitution enlarged the competency of the Apostolic Signatura to include review of contentions arising from the exercise of administrative ecclesiastical authority by one or another of the departments of the Roman Curia.

25. Luke 6:27-31.

26. Mt. 5:3.

27. Mt. 5:9.

28. Mt. 6:12.

29. 1 Cor. 6:1-6.

30. 1 Cor. 6:7-8.

31. C.I.C., c. 1925.

32. C.I.C., c. 1929.

Case 14

Due Process and the Local Ordinary

Bishop Urban Schmidt of the Chester Diocese established a Due Process Board to handle all cases and controversies occurring within the ecclesiastical territory of the diocese other than petitions for annulments of marriages or dispensations from the obligations of sacred orders.

Among the articles of the Due Process Board were the following:

1. The board shall have original and complete jurisdiction over all cases and controversies, except for marriage and holy orders, affecting ecclesiastical life within the Chester Diocese.
2. All members of the diocese residing within the diocese are subject to the board.
3. The board shall have binding authority to decide all cases and controversies presented. Appeal of a decision of the board may be made to the bishop of the Chester Diocese, who, upon receipt of the appeal, shall either affirm the decision of the board or submit the appeal to the diocesan tribunal for judicial determination. Any and all members of the diocese may present cases or controversies to the board for adjudication.

Bishop Schmidt decided that the cathedral, located in a slum area of Chester, needed extensive renovation to the amount of 1.5 million dollars. A group of concerned clergy, religious, and laity (Concerned Christians) opposed such extensive renovation, believing that diocesan money should be used for other purposes, such as education, social projects within the slum area, and support of a diocesan mission in South America. Concerned Christians, therefore, initiated a case with the Due Process Board. The board, realizing the delicate nature of the case, did not wish to decide the issue. Therefore, it indefinitely delayed action on the petition.

Realizing the delay would permit the bishop to proceed with renovation, Concerned Christians initiated suit in Federal District Court on the grounds of denial of due process and breach of contract. The court accepted the petition and ordered the parties to appear.

Meanwhile, the board, hoping to thwart the civil court suit, proceeded to a decision on the petition presented to it. The board decided:

1. That the board did not have authority under canon law to decide an issue against the bishop, notwithstanding the articles of the board;
2. That in no case is an administrative decision regarding expenditures of money a case or controversy;
3. Therefore, the petition is rejected.

Bishop Schmidt affirmed the decision.

Concerned Christians rejected the board's determination, since no hearing was held and since the articles of the board made no exemption for the bishop. The controversy now embraces the entire diocese and affects the very existence of the Due Process Board.

Exercise

1. Under the general law of the Church, may a diocese establish a Due Process Board? If so, what relation does the board have to the juridic structure of the Code?

2. Is the determination of the board legally sound according to the general law of the Church?

3. What authority would a civil court exercise over the ecclesiastical dispute between Concerned Christians and the diocese?

References

Code of Canon Law, canons 335, 1557.

New Catholic Encyclopedia (Supplement), 2nd ed., s. v. "Due Process."

Second Vatican Council, *Dogmatic Constitution on the Church* 18-29 (November 21, 1964).

— — —, *Decree on the Pastoral Office of Bishops in the Church* 8, 11-21 (October 28, 1965).

Maida, A. J., "Rights in the Church," *Chicago Studies* 15 (1976), 255-67.

Walsh, M. J., "Protecting Rights in the Church," *The Month* 11 (1978), 131-34.

Case 15

Precepts and Penalties

Parish Council members of St. Brendan's Church began to receive complaints about the life-style of their associate pastor, Fr. Kevin Smythey. He was often seen in the company of avowed homosexuals and regularly frequented a gay bar in the university area.

Outraged and indignant, some parishioners walked out of the church when Father Kevin appeared for Mass. Others attended Mass at St. Stanislaus Church in town. When the principal advised the disturbed parishioners that they would have to transfer their children from St. Brendan's School unless they became regular supporting parishioners again, they decided it was time to speak with Bishop Oliver Owens.

The bishop summoned Father Kevin and, after a somewhat heated conversation, ordered him to remedy the situation. Angered because he had been reported to the bishop, Father Kevin blurted out, "I'm old enough to take care of myself, and I'll go with whomever I wish and wherever I wish."

Bishop Owens expressed his concern and regrets at the young priest's reaction. Then he told him that he would give him a few days to think the matter over and that he would expect an answer to his order.

At the end of the month, Kevin received a letter from the chancery office. "Under pain of suspension *a divinis*," he read, "you are to shun the company of homosexuals and to desist from going to gay bars."

Three days later the bishop left for Rome. The young priest mused, "He ought to resign. I hope he never comes back here."

Exercise

1. Are Father Kevin's rights to a personal life-style being violated?

2. Using information contained in the problem, draw up a sample precept.

3. Can you support the bishop's action in this case?

4. How long will Father Kevin be held to the precept?

References

Carr, A. M., "Who Can Absolve from This Suspension?" *Homiletic and Pastoral Review* 66 (1966), 696.

Rainer, E., *Suspention of Clerics*. Canon Law Studies, no. 111 (Washington: The Catholic University of America, 1937).

Roelker, E., *Precepts* (Paterson, N.J.: St. Anthony Guild Press, 1955), 202-12.

The Conveyance of Ecclesiastical Goods

Francis G. Morrisey

One of the most difficult sections to apply in the Code of Canon Law is the one referring to the administration of the temporal goods of the Church. A significant number of canons seemed to have had little relevance for North America, and those that did were often too complicated, incomplete, or obsolete to be applied literally.

A characteristic that seems to underlie the norms on administration of temporal goods, and, more particularly, those relating to the alienation or conveyance of such property, is that these norms were promulgated at a time—near the end of World War I—when money was of little value. The patrimony of the Church consisted more in land and property holdings, which were then considered to have a somewhat perennial value, than in liquid assets or invested funds. At the present time, the converse is probably truer. In many instances, land and buildings have become a liability for the Church, especially if they are subject to heavy taxation or other charges.

The entire question of ecclesiastical financial management was brought to the fore dramatically by publicity given in the press to a number of situations faced by dioceses and religious institutes in the U.S.A. and Canada.[1] A recent article in *Fortune,* "There's an Unholy Mess in the Churchly Economy"[2] shows how the matter is causing raised eyebrows in financial circles. The result will be that it will eventually become more and more difficult to obtain loans or float bond issues for Church building and other construction projects if there is any likely risk that the Church or one of its institutions would default on its payments.

One area that seemed to be causing problems was that of financial indebtedness. The contracting of debts, especially through bonds or mortgages, was an area that needed special investigation. Consequently, in view of the difficulties experienced in applying the canons on contracts, especially cc. 1530-1532, a joint committee was established in 1974 by the Conference of Major Superiors of Men, the Leadership Conference of Women Religious, and the Canadian Religious Conference[3] to study the concept of alienation, or "conveyance" as it is now more commonly called, and to prepare interpretations based on present-day practice that would help administrators of ecclesiastical property fulfill their mandate more securely and in accordance with canonical prescriptions. It was thought that a unified form of administration would help restore the credibility of the Church in the area of finances and facilitate the work of diocesan and religious treasurers. The joint committee has completed the first two sections of the project and submitted them to those who commissioned the study. The first part of the report studied the concept of conveyance; the second provided a series of proposed norms that could eventually constitute particular law for the United States of America and Canada in regard to the administration of temporal goods in Religious Institutes. The question of diocesan administration was not directly envisaged in the study, although most of the concepts explained therein would be equally applicable to both sectors.

In the pages which follow, we propose to give a summary of this report, explaining some of the concepts involved, and then proposing applications for contemporary practice. In a third section, we shall examine some of the proposed changes in patrimonial law and make a certain number of general comments.

THE CONCEPT OF CONVEYANCE IN CANON LAW: THE PRESCRIPTIONS

Canons 1530-1532 state that preservable temporal ecclesiastical goods may be alienated or conveyed to others providing there has been at least two appraisals by conscientious experts, there is just cause for disposing of the goods, and the permission of the legitimate superior has been obtained. At the present time, the legitimate superior is the Holy See for goods valued at more than $15,000 in the U.S.A. and $300,000 in Canada.[4]

There has been strong opposition to the prescription requiring permission from the Holy See in certain parts of the Church. Indeed, a number of Episcopal Conferences have not yet reached agreement on the new amounts beyond which the permission of the Holy See would be required. Opposition was based on a number of factors, such as objections to the tax imposed or contribution requested upon receipt of the indult, the difficulty of determining a sum to be used as a basis for transactions, and, especially, disagreement with the very notion that "outside" permission should even be required. Nevertheless, whatever the reasons, the law still remains. One practical consequence of inaction in this regard is that a number of religious communities are hindered in their operations since the recent faculties of Superiors General authorize them to alienate goods or contract debts up to the amount determined by the Episcopal Conference and approved by the Holy See.[5] It often happens that even though dioceses do not request the necessary indults, religious communities are forced to do so. This situation sometimes causes misunderstandings between religious and diocesan authorities. Nevertheless, it is hoped that this inequitable situation will be rectified in the near future. In the meanwhile, though, what do we understand to be the meaning of some of the terms involved in interpreting and applying the canons?

1. Temporal Goods

For the purposes of laws affecting the goods of the Church, temporal goods are considered to be all those non-supernatural things which possess an economic value.[6]

Canonically speaking, money, as such, is not considered a "thing", but a mere medium of exchange. Therefore, as such, money (free capital) is not considered part of the permanent patrimony of an ecclesiastical moral person. Consequently, its use is not governed by the laws on conveyance, but by those on administration, loans, etc. The use of money comes under the laws on conveyance only when money has become part of a stable capital.

It becomes stable capital in the eyes of the Church "only when designated so by an externally manifested act of a competent ecclesiastical authority".[7] Thus, only money which is part of a stable capital comes under the term "temporal goods" in Canon Law.

2. Ecclesiastical Goods and Property

Ecclesiastical goods or property are all temporal goods which belong to any moral person (a canonical corporation) in the Church. The expression "ecclesiastical property" is often used by authors as an equivalent for "ecclesiastical goods". In some particular instances, it is difficult to determine precisely whether certain property is truly ecclesiastical, or only appears to be so.

3. Ownership

Ownership is the radical and fundamental right of enjoying and disposing of temporal goods. Any encumbrance on the goods, such as an easement, mortgage or lien, limits the exercise of the rights of ownership, but not the right itself.

4. Investment of Money

The term "investment of money" applies to any disposition which assures the conservation, at least in equivalent goods, of money, and produces interest or revenues, or provides for capital gains.[8]

Money may be invested in two ways:

a) Temporary Investment

Investment in readily negotiable securities, or a deposit of an annual or temporary surplus, of a gift or of cash on hand, or their putting aside for future needs by the competent ecclesiastical authority. Such money is called free, unstable, or working capital.[9]

b) Permanent Investment

The investment of stable capital or fixed assets to preserve capital and produce income or capital gains. Money so invested is juridically transformed into stable capital or fixed assets by the explicit act of competent authority.

5. Free, Unstable, Fluctuating, or Working Capital

Free or working capital is that money which is cash on hand, or money temporarily invested or put aside for future needs.

If a donor, in making a gift, specified a determined period in which the principal fund must be maintained and the income applied to a specific purpose, upon the expiration of the time specified and the fulfillment of the terms imposed, the fund then becomes free capital.

Money which has been temporarily invested for the general purpose of providing operating funds for the diocese or community (a quasi-reserve fund) should be regarded as free capital. This remains true even if, for purposes of bookkeeping, public relations or information, the administration designates part of these general operating funds as though they were reserved for a specific operating purpose (e.g., deferred maintenance, generalate support, medical fund, mission development, etc.). Likewise, an endowment fund for general operating purposes is considered in Church Law as free capital.

6. Stable, Fixed, or Invested Capital

Stable, fixed, or invested capital is that money which is not being used primarily as a medium of barter or exchange, but which has been invested in property as holdings of some kind.

When money has been invested in this specific way, it is then likened to immovable property, it has been immobilized, and thereupon is subject to the canonical formalities governing conveyance.[10]

Once money or ecclesiastical goods have been permanently or for a lengthy period of time attributed by the donor or the competent authority for a specific purpose, they are said to be immobilized. The money thus earned is a revenue to be used for the same specific purpose (cf. c. 1547).

Immobilization differs from simple investment in the sense that in the former case the principal must be permanently preserved and the income used for the specific purpose (e.g., a scholarship endowment fund, as opposed, for instance, to a quasi-reserve fund or to funds functioning as endowment), or the capital, if spent, must be spent for the specific purpose of the fund (e.g., a building fund or a retirement fund). The instrument in which immobilized funds are invested need not be a long-term instrument.

7. Ecclesiastical Foundations

An ecclesiastical foundation, usually known in law as a "pious foundation", is property (money, stocks, bonds, etc.) given to an ecclesiastical moral person with the obligation of conserving the principal *in perpetuum* or for a long time, and of using the annual income for some specific ecclesiastical function or some determined work of piety or charity (e.g., Mass foundations, founded bursaries, annuities, etc.). A pious foundation is one type of immobilized capital.

When the property itself is to be used or spent for the determined work of piety or charity (for pious causes), this situation is not considered to constitute a pious foundation, but is considered as a gift or donation with a specific purpose.[11]

8. Conveyance (alienation)

In the strict sense, conveyance (i.e., "alienatio", as mentioned in c. 1530) is any act by which the right to ownership of ecclesiastical property is transferred to another.

In the broad sense, conveyance is any act by which the use of the right, or the right itself, of ownership is or could be diminished, restricted or endangered.

For the purposes of Canon Law, the term "conveyance" has been applied to all transactions which may render the rights of a moral person less secure, or to all contracts in which the juridical status of the rights of the Church may become jeopardized.

9. Administration of Ecclesiastical Property

Canon 1527 of the Code of Canon Law refers to ordinary administration, as opposed to acts of extraordinary administration.

The term "ordinary administration" is applied to those acts which may be carried out by administrators in virtue of their office or of delegated powers, and include such items as receiving payments, depositing money in banks, making required sales and purchases, accepting donations or gifts, investing free capital, designating free capital as a reserve fund, leasing or renting ecclesiastical property for a period of less than nine years or for an annual rental amounting to less than one-thirtieth of the amount determined by the Episcopal Conference.[12]

Acts of extraordinary administration which, to be carried out, generally require special authorization of the competent superiors or ecclesiastical authorities, are those acts which are not included in the concept of ordinary administration, or which exceed its limits and extent, such as purchasing or selling of real estate, leasing or rental of property when both the term of the lease is more than nine years and the annual rental exceeds one-thirtieth of the amount the Episcopal Conference has determined, or entering into transactions by which the financial condition of ecclesiastical property becomes less secure (e.g., contracting loans, mortgages, construction or demolition of buildings, etc.). Acts of conveyance in the strict sense are generally classified as acts of extraordinary administration.[13]

Having defined these nine terms, we can now proceed to an examination of their application in contemporary financial practice.

II. Applications of the Definitions

The clearest way of applying the definitions given in the first part of this paper, would be to examine some of the acts which are subject to the canonical prescriptions governing conveyance, and those which are most likely not directly subject to these norms.

1. Acts Subject to the Canonical Regulations Regarding Conveyance[14]

a. Any act by which title to property (ownership) is transferred to another, without prejudice to explanations to be given below.

b. Spending a part or all of immobilized funds for some purpose other than that for which they were immobilized:

- conveying money and investments beyond the amount approved for each country if this money or these investments have become a part of the fixed capital of any canonical corporation;
- withdrawal of money or investments beyond the amount approved for each country, from the fixed capital of any canonical corporation;
- conveyance of money or its equivalent, such as stocks, bonds, bank notes, and the like (beyond the approved amount) received from the sale of property belonging to the fixed capital of a canonical corporation;
- conveyance of money or securities (beyond the approved amount) received in the form of annuities contingent upon the payment of certain annual sums;
- conveyance of money or securities accruing from pious foundations, Mass foundations, burses, endowments, annuities, and the like, particularly if the obligations have not been acquitted;
- conveyance of money and securities (beyond the approved amount) being diverted from specific purposes for which they were originally acquired.

c. Any act which is a preparation for conveyance, such as giving security, a mortgage, an option, compromise, settlement.

d. In general, any act by which Church property is subjected to burdens either *in perpetuum* or for a long time, such as granting the use, the usufruct, or easement of various kinds, again subject to the explanations to be given below.

e. Sale of precious works or conveyance of notable relics.

It is important to mention that, even in the foregoing instances, it is not always necessary to obtain the permission of the Apostolic See. This will depend on the value of the transactions or on the nature of the goods to be conveyed.

2. *Acts Which Are Not Subject to the Canonical Prescriptions Regulating Conveyance*[15]

a. Spending Free Capital

If free capital is transferred, the act of conveyance is not subject to the prescriptions of the Code of Canon Law regarding conveyance (i.e., cc. 1530-1532). It follows that the use of ordinary income or unrestricted movable gifts for operating expenses or capital improvements would likewise not be subject to these prescriptions.[16]

The spending of free capital is not the type of conveyance regulated as such by Canon Law. It does not matter whether the purpose of the action is to reduce debts, meet operating expenses, improve capital assets or make purchases. Nevertheless, the spending of free capital may be regulated by other canons concerning acts of ordinary administration, gifts, investments, etc.

If, for instance, a diocese or a community buys into a Social Security plan retroactive payment, there is no problem in this regard, provided free capital was used, and not securities which were part of the fixed capital—unless this were a specific fund set up for the care of the sick or aged members of the diocese (presbyterium, employees, etc.) or the religious Institute.

b. Transfer of Goods from One Ecclesiastical Moral Person to Another

Unless particular law stipulates otherwise, if the transfer of ecclesiastical goods is from one moral person to another moral person, both part of the same ecclesiastical moral person (i.e., canonical corporation)—other than the universal Catholic Church—this conveyance is not subject to the prescriptions of canons 1530-1532.

Thus, a sale or donation from a parish to the diocese, from a religious house to the religious province to which it is subject, contributions of one religious province to another or to the generalate, transfer when a moral person divides or begets a new moral person (e.g., division of parishes, dioceses), are not acts of conveyance in the sense understood by canons 1530-1532.[17]

Another example would be when one moral person joins another, as when two parishes or dioceses are united.

c. Registering Assests Under a New Title

The mere fact of registering assets under a different civil title is not conveyance in the canonical sense, or at least does not seem to be the kind of transfer contemplated in canons 1530-1532. Thus, when a religious congregation decides to incorporate its motherhouse separately from an adjacent facility, such as a retirement home, college or hospital, the newly established civil corporations may or may not be distinct ecclesiastical moral persons (canonical corporations). The transfer of title to these civil corporations is not an act of conveyance because the same or another—canonical moral person remains the owner. Only when the control of the assets on the part of the ecclesiastical moral person is transferred, diminished or endangered, does the question of conveyance enter.

d. Assuming a Mortgage[18]

If a benefactor gives to an ecclesiastical moral person property to which he held title, but which is heavily mortgaged, the acceptance of such property does not come under the concept of conveyance of ecclesiastical goods, despite the mortgage, since no ecclesiastical funds were invested in it. Rather, the prescriptions of canon 1527 on the administration of ecclesiastical goods must then be observed.

The property acquired may or may not become part of the stable capital or patrimony of the ecclesiastical moral person, depending upon the terms of the gift or the action of competent authority of the same ecclesiastical moral person in aggregating it to its stable capital.

Likewise, the value of the mortgage must be taken into account when computing the value of the real estate to be sold to another owner. The act may become an act beyond the competence of a given authority if the net value exceeds the prescribed sums.

In mortgaging ecclesiastical goods, then, in virtue of canon 1538, the permissions outlined in canon 1532 must be obtained.

e. Transfer of Title

Canonical commentators are generally of the opinion that if a transfer or exchange of titles is for temporal goods of a different category (e.g., exchanging real estate for securities), the prescriptions of canons 1530-1532 must be observed, since this would be conveyance in the strict sense. However, the practice of numerous dioceses and religious Institutes seems to be based on a somewhat different interpretation.

However, when the transfer is confined to temporal goods of the same category (e.g., securities for other securities), this conveyance is generally not governed by the prescriptions of canons 1530-1532. Nevertheless, when title to *real estate* is transferred, this is conveyance in the strict sense of the term, unless the transfer is for another piece of real estate of the same value, in which case the situation of the ecclesiastical goods is not jeopardized.

If ecclesiastical goods are to be transferred for similar ones, then there must be evaluations as prescribed in canon 1530. The evaluation of a government assessor's office, insurance company or real estate broker is generally sufficient.

It also seems that, given the contemporary situation of the Church, the following types of transfer are not considered, in practice, subject to the prescriptions of canons 1530-1532: 1) cases where the sound administration of the goods of the whole moral person require that it be unburdened of certain pieces of property such as land which may no longer be used for Church purposes, vacant land being heavily taxed, land that is creating ill-will toward the Church and its credibility on social concerns, etc; 2) cases where the ecclesiastical moral persons withdraw from certain types of deficit enterprises which risk jeopardizing the goods of the total moral person (e.g., transferring ownership of nursing homes, etc., to Government agencies when there is no other alternative; 3) conversion of capital assets, as will be mentioned in the following section "f".

According to some canonists, however, the examples given in the preceding paragraph simply constitute sufficient reasons for initiating the process of conveyance according to the general norms of the Church. This opinion is not generally followed today.

f. Conversion of Capital Assets

The sale of real estate which is part of the stable capital of the Institute and the application of the proceeds to another *capital* purpose such as capital construction or reduction or liquidation of a mortgage on buildings or to a plant fund, does not constitute a conveyance to which canon 1532 applies, but may be regarded simply as a conversion of capital assets from one form to another.

Some canonists might find difficulty with this interpretation; yet, as it is given here, it is common practice in many dioceses and religious Institutes.

g. Using Ecclesiastical Goods as Collateral for Loans

Since free capital is not considered as ecclesiastical goods, if it is available it may be used as collateral for borrowing.

Likewise, if a moral person borrows or sells bonds to construct a new edifice, puting up *only* the title to the edifice under construction as collateral, this is not the kind of conveyance considered by canons 1530-1532. Indeed, until it exists, the new building is not part of the patrimony of the Church.

However, the simple issuing of bonds constitutes a conveyance, and is subject to the general regulations of canons 1530-1532.

Loans taken out for the purpose of constructing a new edifice would have to be authorized according to the general norms for administration.

This procedure is explained by W. J. Doheny:

> Mortgages are frequently placed on the very structure under actual construc-

tion, such as the church, school, or rectory. In such cases, where the mortgage is clearly and legally limited to the actual edifice under construction, it appears that the status of the church is not really and actually jeopardized. If the element of jeopardy or risk is not present in the mortgage, the special permission of the Holy See would not be necessary, it appears. Hence, if the ecclesiastical corporation has funds on hand for the partial payment of the building (generally about 50 per cent of the total cost), and if it is certain that future payments can be met from the *Ordinary Income* of the corporation, it seems that the special authorization of the Holy See would not be needed.[19]

h. Lending and Borrowing Money[20]

Making a loan is usually exempted from the concept of conveyance. Nevertheless, there are also norms governing this practice (cf. c. 1543).

It does not matter whether invested or free capital is used to make the loan, because if the loan is considered a safe and prudent investment, with a moderate rate of interest, the act of lending is not usually considered as an action endangering title to the goods. Default of payment would give rise to an action to recover the value of the ecclesiastical goods thus lent.

As Doheny states:

> Money invested in stocks, bonds, bank notes, mortgages, and the like may be withdrawn and changed to more lucrative investments, provided that these latter are considered reasonably safe investments.[21]

In other words, lending money is a way of investing money. It is not an act of conveyance, but an act of extraordinary administration and, as such, is regulated by canons 1527 and 1531, par. 3.

On the other hand, borrowing money is an act of conveyance in the sense of canons 1530-1532 when it constitutes an obligation imposed on the properties of the canonical corporation.

There is an exception when money is borrowed for the erection of a building under the terms of a mortgage with the express proviso that the ecclesiastical edifices therewith erected are the objects of the mortgage.[22]

Likewise, some canonists consider that when money is borrowed merely on the general credit of the ecclesiastical corporation, without offering a mortgage as security, this does not constitute conveyance in the sense of canons 1530-1532. This opinion is followed in practice by many dioceses and religious Institutes.

i. Sale of Furniture[23]

The sale of non-precious furniture (cf. c. 1532) in order to replace it with other furniture of equal or greater value is not regarded as conveyance, but is simply an act of prudent ordinary administration. It does not partake of the nature of a genuine transfer of ownership since the moral person still has approximately the same (or greater) assets.

j. Observing the Intentions of Donors[24]

Money given for a specific purpose must be used for that purpose. The spending of money, liquidating of securities or disposal of real estate for the purpose for which it was given by the donors is not an act of conveyance regulated by canons 1530-1532. Thus, if a benefactor willed or gave his home and grounds to further the apostolic activities of a diocese or religious community, these may be sold and the money used for the apostolic activities of these bodies.

k. Curtailment of Property Rights Through Negligence

Permitting the process of prescription would not be conveyance because there is no contract; however, it could be classified as bad administration and must be avoided (cf. cc. 1508-1512, 1523).

Religious and diocesan administrators must be fully sensitive to the requirements of social justice and the demands of Christian charity. Nevertheless, certain acts can be acts of negligence and classified as poor administration even though they do not constitute conveyance in the sense of canons 1530-1532. For instance, an ecclesiastical moral person could let the neighbourhood children use the grounds as a public park with such abandon or prodigality as to create such expectations or attitudes as will make it morally impossible, or at least extremely difficult, for the moral person ever to exercise the rights of ownership in relation to the land in question.

l. Refusal of Gifts[25]

The refusal to accept a gift or a profit is not considered a conveyance since ownership is not transferred; it is merely not acquired. However, the prescriptions of canon 1536 requiring the permission of the competent superior, must be observed before a gift may be refused.

m. Acceptance of Foundations[26]

The norms for accepting foundations should be carefully applied to avoid imposing undue hardship in the future on a diocese or religious Institute (cf. cc. 1545-1546). These acts are not considered as conveyance in the sense of canons 1530-1532.

n. Involuntary Surrender of Property

Curtailment on the use of property by ecological covenants and certain types of easements does not constitute conveyance in the sense of canons 1530-1532, provided this restriction of rights is imposed by public authorities or required for public utilities. The same could probably be said in the case of expropriations of land, hospitals and colleges.

* * *

A study of various financial transactions reveals that there are many types of such acts. The concept of conveyance is one such type, applied to a limited number of transactions. It is part of the overall norms regarding contracts. There are also other acts mentioned in the law, such as renting immovable property, lending or mortgaging ecclesiastical goods, and so forth.

Permissions required in one instance are not necessarily applicable in another. However, although a specific act does not fall under the concept of conveyance (cc. 1530-1532), this does not mean that no prescriptions of law are applicable. Permissions do vary from act to act. When a specific permission is required, in each case the precise prescriptions of law must be observed.

This being what seems to be the actual situation, what significant changes are proposed for the new law on the subject?

III. Proposed Changes in the New Law

The journal *Communicationes*[27] has presented a general overview of the fifty-four proposed new canons regarding the administration of the patrimony of the Church.

A number of the present norms have been substantially simplified, or even eliminated. Regarding conveyance or alienation, many interesting changes have been proposed.

Still, canon 33 would require the permission of the competent superior for the alienation of goods which have been legitimately assigned to the stable patrimony of an ecclesiastical moral person.

Canon 34 would state who the competent superior is. He is the local Ordinary, who would have to seek the advice of the council of administration and receive the required consent. In the case of temporal goods whose value exceeds the amount determined by the Episcopal Conference and approved by the Holy See, the consent of the local Ordinary will have to be confirmed by a special commission to be established by the Conference. The nature of this special commission does not seem to be determined in the new law. However, the canons might well provide more details on the subject; it is difficult to tell at this time because the *Schema* has not been distributed for comments.

In the case of temporal goods given to the Church as *ex voto* offerings, or of goods exceeding twice the amount approved by the Conference, the permission of the Holy See would also be required for validity.

This prescription regarding a special commission has advantages. It provides a guarantee against rash actions; it also demonstrates the solidarity that should exist among all dioceses of a country or region. Objections will probably be raised against its existence because it restricts somewhat a bishop's freedom. Nevertheless, recent events in the Church show the wisdom in promoting such a norm.

Taking the proposed new law as a whole, and not considering only the canons on contracts, a number of observations could now be made concerning the norms and the manner in which ecclesiastical temporal goods are administered in the Church today.

1. The Principle of Accountability

The principle of accountability for one's actions that the Church has implemented in so many other areas, will also have to be introduced in the area of ecclesiastical financial administration. It is almost unbelievable that one person, who often has not been trained in the area, although he might have acquired great experience, has final say alone in transactions involving millions of dollars, and that often no accounting need be rendered. This situation is being corrected, but much more remains to be done to reestablish our credibility in this regard.

2. Indebtedness of Dioceses and Religious Institutes

The principal financial problem in the Church today is not caused by selling of property. Rather, it is probably the indebtedness of dioceses and religious Institutes. Norms could well be proposed governing the total amount of debts to be carried by an ecclesiastical moral person.

The joint committee established by the C.M.S.M., L.C.W.R., and C.R.C., proposed the following norms:

> Unless particular law determines otherwise, an Institute of Consecrated Life or an ecclesiastical moral person of the same Institute may not contract debts without the permission of a joint commission of representatives of the National Episcopal Conference, and of the Conference of Major Superiors, even within the limits prescribed above, if the total debts of the same moral person are the equivalent, for each active member of the same, to one-thirtieth of the amount approved by the Episcopal Conference as the amount beyond which a review of the proposed conveyance and action of the special commission . . . is required before action is taken by the Superior General and the Council of the Institute.
>
> The consent of the Holy See shall be obtained in each case where the total debts of an Institute of Consecrated Life or of an ecclesiastical moral person which is part of the same Institute, exceed the equivalent, for each active member of the same, of one-fifteenth of the same amount approved by the Episcopal Conference.[28]

3. Size of a Diocese or Institute

The law should take into account the size of a diocese or of an Institute and the number of persons involved in a given ecclesiastical moral person. For instance, a diocese with 2,000,000 Catholics should have proportionately more extensive powers than one of 20,000 Catholics. Likewise, a religious Institute of 4,000 members as opposed to one of 40 members.

4. Unlimited Use of Free Capital

It seems surprising in today's world that a diocese or an Institute may spend unlimited amounts of free capital if it is available, while at the same time being subjected to more stringent prescriptions regarding the sale of real estate or other property. Some norms could probably be prepared in this regard so that, at least, the particular law of each country or diocese would have to consider the question.

5. Independence in Financial Matters

The recent financial tragedies affecting dioceses and religious Institutes demonstrate only too clearly the importance for the Church to have trained and competent administrators who will follow the prescriptions of both civil and canon law. No legislation can provide for this, but greater accountability might be helpful. Is it naive to suggest that the financial statements of each diocese and religious Institute should be examined annually or regularly by specially appointed committees?

Dioceses and Religious Institutes can no longer afford to be completely independent in financial matters because of the effects on all ecclesiastical institutions when one of them defaults or goes into bankruptcy.

6. Catholic Ownership of Property

It will also be important in the near future to reach agreement on what constitutes Catholic ownership of property, especially in the case of publicly funded hospitals or educational institutions under partly lay boards.

CONCLUSION

The norms on conveyance and alienation can be observed without too much difficulty if they are understood correctly and have reasonable limits within which to operate. In a number of cases, the interpretation of the canonists differs on the intent or prescriptions of the law. It is certain that the law cannot be interpreted exclusively on a basis of practice. Nevertheless, if the practice differs radically from the letter of the law, then efforts must be made to have the law revised.

Where the opinions differ, as pointed out in this study, it is probably quite acceptable to follow the broader opinion. However, the problem does not lie there as much as it does in not having sufficiently high sums of money authorized as a basis upon which to apply the canons.

We are stewards of the patrimony of the Church. We all have at heart the protection of these goods so that they may be used to further the Church's apostolic mission. May we apply all available means so as to fulfill our role faithfully and prudently, and spare no effort to strive for better legislation in this delicate, yet important, area.

NOTES

*Paper presented at the Thirty-Eighth Annual Convention, Canon Law Society of America, Philadelphia, Penna., October 11-14, 1976.

1. *Cf. National Catholic Reporter,* 12 (1976), Nos. 14, 16; January and February, 1976.
2. James Gollin, *There's an Unholy Mess in the Churchly Economy,* in *Fortune,* May, 1976, p. 223-248.
3. Members of the Task Force on the Alienation of Ecclesiastical Goods: Very Rev. Paul M. Boyle, C.P.; Sister Marie-Paule Levaque, S.P.; Rev. William Lewers, C.S.C.; Sister Mildegarde Marie Mahoney, S.C.; Rev. Francis G. Morrisey, O.M.I.; Sister Mary Assunta Stang, S.C. The report of this task force was distributed by the Canadian Religious Conference on April 12, 1976, Document 12-4-76, Administration. Certain amendments were made to the report, August 16, 1976.
4. Cf. *Commentarium pro Religiosis,* 55 (1974), p. 364.
5. Cf. *A.A.S.,* 59 (1967), p. 362-376.
6. Cf. T.L. Bouscaren, *et al., Canon Law. A Text and Commentary,* Milwaukee, Bruce, 4th revised edition, 1966, p. 805.
7. W.J. Doheny, *Practical Problems in Church Finance,* Milwaukee, Bruce, 1941, p. 43.
8. Cf. T.L. Bouscaren, *op. cit.,* pp. 838, 849.
9. Cf. W.J. Doheny, *op. cit.,* p. 43.
10. Cf. *Ibid.,* p. 43-44.
11. Cf. T.L. Bouscaren, *op. cit.,* p. 853.
12. Cf. canon 1532, par. 2-3; *Canon Law Digest,* VI, p. 822-823: decree of the Sacred Consistorial Congregation, July 13, 1963.
13. Cf. T.L. Bouscaren, *op. cit.,* p. 835-836.
14. Cf. *Ibid.,* p. 838; W.J. Doheny, *op. cit.,* p. 44-45.
15. Cf. T.L. Bouscaren, *op. cit.,* p. 838-839.
16. Cf. *Ibid.,* p. 838.
17. Cf. A. Larraona, in *Commentarium pro Religiosis,* 1932, p. 184 sqq.
18. Cf. T.L. Bouscaren, *op. cit.,* p. 838.
19. W.J. Doheny, *op. cit.,* p. 56-57.
20. Cf. T.L. Bouscaren, *op. cit.,* p. 838.
21. W.J. Doheny, *op. cit.,* p. 53.
22. Cf. *Ibid.,* p. 48.
23. Cf. T.L. Bouscaren, *op. cit.,* p. 838.
24. Cf. *Ibid.,* p. 839.
25. Cf. *Ibid.,* p. 839
26. Cf. *Ibid.*
27. *Communicationes,* 5 (1973), p. 94-103.
28. C.R.C., *Report 12-4-76 Administration,* Part II, p. 3, Norm 16.

Case 16

Ownership of Church Property

St. John's Church in Winslow was built in 1860 and can seat 125 people. After World War II small industries moved into the area. The Catholic population has grown steadily and now numbers over eleven hundred souls. Two Saturday evening Masses and six Sunday Masses have been crowded for years. Something has to be done for the good of the people.

Fr. Thomas Wells wrote to his bishop concerning the need of a larger church. Responding for the bishop, the chancellor stated: "Bishop Casey has decided that the first step before seeing you concerning this would be for the Diocesan Finance Committee to make a study of the parish to ascertain its ability to pay for any property or structure that you should purchase or build."

The chancellor continued in his letter: "As I discussed with you, the Kearns Charity Fund will not be used for a parish project. The Kearns Charity Fund and property is diocesan property and will be used in Winslow for a Social Service Center. I would like to remind you that by canon law the bishop is the sole owner of all church properties in the diocese and the sole dispenser of all bequests left for charitable purposes in the diocese."

Fr. Wells dug up Mr. Kearns' last will and testament and read: "All the rest of my property both real and personal to be divided equally as follows: To Mamie Huggins, one-third; to Cynthia Porter, her sons Preston and Floyd, one-third; to the St. John's Catholic Parish, one-third—the St. John's one-third to be used for a fund known as the Marcia Kearns Charity Fund."

Exercise

1. Explain the canonical principle concerning the ownership of church property.

2. What are the rights and obligations of administrators of church property?

3. How would you advise Father Wells?

4. Comment on the significant portions of the chancellor's letter to Father Wells.

References

Bartlett, C. J., *The Tenure of Parochial Property in the United States.* Canon Law Studies, no. 31 (Washington: The Catholic University of America, 1926).

Korth, F. N., *Canon Law for Hospitals* (St. Louis: The Catholic Hospital Association of the United States and Canada, 1961)

McGrath, J. J., "Canon Law and American Church Law: A Comparative Study," *The Jurist* 18 (1958), 260-78.

PART IV: *Sacramental and Liturgical Law*

A. SACRAMENTAL LAW

The Canonical Ordering of the Sacraments

Tomás Garcia Barberena

I. Sacraments and Structure

In the ecclesiology of the manuals, the sacraments are means given by God to the Church for the sanctification of man, vehicles or channels of sanctifying grace, each with the form appropriate to its particular character. The Codex, faithfully following this conception of them, considers the sacraments as *praecipua sanctificationis et salutis media* (c. 732, § 1), and classifies them among the *res* which are *media ad Ecclesiae finem consequendum* (c. 726). They therefore appear in Book III, *De Rebus*.

This conception seems to assume that God at a given moment established the Church as a visible and hierarchically ordered society, and that later seven means of sanctification were placed at the disposal of this ready-made Church, and these are what we call the sacraments. Now this understanding of the sacraments is not that of Vatican Council II, and one might even call it erroneous, because the sacraments are part of the essential, inner structure of the Church, and are precisely what gives the Church her outer, visible character—that is, her juridical character.

The theological bases of this understanding of the Church are the incarnation, Christ as the primary sacrament of salvation, the Church herself as "the universal sacrament of salvation" (*Constitution on the Church,* n. 48), and the sacraments as concrete embodiments of the Church.[1]

The sacraments are not only seven channels of grace, but are at the same time seven juridical acts which define the position of the Christian in the

1. There is an abundant bibliography on the subject matter of this article. I am principally indebted to the following works: K. Rahner, *The Church and the Sacraments* (London and New York, 1965); P. Smulders, "The Church as the Sacrament of Salvation", in Barauna (ed)., *The Church of Vatican II* (not yet published in English; French and Spanish versions are available); *idem,* "Sacramenta et Ecclesia" in *Periodica* 48 (1959) pp. 3-55; E. Schillebeeckx, *Christ, the Sacrament of the Encounter with God* (London and New York, 1963); M. Useros Carretero, *Sacramenta Ecclesiae et Statuta Ecclesiae en la Eclesiologia de Santo Tomás* (Rome, 1962); R. Schulte, "Kirche und Kult", in *Mysterium Kirche* II (Salzburg, 1962), pp. 714ff.; St. Thomas Aquinas, in IV sent. dist, 17 & 18 and *Summa* II-II, 39, 3, and various well-known treatises of sacramental Canon Law.

Church. Article 11 of the *Constitution on the Church* explains this for each one of the sacraments: baptism makes him a member of the Church with the obligation of confessing the faith he has received; confirmation binds him more closely to the Church and increases his obligation to defend and propagate his faith—it must be received before he can marry or take orders (cc. 1021, §2 and 993, §1) and some would maintain that it should precede the eucharist. The eucharist is participation in the Church's greatest social act: it is both a sacramental institution and a juridical one, since participation in the eucharist is the juridical realization of the unity of the Church, as is stated in n. 2 of the *Decree on Ecumenism.*

This is why excommunication means above all exclusion from the eucharistic communion, and the prohibition to participate *in sacris* with non-Catholics (c. 1258) refers principally to the sacramental aspect, and particularly the eucharist, the sign of unity.

On the subject of penance, the *Decree on the Ministry and Life of Priests* (n. 5) says that through it "sinners are reconciled to God and the Church, the reconciliation with the Church being a sign and cause of reconciliation with God. The anointing of the sick likewise binds the sick person to the Church in a special way; his attitude should be one of obedience to and confidence in God so as to bear with illness and death, and his attitude to the Church should be of one who is dying with Christ who bore death", while "the whole Church commends those who are ill to the suffering and glorified Lord, asking that he may lighten their suffering and save them" (*Constitution on the Church,* n. 11).

The juridical aspect of matrimony is so clear that there is no need to describe it here, and the same goes for the sacrament of orders which places the ordained person in the clergy with the power of orders and the possibility of exercising jurisdictional powers, thereby establishing the principal, divinely originated, division of the members of the Church into clergy and laity (cc. 107 and 548).

Taking their stand on patristic and Scholastic teaching, modern theologians attribute a sacramental structure to the Church. A sacrament is not something that the Church holds as a deposit, but something that belongs to her very being and that makes the Church present every time it is produced. The Church is visible, external and juridical through her sacramental nature, and, as St. Thomas says, all law in the Church is based (*consistit*) on the sacraments; it is either sacramental of itself or can be reduced to what is sacramental, and, in the final analysis, to the eucharist, "the center and summit of the sacraments" (*Decree on the Church's Missionary Activity*).

The juridical consequences deriving from this approach are extremely important. In this article I just want to make some observations on its application to the sacramental structure of the Church and her constitutional law.

Modern writers have a very high opinion of the teaching of St. Thomas, who affirmed on various occasions that the Church was "fabricated", "founded", "built" and "instituted" by faith and the sacraments of faith. Vatican Council II affirmed that the Church should be regarded as a "visible structure" in which are to be found juridical agencies and the mystical body of Christ (*Constitution on the Church,* n. 8).

The same ingredients and the same problem of unity are to be found in the sacraments, which are also external and visible signs with the divine and invisible gift of grace hidden in them. This likeness indicates that Church and sacrament are really the same thing: the Church the proto-sacrament and the seven sacraments so many more actualizations and realizations of the Church making contact with individuals to offer them the life of God in the lives of each one of them. In Christ the divine and the human are unconfused but inseparable, because the hypostatic union is everlasting; so, too, in the Church are the hierarchical society and her power of saving, and also sign and grace in the sacraments.

Since 1940, the works of Carnelutti and Fedele have reanimated the discussion from the canonical point of view; yet, though fruitful, we have the impression today of having failed to get to the root of the problem owing to our defective ecclesiology. The characteristics of canonical ordering and its differences from secular law were sought in the *different ends* of the Church and secular society. The method is not illegitimate, but the "why" of things does not always explain their "what". Canon Law is not the same sort of thing as secular law, but only analogous to it, because of its sacramental character.

The juridical constitution of the Church is in fact an expression of its sacramentality. The Church is visible and hierarchical *through* the sacraments. I shall examine later how the hierarchy stems from the sacraments, here I want to show that the external visibility of the Church is that of the sacraments. Neither the Church nor the sacraments are the juxtaposition of two elements, one visible (the sign) and the other invisible (grace). The reason the Church is visible is not that she *has* some visible elements. The formal visibility of the Church consists in the fact that her mystery is made apparent in her organization, in her hierarchical and juridical relations, because everything in the Church—people, things, structures—is informed by a supernatural principle that effects an interior transformation. Without this inner supernaturalization, the people, things and structures would not form a Church, nor would the Church be formally visible with a visibility that would distinguish her from other purely human societies. From all this it follows that constitutional law in the Church is not limited to "hierarchology"; the basic norms of the sacraments belong to the sphere of the Church's law and should be incorporated in her revised Codex, if it is finally decided to proceed with one.

II. Sacraments and the Liturgy

The canons dealing with liturgical celebration are also to be found in

Book III of the Codex, *De Rebus.* The rules laid down in them are generally superficial and concerned with detail. Now the liturgical aspect is an important zone of coincidence between the sacraments and the Church, since both are institutions of worship. As Schillebeeckx writes: "A sacrament is the manifestation of the divine love that Christ feels for men [the gift of grace] and of the human love that he feels for God [worship]". The *Constitution on the Sacred Liturgy* (n. 59) affirms that the sacraments are acts of worship, modern theologians regard the Church as a worshiping society, and Vatican Council II fully endorsed this point of view (*Constitution on the Sacred Liturgy,* n. 59; cf. nn. 7, 10 and 99, as well as the *Constitution on the Church,* n. 10), even though it made a careful distinction between the hierarchical priesthood and the common priesthood of all believers. The theological bases are the same as those noted in the previous section. Everything stems from the incarnation, since Christ is a priest because he is is man and precisely in virtue of the hypostatic union. "In Christ there came forth the perfect satisfaction needed for our reconciliation, and we received the means for giving worthy worship to God" (*Constitution on the Sacred Liturgy,* n. 5). The priesthood of Christ is present in the Church as in an organically structured unity which "through Christ offers worship to the eternal Father", and so "in the liturgy full public worship is performed by the mystical body of Jesus Christ, that is, by the head and its members" (*Constitution on the Sacred Liturgy,* n. 7).

What is the link between the liturgical aspect and that of sanctification by grace common to the Church as proto-sacrament and the sacraments as manifestations of the Church? The sacraments sanctify through being acts of Christ and acts of the Church. They are not a form of magic; they are external signs that are valid only if, in the bosom of the Church, they are impregnated with the faith and merits of Christ. This way they fit into the Church is described by the term *res et sacramentum,* an intermediary element between the outward sign and the sanctifying gift of grace, since it is *signifying* in relation to grace and *signified* in relation to the outward sign.

The water of baptism, for example, is first an outward sign bringing juridical membership in the Church, a membership that both signifies and produces the grace of baptism. Smulders has traced the parallelism between these three trilogies of concepts: law-worship-spirit; outward sign-character-grace; juridical society-worshiping society-society of grace. In this systematic construction the liturgy of the Church and the sacraments form the intermediary element—*res et sacramentum*—linking the extreme elements of sign and grace, law and charism. It consists in the character in the three sacraments that stamp it on and in the equivalent or *ornatus* entity in the other sacraments.

Here I want to consider only the fact that the liturgical aspect is inseparable from the sacramental and ecclesial reality, and the liturgy is the same as that performed by Christ the priest on the cross, his priesthood perpetuated in the Church in time. The Church is a worshiping society with a sacramental structure; thus the basic norms of the liturgy must be in the fundamental code of the Church, with the primacy given to eucharistic worship.

But the Codex does not mention the priesthood of all the faithful or their active priestly role in the liturgy; they are only granted the right of receiving spiritual goods and aids to salvation from the clergy (c. 682). Vatican Council II took a different approach, calling the Church a priestly community with a sacred nature and an organic structure, and affirming that this community is brought into operation by the sacraments (*Constitution on the Church,* n. 11). The *Decree on the Apostolate of the Laity* says that the laity are "consecrated into a royal priesthood and a holy people" and that they have an active part to play in the life of the Church as sharers in the threefold office of Christ—priest, king and prophet.

The present Codex does not treat the sacraments as liturgical actions either, not even the eucharist; it seems rather to exclude them from the concept of liturgy, since c. 1256 defines liturgical acts as "instituted by the Church". Instead it abounds in minutely detailed rulings that would better be left to individual bishops. It is to be hoped that the new Codex will base the ordering of the liturgy on the principles of the *Constitution on the Sacred Liturgy* and emphasize the sacramental basis of Christian liturgy. The ecumenical demands of worship in common with other Christians (*Decree on Ecumenism,* nn. 8 and 13), will also have to be borne in mind, particularly common worship with the Eastern Churches, which, "though separated, possess true sacraments" (*Decree on Ecumenism,* n. 15).

III. Sacraments and the Hierarchy

The Church is not made up of the sum of two elements, one juridical (legislative, judicial and coactive power) and the other supernatural (the power of orders and of the magisterium). Any exclusively temporal power in the Church is an unacceptable hypothesis on any grounds. The power of the Church must be supernatural and visible at the same time. Therefore, in the hierarchy all power is raised to the supernatural order: subjects, authority, juridical relationships and the ends of hierarchical action and of all canonical ordering. One must beware of certain juridical formalisms which have been introduced too definitely in Canon Law as they have in civil law.

Basically, the hierarchy is unique (cc. 108, §3 and 109). Ordination and ordination alone is what introduces a man to it and enables him to receive a canonical mission. The history of the concept of hierarchy would show that the present distinctions between orders and jurisdiction stem from the dislocation into autonomous powers of what were originally acts of one sole power. There are not some "king" hierarchs sharing the kingship of Christ and other "priest" hierarchs sharing in his priesthood. The bishop, by virtue of being a bishop, directs the regular and fruitful distribution of the sacraments by his authority (*Constitution on the Church,* n. 26); his authority is exercised "in the name of Christ" and is "proper, ordinary and immediate" (*Constitution on the Church,* n. 27) so that, represented by the presbyter, he is in a certain sense present in every local assembly (*Decree on the Ministry and Life of Priests,* n. 5).

Orders does not of itself include the power of jurisdiction, but this is rooted in orders without which it would have no *raison d'être.* Orders is the immediate cause of what St. Thomas calls the *praeminentia dignitatis,* and this produces the *praeminentia virtutis* or jurisdiction. St. Thomas likewise states that the spiritual power of the Church is based *in aliqua consecratione,* a consecration that exists in the first place for the eucharist, then for the other sacraments as liturgical actions, and finally for pastoral care.

The distinction between the powers of orders and of jurisdiction will certainly have to stay, but they should no longer be considered two totally distinct realities, because jurisdiction is subordinate to orders since it springs from it and serves it. This service, being juridical in kind, is carried out through the medium of authority, from which it follows that the acts of the power of orders are frequently conditioned by the exercise of jurisdiction, even in what concerns their very validity. But jurisdiction supposes a hierarchical consecration and is based on the sacramental character of holy orders. The canonical mission does not create power, but supposes it by virtue of its basic sacramentality, which is sometimes active (holy orders) and sometimes passive (baptism of the laity into a common priesthood). As the same way, the pastoral authority of the Church serves the sanctifying mission she exercises through her sacramental power.

The powers and laws of the Church are in fact ordered to this end—even those that at first sight seem furthest away from the sacraments, such as those governing tribunals and ecclesiastical goods. A good number of these rules have no immediate theological support, but are the product of natural justice and the judicial customs of each country; this is the case of civil laws that have passed into Canon Law. But even in these cases the law of the Church cannot dissociate itself from its sacramental meaning, since it exists to rule the People of God, a sanctifying society, worshiping God the Father through the Son in the Holy Spirit. This is why the revision of the Codex should bring out more clearly the connection and dependence between the ecclesiastical hierarchy and the sacrament of orders, since the present Codex makes orders and jurisdiction independent of each other, and the actual physical distance that separates some rules from others accentuates this impression of disconnectedness. Even the rights and duties of the clergy could be given next to the sacrament of orders, as deriving from it and being required by it, rather than, as at present, being merely disciplinary rules.

IV. The Sacraments as a Function of the Church

The foregoing has dealt with the sacraments as institution, corresponding to the constitutional aspect of the Church's law. When the sacrament is realized in an individual, it functions as an action of the Church, by which the saving act of Christ is made present in the person receiving the sacrament.

Seeing the sacrament in this way as a function of the Church is to take the viewpoint of the Codex and so to consider what is called sacramental law and liturgical law. Here the rules of Part I of Book III of the Codex apply, and also some part of the penal clauses, such as cc. 2261 and 2364-74. I have already shown how what is basic in these rules should be transferred to the constitutional section. All that can be said about these rules here is that it is most important to insist on their basis in theology.

This functional aspect of the sacraments shows what is dynamic and contingent in the Church, just as the basic norms indicate what is fundamental and permanent. The sacramental sign is repeated and happens every time the sacrament is used; this sign is only sanctifying if its basic roots are in the Church, the permanent sacrament. Sacramentality only has meaning in a human context, because the sacraments exist to bring about a relationship between God and man. Man happens; he has a history—yet not so much a history as a structure, with a permanent consciousness of his personality. His existence comes about moment by moment in the flux of time. If sacramentality is to respond to human characteristics, it too has to be an organism with a permanent structure, but bringing about its happenings within the compass of the human event. God comes to meet our great human experiences in the sacraments, because "until there is a new heaven and a new earth where justice dwells, the pilgrim Church in her sacraments and institutions, which pertain to this present time, takes on the appearance of this passing world" (*Constitution on the Church,* n. 48).

Case 17

Refusal of Baptism

Tom and Mary arrived at Sacred Heart Rectory to discuss the baptism of their new daughter Sarah. Fr. Ron Peterson received them in his office and obtained preliminary information from them. At age 18, Tom and Mary, both baptized Catholics, were married before a justice of the peace. This was seven years ago. At that time Mary was pregnant; she later had a miscarriage.

"Is there a reason why the two of you haven't had your marriage blessed in the Church?" Father Ron asked.

"Well," Tom replied, "we haven't been regular churchgoers, maybe Christmas and Easter, if we are home with the folks. Actually, Father, I see little purpose in going to church. And I have many problems with beliefs of the Catholic Church."

"Why, then, do you want Sarah baptized?"

"I guess because we can't get rid of all our Catholic beliefs. If Sarah isn't baptized, she'll not get to heaven. I mean . . . I might not be religious, and I may mess up my life, but Sarah can't make that decision now. So I want to get her baptized because she has a right to heaven. Besides religion is a good conveyor of moral values."

Father Ron was somewhat puzzled. He asked, "Do you intend to teach the Catholic religion to Sarah and help her practice our religion?"

"I guess so," Mary responded. "When she gets old enough she can choose to go to religious studies. Besides I'm sure our folks will take her to church and teach her some prayers. What difference does teaching make? If she is baptized and leads a good life, she'll get to heaven!"

Father Ron discussed the situation further with Tom and Mary, explaining to them that baptism was a rite of initiation to the practice of faith, that it involved the necessity to educate Sarah in Catholicism, and that non-baptism wouldn't prevent Sarah's getting to heaven. But Tom and Mary insisted on baptism and pretty well stated that their practice of religion wouldn't change.

Father Ron started weighing the issues: not baptizing Sarah because there is no indication she will be raised a Catholic versus baptizing Sarah because she should have that right, and further, it may bring Tom and Mary closer to the Church.

Exercise

1. Research the theology of baptism.

2. What is the law concerning baptism in this situation?

3. Pastorally, what would you do in this situation?

References

The Code of Canon Law, canons 682, 731, 737-79.

Rite of Baptism for One and Several Children (Collegeville, Minnesota: The Liturgical Press, 1970).

Buckley, F. J., "The Right to the Sacraments of Initiation," *Canon Law Society of America, Proceedings, 1978,* 60-73. Also in *Origins* 8 (1978), 329-36.

Carr, A. M., "On Refusing Baptism to Children of Unmarried or Lapsed Catholics," *Homiletic and Pastoral Review* 77 (1977), 69-72.

———, "Baptism of Children of Non-Practicing Catholics," *Homiletic and Pastoral Review* 76 (1976), 61-68.

Challancin, J., "Infant Baptism: More Difficult Requirements?" *Homiletic and Pastoral Review* 77 (1977), 61-68.

Green, T., "The Revision of Sacramental Law: Perspectives on the Sacraments Other Than Marriage," *Studia Canonica* 11 (1977), 261-328.

Shaughnessy, J. D., "Christian Initiation: Its Meaning in the Church Today," *Studia Canonica* 7 (1973), 75-91.

Case 18

Sacrament of Reconciliation and Abortion

St. Peter's Church is located in a major metropolitan area. Four priests care for over three thousand families. Further, numerous people, not members of the parish, seek out the ministry of these priests. People regularly call on them for counseling and for private reception of the sacrament of reconciliation.

Fr. Ron Miller is on house duty Tuesdays. One Tuesday, as he sits in his office preparing a wedding homily, the doorbell rings. A young woman asks the parish secretary if she could see a priest. Her voice seems somewhat hesitant and very nervous. The secretary buzzes Father Miller that a "walk in" wishes to see a priest. Father tells the secretary to show her in.

Hesitantly the young woman says, "I need you, Father, I need God's forgiveness—Oh, will he ever forgive me! You see, Father, I killed, I killed my baby. Father, I had an abortion. Please, Father, give me absolution. I'm sorry, so sorry for my sin."

"Please sit down. Now let's just take it easy for a minute. My name is Ron Miller. Yours?"

"Lucy."

"Now, Lucy, just calmly begin from the beginning."

"Well, you see, Father, I've been going with Tom, who is a senior at the academy. I really love him, and he loves me. We plan to be married after he graduates. You see, he cannot marry until after graduation. Anyway, about three months ago I got pregnant. We really wanted to get married then, but the commanding officer said no; it is against regulations. I'm a senior in college. I did not want a baby out of wedlock. Tom and I didn't want to marry and already have a baby. What could I do, Father, what could I do? Ruin Tom's career, my career, our future marriage? I don't know. I just went to the doctor's office. I felt like I was getting a check-up. But, Father, it was my baby. I murdered my baby. I need God's forgiveness. Will God ever forgive me? Father, please forgive me. Bless me, Father, I have sinned. My last confession was six months ago. I had an abortion. Please forgive me. Please."

"Lucy, the Lord does forgive."

"But Father, can he forgive me, I killed an innocent, helpless child. My baby."

Father Miller continues to talk with Lucy. After approximately an hour, Lucy still asks, "Father, can you forgive me."

Father Miller, a diocesan priest, realizes that a person who has received an abortion is automatically excommunicated, which is a reserved penalty.

But Father Miller also realizes that Lucy is hurting, that she really is sorry, and really wants forgiveness now. Father Miller feels that he should talk with her again but also that now is the time for absolution. Yet, he does not know whether he could grant absolution now without seeking authorization from the bishop.

Exercise

1. What is the canon law concerning abortion and its effects on Lucy?
2. Under the general law of the Church, can abortion also be a reserved sin?
3. What are the various possibilities Father Ron could follow?
4. Pastorally, which option should be used with Lucy?

References

The Code of Canon Law, canons 2350, 2245-54, 893, 895-96, 899-900.
Coriden, J., "Church Law and Abortion," *The Jurist* 33 (1973), 184-98.

Case 19

Clergy, Religious, Confidentiality

Leo Murphy, a senior at St. Mark's High School, had a bad relationship with his father. The difficulty arose because the father beat his wife repeatedly before they separated. Leo was befriended by Sister Ann Pontiac, a teacher, and Fr. Frank Draper, the school counsellor. One evening, Leo's father came home drunk, and beat his wife. Leo took a baseball bat, hit his father, and ran out. His father later died. Leo ran to the convent and told Sister Ann what happened. She took him to Father Draper who talked to him about an hour. Leo did not ask to receive the sacrament of penance, but at the end of the conversation he asked for absolution.

Later the police arrested Leo and he was charged with second-degree murder. The district attorney asked Sister Ann and Father Draper to testify. Both refused, claiming the clergy-penitent privilege. In a contempt proceeding, the district attorney argued that a religious could make no claim of privilege under church law or state law and that Father Draper could only claim the privilege for the communication which followed the request for absolution. The district attorney says he needs the evidence of Sister Ann and Father Draper because the mother was not in the room when Leo and his father were fighting and Leo will not testify.

Exercise

1. Is Father Draper or Sister Ann free to testify under current church law?

2. Is there any civil law privilege of confidentiality for Father Draper or Sister Ann?

References

Callahan, M. "Historical Inquiry into the Priest-Penitent Privilege," *The Jurist* 36 (1976), 328-37.

Campbell, S., "Catholic Sister, Irregularly Ordained Women and the Clergy—Penitent Privilege," *University of California, Davis, Law Review* 9 (1976), 523-47.

Hogan, E., "A Modern Problem on the Privilege of the Confessional," *Loyola Law Review* 6 (1951), 1-14.

Stoyles, R., "The Dilemma of the Constitutionality of the Priest-Penitent Privilege—the Application of the Religion Clauses," *Pittsburgh Law Review* 29 (1967), 27-63.

Case 20

Denial of the Eucharist

The National Organization of Women (NOW) promotes the equal rights for women in American society. Among other things, NOW actively advocates the passage of the Equal Rights Amendment and also freedom of choice in the matter of abortions. Women from various backgrounds hold membership in NOW, and each member does not necessarily advocate or even favor each position held by NOW. Thus, a member may be for the ERA but not for freedom of choice in the matter of abortions. Each year NOW participates in International Woman's Day.

In the River City Diocese, NOW is especially active in activities advocating freedom of choice in abortions. The diocese is both metropolitan and rural. Its Priests' Senate is discussing NOW's position on abortion. The senators feel that membership in NOW would be inconsistent with membership in the Roman Catholic Church. Further, because of NOW's position on abortion, membership in NOW is tantamount to incurring the penalty of canon 2350, §1. The senate, therefore, passes a resolution calling the priests of the diocese to deny reception of Communion to any and all women who present themselves for reception of the Eucharist if the woman is wearing a NOW button. This resolution, if effective, will affect participation of NOW members in International Woman's Day.

The senate presents the resolution to the bishop for approval and promulgation. Although the bishop believes Catholic women should not be members of NOW, he has serious reservations about denial of Communion. His reservations are based on political, pastoral, and canonical reasoning. Politically, it is unwise to give NOW a *cause célèbre*. Pastorally, a positive approach is needed rather than negative reaction. Canonically, the right to receive the Eucharist is not to be taken away except under certain circumstances. Therefore, the bishop ponders the matter and seeks outside advice.

Exercise

1. What are the rights of the faithful regarding reception of the sacraments?

2. Under what circumstances may Communion be denied a person? May Communion be denied a person wearing a NOW button at the Eucharist?

3. Has the penalty of canon 2350, §1 been incurred by Catholic women who are members of NOW?

4. Apart from the canonical issue, what is politically and pastorally most advisable for the bishop to do?

References

The Code of Canon Law, canons 682, 2370, 853, 855.

Turney, T., "The Right of the Faithful to the Sacraments," *The Catholic Lawyer* 23 (1977), 57-68.

Case 21

Non-practicing Catholics and the Sacraments

Sister Joan William was exhausted and discouraged when she returned to the rectory after a long afternoon making home visitations. She had discovered that there were many more lapsed Catholics in Sacred Heart Parish than she had anticipated. She was especially saddened by the religious indifference and the neglect of the children of the parish. What could she do? What should she do to prevent the manifest drifting away from the Church?

She expressed her concern to Fr. Carl Malley, her pastor. The veteran priest smiled and then ticked off rules he had drawn up and lived by to meet the leakage problems:

1. He would not allow baptized Catholic children to make their first confession and Communion if they never went to Mass or did so rarely.
2. He would not assist at the marriage of Catholics who, in his estimation, would not educate their children as Catholics.
3. He would not receive converts into the Church until after at least six months' instruction and unless he was confident they would remain good Catholics.
4. He would not bury divorced Catholics remarried outside the Catholic Church.

Joan listened attentively. She was amazed at Father Malley's determination. When she returned to her study, she wondered, "What about the needs of the people? Haven't they any rights to my ministry?"

Exercise

1. Cite and explain the principles of the Code governing the rights of baptized persons to the sacraments.

2. What are the obligations of ministers to administer the sacraments?

3. When must a person be received into the Church?

4. What are the rights of baptized persons to ecclesiastical burial?

References

The Code of Canon Law, canons 1239-41.

Bevilacqua, A. J., "Problem Areas in Chancery Practice (Refusal or Deferral of Baptism and Marriage)," *Canon Law Society of America, Proceedings, 1976,* 52-73.

Buckley, F. J., "The Right to the Sacraments of Initiation," *Origins* 8 (1978), 329-36.

Cuenin, W. H., "Marriage and Baptized Non-Believers—Questions: Faith, Sacrament, and Law," *Origins* 8 (1978), 321, 323-28.

B. LITURGICAL LAW

Liturgical Law and Difficult Cases

Frederick R. McManus

A decade after the Second Vatican Council's Constitution *Sacrosanctum Concilium* on the Sacred Liturgy there are certainly more significant liturgical issues than the question of authority, discipline and law. The great questions of liturgical growth are how to use to best advantage the wealth of pastoral-liturgical reform embodied in the revised service books of the Roman liturgy; how to develop communities of believers who can authentically express (and surpass) the religious thoughts and emotions set down in the appointed words and rites; how to marry catechesis and liturgical celebration; how to be ritually creative without being mindlessly iconoclastic. Compared to the demands of such questions, liturgical discipline as such appears slight indeed.

Nevertheless liturgical norm does remain a serious question for the majority of priests, other ministers and those with special roles in the celebration. It can be a grave obstacle in the way of living liturgy. It can worry the consciences of those who respect tradition and good order and church communion.

Needless to say, liturgical norm means little to contemporary antinomians. Presumably they see a role for church law only in the protection of rights and not in the realm of responsibility and accountability. Perhaps in this category we must also place some ordained ministers who, unintentionally or witlessly, find themselves presiding over the celebration of the Christian liturgy but are truly ignorant of its theology, history, structure and current order.

Still there are parish priests, campus ministers, chaplains of religious communities, together with those who work with them in planning and celebrating, who are conscientious in their concern for liturgical and

An associate editor of *Worship,* Fr. McManus is director of the Secretariat, Bishops' Committee on the Liturgy, Washington, D.C. He is vice provost of The Catholic University, Washington, D.C., and dean of the Graduate School; he is professor of canon law in the School of Religious Studies.

sacramental order. Some of them find this order incompatible with the concrete pastoral situation. The purpose of this article is to explore some avenues of relief.

Without undermining legitimate and necessary liturgical discipline, it is still possible to find unexpected flexibility and opportunities of escape from the rigid norm. It is possible to uncover circumstances in which apparent nonobservance of the liturgical law is a higher moral and canonical imperative.[1] First, then, what are the difficult cases? What are the pastoral situations in which strict compliance with the liturgical discipline can be pastorally hurtful rather than helpful? What are the liturgical rites or rules which occasion most discomfort or dissatisfaction?

1. A first huge area is that of special liturgies with children or, in a situation not entirely dissimilar, with congregations of retarded persons, whether these are children or adults. The argument is simple enough: there are elements in the ordinary Christian liturgy—perhaps above all its increasing quantity of words—which are entirely beyond the comprehension and attention of very young children. To put it in another way, there are large numbers of the believing community who now appear to be unable to celebrate the eucharistic liturgy unless it is radically adapted and simplified.

Various facile answers have been given to this problem: very young children should not even come to the liturgy; if they do, their passive presence at adult eucharists will gradually develop into understanding participation; such children understand more than we think they do; the gravity and dignity of the sacred ministries may not be compromised for the sake of children. Such answers have not satisfied teachers or priests with a fierce pastoral commitment to religious formation of the very young. Nor of course were such answers of much help in the somewhat parallel case of liturgies with the mentally retarded. Another response, that simplified rites would be puerile, missed the point completely; no reputable person was suggesting anything in an adapted liturgy for children that was childish, unworthy or improper.

In the case of liturgies with young children, preadolescents and the mentally or physically retarded, the recent Roman Directory *Pueros baptizatos* for Masses with Children has probably resolved most of the major difficulties.[2] Except in the matter of the eucharistic prayers (no. 52) and the paraphrasing of Scripture (no. 45), it is remarkably free and open. At the same time, the Directory makes tremendous demands upon the ingenuity and creativity of those who plan liturgical celebrations with children. It is an

1. For an article summarizing the contemporary challenge to liturgical law, see Walter J. Kelly, "The Authority of Liturgical Law," *The Jurist* 28 (1968) 397-424. For a treatment of the historical question, see John E. Rotelle, "Liturgy and Authority," *Worship* 47 (1973) 514-526.

2. Congregation for Divine Worship, November 1, 1973 *[Acta Apostolicae Sedis: AAS* 66 (1974) 30-46]. The Directory for Masses with Children was prepared as a supplement to the General Instruction of the 1969 *Missale Romanum* (no. 4).

extraordinarily balanced document, with the avowed purpose of developing simple eucharistic celebrations which will parallel the ordinary eucharist closely. This practice should lead the children gradually to the point when they can participate with the larger, heterogeneous eucharistic assembly.

Yet the Directory is not, according to its own terms, applicable to eucharistic liturgies with adolescents or with young adults. (No service is done to law or truth by pretending that the Roman document, in its letter or spirit, is so applicable. The document is clear enough on this point.)[3] And while the psychological or cultural needs may be different in somewhat older groups, these needs may be greater than with small children. In the face of alienation or disaffection or simple lack of comprehension, what innovations can be judged legitimate? We believe that the eucharist is not only the expression of the faith and worship of a Christian community that is already formed but also the source of divine favor and a stimulus to Christian formation, deeper faith and action. Therefore it may be necessary to question a rigid liturgical discipline that appears to be an insuperable obstacle to participation by certain groups. In the concrete situation, many priests certainly resolve the problem in what they judge to be a commonsense manner. Others seek to respect both church law and pastoral demands, and this essay is intended to help them.

2. A second example is the problem still created in some dioceses by normative directions which require confession before first communion—an issue precipitated by the Appendix to the 1971 General Catechetical Directory[4] and by a joint Declaration of two Roman congregations.[5]

After the dust had settled, it was clear that the Roman congregations and certainly Pope Paul had not created an entirely novel canonical decree, as if to oblige a child not conscious of grave sin to go to confession before communion. In fact, thanks in some measure to the moderating efforts of the Division of Religious Education (Confraternity of Christian Doctrine) of the United States Catholic Conference,[6] the reasonable intent of the Roman documents became much clearer: since the child *may* be obliged to annual confession at an early age and should certainly be *free* to receive the sacrament of penance as soon as he or she is able, adequate preparation for the sacrament should not be delayed, nor should access to the sacrament ever be denied or impeded.

A pastoral problem did exist for a considerable period, especially where parents with sufficient religious education had already welcomed the postponement of first penance. The law said or appeared to say one thing,

3. *Ibid.*, nos. 1, 2, 6. The Directory is not designed for, but may be applied to, the retarded (no. 6).

4. Congregation for the Clergy, April 11, 1971 [*AAS* (note 2 above) 64 (1972) 173-176].

5. Congregation for the Clergy and Congregation for the Discipline of the Sacraments, May 24, 1973 [*AAS* 65 (1973) 410].

6. *A Study Paper for First Confession* (Washington: U.S.C.C. Publications Office 1973).

and respect for the freedom, conscience and developing mentality of the child said something different. In some places the problem may persist for the priest, teacher or parent—who in other circumstances is asserted to have primary responsibility in these matters.

3. The third instance is in itself much less significant but extremely sensitive. It is the introduction of the practice of receiving communion in the hand. For a brief period several years ago it was argued rather speciously that, since no written direction of the kind existed, church discipline did not require that lay people (and bishops, priests and deacons who are not liturgical celebrants) receive communion directly on the tongue. Even as the practice spread, however, it was evident, from the very terms in which the Apostolic See offered the opportunity to restore the traditional practice, that the customary discipline had the strongest force of unwritten law.

Twice the National Conference of Catholic Bishops failed to take the action necessary to give canonical legitimacy to this practice in the United States. Once the majority vote did not reach the requisite two-thirds; once a simple majority was not obtained. One may regret the reasons offered for opposition to the practice of communion in the hand. The charge of irreverence, so often repeated in the right-wing press, was an offensive affront to devout Catholic believers in other countries, to the episcopal conferences of most of the major non-Latin countries and to the Pope himself. Nevertheless the decision of the episcopal conference, or rather the absence of a decision, was perfectly clear. In this country the general law is in effect, as restated in the revised Roman Ritual: "In the distribution of holy communion there shall be observed the custom of placing the particle of consecrated bread on the tongue of those who receive communion, because it is based upon a usage handed down over many centuries."[7]

The mode of receiving communion is a secondary matter, and the controversy has been largely a symbol of the respective positions of support for and opposition to liturgical reform. Granted all this, the pastoral problem was and is a genuine one. What is the minister of the eucharist to do in places where the practice has become deeply entrenched. How should believers in perfect good faith be treated at the Lord's table when, whether because they are strangers or because they have a strong conviction in the matter, they reverently and humbly extend their hands to receive the consecrated bread. What help can be offered to the campus minister who is convinced in conscience that this issue, even if only token, serves to estrange disaffected young people whose judgment about the reasonableness of church authority is already negative?

4. Still another example of what have been called "standard deviations" in current liturgical usage is the original or even spontaneous eucharistic

7. *De sacra Communione et de cultu mysterii eucharistici extra Missam* (1973), Chapter 1 on Holy Communion Outside of Mass, no. 21 [*Notitiae* 9 (1973) 314].

prayer. This is clearly unauthorized by legitimate church authority. The anaphora is the central and crucial presidential prayer. The texts (Latin or now vernacular) of the presidential prayers have been rigidly restricted by both old and new liturgical discipline. In the new Roman service books every kind of freedom seems admissible for the choice of song texts. Broad flexibility has been introduced for the selection of readings. The addition of minor ritual acts, music and art forms has been accepted in a much more relaxed spirit. But there has been little weakening of the firm rule that there is one authentic text of the liturgical prayers spoken by the presiding priest.[8]

We are not directly concerned with the actual erosion of liturgical discipline which is evident in the use of original texts. In practice fewer and fewer priests hesitate to take minor liberties—all the way from those who will say "my sacrifice and yours," in place of the official text approved by the episcopal conference and confirmed by the Apostolic See, to those who simply compose original presidential prayers, including the eucharistic prayer. For completeness, however, two points should be made:

First, a large proportion of original presidential prayers are apparently untheological, unliturgical and out of context. There seem to be a good many priests who do not even know whether they are addressing God the Father of God the Son. Similar weaknesses are found in original eucharistic prayers which have been published or reported. One extreme example is supposed to consist of a lengthy exhortation to the people rather than a *confessio* addressed to God; it is a series of invitations to the assembled congregation, interrupted once, perhaps because of a minimalistic sacramental theology, by the Last Supper narrative. Priests who employ such texts or compose them are unlikely to be concerned with the pastoral or moral problems that may be associated with liturgical law.

Second, a principle of the adaptation and simplification of the liturgical prayers—apart from the eucharistic prayer—has been carefully enunciated for the special case of liturgical celebrations with children. In these circumstances the other presidential prayers may be altered by the minister to make them intelligible to a congregation of children. The purpose and thrust of the original must be respected. The literary character of the prayer may not be distorted (for example, by multiplying petitions, by turning a prayer after communion into a thanksgiving prayer, by distorting the liturgical elements of the collect-style prayer by moralizing).[9] This is a sound rule, although it is literally applicable only to rather special occasions.

8. See canon 733, § 1, of the Code of Canon Law (1917). This rigidity was enforced by the Second Vatican Council in the frequently quoted no. 22, § 3, of the Constitution on the Liturgy: "Therefore, absolutely no other person, not even a priest, may add, remove, or change anything in the liturgy on his own authority" [*The Documents of Vatican II,* ed. W. M. Abbott (New York 1966) 146].

9. See Directory (note 2 above), no. 51.

The variety that is provided in new preface texts and the opportunity to introduce the eucharistic prayer with an appropriate *monitio*[10] make original eucharistic prayers less crucial. There is legitimate fear of the aberrations often found in original presidential prayers. One is therefore inclined to hesitate over the exploration of reasons which might make such practices legitimate.

At the same time, there are communities where stilted phrases and foreign images and inapplicable or inauthentic language in the four authorized eucharistic prayers appear to be grave obstacles to the living, genuine Christian worship of the participants. The situation is not imaginary. It is asserted by campus ministers, by those who lead children in the eucharistic celebration and by others. Like the instances mentioned above, the situation is sufficient reason to explore, even from a narrowly canonical viewpoint, some avenues of relief. The liturgical discipline appears to be, or is asserted in all honesty to be, too rigid and restrictive.

The four broad examples given above are rather common and important. The question in all cases is the same: whether it is possible to combine complete respect for the legitimacy of liturgical authority with opportunities or occasions for freedom from that discipline. To put it another way, how restrictive and how rigid is the liturgical legislation? The answer seems to lie in reflection upon a whole series of reminders and possibilities which can only be summarized here. Apart from explicit conciliar developments, they are neither novel nor original.

Matters of Minimal Significance

A canonical axiom derived from Roman Law reads: *De minimis non curat praetor*. In the context of church law, this means that there are matters of such minimal significance that they are not suitable to be the object of legislation or norm. While this consideration is of little usefulness in resolving great issues, modern liturgical discipline has contained much that is of trifling weight.

The concern with minutiae in past legislation was fantastic. Sober rubricians—there were happy exceptions like the late Joachim Nabuco and the still flourishing J. B. O'Connell— hardly dared to point out some of the more ludicrous examples: which arm the priest should put into the alb first, whether a deacon with the privilege of a skullcap should wear it when assisting a priest who did not enjoy the privilege, what precise sequence to follow in lighting candles, how the celebrant should cast his eyes down when

10. See Congregation for Divine Worship, Circular Letter *Eucharistiae participationem* to the Presidents of Episcopal Conferences on the Eucharistic Prayers, April 27, 1973 [*AAS* 65 (1973) 340-347 = *Notitiae* 9 (1973) 193-201: the rest of the June *Notitiae* (84) is devoted to comments and articles on the Circular Letter].

greeting the people, and so forth.

Today it is not always remembered that many of the solemn, formal prescriptions of such minutiae were simply neglected or disobeyed. A generation ago few priests bothered to bow their heads at the name of the saint of the day; in this country no one genuflected to the diocesan bishop in the course of the liturgy; the ritual kisses were largely and happily ignored; the deacon did not remove the bishop's mitre, etc.

The above examples are deliberately extreme, and the revised rubrical directions have suppressed huge quantities of minute prescriptions. Flexibility and a more human and relaxed style of ritual celebration, without sacrifice of dignity or propriety, have been preferred. Yet with the proliferation of lengthy *praenotanda* in the revised liturgical books, the running rubrics of new rituals and complex Roman instructions, the same question can still be raised. Are some of the matters touched upon, with formal if less solemn directions, so minute or trifling that they are simply not appropriate objects of ecclesiastical norm?

Nature of the Document

In a broader context the whole issue of distinctions among canonical sources has been raised.[11] In recent years, too little discrimination has been shown between the most solemn pronouncement affecting general church order and the most casual and secondary Roman response to a private inquiry. There is a vast difference between a solemn conciliar decree, at one extreme, and an individual rescript or private letter of a Roman congregation or bishop. There is a vast difference between formal canons and any kind of supplementary documents of guidance, directories, instructions and the like.

These distinctions are especially applicable to liturgical legislation. Again, at one extreme is the solemn conciliar decree, the Constitution on the Liturgy, along with the Roman liturgical books issued by mandate of the Council and published by papal authority, or for that matter the national or regional liturgical books approved by authority of episcopal conferences and confirmed by the Apostolic See. At the other extreme are the helpful replies published in *Notitiae,*[12] the cautionary private letters of curial officials, nuncios and others. As it happens, the streams of supplementary and interpretative instructions on liturgical matters since 1964 have been informative, but these materials simply do not have the weight or

11. See "Canonical Reflections on Priestly Life and Ministry," *American Ecclesiastical Review* 166 (1972) 365; James A. Coriden, "The Future of the Law," *The Jurist* 34 (1974) 156.

12. Early issues of *Notitiae* carried a very careful disclaimer before the *dubia* or *documentorum explicatio*: "The solution which is proposed bears no official character. It has only an orientative value, since solutions will be made public *ex officio,* if necessary, by the competent authority in the *Acta Apostolicae Sedis.*"

force of the definitive norms of the official service books,[13] much less the authority of a conciliar decree or papal constitution.

Some of the careful distinctions which are possible among the various grades of documents in which liturgical discipline is articulated may well appear to require hairsplitting. In general, however, the principle at stake is a sound one. Perhaps relief from the apparent rigidity of liturgical pronouncements can be found precisely in this way, that is, by understanding that there are such distinctions.

Rubrical Directives

Long before contemporary pastoral problems of liturgical diversity and flexibility were experienced, there was much theoretical discussion of a rather specialized distinction. It was between those norms of the official liturgy which were to be considered preceptive and those regarded as directive or nonpreceptive.[14]

The preceptive rubric was a formal and obligatory norm of ecclesiastical law. It might be of greater or lesser significance, depending upon its content, but nonetheless it was a genuine canonical law. On the other hand, the liturgical service books contained much that was secondary, although not necessarily minuscule in the sense described above. These rubrics constituted important and useful directions or guidelines; they were norms and principles which should ordinarily be followed but which could hardly be considered a part of church law.

Past controversies over such distinctions are no longer of great concern. One position, for example, limited the so-called directive rubrics to the preliminaries of the Roman Missal and spoke of the preceptive rubrics of the celebration itself. Still another category of norms was described—namely, those rubrics which provided an option or choice. This category of facultative rubrics has multiplied many times over in the current revision of the service books.

The present significance of the old distinction between preceptive and directive rubrics is this. It suggests one more way to scrutinize the language and content of the liturgical books in order to see whether some of these rubrics are intended as binding precepts necessary for church order, communion and legitimacy of celebration. Perhaps they may be only useful and helpful guidelines for more effective celebration.

13. A comparison between the contents of the several liturgical "Instructions" since 1964 and the distillation of such material in the official service books would be interesting.

14. See P. Oppenheim, *Institutiones Systematico Historicae in Sacram Liturgiam* (Turin 1938-41) 356; I. B. Menghini, *Elementa Iuris Liturgici* (Rome 1906) 118-119; J. B. O'Connell, *The Celebration of Mass* (Milwaukee 1966) 20-26.

Descriptive Rubrics

Another avenue of relief can be found in the way rubrical directions are expressed. It is hard to say why objections have been raised to the large quantity of such red matter (now printed in the Latin liturgical books in a somewhat more attractive color). Most of this new material which has appeared since 1968 (the date of the first revised service book decreed by the Second Vatican Council) is of high quality and extremely valuable for the liturgical minister. Moreover, many of the new rubrics are couched in declarative rather than in jussive terms. Such a change by itself limits somewhat the burden of formal norms.

The matter may be stated somewhat differently. Even where the rubrics are couched in rather preceptive language—in English, "shall," "must," "should"—it is still possible in some cases that the material is descriptive rather than preceptive. In the distant past a major instance of this was the Roman *Ceremonial of Bishops,* a liturgical book issued in 1600 with all the formality of the post-Tridentine Roman missal, breviary and pontifical; it was applicable to services celebrated by priests as well as bishops. As a result of the rather graphic and discursive nature of this book, however, many of its norms fell into desuetude. Its detailed accounts of rites, insignia and the various elements of liturgical celebration seem to have been accepted as mere descriptions. These were to be followed ordinarily as a pattern and norm but clearly did not have the solemn weight of an ecclesiastical canon.

Perhaps a similar approach can be taken to certain parts of the new liturgical books, especially when there is a simple description of the best way of doing something. If indeed they are seen to be simple descriptions, not necessarily normative, it may help to relieve some of the conflict and tension that arises from the present weight of church discipline.

Custom and Usage

This is hardly the place to give even a summary treatment of the doctrine of ecclesiastical custom. In the Code of Canon Law, for example, custom in the church has been hedged in very carefully.[15] It has been limited by a theory of ecclesiastical law in which primacy is given to the lawmaker's will rather than to the reasonableness of the norm. It has also been hedged in by requirements of continuity and length (forty years as a minimum) for custom to abrogate the written law.

Even so, church law is considerably more generous and liberal than some other systems of law. In the church, custom is unwritten law. It has the same force as the written law, at least in theory, and it can abrogate the written law of popes and councils. Because of the understandable desire of

15. Canons 25-30.

church authorities to safeguard their own written legal enactments, it is difficult to satisfy all the conditions for so-called legal custom. Thus it is also difficult to find in this precise area any escape from the official precepts of liturgical discipline.

But there is another facet to custom in the church, which is prior to and more significant than the limited legal custom. It is the actual usage of the Spirit-guided community, which canonists call factual custom. This kind of usage is considered as the best interpreter of church law[16] because the way in which the Christian people behave should be the clearest sign of what is needed by way of church order and discipline.

In addition, the revised liturgical books refer rather frequently to customary usage. By this they do not mean, as the context shows, the kind of legal custom that satisfies all the demands of binding canonical custom. Rather they show respect for the usage actually present and developing. Such usage may not perhaps be of very long standing, but it is the practice in various local churches (i.e., dioceses) or even in local congregations and parishes. In this respect the new service books are following a Roman tradition. In the early days of the Congregation of Rites (1588), questions were resolved rather often by reference to customary usage or to the opinion of commentators in preference to possibly arbitrary, if authentic, interpretations.

In any event, those who are faced with the constraints or obstacles imposed by liturgical discipline may profitably explore the possibility of usage or custom. Its evaluation depends on many things—the objective of goodness of the practice, the stability which it enjoys, the degree of variance with the prescribed liturgical norm, the significance of the matter involved. But church law is never intended to be an end in itself or the highest goal. It is possible to discern the workings of the Spirit in the actions, including the liturgical inspirations, of the smallest congregations and the least members of the community.

Cessation of Law

There is a common-sense ring to the canonical rules which speak of the way in which ecclesiastical law—ordinarily the written law found in canons and decrees—ceases. One way is through the operation of contrary customs, mentioned above. More usual is the introduction or promulgation of new law. The Code of Canon Law sums this matter up rather simply: "A later law . . . abrogates an earlier law [1] if the later law expressly decrees this or [2] if the later law is directly contrary to the former law or [3] if the later law rearranges the complete matter of the earlier law in its entirety. . . ."[17] (What is not so generally understood is that a new general

16. Canon 29.

17. Canon 22.

law—for example, a papal law—does not abrogate an existing particular law, for example, the law of an episcopal conference or of a diocese.) Controversies over doubtful suppression of existing law apart, the canonical principle is evident enough, and canonists speak of this as the "extrinsic" cessation of law.

There is, however, a quite different manner in which ecclesiastical law ceases to have force and effect. Technically called the "intrinsic" cessation of law, this occurs when a church law, canon or decree has outlived its usefulness. When a norm is no longer suitable for its purpose, when it has become obsolete or useless, when it has become—to use current jargon—counterproductive, canonists will agree that it is no law.[18]

As with almost every one of the opportunities for relief enumerated here, it may be perilous to invoke the principle of intrinsic cessation of law arbitrarily. Individuals are often the worst judges of the validity or applicability of a law when it comes to their own case. But the principle is sound. Unlike civil law, which can invoke a statute which has been in total disuse for a hundred years, canonical doctrine in the church recognizes that laws do become obsolete and, even without the formal (extrinsic) act of abrogation, cease to have force for the Christian community.

One need not assert the requirement of community acceptance of church law—a doctrine much more at home in the East than in the West—to recognize that a point may be reached when a given law is so far removed from the purposes, experiences and genuine situations of the church community that it is no longer a law. This may take a long time or it may happen quickly; an example from the not so distant past is the Apostolic Constitution *Veterum sapientia* of Pope John XXIII on Promoting the Study of Latin (1962). Again, intrinsic cessation of law is a possibility which needs discussion when problems of authentic liturgical celebration are faced.

Dispensation from the Law

Much of what has been said refers directly to the general liturgical law of the Latin or Western Church. It assumes a liturgical discipline now chiefly embodied in the revised service books of the Roman liturgy. Much of it is equally applicable to diocesan and national liturgical law. But attention must also be paid to what was, by modern canonical standards, a revolutionary turn taken by the Second Vatican Council. This change is sometimes referred to as decentralization or subsidiarity. It is better to see it in more theological terms as a rediscovery of the meaning of the local church, which is the community of Christian believers assembled under the presidency of its bishop together with the body of ordained ministers—the congregation

18. See G. Michiels, *Normae Generales Juris Canonici* (Paris 1949) I.646-649.

of God's people in which the church is made present and real.[19]

The enumeration of the above avenues of relief began with the slight matter of rubrical minutiae and went in the direction of the more profound meaning of liturgical custom and the stability of liturgical legislation. In connection with the local church also, it is possible to begin with the rather secondary matter of dispensation.

Dispensation is a traditional and valuable institute of church order. In some ways it corresponds to the "economy" of Eastern theology and canon law, but it has taken on its own characteristics. Prior to the Second Vatican Council the received canonical doctrine was that the individual bishop in the local church could dispense from general church laws (for all practical purposes, papal law) only in certain cases of doubt and only when some clear concession of authority had been given to the bishop. For the most part, such concessions were embodied in faculties. Some of these faculties were rather generous and stable; some were embodied in the common Code of Canon Law; others were quite occasional and individual.

The principle, however, was that jurisdiction over the more general law belonged in the local church or diocese only by way of exception and concession. At Vatican II much of the discussion, derived from the preparatory stages of the Council, centered on the bishops' desire to increase substantially the faculties or concessions which they already enjoyed. It was even planned to add to the conciliar decree on the matter a lengthy list of such faculties.

Instead the whole principle was reversed. The conciliar Decree *Christus Dominus* on the Bishops' Pastoral Office in the Church (1965) recognizes that the bishops, each one for his respective church, have the right to dispense the faithful, for their spiritual good and in particular cases, from the general law of the church—unless there is some clear intervention or exception to the rule made by the higher authority of pope or council.

As yet, one could hardly say that bishops have exhausted the opportunities afforded them by this conciliar decision. Perhaps this is as well, because often the meaning of dispensation is not understood, especially the concept that canonical dispensation depends upon the reasonable discretion of the church authority. If the law or the element of church order from which dispensation is sought is itself sound, then dispensation is indeed the exception: the bishops or others who dispense must reflect seriously upon the importance of the issue, the reason for the dispensation, the needs, and the like.

The following is the conciliar text: "Individual diocesan bishops possess the faculty to dispense from the general law of the church, in a particular case, the faithful over whom they exercise authority according to the norm of law, whenever they judge that this will be for their spiritual benefit,

19. See Dogmatic Constitution *Lumen gentium* on the Church (1964), no. 23 [Abbott (note 8 above) 44-46]; Constitution on the Liturgy, no. 41 [*ibid.* 152].

unless a special reservation has been made by the supreme authority of the church."[20]

Without a careful reading of the text, some have taken this to mean that the bishop may practically abrogate and suppress general laws of the church or that he might, for example, create a new liturgical rite of the sacraments, simply ignoring the common rite. The conciliar enactment means less than this; it means, in the traditional sense, that the bishop may in a particular case lift the binding force of a given general law of the church. This he may do for cause and without affecting the validity or force of the law as law. What is untraditional, or at least quite contrary to the modern tradition, is that no general ecclesiastical law is exempt from the dispensing power of the bishop unless the supreme authority of pope or council makes special reservation.

Moreover, the breadth of this dispensing authority is larger than may appear by the reference to its use "in a particular case." While the bishop may not dispense so generally as to revoke the law (except of course to revoke a diocesan law), he may issue a single dispensation on a single occasion which has a multiple and indeed a very broad effect. This the bishop does by dispensing each individual person who meets the conditions or circumstances of the cause or reason for which the dispensation is granted. This cause will be, in broad terms, the spiritual good of the individual; specifically it will be determinable according to circumstances. Such a generous understanding of the dispensing authority is ordinary canonical doctrine,[21] although it is hardly favored by curialists who are anxious to maintain the rigidity of the law and to minimize the conciliar decision.

In 1966 Pope Paul VI, in very careful and correct implementation of the above regulation, listed the special reservations to which the Council had referred.[22] These included some twenty rather specific matters plus some broad areas known as constitutive and procedural law. Neither liturgical law in general nor specific areas of legislation for the ritual celebration of the eucharist and the other sacraments was involved in the reservation by Pope Paul.

Those anxious to restrict the local episcopal authority and perhaps those hesitant to employ it might not be so ready to acknowledge that the conciliar recognition of the biships' dispensing authority is applicable to liturgical discipline. Long before this particular issue was raised, however, the following was sound canonical teaching: [1] the liturgical discipline is in fact ecclesiastical legislation, that is to say, "canon law"; [2]

20. Decree *Christus Dominus,* no. 8 (b), in the author's translation [Abbott 401].

21. See E. F. Regatillo, *Institutiones Iuris Canonici* 2 (Santander 1951) 68; A. Vermeersch-I. Creusen, *Epitome Iuris Canonici* 2 (Malines 1934) 393.

22. Motu proprio *De Episcoporum muneribus,* June 15, 1966 [*AAS* 58 (1966) 467-472]. For one instance of broadening particular cases, see no. VI: "A 'particular case' is one referring not only to individual persons but also to many individuals who form a community in the strict sense" [*ibid.* 469].

the broad norms for church law—such as interpretation, cessation, the force of custom[23]—are equally applicable to liturgical discipline. In fact, if one is to judge liturgical discipline as having the same force and weight as the rest of church order, it is rather obvious that the dispensing authority of the bishop is applicable. If one holds, on the contrary, that liturgical discipline is somehow or other less than ordinary church law, a fortiori the bishop may dispense.

This canonical *discursus* may seem far afield. But it should be understood in terms of the local church and the role of the diocesan bishop in celebrating and moderating the liturgy, to which reference is made below. In the Latin Church dispensation is a hallowed canonical institute, exercised in somewhat the same way as the doctrine of economy is invoked by episcopal authority in the Eastern Churches. It provides relief, always for cause, from the burdens of the law in a way unknown to civil law. In the liturgical context, it means that the bishop can resolve conflicts which arise in the concrete liturgical situation of individual congregations, just as he is empowered to act in cases of interconfessional liturgical sharing.[24]

THE BISHOP AS MODERATOR OF THE LITURGY

Attention has also to be drawn to the broader context in which the bishop's dispensing authority is exercised—namely, his office as president of the liturgy. The bishop presides, personally or through the presbyters, over the eucharistic and other assemblies of the diocese. In a substantial reversal of the previous canon law, the Second Vatican Council developed the canonical or disciplinary implications of the bishop's sacramental role. Just as the Council sought to root the canonical authority of the bishop in his sacramental consecration or ordination,[25] so in the Constitution on the Liturgy there are twin statements susceptible of the same explanation:

[1] According to the conciliar doctrine of the episcopal order, the bishop is the high priest of the diocese, and "the pre-eminent manifestation of the Church consists in the full active participation of all God's holy people in the liturgical celebrations, especially in the same eucharist, in a single prayer, at one altar, at which there presides the bishop surrounded by his college of priests and by his ministers"[26] [2] At law, canon 1257 of the Code of Canon Law ("It is for the Apostolic See alone to order the sacred liturgy and to approve the liturgical books") is replaced by the following norm:

23. See F. X. Wernz, *Ius Decretalium* (Rome 1898-1914) 3.357; A Van Hove, *De Consuetudine et de Temporis Supputatione* (Malines 1933) 199-201; P. Oppenheim, *Institutiones* (note 14 above) 3.136; G. Michiels, *Nomae Generales* (note 18 above) 2.188.

24. Decree *Unitatis redintegratio* on Ecumenism, no. 8 [Abbott 352-353].

25. Dogmatic Constitution *Lumen gentium,* no. 21 [Abbott 40-42].

26. Constitution on the Liturgy, no. 41, as translated in a 1963 Liturgical Press Latin-English edition, p. 27 [Abbott 152].

"Regulation of the sacred liturgy depends solely on the authority of the Church, that is, on the Apostolic See and, as laws may determine, on the bishop."[27]

Apart from the liturgical context, the same point is made—perhaps even more strongly—in the conciliar Decree *Christus Dominus* on the Bishop's Pastoral Office in the Church, just before the above reference to the bishop's dispensing authority, when this central and crucial decision was made concerning the governance of the local church: "*Per se* all ordinary, proper and immediate power which is required for the exercise of their pastoral office belongs to the bishops, as successor of the apostles, in the dioceses committed to them; the power which, by virtue of his office, the Roman Pontiff has of reserving cases to himself or to some other authority always remains intact in every respect."[28]

This is not the place to draw out the implications of the decree's acknowledgement of responsibility within the local church in relation to the shepherding role of the chief bishop. In fact the relationship between the Roman see and the local church, between the bishop of Rome, and the diocesan bishop, demands compromise, exchange and dialogue. The relationship almost implies a measure of tension, and, nearly a decade after Vatican II, the principle has barely been tested.

Nevertheless the governing role of the local bishop as the shepherd of the individual church or diocese is now much more broadly based. It is a governing role which we may hope will be exercised in closest collaboration with the presbyters and the deacons (this is the conciliar image of local church leadership) and with the fullest participation of the unordained faithful.[29] In a period when priority has had to be given to a thorough revision of the traditional Roman liturgy (a revision that was centuries overdue), no one should expect a sudden development of diocesan liturgies as such. Nor is liturgical fractionalism necessarily desirable, a fact which explains in some measure the conciliar decision to place many matters of church discipline, including the liturgy, partly in the hands of the supradiocesan regional authority known as the episcopal conference.[30]

It still remains important that, even in the very traditional ecclesiastical and canonical terms of the Second Vatican Council, the direct moderation or regulation of the liturgy does belong to the local bishop and—as in other matters of church discipline—the reservation made by the church's supreme authority in favor of the pope or of the episcopal conference should not be presumed.

27. *Ibid.*, no. 22, § 1, from the same 1963 edition, p. 17 [Abbott 146].

28. Decree *Christus Dominus*, no. 8 (a), in the author's translation [Abbott 401]; cf. note 20 above.

29. See "Canonical Reflections," *American Ecclesiastical Review* 166 (1972) 367-372.

30. Constitution on the Liturgy, no. 22, § 2 [Abbott 146].

Perhaps the local episcopal authority may be a means of resolving some of the tensions and conflicts in the pastoral situation of the liturgy.

EPIKIA

There are as many meanings of *epikia* (Greek *epieíkeia*: reasonableness, equity) as there are spellings of the word. With it we come to considerations which may be more immediately or directly helpful to the individual minister than recourse to episcopal authority. By the same token they are means which must be exercised with all the greater care in order to avoid disruption or discord among the congregations of the local church.

Epikia is often considered to be related to equity, either [1] natural equity, which mitigates justice and is a generous, merciful and Christian application of the law, or [2] canonical equity, which is the equity recognized, acknowledged an even required by the ecclesiastical canons.[31] This kind of equity is exercised and applied by church authority, by bishops and judges. For example, the bishop who recalls a cleric serving in the ministry of another diocese is canonically bound to observe "natural equity";[32] the bishop who transfers or removes pastors for the needs and welfare of the people must, in following the due process of canon law, observe "natural and canonical equity."[33]

Epikia, however, is not exercised by church authority but by those who are trying to observe the prescriptions of church discipline, including liturgical discipline. It is defined in traditional terms as "'a correction or emendation of a law which in its expression is deficient by reason of its universality, a correction made by a subject who deviates from the clear words of the law. . . ."[34] To make such a judgment and to act upon it may be an act of virtue. However great the possibility of self-deception, to interpret or, better, to correct the law in the light of unforeseen conditions or conditions not originally comprehended is not to use a shabby escape-clause. It is to discern a deeper purpose in church discipline.

When are these ordinary and rather old-fashioned principles applicable to liturgical discipline? At what point does the literal observance of a norm become impossible or harmful or truly disadvantageous to the liturgical assembly or the Christian community or congregation? When must the president of the assembly make such a decision? These are extremely difficult questions to answer. The fact that, with all the current defections from religious practice, they are still being asked is a positive indicator. At

31. See the reflections on canonical equity by Pope Paul VI in the Allocution *Vivissima gioia* of February 8, 1973 [*AAS* 65 (1973) 95-103, esp. 98-100]; English translation: "Canonical Equity," *The Jurist* 34 (1974) 1-9.

32. Canon 144.

33. Decree *Christus Dominus,* no. 31 [Abbott 419-420].

34. Lawrence J. Riley, *The History, Nature and Use of EPIKEIA in Moral Theology* (Washington 1948) 459.

least the opportunity of resolving difficult liturgical cases should be kept open, within the framework of lawful church discipline and communion.

The most traditional understanding of *epikia* is enough to justify some deviations from the letter of liturgical discipline if, for example, such laws "occasion the rejection of the liturgy by large numbers of people."[35]

EXCUSING CASES

Both canonists and moralists, again in very traditional ways, recognize how often one may be "excused" from the observance of church law. Their hesitance to pursue the principle far enough in the case of liturgical discipline does not detract from its importance.

Thus the preconciliar moralists spoke of the moral impossibility or of "the serious damage or inconvenience in proportion to the law"[36] which excuses an individual from the observance of a law. The key phrase is "in proportion to. . . ." As the bishop who dispenses must have "a just and reasonable cause, taking into account the seriousness of the law from which he dispenses,"[37] so the individual can judge himself or herself excused only for cause. Writers—and church authorities—have been reluctant to draw the logical conclusions or to make a thorough application of these staid and abstract principles to liturgical situations. This should not deter those who honestly feel that there is greater harm than good in a given aspect of the law.

This recital of avenues of relief from rigidity has been in terms which would have been comprehensible and recognized in 1960 or 1900—with the sole exception of the new conciliar acknowledgement of much more extensive authority in the local church. More radical approaches to liturgical discipline are possible.[38] For the purpose of this article, however, it is sufficient to point out that apparent inflexibility (in the liturgical forms which have not been relaxed and opened up to options and adaptations) is susceptible of legitimate deviation under several formalities—from the dispensation conceded by the local bishop to the excusing causes an individual may find in the concrete circumstances.

Listing or reporting these possibilities requires a very large disclaimer. One aspect of the disclaimer arises from the fear, hinted at above, that the relief or escape from liturgical discipline may come too easily and too perilously; another aspect is the honest conviction that the reformed liturgy has within its formal limits an unrealized freedom and potential.

35. Kelly (note 1 above) 418.

36. H. Noldin-A. Schmidt, *Summa Theologiae Moralis* 1 (Vienna 1940) 179-180: see B. H. Merkelbach, *Summa Theologiae Moralis* 1 (Bruges 1949) 325-327.

37. Canon 84, § 1.

38. See, for example, A. Turck, "Le Probleme de la loi: Réflexions pastorales, *Paroisse et Liturgie* 47 (1965) 3-13; Thomas Vismans, "Liturgy or Rubrics?" *Concilium* 12 (1966) 83-91.

First of all, there are dangers inherent in the ready use of canonical or moral escapes from liturgical legislation. Even if one is not easily deceived, even if the need is proportionately serious, there is one element of the proportion which must be asserted strongly. It is the need for church unity and concord, for communion among the communities and congregations of the local church, among the local churches and with the primatial see of Rome. Often the best of cases for liturgical deviation or innovation may fail on this account: there is need for concord among the congregations and churches, even at the expense of some inconvenience in the particulars of church discipline. And, by the same token that disavows the canonical force of minuscule precepts, those precepts which are truly insignificant can hurt no one by their observance.

The other aspect of the disclaimer is more important. It is somewhat wearisome to hear the conciliar and Roman liturgical reform criticized for being insufficiently creative when the opportunities it affords for creativity have been neglected. If the new rubrics were read and taken seriously about song and rite and silence, there would be fewer distortions and perhaps less need for the relief from rigidity described above. To put it differently, the new rituals attempt and often achieve a pastoral balance between freedom and fixed order. Until the freedom is employed, it is hard to reject the fixed order. Until the fixed order is celebrated well, it is hard to explore the possibilities of relief from it.

Perhaps this does sum up our contemporary liturgical situation. More important things than discipline and order do call us: catechesis, creative growth. When there are grave inhibitions in the present rite, no one should hesitate to consider the several possibilities of relief for the good of the praying and worshiping people. But more often the solution is in trying to celebrate effectively the received rite.

Case 22

Liturgical Norms—the Eucharist

Fr. Peter Lynch is an avid outdoorsman. He enjoys hunting, fishing, and camping. Prior to ordination he went on a backpacking trip each summer. However, because of parish duties he has been unable to do so for the first three years of his priesthood. Father Peter is now able to take a two-week backpacking-canoe expedition into Canada as part of his summer vacation. Three other Catholic men also are making the trip.

Since the four men will be in the wilderness for two weeks, plans for adequate supplies which are portable must be carefully made. Father Peter decides that among his personal items must be his breviary. He also realizes that the expedition will be over two Sundays and the Feast of the Assumption. He should celebrate the Eucharist at least on these days. However, portage of Mass equipment would be too much: a chalice, paten, candles, lectionary, sacramentary, hosts, wine, crucifix, plus vestments. Minimally, he decides that he needs a missalette, hosts, and wine. However, the Order of the Mass and other liturgical laws should be followed. He feels that he should not disregard the liturgical laws, yet he cannot realistically carry all the requisites. He could ask the bishop, but then he might appear dumb or rebellious, depending upon the bishop's point of view.

Father Peter suddenly realizes that the Holy Day and Sunday obligation can only be fulfilled in certain places, namely, churches and certain oratories. Certainly under God's sky is not included in canon 1249. Now Peter could ask the bishop for permission to hold Mass, but again it seems ridiculous to ask for such permission.

Father Peter realizes that normally he should not celebrate Mass without vestments, but this expedition seems a reasonable exception. As an afterthought Father Peter wonders whether he could use regular bread (camper's "from scratch bread") if the hosts run out or are lost or ruined in portage.

Exercise

1. What are the specific requisites for a valid celebration of the Eucharist?

2. What are the specific requisites for a licit celebration of the Eucharist?

3. Applying canonical principles, what must Father Peter bring along in order to celebrate a valid Eucharist? A licit Eucharist?

4. May Father Peter use regular leavened bread rather than unleavened hosts under the circumstance?

5. May the bishop dispense Father Peter from the various liturgical laws?

References

"Actio Pastoralis Ecclesiae" (May 15, 1969), *Canon Law Digest* VII, 637.

"Liturgical Instaurationes" (September 5, 1970), *Canon Law Digest* VII, 40.

Notitiae 10 (1974), 306-7.

The Roman Missal: General Instructions and the Order of the Mass (April 6, 1969), (March 27, 1975, 2nd ed.).

Case 23

Mass Stipends

The River City Diocesan Priests' Senate decided to establish a policy concerning Mass stipends. The senators hotly debated the issue since some favored the abolition of stipends, others favored the present general church law, and still others favored retention of stipends with the monies going to the parish.

Fr. Damian Walsh argued that stipends by law belong to the priest offering the Mass and that particular laws cannot change this. Fr. David Franta stated that present church law, especially the law stated in *Christus Dominus* 8a of Vatican II, gives the bishop authority to change the law on stipends. Just recently the bishop changed the policy on stole fees by requiring these monies to be entered into parish income. The bishop could do the same regarding Mass stipends. Since the priests of the diocese receive an adequate salary of $400 a month, plus expenses and an annual cost-of-living increase, stipend money is no longer needed.

Fr. Raymond Moorse spoke in favor of the abolition of Mass stipends:

> The retention of Mass stipends is inconsistent with the theology of the Eucharist. The concept of the "fruits" of the Mass emphasizes the Eucharist as an object which can be divided up according to participation level. Rather, the Eucharist is the participation of those present in the mystery of faith during which the people pray for themselves and others, and the efficacy of such prayer cannot be determined or given a grade of participation value. Stipends merely continue the superstitious belief in the sacrificial efficacy of the Mass.

After lengthy discussion, the senate approved the norm that "all stipends which are offered for Masses celebrated at a particular parish or chaplaincy shall be received as income to the parish or chaplaincy and belong to the parish or chaplaincy."

Bishop John McRaul doubted whether he could approve such a diocesan regulation because of the tradition that the stipend belongs exclusively to the celebrating priest. The bishop, therefore, asked the opinions of the two canon lawyers of the diocese. However, this was not very helpful since they disagreed, one holding the regulation permissible in light of *Christus Dominus* and subsequent legislation, the other maintaining that the stipend belongs to the celebrating priest according to the Code and universal customary law.

Exercise

1. Research the law on Mass stipends.

2. Evaluate the opinions of the two canon lawyers as regards the bishop's authority to establish such legislation.

3. Evaluate the various positions suggested by the senators.

4. Present your own view on Mass stipends.

References

The Code of Canon Law, canons 824-44.

Decree on the Pastoral Office of Bishops in the Church, Vatican II, par. 8.

"Firma in Traditione" (June 15, 1974), *The Canon Law Digest,* Supplement through 1974, canon 824.

Gilpatric, C. E., "Mass Stipends and Mass Intentions," *Worship* 38 (1964), 190-201.

Rahner, K. and Haussling, A., *Celebration of the Eucharist* (New York: Herder and Herder, 1968).

Van der Marck, W., "The Classic Meaning of Stipends," *Theology Digest* 14 (1966), 52-53.

Glossary

ABBACY NULLIUS: a territory which is set apart from any diocese and in which the clergy and the people are subject to an abbot as their local ordinary

ADMINISTRATION (of property): the care and control of church goods or property to fulfil the purpose for which they were given or acquired. Administration may be ordinary or extraordinary

ALIENATION (of property): any act by which the right to ownership of stable or fixed church property is either transferred to another or diminished

APOSTATE from religion: a religious with perpetual vows who leaves the religious house without permission and with the intention of not returning, or who has left with permission but does not return because he or she intends to withdraw from religious obedience

APOSTOLIC ADMINISTRATOR: an ecclesiastic, who, for serious and exceptional reasons, is appointed by the pope to govern a canonically erected diocese

APOSTOLIC DELEGATE: a prelate sent by the pope to countries which do not have diplomatic relations with the Holy See and whose ordinary function is to keep the pope informed about the condition of the Church in their territory

APOSTOLIC SIGNATURA: the supreme tribunal of the Church

APPEAL: a demand that a higher court pass upon the justice of a sentence of a lower court

AUDITOR: one who draws up the record of a trial, summoning and hearing witnesses, and drawing up the record of the case

CANONICAL MISSION: the conferring of an ecclesiastical office by the competent church authority in accordance with the sacred canons

CANON LAW: the body of law enacted by legitimate church authority for the pastoral ministry and proper organization and government of the Church as a visible society

CELEBRET: a document with which a local ordinary or religious superior testifies that a priest is in good standing and requests that he be admitted to the celebration of Mass (*celebret:* let him celebrate) or perform other priestly functions

CENSURE: a penalty which deprives a baptized person who has committed a crime and is contumacious of certain spiritual goods until he repents of his misdeed and is absolved. The purpose of a censure is the correction of the delinquent; thus it is medicinal. There are three classes of censures: excommunications, suspensions, and interdicts.

CLERICAL INSTITUTE: an institute of consecrated life the majority of whose members are ordained to the priesthood (Code of Canon Law); an institute which, by reason of the aim or purpose envisaged by its founder or by reason of legitimate tradition, assumes the service of sacred orders and is recognized as such by church authority (Proposed Norms)

CLOISTER: the enclosure of a monastery or convent, which members of the community may not leave and which non-members may not enter without proper permission

COMMON ERROR (as opposed to private error): an error in some sense common to the people of a place (parish, religious community) where an act of jurisdiction is placed. The Church supplies jurisdiction, thought erroneously to be possessed, as far as it is needed.

COMMON GOOD: "the sum of those conditions of social life which allow social groups and their individual members relatively thorough and ready access to their own fulfillment" (*Gaudium et Spes,* n. 26)

COMMON WORSHIP: taking part in the liturgical worship or in the sacraments of a separated Church or community (*communicatio in sacris*). Sharing of spiritual activity and resources (*communicatio in spiritualibus*) is the term used to signify prayer offered in common, common use of sacred places and objects, as well as *communicatio in sacris* in the strict sense.

CONCORDAT: an agreement between the Church and a sovereign state having the force of law regarding matters of mutual concern, such as the appointment of bishops, legal action against clerics and religious, the Church's exclusive right to handle matters of church law

CONSTITUTIONS: the principal code of an institute of consecrated life; it contains the fundamental juridical norms concerning the discipline of an institute and its members, its government, the incorporation and training of its members, and the proper object of the vows or sacred bonds. Constitutions must be approved by competent church authority and may not be changed without the approval of the same authority.

COUNCIL: a group of advisors whose consent or advice one in authority must seek as required by general or particular law

CRIME (delict): an external and morally imputable violation of a law to which a sanction, at least indeterminate, has been attached

CUSTOM (legal sense): an unwritten law introduced by a uniform course of conduct in a community

DECREE: a command; a generic term which can include laws, precepts, and judicial pronouncements

DIMISSORIAL LETTERS: letters in virtue of which one may be lawfully ordained a deacon or priest by a bishop other than his proper ordinary. Theses letters testify, at least virtually, to the ordinand's fitness, completion of studies, freedom from irregularities, canonical title.

DIOCESAN ADMINISTRATOR: a priest or bishop, appointed by the board of diocesan consultors, who governs the diocese during its vacancy

DIOCESAN CONSULTORS: priests, appointed by the bishop in dioceses without a cathedral chapter, who counsel the bishop in cases determined by law and who govern the see during its vacancy

DIOCESAN CURIA: the personnel and the offices through which a bishop conducts the affairs of his diocese. Among the principal officials are the vicar-general, chancellor, chief judge of the court, consultors.

DIOCESAN INSTITUTE: an institute of consecrated life established, or approved, by a local ordinary

DIOCESAN SYNOD: a consultative body called by the bishop to consider matters for the welfare of the clergy and people of the diocese

DIOCESE: a fully organized church district in which pastoral ministry is exercised by a bishop as local ordinary

DISPENSATION: a relaxation of the law in a particular case by the legislator, his successor or superior, or any person to whom one of the foregoing may give the faculty to dispense

DOMICILE: the place where a person has a fixed and permanent home and principal establishment, to which, whenever he is absent, he has the intention of returning. QUASI-DOMICILE: a less permanent place of residence

DOMINATIVE POWER: power which rests upon the free agreement of subjects to obey their superiors

DOUBT: a state of mind in which the intellect suspends judgment for fear of erring. DOUBT OF LAW (*dubium iuris*): doubt about the existence or meaning of a law; DOUBT OF FACT (*dubium facti*): doubt about the existence of a concrete fact

ECUMENISM: the movement of Christians and Christian churches towards unity. The ECUMENICAL MOVEMENT embraces "the initiatives and activities encouraged and organized, according to the various needs of the Church and as opportunities offer, to promote Christian unity" (*Decree on Ecumenism,* n. 4).

EPIKEIA: a benign interpretation of the mind of the legislator prudently considered not to intend a positive law to bind in certain circumstances

EQUITY (canonical): "justice tempered by the sweetness of mercy" (Hostiensis); the prudent moderation of the written law against the rigor of the words of the law

ERROR: a false judgment of the mind

EXCLAUSTRATION: permission to leave a religious institute temporarily

EXCOMMUNICATION: a censure by which a Christian is excluded from communion with the faithful within the limits determined by the law

EXEMPT INSTITUTE: an institute of consecrated life which has been withdrawn from the jurisdiction of the local ordinary within the limits specified by the law

FACULTIES: grants of jurisdiction or authorization made by church law or by a competent superior to perform ministerial acts such as hearing confessions, officiating at weddings, granting dispensations

FORUM: a sphere in which jurisdiction or authority is exercised. INTERNAL FORUM: the activity is juridically occult; EXTERNAL FORUM: the activity is juridically public

FUGITIVE from religion: a religious who leaves the religious house without permission but with the intention of returning

GOOD FAITH: a prudent judgment by which one holds that he is acting rightly

HOLY SEE: the Roman pontiff and/or the bodies of the Church's central administration, the Roman curia, which act by the authority and in the name of the pope

IGNORANCE: lack of due knowledge

IMPEDIMENT: a condition or a fact considered by the law an obstacle to marriage, ordination, or entrance into an institute of consecrated life. IMPEDIMENT and DIRIMENT impediments both gravely forbid marriage, for example, but only DIRIMENT impediments render marriage or entrance into a novitiate invalid.

INCARDINATION: the affiliation of a cleric to a diocese for service in that diocese. EXCARDINATION: breaking of the affiliation of a cleric to a diocese as a preparation for incardination into another diocese or for affiliation to a religious order or congregation

INDULT: a concession (dispensation, permission, faculty, privilege) granted by a competent superior to do something not permitted by the common law of the Church

INTERDICT: a penalty by which a member of the Church is forbidden to take part in certain liturgical services and to administer or to receive certain sacraments (personal interdict), or by which certain liturgical services or the celebration or reception or certain sacraments is forbidden in certain places (local interdict)

IRREGULARITY: an impediment to the reception or the exercise of holy orders

JURIDICAL PERSON: a subject of rights and obligations, constituted by the law itself or by a formal decree of a competent ecclesiastical superior, and distinct from all natural or physical persons

JURISDICTION (in the Church): the power, right, or authority to govern the faithful for the attainment of the end for which the Church was founded. ORDINARY jurisdiction: that which the law attaches to an office; DELEGATED jurisdiction: that which is granted to a person without reference to any office he may, or may not, have. JURISDICTION IN THE EXTERNAL FORUM: provides directly and primarily for the common good by public exercise of power with public juridical effects; JURISDICTION IN THE INTERNAL FORUM: provides directly and primarily for the welfare of the individual faithful by confidential or private exercise of power with juridical effects which are not publicly known. Jurisdiction in the internal forum may be sacramental or extra-sacramental.

JUSTICE: a cardinal virtue by which a person gives to others that which is due to them as a matter of right

LAICIZATION: the procedure by which one in sacred orders is returned to the status of a lay person and is relieved of the obligations of his order

LAW: an ordinance in accordance with reason promulgated by the head of a community for the sake of the common good

LICIT ACTION: lawful action, or an action performed according to the requirements of the law

MAJOR SUPERIOR: abbot, superior general, provincial superior, and their vicars

MASS STIPEND: an offering given to a priest for celebrating and applying a Mass according to the intention of the donor

"MISSA PRO POPULO" (Mass for the people): the Mass which pastors are required to celebrate on Sundays and on certain feasts throughout the year for the faithful committed to their care

NOVICE: a person preparing, during a formal period of formation called the novitiate, for admission into an institute of consecrated life

OFFICE (ecclesiastical): a function legitimately exercised for a spiritual purpose (broad sense); a function permanently established by either divine or church law, entailing some participation in the power of orders or of jurisdiction, and conferred according to law (strict sense); any function which has been permanently assigned and is to be exercised for a spiritual purpose (*Decree on Priestly Ministry*, n. 20)

ORDINARY: one who has ordinary jurisdiction: the Roman pontiff, residential bishops, abbots and prelates *nullius,* vicars and prefects apostolic; those who temporarily fill the office vacated by one of the foregoing (a diocesan administrator, for example), vicars-general, major superiors in clerical exempt institutes of consecrated life. By LOCAL ORDINARY is meant all the above except major superiors.

PASTOR: a priest or a juridic person upon whom, as its proper titular, a parish has been conferred with the care of souls to be exercised under the authority of the local ordinary

PENALTY: the deprivation of some good or benefit for the correction of the delinquent or for the punishment of a crime, inflicted by lawful church authority

PIOUS CAUSE (*causa pia*): anything done principally in consideration of God and a supernatural end, for example, building churches, orphanages, schools, convents, hospitals; establishing associations to assist the youth, poor, aged

PIOUS FOUNDATION: temporal goods given to a juridical person in the Church with the perpetual or long-standing obligation to use the income to have Masses celebrated, to conduct religious services, or for the performance of works of piety and charity

PONTIFICAL INSTITUTE: an institute of consecrated life which has received the approbation or at least the *decretum laudis* (decree of praise) from the Holy See

PRECEPT: a command given by a competent superior to an individual, to a group of persons, or to a community only for a time

PRELATE: a cleric, either diocesan or a member of an institute of consecrated life, who possesses jurisdiction in the external forum. The title of prelate, without jurisdiction, is granted by the Holy See to some clerics as an honorary distinction

PRESCRIPTION: a mode of acquiring ownership of property by possessing it for a required period of time under conditions prescribed by the law; also a mode of freeing oneself from an obligation

PRESUMPTION: the probable conjecture of an uncertain fact

PRIVILEGE: a favor, contrary to or outside the law, granted by competent authority to determined persons, places, or things; a favorable rule

PROFESSION: incorporation into an institute of consecrated life; an act by which a person embraces life consecrated by the profession of the evangelical counsels, enters upon an agreement made with the institute through its competent superior (moderator), and accepts rights and obligations in the institute

PROPERTY: (Church): temporal goods belonging to the Church universal, the Apostolic See, a diocese, parish, institute of consecrated life, or some other juridical person in the Church

PROVINCE: a division of the Church, comprising an archdiocese (the metropolitan see) and one or more dioceses (suffragan sees); a division of an institute of consecrated life under the authority of a provincial superior

RECOURSE: a demand for a review of a decree, precept, or other nonjudicial decision

RESCRIPT: a written reply from the Holy See or from an ordinary, granting a dispensation or a favor, or giving information or a decision

RESERVED CASE: a censure or a sin, absolution from which is reserved to the pope, bishop, superior of an institute of consecrated life, or to a confessor having special faculties

RITE: in a very broad sense rite denotes the entire system of government, law, liturgy, and church life of a particular Church (for example, the Ruthenian Rite, the Byzantine Rite, the Greek Rite, the Latin Rite) or of a group of Churches (for example, the Latin Rite Churches and the Oriental Rite Churches). Rite also means the ceremonies used in public worship.

SANATION: an action rectifying an invalid act such as an invalid contract, profession in an institute of consecrated life, or marriage

SEAL OF CONFESSION: the canonical obligation of secrecy to be observed concerning whatever is learned in connection with the confession of sin in the sacrament of reconciliation

SECULAR INSTITUTE: a form of consecrated life, canonically erected by competent church authority; members, men and women, laity and clergy, make profession of the three evangelical counsels by means of vows or other sacred bonds; by their presence and action within the world, they are committed to the human growth of the world according to God's plan

SECULARIZATION: permission to leave a religious institute permanently; a permanent and total release from the religious institute

SEE: a diocese or archdiocese

SENTENCE: a legitimate pronouncement in which a judge, in a judicial manner, decides a case proposed to him

STOLE FEES: offerings made by the faithful especially on the occasion of the celebration of certain sacraments and sacramentals

SUBSIDIARITY (principle of): "It is a fundamental principle of social philosophy . . . that one should not withdraw from individuals and commit to the community what they can accomplish by their own enterprise and industry. So, too, it is an injustice . . . and a disturbance of right order to transfer to the larger and higher collectivity functions which can be performed and provided for by lesser and subordinate bodies. . ." (*Quadragesimo Anno,* n. 79).

SUPPLIED JURISDICTION: the Church supplies (*ecclesia supplet*) jurisdiction both for the external forum and the internal forum in common error or in a positive and probable doubt whether of law or of fact

SUSPENSION "A DIVINIS": a censure by which a cleric is forbidden to perform any act of the powers of orders. SUSPENSION "*A IURISDICTIONE*": a censure which forbids every act of jurisdiction

TITULAR SEE: a diocese which exists only in name or title, given to a bishop without a territorial or residential diocese of his own

VALID ACT: an act performed in compliance with requirements of the law stipulated for the juridical value of such an act. Noncompliance with a requirement necessary for validity results in an action which is null and void.

VICAR-GENERAL: a bishop or priest appointed by a residential bishop to assist him as a deputy in the administration of his diocese

VINDICTIVE PENALTY: a penalty whose aim is the expiation of crime. A vindictive penalty ceases when expiation has been made or a dispensation is granted by competent authority.

VOW: a deliberate and free promise made to God, having as its object a moral good which is possible and better than its omission. PUBLIC VOWS: those made before a competent ecclesiastical superior and accepted by him in the name of the Church; PRIVATE VOWS: vows made without public recognition by the Church. SOLEMN VOWS: render contrary acts unlawful and invalid; SIMPLE VOWS: render contrary acts unlawful but not invalid. RESERVED VOWS: only the Holy See can grant dispensations from them

Selected Bibliography

Part I: Foundations of Church Law

Bassett, W., "Law and Institutions in the Apostolic Church," *The Jurist* 32 (1972), 224-33.

Berman, H. J., *The Interaction of Law and Religion*. Nashville: Abingdon Press, 1974.

Bishop, J., "Canon Law: Pluralism or Uniformity? *The Jurist* 27 (1967), 77-81.

Boyle, P. M., "The Relationship of Law to Love," *The Jurist* 25 (1965), 393-406.

Bradley, R., "The Relation Between Natural Law and Human Law in Thomas Aquinas," *The Catholic Lawyer* 21 (1975), 42-55.

Caron, A., "Canon Law and Moral Theology," *The Jurist* 22 (1962), 319-32.

Carroll, J., "Revision of the Code of Canon Law" *Australasian Catholic Record* 45 (1968), 237-56.

Cicognani, A., *Canon Law,* 2nd ed. Philadelphia: The Dolphin Press, 1935, 182-437.

Cross, F., "History and Fiction in the African Canons," *Journal of Theological Studies* 12 (1961), 227-47.

Cunningham, R. G., "The Principles Guiding the Revision of the Code of Canon Law," *The Jurist* 30 (1970), 447-55.

Echevarria, L. de, "The Theology of Canon Law," *Renewal and Reform of Canon Law. Concilium* 28, N. Edelby, T. Jiménez-Urresti, P. Huizing, eds. New York: Paulist Press, 1967, 7-15.

Encyclopaedia Britannica, 15th ed., s.v. "Canon Law" by P. Huizing.

Fitzmyer, J., "Saint Paul and the Law," *The Jurist* 27 (1967), 18-36.

Gallagher, C., "Canon Law and the Christian Community. I. A Classical View," *The Heythrop Journal* 12 (1971), 281-96.

———, "Canon Law and the Christian Community. II. Current Views on the Role of Law," *The Heythrop Journal* 12 (1971), 401-24.

Gilchrist, J., "Canon Law Aspects of the Eleventh-Century Gregorian Reform Program," *The Journal of Ecclesiastical History* 13 (1962), 21-38.

Green, T. J., "Reflections on the People of God Schema," *Canon Law Society of America Proceedings,* 1978. Toledo: CLSA, 1979, 13-33.

———, "Revision of Canon Law: Progress and Problems," *The Priest* 33 (1977), 34-41.

Huizing, P., "Comments on the Revision of Canon Law," *Ongoing Reform of the Church. Concilium* 73, A. Müller and N. Greinacher, eds. New York: Herder and Herder, 1972, 97-106.

———, "The Revision of Canon Law," *Contestation in the Church. Concilium* 68, T. Jiménez-Urresti, ed. New York: Herder and Herder, 1971, 124-32.

Jiménez-Urresti, T., "Canon Law and Theology: Two Different Sciences," *Renewal and Reform of Canon Law. Concilium* 28, N. Edelby, T. Jiménez-Urresti, P. Huizing, eds. New York: Paulist Press, 1967, 17-24.

Jukes, J., "Fulfilling the Law and the Prophets," *The Clergy Review* 63 (1978), 187-91.

Kemmeren, C., "Recent Trends in the Science of Canon Law Towards a Theology of Canon Law," *The Jurist* 25 (1965), 25-45.

King, G., "The Acceptance of Law by the Community: A Study in the Writings of Canonists and Theologians, 1500-1750," *The Jurist* 37 (1977), 233-65.

Kuttner, S. G., "The Code of Canon Law in Historical Perspective," *The Jurist* 28 (1968), 129-48.

———, "The Father of the Science of Canon Law," *The Jurist* 1 (1941), 2-18.

LaDue, W. J., "A Written Constitution for the Church?" *The Jurist* 32 (1972), 1-13.

McGrath, J. J., "Canon Law for the Church and the Churches," *The Jurist* 26 (1966), 454-59.

McKenzie, J. L., "Law in the New Testament," *The Jurist* 26 (1966), 167-80.

Morrisey, F. G., "Preparing Ourselves for the New Law: 'Law Alone Will Not Hold the Church Together,'" *Studia Canonica* 7 (1973), 113-28.

———, "The Revision of the Code of Canon Law," *Studia Canonica* 12 (1978), 177-98.

New Catholic Encyclopedia, 2nd ed., s.v. "Canon Law, History of" by C. Vogel et al.

Onclin, W. H., "Church and Church Law," *Theological Studies* 28 (1967), 733-48.

Orsy, L. M., "The Creative Role of Constitutional Law in the Church," *Studia Canonica* 2 (1968), 307-24.

———, "Law in the Church — Theological Reflections," *The Way* 11 (1971), 313-23.

———, "The Life of the Church and the Renewal of Canon Law," *The Jurist* 25 (1965), 46-65.

———, "The Problem of Constitutional Law in the Church," *The Jurist* 29 (1969), 29-56.

———, "The Reform of Canon Law," *Clergy Review* 48 (1963), 750-67.

———, "Theology and Canon Law," *The Furrow* 16 (1965), 149-53.

———, "Towards a Theological Conception of Canon Law," *The Jurist* 24 (1964), 383-92.

Peter, C. J., "Dimensions of 'Jus Divinum' in Roman Catholic Theology," *Theological Studies* 34 (1973), 227-50.

Pontifical Commission for the Revision of the Code of Eastern Canon Law, "Guidelines for the Revision of the Code of Oriental Canon Law," *The Jurist* 37 (1977), 172-80.

Rahner, K., "Reflections on the Concept of 'Ius Divinum' in Catholic Thought," *Theological Investigations* 5. Baltimore: Helicon Press, 1966, 219-43.

Rodes, R. E., "A Suggestion for the Renewal of the Canon Law," *The Jurist* 26 (1966), 272-307.

Stuhlmeyer, C., "Biblical Approaches Towards Law," *Homiletic and Pastoral Review* 65 (1965), 815-25.

Taylor, J., "Canon Law in the Age of the Fathers," *Australasian Catholic Record* 54 (1977), 151-68.

Taylor, R. J., "Law in the New Testament," *Clergy Review* 65 (1971), 182-90.

Vella, D. J., "Canon Law and the Mystical Body," *The Jurist* 22 (1962), 412-32.

Vischer, L., "Reform of Canon Law — An Ecumenical Problem," *The Jurist* 26 (1966), 395-412.

Part II: The People of God

Aerts, H. G., "Pastoral Care of the Oriental Faithful," *Australasian Catholic Record* 54 (1977), 133-41.

Barbarena, T. G., "Collegiality at Diocesan Level: The Western Presbyterate," *Pastoral Reform in Church Government. Concilium* 8, T. Jiménez-Urresti and N. Edelby, eds. New York: Paulist Press, 1965, 19-32.

Barker, A., "The Superior and Government: Some Reflections on 'The Superiorless Community,'" *The Clergy Review* 57 (1972), 35-40.

"Basic Bylaws for Parish Councils," *The Jurist* 28 (1968), 352-61.

Belcasto, J., *The Relationship of Baptism to Church Membership*. St. Louis: Bethany Press, 1963.

Bourke, M. M., "The Catholic Priest: Man of God for Others," *Worship* 43 (1969), 68-81.

Boyle, J. P., "Presbyters, Pastors, the Laity and Decision-Making in the Church," *American Ecclesiastical Review* 169 (1975), 592-609.

Brunett, A. J., "The Diocesan Synod of Detroit: The Theology Underlying the Synod Document," *The Canon Law Society of America Proceedings,* 1969. Hartford: CLSA, 1970, 112-15.

Campbell, C., "The Parish Council Syndrome," *Homiletic and Pastoral Review* 79 (1979), 49-54.

"Canonical Reflections on Priestly Life and Ministry," *American Ecclesiastical Review* 166 (1972), 363-92.

Carter, A., "Bishop-Priest-Laity Relationship in the Light of Vatican II," *Studia Canonica* 1 (1967), 79-95.

Collins, P. W., "The Diocesan Synod — An Assembly of the People of God," *The Jurist* 33 (1973), 399-411.

Congar, Y., "What Belonging to the Church Has Come to Mean," *Communio* 4 (1977), 146-60.

Congregation for Bishops — Congregation for Religious and Secular Institutes, "The Relationship of Bishops/Religious Orders," *Origins* 8 (1978), 161, 163-75.

Cora, G. F., "Team Ministry: Theological Aspects," *American Ecclesiastical Review* 167 (1973), 684-90.

Coriden, J. A., "The Diocesan Synod. An Instrument of Renewal for the Local Church," *The Jurist* 34 (1974), 68-93.

———, "Ministries for the Future," *Studia Canonica* 8 (1974), 255-75.

Crehan, J., "Ministerial Priesthood: A Survey of Work Since the Council," *Theological Studies* 32 (1971), 489-99.

Crowley, P., "The Diaconate for the Present Age," *The Clergy Review* 59 (1974), 787-803.

Cuneen, J. E., "The Role of Lay People in the Church," *Catholic Mind* 74 (1976), 26-35.

Donnelly, F. G., *The Diocesan Synod. An Historical Conspectus and Commentary.* Canon Law Studies, no. 74. Washington: The Catholic University of America, 1932.

Dufault, W. J., "The Superiors General and 'Renovationis Causam,'" *Studia Canonica* 3 (1969), 269-75.

———, "The Unity of Apostolic Religious Life in the Instruction 'Renovationis Causam,'" *Studia Canonica* 3 (1969), 319-23.

Echlin, E. P., "Theological Frontiers of the Deacon's Ministry," *American Ecclesiastical Review* 166 (1972), 479-91.

Fogarty, G. P., "American Conciliar Legislation, Hierarchical Structure, and Priest-Bishop Tension," *The Jurist* 32 (1972), 400-9.

Ford, J. T., "Infallibility: Primacy, Collegiality, Laity," *The Jurist* 30 (1970), 436-46.

Frison, B., "The Challenge of Change. Renewal of Structures of Government in Religious Institutes," *Studia Canonica* 1 (1967), 223-43.

———, "Renewal of Religious," *Studia Canonica* 1 (1967), 45-78.

Gallen, J. F., "New Canon Law for Religious in Detail," *Review for Religious* 35 (1976), 232-50.

Graham, R. A., *Vatican Diplomacy: A Study of Church and State on the International Plane.* Princeton: Princeton University Press, 1959.

Granfield, P., "Papal Resignation," *The Jurist* 38 (1978), 118-31.

Green, T. J., "Reflections on the People of God Schema," *Canon Law Society of America Proceedings,* 1978. Toledo: CLSA, 1979, 13-33.

Gula, R. M., "A Theology of Diaconate," *American Ecclesiastical Review* 169 (1975), 621-35, 669-80.

Hayes, J. M., "Religious and the Diocesan Administration," *Studia Canonica* 3 (1969), 251-58.

Howes, R. G., "Consultative Process in the Church," *American Ecclesiastical Review* 168 (1974), 422-30.

———, "Pastoral Councils Revisited," *Pastoral Life* 25 (1976), 7-12.

———, "Shared Responsibility: Diamond in the Rough?" *Homiletic and Pastoral Review* 78 (1977), 56-65.

Hudson, E. R., "Women and the Diaconate," *The Clergy Review* 56 (1971), 886-90.

Hughes, M., "The Juridical Nature of the Act of Joining the Catholic Church," *Studia Canonica* 8 (1974), 45-74.

Huizing, P., "Church and State in Public Ecclesiastical Law," *Structures of the Church. Concilium* 58, T. Jiménez-Urresti, ed. New York: Herder and Herder, 1970, 126-35.

———, "Divine Law and Church Structures," *Theology Digest* 18 (1970), 144-50.

Hünermann, P., "Conclusions Regarding the Female Diaconate," *Theological Studies* 36 (1975), 325-33.

Huysmans, R., "The Diocese as an Administrative Unit," *The Unifying Role of the Bishop. Concilium* 71, E. Schillebeeckx, ed. New York: Herder and Herder, 1972, 89-98.

Hypher, P., "The Restoring of the Diaconate," *The Clergy Review* 63 (1978), 390-94.

Jong, A. de, "Concordats and International Law," *Structures of the Church, Concilium* 58, T. Jiménez-Urresti, ed. New York: Herder and Herder 1970, 104-12.

Jukes, J., "A Commentary on the 'Notae Directivae' on the Mutual Relations Between Bishops and Religious in the Church," *The Clergy Review* 63 (1978), 472-77; 64 (1979), 21-31.

Kagithapu, M., "International Unions of Superiors," *Apollinaris* 49 (1976) 133-62.

Kaufmann, L., "The Ministerial Priesthood at the Bishops' Synod," *The Clergy Review* 56 (1971), 593-603.
Kelly, G. A., "The Parish: New Life from Old Roots," *The Clergy Review* 64 (1979), 45-59.
Kennedy, R. T., "Experimental Parishes and the Law of the Church," *Dunwoodie Review* 14 (1974), 123-34.
Kilmartin, E. J., "Apostolic Office: Sacrament of Christ," *Theological Studies* 36 (1975), 243-64.
LaDue, W. J., "The Right of the Church People to Participate in Ecclesial Decision-Making," *Studia Canonica* 7 (1973), 179-90.
Lapierre, M. J., "Why Religious Life," *Studia Canonica* 2 (1968), 289-306.
Leclercq, J., "The Role of Monasticism in the Church of Today," *Australasian Catholic Record* 54 (1977), 63-83.
Legrand, H. M., "The Revaluation of Local Churches: Some Theological Implications," *The Unifying Role of the Bishop. Concilium* 71, E. Schillebeeckx, ed. New York: Herder and Herder, 1972, 53-64.
Ligier, L., "Women and the Ministerial Priesthood," *Origins* 7 (1978), 694-701.
Lombardia, P., "Rights of the Layman in the Church," *Contestation in the Church. Concilium* 68, T. Jiménez-Urresti, ed. New York: Herder and Herder, 1971, 115-23.
Lynch, J. E., "Marriage and Celibacy of the Clergy: The Discipline of the Western Church: An Historico-Canonical Synopsis," *The Jurist* 32 (1972), 14-38, 189-212.
Malloy, E. A., "The Character of a Religious Community," *Review for Religious* 37 (1978), 748-52.
Martinell, M., "Women and Ministries in the Church," *The Clergy Review* 59 (1974), 610-20.
McDermott, R., "Internal Ministry and Legislation in the Church Today," *Review for Religious* 38 (1979), 247-55.
Morrisey, F. G., "The Spirit of the Proposed New Law for Institutes of Consecrated Life," *Studia Canonica* 9 (1975), 177-94.
Müller, A., "Obedience to the Bishop," *The Unifying Role of the Bishop. Concilium* 71, E. Schillebeeckx, ed. New York: Herder and Herder, 1972, 79-88.
Murray, L., "The 'Superiorless' Community," *The Clergy Review* 56 (1971), 671-85.
"National conference of Bishops: Statutes and By-Laws," *The Jurist* 32 (1972), 108-28.
New Catholic Encyclopedia (Supplement), 2nd ed., s.v. "Women as Priests" by A. Cunningham.
Nicholl, D., "The Layman and Ecclesiastical Authority," *The Clergy Review* 49 (1964), 393-415.
Nuns of the Poor Clare Federation of Mary Immaculate, "With Light Step and Unstumbling Feet," *Review for Religious* 37 (1978), 371-88.
O'Brien, J. D., *The Exemption of Religious in Church Law*. Milwaukee: The Bruce Publishing Company, 1942.
O'Connell, P., "The Role of Senates: Consultation and Collegiality," *African Ecclesiastical Review* 4 (1971), 337-43.
O'Connor, D. F., "Developing Constitutions and Directories," *Review for Religious* 37 (1978), 753-76.

Onclin, W., "The Power of Decision in the Church at the Supra-Diocesan Level," *Studia Canonica* 4 (1970), 279-96.

O'Reilly, M., "Faculties in Favour of Religious," *Studia Canonica* 7 (1973), 93-111.

Pennington, M. B., "The Evolution of Monastic Law," *Studia Canonica* 8 (1974), 349-62.

———, "Renovationis Causam: Instruction on the Renewal of Religious Formation — A Practical Commentary," *Studia Canonica* 3 (1969), 107-24.

———, "'Venite Seorsum' — An Evaluation," *Studia Canonica* 5 (1971), 245-57.

Poel, C. J. Van der, "Exemption and Institutes of Pontifical Law," *The Jurist* 25 (1965), 439-52.

Prince, B., "Episcopal Conferences and Collegiality," *Studia Canonica* 2 (1968), 125-32.

Provost, J. H., "The Involvement of Dispensed Priests in the Official Ministry of the Church," *The Jurist* 34 (1974), 143-53.

Purcell, J. W., "The Institute of the Senate of Priests," *The Jurist* 38 (1978), 132-52.

Rahner, K., "Membership of the Church According to the Teaching of Pius XII's Encyclical 'Mystici Corporis Christi,'" *Theological Investigations* 2. Baltimore: Helicon Press, 1963, 1-88.

Reed, J., "The Laity in Church Law," *Theological Studies* 24 (1963), 612-15.

Reese, J. M., "Patterns of Ministry in the New Testament as Interpreting the Role of the Permanent Diaconate," *American Ecclesiastical Review* 166 (1972), 174-84.

Rooney, J., "In Search of Authenticity," *The Clergy Review* 63 (1978), 125-31.

Rothluebber, F. B., "The Power of Decision in Religious Communities," *Studia Canonica* 4 (1970), 297-307.

Russell, E. A., "Church and State in the New Testament," *The Irish Theological Quarterly* 44 (1977), 192-207.

Sacred Congregation for Bishops, *Directory on the Pastoral Ministry of Bishops,* tr. Publications Service of the Canadian Catholic Conference. Ottawa: Canadian Catholic Conference, 1974.

Said, M., "Particular Law of Institutes in the Renewal of Consecrated Life," *Review for Religious* 36 (1977), 924-47.

———,"The Present State of the Reform of the Code Concerning the Section 'De Institutis Perfectionis,'"*Studia Canonica* 8 (1974), 213-35.

Schillebeeckx, E., *Collaboration of Religious Among Themselves, With the Episcopacy and With Secular Priests.* Chicago: Franciscan Herald Press, 1965.

Seasoltz, R. K., "Monastic Autonomy and Exemption: Charism and Institution," *The Jurist* 34 (1974), 316-55.

Sheets, J. R., "Ordination of Women: The Issues," *American Ecclesiastical Review* 169 (1975) 17-36.

———, "The Ordination of Women," *Communio* 3 (1976), 3-15.

Smith, G. F., "Why Permanent Deacons?" *Homiletic and Pastoral Review* 78 (1978), 63-67.

Théoret, J. M., "The Post-Conciliar Parish," *Studia Canonica* 1 (1967), 191-203.

Tillard, J.M.R., "Jurisdiction of the Bishop of Rome," *Theological Studies* 40 (1949), 3-22.

Ullmann, W., "Medieval Views on Papal Abdication," *Irish Theological Record* 71 (1949), 125-33

Vasquez, L., "The Position of Women According to the Code," *The Jurist* 34 (1974), 128-42.

Walter, J. J., "The Church: A Power Structure," *American Ecclesiastical Review* 169 (1975), 102-17.
Wright, J. H., "Church and Priesthood: A Perspective on Ordained Ministry," *Communio* 4 (1977), 261-74.

Part III: Canonical Norms and Select Procedures

Amens, M., "Canonical Equity Before the Code," *The Jurist* 33 (1973), 1-24.
Bearsley, P., "Canon Law as a Sign and Its Presuppositions," *The Australasian Catholic Record* 54 (1977), 256-69.
Betrams, W., "Subsidiarity in the Church," *Catholic Mind* 59 (1961), 358-63.
Bourke, M., "Reflections on Church Order in the New Testament," *The Catholic Biblical Quarterly* 30 (1968), 493-511.
Cann, H. V., "Changing Emphasis on the Concept of Authority in the Church," *The Jurist* 23 (1963), 377-93.
Comyns, J. J., *Papal and Episcopal Administration of Church Property,* Canon Law Studies, no. 147. Washington: The Catholic University of America, 1942.
Congar, Y., "The Historical Development of Authority in the Church," *Problems of Authority,* J. M. Dodd, ed. Baltimore: Helicon Press, 1962.
Coriden, J., "Towards Constitutional Development Within the Church," *We the People of God,* J. A., Coriden, ed. Huntington, Ind.: Our Sunday Visitor, Inc., n.d., 5-18.
Deutsch, B., *Jurisdiction of Pastors in the External Forum,* Canon Law Studies, no. 378. Washington: The Catholic University of America, 1957.
Frison, B., *Selection and Incorporation of Candidates for the Religious Life.* Milwaukee: The Bruce Publishing Company, 1962.
Hubbell, S. D., "Civil Rights Impact on the Church," *The Catholic Lawyer* 21 (1975), 339-49.
Huhmann, J. F., *The Pastor's Power of Dispensing.* Rome: Pontificium Athenaeum Angelicum, 1956.
Huizing, P., "The Problem of the Division of Governmental Functions in the Church," *Democratization of the Church. Concilium,* 63, A. Müller, ed. New York: Herder and Herder, 1971, 127-34.
Kennedy, R. T., "The Art of Church Government," *America* 126 (1972), 34-37.
Kenyon, R. A., "A Compendium of Episcopal and Presbyteral Powers of Dispensation," *The Jurist* 38 (1978), 190-202.
McFarland, N. F., *Religious Vocation—Its Juridic Concept,* Canon Law Studies, no. 328. Washington: The Catholic University of America, 1953.
Mallon, V. T., "Easy Exit for Priests," *Homiletic and Pastoral Review* 78 (1978), 14, 16-26.
Metz, R., *What Is Canon Law?* New York: Hawthorn Books, 1960.
New Catholic Encyclopedia (Supplement), 2nd ed., s.v. "Due Process" by R. T. Kennedy.

New Catholic Encyclopedia (Supplement), 2nd ed., s.v. "Subsidiarity in the Church," by J. S. George.
O'Connor, E. D., "Charism and Institution," *American Ecclesiastical Review* 168 (1974), 507-25.
Pfaller, B. A., *The "Ipso Facto" Effected Dismissal of Religious,* Canon Law Studies, no. 259. Washington: The Catholic University of America, 1948.
Plöchl, W. M., "The Fundamental Principles of the Philosophy of Canon Law," *The Jurist* 4 (1944), 70-100.
Quinn, H., *The Particular Penal Precept,* Canon Law Studies, no. 303. Washington: The Catholic University of America, 1953.
Range, J. A., "Legal Exclusion of Women from Church Office," *The Jurist* 34 (1974), 112-27.
Riemslag, A. C., "Contestation and the Church," *American Ecclesiastical Review* 166 (1972), 550-60.
Rodes, R. E., "The Canon Law as a Legal System—Functions, Obligations, and Sanctions," *Natural Law Forum* 9 (1964), 45-94.
Roelker, E., *Precepts.* Paterson, N. J.: St. Anthony Guild Press, 1955.
Ryan, R. R., "The Dispensing Authority of the Residential Bishop of the Latin Rite Regarding General Laws of the Church," *The Jurist* 35 (1975), 175-211.
Schillebeeckx, E., "The Catholic Understanding of Office in the Church," *Theological Studies* 30 (1969), 567-87.
Staffa, D., "The Supreme Administrative Tribunal," *The Catholic Lawyer* 23 (1977), 69-77.
Stevens, C., "The Anatomy of a Vocation," *Review for Religious* 34 (1975), 140-45.
Tartre, R. A., "Church Laws — A Service," *Homiletic and Pastoral Review* 74 (1974), 51-55.
Tierney, T. E., "Should Church Law Adopt Articles of Impeachment?" *The Catholic Lawyer* 21 (1975), 229-34.
Walsh, M. J., "Protecting Rights in the Church," *The Month* 11 (1978), 131-34.
Wiggins, U. C., *Property Laws of the State of Ohio Affecting the Church,* Canon Law Studies, no. 367. Washington: The Catholic University of America 1956.
Wild, R., "Office and Charism," *American Ecclesiastical Review* 167 (1973), 275-83.
Zapp, H., "Diocesan Jurisdiction: An Historical Survey," *Judgment in the Church. Concilium* 107, W. Bassett and P. Huizing, eds. New York: Seabury Press, 1977, 9-19.

Part IV: Sacramental and Liturgical Law

Austin, G., "What Has Happened to Confirmation?" *Worship* 50 (1976), 420-26.

Bauer, N. R., "Intercommunion: Possibilities and Practicalities," *The Clergy Review* 63 (1978), 426-30.

Becker, K. J., "Necessity of Integral Confession According to Trent," *Theology Digest* 21 (1973), 204-9.

Beeck, F. J., van, "Sacraments, Church Order, and Secular Responsibility," *Theological Studies* 30 (1969), 613-34.

———, "Towards an Ecumenical Understanding of the Sacraments," *Journal of Ecumenical Studies* 3 (1966), 57-112.

Brusselmans, C., "Children and the Sacrament of Reconciliation," *Worship* 49 (1975), 149-57.

Buckley, F. J., "The Right to the Sacraments of Initiation," *Origins* 8 (1978), 329-36.

———, "Recent Developments in the Sacrament of Penance," *Communio* 1 (1974), 83-98.

———, "What Age for Confirmation?" *Theological Studies* 27 (1966), 655-66.

Buswell, C. A., "Pastoral Suggestions for the Celebration of Confirmation," *Worship* 46 (1972), 30-34.

Callahan, M. J., "Historical Inquiry into the Priest-Penitent Privilege," *The Jurist* 36 (1976), 328-37.

Campbell, J. F., "Reconciliation: New Rite, New Perspectives," *The Priest* 32 (1976), 14-22.

Challancin, J., "Infant Baptism: More Difficult Requirements?" *Homiletic and Pastoral Review* 77 (1977), 61-68.

Connolly, J. M., "Liturgical Law and Liturgical Practice," *The Dunwoodie Review* 12 (1972), 112-22.

Crichton, J. D., "The Christian Initiation of Adults. A Pastoral Opportunity," *Life and Worship* 41 (1972), 8-12.

Curran, C. E., "The Sacrament of Penance Today," *Worship* 43 (1969), 510-31, 590-619; 44 (1970), 2-19.

Dallen, J., "Eucharist and Penance," *Worship* 50 (1976), 316-29.

Dease, D., "General Confession and Absolution," *Worship* 51 (1977), 536-45.

Devlin, A., "Roman Declaration on the First Sacraments," *The Furrow* 24 (1973), 733-37.

Driessche, G. van, "Confession and Adolescents: Enquiry Among Pupils of Catholic Schools," *Lumen Vitae* 22 (1967), 503-28.

Dulles, A., "Ministry and Intercommunion: Recent Ecumenical Statements and Debates," *Theological Studies* 34 (1973), 643-78.

Gilpatric, C. E., "Mass Stipends and Mass Intentions," *Worship* 38 (1964), 190-201.

Gusmer, C., "Liturgical Traditions of Christian Illness: Rites of the Sick," *Worship* 46 (1972), 528-43.

Gwinnel, M., "The Age or Stage for Confirmation," *The Clergy Review* 55 (1970), 10-26.

Hardon, J. A., "First Confession: An Historical and Theological Analysis," *Eglise et Théologie* 1 (1972), 69-110.

Hughes, J. J., "Ministerial Intention in the Administration of the Sacraments," *The Clergy Review* 51 (1966), 763-76.

Huizing, P. J., "The Sacramental Structure of Church Order and Its Implications," *The Jurist* 32 (1972), 479-93.

Kavanagh, A., "Christian Initiation of Adults: The Rites," *Worship* 48 (1974), 318-35.

———, "Initiation: Baptism and Confirmation," *Worship* 46 (1972), 262-76.

Kelly, B., "The Confession of Devotion," *Irish Theological Quarterly* 33 (1966), 84-90.

Kelly, W. J., "The Authority of Liturgical Laws," *The Jurist* 28 (1968), 397-424.

Kiesling, C., "Infant Baptism," *Worship* 42 (1968), 617-26.

Landini, L., "Baptismal Practices in Catholic Hospitals: A Theological Reflection on Canons 752 and 750," *The Jurist* 35 (1975), 296-309.

Lynch, J. E., "Ecumenical Guidelines," *Chicago Studies* 15 (1976), 330-48.

McAuliffe, C., "Penance and Reconciliation with the Church," *Theological Studies* 26 (1965), 1-39.

McManus, F. R., "The Juridical Power of the Bishop in the Constitution on the Sacred Liturgy," *The Church and the Liturgy. Concilium* 2, J. Wagner, ed. Glen Rock, N. J.: Paulist Press, 1965, 33-49.

———, "The Law, the Liturgy and Participation," *The Jurist* 20 (1960), 42-54.

———, "Liturgical Law and Difficult Cases," *Worship* 48 (1974), 347-66.

———, "The Sacraments of the Church," *Chicago Studies* 15 (1976), 330-48.

———, *Sacramental Liturgy*. New York: Herder and Herder, 1967.

McMorrow, K., "Sacrament of the Anointing of the Sick: Historical-Theological Considerations," *American Ecclesiastical Review* 169 (1975), 507-21.

McReavy, L. L., "Notes on Roman Documents. The Matter and Form of Confirmation," *The Clergy Review* 57 (1972), 141.

Marck, W. van der, "The Classic Meaning of Stipend," *Theology Digest* 14 (1966), 52-53.

Marsh, T., "The History and Significance of the Post-Baptismal Rites," *Irish Theological Quarterly* 29 (1962), 175-206.

———, "A Study of Confirmation," *Irish Theological Quarterly* 39 (1972), 149-63, 319-36; 40 (1973), 125-47.

Morrisey, F. G., "Ten Years of Liturgical Legislation (1963-1973)," *Studia Canonica* 7 (1973), 289-308.

Newns, B., "General Absolution: Traditions and Recent Trends," *The Clergy Review* 62 (1977), 62-68.

Nocent, A., "Confirmation: The Difficult Catechesis," *Lumen Vitae* 28 (1973), 97-112.

O'Hanlon, D. J., "A New Approach to the Validity of Church Orders," *Worship* 41 (1967), 406-21.

O'Leary, H. M., "The Tridentine Mass Today," *Australasian Catholic Record* 53 (1976), 370-81.

O'Neil, C., "The Role of the Recipient and Sacramental Signification," *The Thomist* 21 (1958), 257-301.

Orsy, L. M., "The Sacrament of Penance in Religious Communities," *Worship* 42 (1968), 159-68.

Osborne, K. B., "Why Confess to a Priest?" *Chicago Studies* 14 (1975), 260-78.

Palmer, P. F., "Who Can Anoint the Sick?" *Worship* 48 (1974), 81-92.

Patino, J., *The New Order of Mass*. Collegeville: The Liturgical Press, 1970.

Peter, C. J., "Integrity Today?" *Communio* 1 (1974), 60-82.

Rahner, K., "Forgotten Truths Concerning the Sacrament of Penance," *Theological Investigations* 2. New York: Seabury Press, 1975, 135-74.

———, "The Meaning of Frequent Confession of Devotion," *Theological Investigations* 3. New York: Seabury Press, 1974, 177-89.

———, "Problems Concerning Confession," *Theological Investigations* 3. New York: Seabury Press, 1974, 190-206.

Redmond, R., "Infant Baptism. History and Pastoral Problems," *Theological Studies* 30 (1969), 79-89.

Richstatter, T., *Liturgical Law Today: New Style, New Spirit.* Chicago: Franciscan Herald Press, 1977.

Rotelle, J. E., "Liturgy and Authority," *Worship* 47 (1973), 514-26.

Ryder, A., "Parents' Faith and Infant Baptism," *The Clergy Review* 58 (1973), 746-59.

Sacramentum Mundi, s.v. "Anointing of the Sick" by P. DeLetter.

Schmitz, W. J., and Tierney, T. E., *Liturgicon.* Huntington, Ind.: Our Sunday Visitor, 1976.

Smith, P., "General Sacramental Absolution," *Studia Canonica* 12 (1978), 225-63.

Smits, K., "Confirmation Re-examined: An Evolving Theology and Practice," *Worship* 48 (1974), 21-29.

Sullivan, E. H., *Proof of the Reception of the Sacraments.* Canon Law Studies, no. 209. Washington: The Catholic University of America, 1944.

Sullivan, T. F., "The Directory and First Confession," *The Living Light* 16 (1979), 192-208.

———, "The First Confession: Law and Catechesis," *America* 137 (1977), 128-30.

Tierney, T. E., "The Right of the Faithful to the Sacraments," *The Catholic Lawyer* 23 (1977), 57-68.

Tillard, J. M., "Sacramental Questions: The Intentions of Minister and Recipient," *The Sacraments in General: A New Perspective. Concilium* 31, E. Schillebeeckx and B. Willems, eds. New York: Paulist Press, 1967, 117-33.

Vanyo, L. V., *Requisites of Intention in the Reception of the Sacraments.* Canon Law Studies, no. 391. Washington: The Catholic University of America, 1965.

Vries, W. de, "*Communicatio in Sacris:* An Historical Study of the Problem of Liturgical Services in Common with Eastern Christians Separated from Rome," *The Church and Ecumenism. Concilium* 4, H. Küng, ed. New York: Paulist Press, 1965, 18-40.

Žužek, I., "The Sacramental Canon Law of the Christian East," *The Sacraments in Theology and Canon Law. Concilium* 38, N. Edelby, T. Jiménez-Urresti, and P. Huizing, eds. New York: Paulist Press, 1968, 146-60.

The AUTHORS

JORDAN F. HITE, T.O.R., L.L.M., J.C.L., is director of formation for the Franciscan friars (Sacred Heart Province) and a lecturer on constitutional law at St. Francis College, Loretto, Pennsylvania. He is a member of the Bar of the State of Virginia and of the United States Supreme Court. Father Hite has published articles in *Studia Canonica*, *The Cord*, and the *Review for Religious*.

GENNARO J. SESTO, S.D.B., J.C.D., S.T.L., is the associate academic dean of the Pontifical College Josephinum, Columbus, Ohio, and a professor of canon law and pastoral education at that college. He is a procurator and advocate of the Sacred Roman Rota. Father Sesto is a past president of Don Bosco College, Newton, New Jersey, and a former professor of canon law at the Pontificium Athenaeum Salesianum, Turin, Italy.

DANIEL J. WARD, O.S.B., J.D., J.C.L., is an assistant professor of theology and government and assistant to the president for legal services at St. John's University, Collegeville, Minnesota. Father Ward is a judge of the Tribunal of the St. Cloud Diocese and a member of the Bar of the State of Minnesota.

Cover by Br. Placid Stuckenschneider, O.S.B.